Iron Age Burials from Mill Hill, Deal

Frontispiece. The Deal Crown: a replica of the crown photographed on the skull from Grave 112.

Iron Age Burials from Mill Hill, Deal

Keith Parfitt

with contributions by
Janet Ambers, T. Anderson, D. Holman, A. J. Legge, Valery Rigby, I. M. Stead and Sheelagh Stead

Published for the Trustees of
the British Museum by
BRITISH MUSEUM PRESS

Published by British Museum Press
A division of British Museum Publications
46 Bloomsbury Street, London WC1B 3QQ

British Library Cataloguing in Publication Data
A catalogue record for this book is available from the British Library

ISBN 0 7141 2304 8

Designed by Andrew Shoolbred
Typeset and printed by Henry Ling Ltd, Dorset

Contents

List of Contributors

Janet Ambers	Dept of Scientific Research, The British Museum, London, WC1B 3DG
T. Anderson	Canterbury Archaeological Trust, 92a Broad Street, Canterbury, Kent CT1 2LU
D. Holman	c/o Dover Archaeological Group, 8 Castle Avenue, Dover, Kent, CT16 1HA
A. J. Legge	Centre for Extra-Mural Studies, Birkbeck College, 26 Russell Square, London WC1B 5DQ
K. Parfitt	Dover Archaeological Group, 8 Castle Avenue, Dover, Kent, CT16 1HA
Valery Rigby	Dept of Prehistoric and Romano-British Antiquities, The British Museum, London, WC1B 3DG
I. M. Stead	Dept of Prehistoric and Romano-British Antiquities, The British Museum, London, WC1B 3DG
Sheelagh Stead	Ratcliffe House, Ashwell, Hertfordshire, SG7 5NP

List of Plates

List of Figures

forthcoming); 25. Sutton, Notts (582×37mm) Fox 1958, pl. 21; 26, River Witham, Lincs (530×45mm) Kendrick 1939; Fox 1958, pl. 22b.

19. Plan showing the distribution of bronze fittings of the shield within Grave 112. The main shaded area shows the limits of the distribution of decorated sheet bronze fragments; the shaded areas numbered 15 show where fragments from the cover of the boss were found. (Scale 1/6)
20. The shield from Grave 112: (a) and (b) diagrams showing the distribution of bronze fittings in section, as excavated in two levels; (c) and (d) a hypothetical reconstruction of the shield as deposited – indicating in (c) the two levels as excavated and the grave filling lost before excavation.
21. Bronze bindings from three corners of the shield. (Scale 1/2)
22. Bronze clamps and other fittings from the shield. (Full size)
23. Sheet bronze cut-out ornament from the shield: 15. from the boss; 16. from near a corner; 17. from the main area shaded on fig. 19. (Full size)
24. Reconstruction of the shield from Grave 112; for the high and low level, as excavated, see the section, fig. 20. (Scale 1/6)
25. Crown from Grave 112: drawings to illustrate its construction. (Scale 2/5)
26. The distribution of mineral-replaced hair on the inner surface of the crown (b), its limits indicated by shading in (a); and a detail of the mineral-replaced hair (c). (Scales, (a) and (b), 2/5; (c), full size)
27. The decoration on the band of the crown. (Full size, apart from the diagram at the top)
28. The decoration on the band of the crown. (Full size, apart from the diagram at the top)
29. The remains of a crown from Hounslow. (Full size; reconstruction, about 1/4).
30. Fragments of the Hounslow crown, see fig. 29. (Full size)
31. Typology of Iron Age and Roman crowns: (a) Hockwold; (b) Leckhampton; (c) Cavenham Heath; (d) Stony Stratford; (e) Wanborough; (f) Ogmore Down; (g) Cerrig-y-Drudion. (Scale 1/4).
32. Bronze artefacts from Grave 112: 4. brooch; 5. suspension ring; 6. strap-link. (Full size)
33. The Newnham Croft bracelet, with details of surviving ornament. (Full size; the diagram at the top is approximately 2/3)
34. The Newnham Croft bracelet: suggested reconstructions of the designs on bands 3, 4 and 7. (Full size)
35. Diagonally balanced designs centred on opposed triangles: (a) Deal brooch; (b) Fiskerton sword handle; (c) Camp de Châlons torque; (d) Sutton scabbard-plate; (e) Toome scabbard; (f) Newnham Croft bracelet. (Not to scale)
36. Showing how the design on the Deal crown (e) is constructed from lobe and cusp motifs (b) derived from a palmette ((a) = a half-palmette, Saulces-Champenoises).
37. Showing the relationship between two designs on the Sutton scabbard-plate (a) and (b) and the derivation of the central double-lobe motif.
38. The design on the Deal scabbard: (a) simplified version to emphasise the lobes and cusps; (b) detailed design; (c) emphasising the infilling of the lobes and cusps; (d) trumpet voids in the circular terminals and central node.
39. Trumpet voids on the open-work plaque that covered half of the shield-boss. (Full size)
40. Bronze (1 and 4) and iron (3, 5–7) brooches from Deal. (Full size)
41. Distribution of involuted brooches: 1. Burton Fleming, Humberside (Stead 1991a, 87); 2. Rudston, Humberside (ibid. 83–9); 3. Danes Graves, Humberside (Stead 1979, 68–9); 4. Eastburn, Humberside (ibid. 68); 5. Garton Slack, Humberside (Hull and Hawkes 1987, 159 and 161, nos. 1527 and 1599 – the same brooch illustrated twice; Dent 1983, 11, fig. 8, A–D); 6. Wetwang Slack, Humberside (Dent 1982, 441–4); 7. Ancaster, Lincolnshire (Hull and Hawkes 1987, 161, no. 9220); 8. Thetford, Norfolk (Gregory 1991, 123–4, no. 27); 9. The Breiddin, Powys (Musson 1991, 142–4); 10. Twyn-y-Gaer, Gwent (Probert 1976, 115); 11. Croft Ambrey, Hereford and Worcester (Stanford 1974, 162–4); 12. Wood Eaton, Oxon (Hull and Hawkes 1987, 163 and 164, nos. 3070 and 4281); 13. Beckley, Oxon (ibid. 163, no. 2244); 14. Frilford, Oxon (ibid. 158, no. 3071); 15. London (ibid. 166, no. 2242); 16. Stokeleigh Camp, Avon (Haldane 1975, 59, fig. 19, M49); 17. Meare East, Somerset (Coles 1987, 75, no. EE15; 77, no.EE 66.56; 127, no. 184); 18. Cold Kitchen Hill, Wiltshire (Hull and Hawkes 1987, 160, no. 2247; 162, nos. 5475 and 5477; 165, nos. 3194 and 5476 [?the same brooch]; 166, no. 2246); 19. Hod Hill, Dorset (ibid. 158, no. 3071); 20. Trevone, Cornwall (ibid. 158, no. 6889); 21. Trethellan Farm, Newquay, Cornwall (Nowakowski 1991, 222, fig. 84, no. 205); 22. Shoreham, Sussex (Hartridge 1978, 99, nos. 7–9); 23. Farningham Hill, Kent (Philp 1984, 35, no. 6); 24. Deal, Kent (Grave 127).
42. Bronze brooches from Deal; drawn by Frank Gardiner. (Full size)
43. Bronze brooches from Deal; no. 16 drawn from a photograph. (Full size)
44. Bronze brooches from Deal; no. 22 drawn from a photograph and no. 25 from a sketch by Newington. (Full size)
45. Bronze pin. (Full size)
46. Bronze spoon. (Full size)
47. Bronze spoon. (Full size)
48. Bronze objects: 1. toilet set; 2. bracelet with suspended rings; 3. finger-ring; 4. handle. (Full size)
49. Iron objects: 1. blade of a knife; 2. triangular knife with bronze handle. (Scale 2/3)
50. Distribution of bronze coins of Eppillus (VA 451; M 310) in Kent and Essex: 1. Harlow; 2. Colchester; 3. Cliffe; 4. Teston; 5. Boxley; 6. Birdcage Marsh, Lower Halstow; 7. Isle of Sheppey; 8. Faversham; 9. Canterbury; 10. Bishopsbourne; 11. Margate; 12. Broadstairs; 13. Archer's Low, Sandwich; 14. Worth; 15. Ham; 16. Deal; 17. Folkestone.
51. Iron Age horses, metacarpal measurements.
52. Iron Age horses, tibia measurements.
53. Iron Age horses, radius measurements.
54. Calibrated age ranges for the radiocarbon results shown as simple lines for summed 68% and 95% confidence limits.
55. Calibrated age ranges for the radiocarbon results given as probability distributions of possible calendar age.
56. Central Cemetery, grave plans. (Scale 1/20)
57. Central Cemetery, grave plans. (Scale 1/20)
58. Grave 131, plan and section, and pottery from Graves 15, 30, 131 and 132. (Scales, pottery 1/4; plan and section of Grave 131, 1/20)

List of Tables

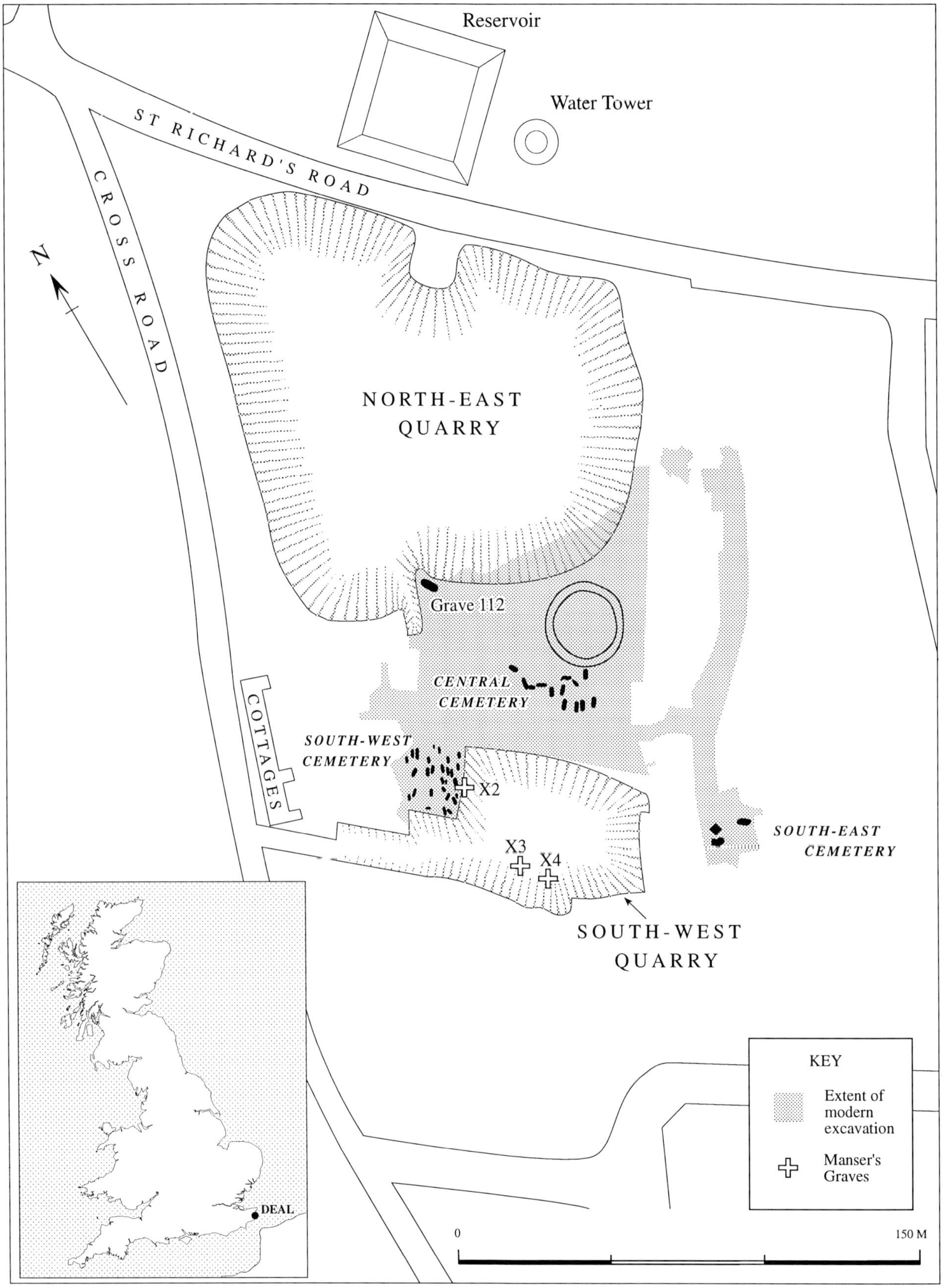

Figure 1. Mill Hill, Deal, showing the two quarries, the extent of the recent excavations (1984–9), and the positions of some of the main features. (See also figs 2 and 10).

INTRODUCTION

This report describes a series of Iron Age burials located during rescue excavations by the Dover Archaeological Group on two adjoining housing-development sites along the southwestern side of St Richard's Road (formerly Waterworks Road), on Mill Hill at Deal, in east Kent (fig. 1). These sites (now called 'Walmer Way' and 'Fairview Gardens') were examined successively between 1984 and 1989, with Group members working on an essentially amateur basis, without any official financial assistance. Excavations revealed an extensive multi-period complex, the limits of which were not located in any direction (Parfitt 1990; Parfitt 1991). The graves described here form just one element of the complex and the other features on the site, including an extensive series of pagan Anglo-Saxon burials, will be described in future reports.

The excavated area (centred on NGR TR 3631 5074) lies upon the top of the Mill Hill ridge on the outskirts of Deal and overlooks the sea at an elevation of between 34 and 36 metres above Ordnance Datum. The ridge consists of Upper Chalk and is situated close to the foot of the North Downs dip-slope. It is about 2km in length, the main axis being northwest by southeast. From earlier discoveries made during the course of chalk quarrying and building work it has long been clear that the entire length of Mill Hill was intensively occupied by ancient man (Stebbing 1937, 5).

The present excavations were conducted between and immediately adjacent to, two disused chalk quarries opposite Deal Waterworks which formerly belonged to local builders, Messrs G. H. Denne. The larger of the two (the North-East Quarry) fronting onto St Richard's Road had by the 1980s been almost completely filled in, whilst the smaller pit (the South-West Quarry) remained open but had been abandoned for many years. Significantly, the quarries, when worked in the late nineteenth and early twentieth centuries, produced many archaeological finds, mostly in the form of brooches and complete pots, apparently derived from a series of Iron Age and Roman burials (Woodruff 1904; Newington's notebook, see p. 171; Bushe-Fox 1925, 18–19). The precise position of the earlier discoveries within the extensive quarry complex was never accurately recorded; some of the individual finds are nevertheless of considerable importance (Birchall 1965; Stead 1976). In view of their significance in relation to the most recent discoveries, some renewed investigation into the provenance of the earlier finds has been undertaken and the most useful results are included below. A number of the more important Iron Age objects have been reassessed and are republished here.

More than 500 individual archaeological features, ranging in date from the earlier Neolithic to the post-Roman period, were revealed during the present investigations. Some 132 burials were also excavated, the great majority being inhumations. Over half were readily dateable to the sixth century AD, belonging to a major Anglo-Saxon cemetery of a type for which east Kent is famous. Forty-two other inhumations, initially thought to be of similar age, now appear to belong principally to the Iron Age period. These, together with five pre-Roman cremations and a horse burial, are detailed in the following chapters.

Occupation on the site during the Iron Age seems to have been fairly widespread in both time and space but it was apparently never of any great intensity. A few pits contained pottery dateable to the early, middle and late Iron Age periods (Parfitt 1985); several four-post structures and one six-post structure, typical Iron Age forms, were widely spaced across the site (fig. 2). The fairly slight evidence for Iron Age occupation is perhaps partially explained by the presence of a significant number of Iron Age graves, implying that the area was then considered more appropriate for burial than settlement.

Acknowledgements

The excavations on Mill Hill will long stand as a splendid example of what can be achieved by a local, amateur group. With the aid of specialists who have been largely prepared to undertake extensive research on the material recovered at no cost to the excavators, it has been possible to set the recorded discoveries in their cultural background and provide the detailed report below.

The Dover Archaeological Group would like to record its sincere thanks to the developers of the site, Dunsthorpe Ltd of Canterbury and Mr Noel Farmer and Mr Peter Clark of Margate, who readily gave permission for excavations on their respective properties. They have generously waived their claim to the finds, allowing them to be donated to Dover Museum (with the exception of the material from Grave 112 which has been given to the British Museum). Messrs Farmer and Clark made available, free of charge, their Case mechanical excavator for the initial site-clearance work, without which little of the area could have been fully investigated. Indeed, the level of developer cooperation seen on this site has rarely been exceeded in Kentish archaeology.

Of the Dover Group members who undertook the excavations Messrs Mike Halliwell, Geoff Halliwell, Ben Stocker, Howard Jones, Pat Mungovan, David Holman, Garry Marshall, Chris Huff, Peter Godden, David Woodcock, Andrew Rowing, together with Mrs Pat Godden, Mrs Tina Parfitt, Mrs Jill Bowers and Miss Clare Bowers all deserve a special mention for their sustained hard work over many weekends. Without their efforts little could have been achieved. In addition, Mike Halliwell spent many hours machine-stripping areas ready for excavation and backfilling as necessary.

The writer would like to add his personal thanks to the various contributors who have provided in-depth studies on the material recovered, and in particular to Jo Bacon who drew the pottery and did preparatory work on the grave- and site-plans, and Karen Hughes who drew all the other illustrations in this report. The Frontispiece and pls VII–X are taken from photographs by Sandra Marshall; pls I–V and XI–XIX by Mike Halliwell, and pls VI, VII and XX–XXII from archive photographs in the British Museum. Trevor Anderson acknowledges the contribution of Dr Jon Andrews, a practising dental surgeon, who recorded the dental remains; the radiographs that were kindly provided by Mr Stuart Capel, Senior Lecturer, Radiography Department, Christ Church College, Canterbury; and discussion and interpretation of the radiographs carried out by Dr Adrian Carter, Consultant Radiologist at Kent and Canterbury Hospital. Dr N. Garland and Dr N. Chandler provided a detailed archive report on the bones from Grave 5.

Jessica Vale, formerly Heritage Development Officer for Kent County Council Heritage Services, and Maggy Taylor, English Heritage Museums Division, made available the Deal finds from the earlier excavations and the associated archive. The staff of Dover Museum have given much support and encouragement throughout the course of the project, and artefacts and documents were made available at the Cambridge University Museum of Archaeology and Anthropology, Canterbury City Museum, Dartford Borough Museum, Folkestone Museum, Guildford Museum, Museum of Sussex Archaeology, Lewes, Maidstone Museum and Art Gallery and the Guildhall Museum, Rochester. The artefacts from Grave 112 were conserved by Ruth Goldstraw in the Conservation Department, British Museum.

D. Holman would like to thank Andrew Burnett of the British Museum and Simon Bean of Liverpool Museum for reading through earlier drafts of his report; their comments have been gratefully noted and accepted.

1

EXCAVATIONS 1984–89

The bulk of the excavation work undertaken between 1984 and 1989 was in the form of large-scale open stripping, using a Case excavator to remove the thin layer of topsoil overlying the natural chalk. An area of more than 5,000 sq. metres was cleared and examined, supplemented by salvage recording within builder's trenches. Fortunately, all the burials discovered were located in the main excavations and could be investigated under reasonably controlled conditions.

Figure 2. Mill Hill, Deal, showing the extent of excavations and distinguishing (in black) the Iron Age graves. (For more detail see figs 4, 5 and 7).

The Large Round Barrow

A major prehistoric feature excavated in 1988 on the Fairview Gardens estate occupied the highest part of the site, standing at an elevation of 36m above Ordnance Datum. It consisted of a large ring-ditch, some 20m in diameter, which almost certainly defined a now otherwise destroyed round barrow, presumably of Bronze Age date (Grinsell 1992, Deal 3) (pl. I). Judging by the size of the enclosing ditch this barrow must once have been substantial and would have formed a prominent local landmark. Indeed, it occupies a classic site for such a monument, on a hilltop which is visible from a considerable distance in most directions (F. 200, fig. 2).

Unfortunately, nothing of the mound or any contemporary burials had survived the ploughing of more recent centuries, but it seems clear that the barrow had remained largely intact until at least the sixth century AD, when it provided the focus for a large pagan Anglo-Saxon cemetery (fig. 2). Moreover, the local field name 'Whiteberry Field' (1839) or 'The White Barrow' (1855) must record the former existence of a round barrow in this area. The last surviving element of the barrow, its encircling ditch, was of substantial proportions, ranging in width from 1.5m to 2.5m and in depth from 0.83m to 1.31m. It was of broadly V-shaped profile, with convexly sloping sides and a slightly rounded or flat base. The finds in the filling show that the ditch was almost completely silted by the end of the Iron Age. Subsequently, in the Roman period, an enclosure ditch and several shallow chalk quarries encroached upon the filled-in ditch but it seems probable that the mound was preserved and treated with some reverence as an ancient burial place until well into historic times.

The positioning of the Anglo-Saxon burials, within the immediate area of the ancient barrow, seems a very deliberate act and the same arrangement has been noted on a number of other Saxon cemetery sites in Kent and beyond (Evison 1987, 154). At Mill Hill, however, the desire to use a pre-existing burial place and so provide perhaps vital links with ancestors seems to be clearly discernable before the Anglo-Saxon period. Indeed, the construction of the original prehistoric barrow on this part of Mill Hill began a long tradition of burial and appears to have been ultimately responsible for its choice as a burial site over the next two and a half millennia.

During the Iron Age a considerable number of graves were cut in the vicinity of the barrow. It seems quite possible that a few small satellite barrows were erected, creating a small barrow cemetery around the main mound, which would have emphasised the importance of the place to later settlers with dead to bury.

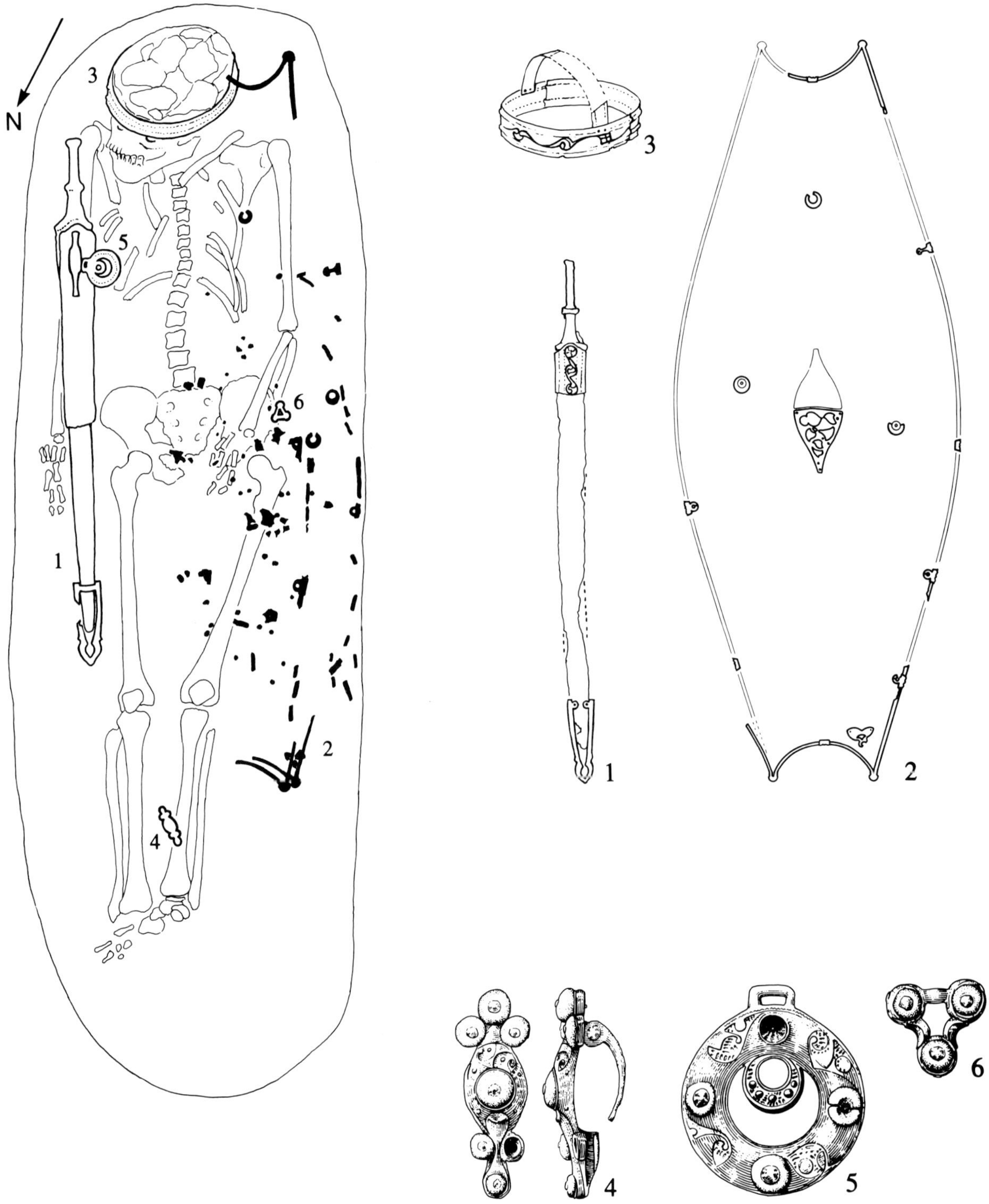

Figure 3. Grave 112 in plan, and the grave-goods. (Plan, and nos. 1–3, scale 1/10; nos. 4–6, scale 2/3).

The Warrior Burial, Grave 112

This isolated inhumation, excavated in late December 1988, was situated near the highest part of the ridge, close to the barrow circle and about 105m to the southwest of the centre of St Richard's Road. It lay upon the southwestern edge of the North-East Quarry, on the Fairview Gardens estate.

Predictably, the grave was discovered during rapid machine trenching, in an area thought to be devoid of archaeological features and too disturbed to warrant any detailed investigation. The survival of the grave had indeed been highly fortuitous, for it occupied a small projecting spit between the two main cuts of the original quarry face. Early editions of the 25 inch OS map show that this projection of undug chalk was related to a long-established boundary marking a division in the ownership of separate sections of the quarry (see p. 30; figs. 2, 10). Moreover, the grave was surrounded by a number of other modern intrusions, including two large machine-cut soil-test trenches dug several months previously and a substantial post pit (complete with surviving wooden post stump). If positioned only a little differently, the quarry edge or any one of these modern disturbances could have destroyed the grave totally. But the burial deposit had survived reasonably untouched, apart from being cut by a shallow field boundary gully (Feature 504) at some time in the Roman period. Recent chalk quarrying had led to the removal of all the original covering topsoil and a slight reduction in the level of the natural chalk surface here, with the consequent destruction of the upper levels of the grave.

When it was found, the grave was sealed by just 0.4m to 0.5m of mixed soil and rubble from the mid-twentieth-century backfilling of the chalk quarry. A hand-dug slot, rapidly cut to eliminate what at first sight appeared to be yet another modern intrusion, soon revealed the true nature of the present feature, but unfortunately led to some damage of the sword and scabbard chape which accompanied the burial. The grave was fully excavated, recorded and lifted over a period of three short, winter days during the Christmas holidays of 1988 (pl. II).

As with all the burials excavated, a one-tenth scale plan and section of the grave and its contents was drawn, with each find being plotted and given an identifying code letter (a) to (gg). This record was supplemented by photographs and written notes. The broad date and significance of the burial was fully apparent by the end of its excavation and expert assistance was sought from staff of the British Museum immediately after the Christmas break. In view of the importance of the burial, arrangements were made with the landowners for the donation of the find to the British Museum. The grave-goods arrived at the Museum in October, 1989 and conservation work, in preparation for publication and permanent display, began immediately and was completed within three years.

The unimposing grave pit was sub-rectangular in plan, with rounded corners and measured 1.73m in length by 0.59m in width (fig. 3). It was aligned roughly northwest by southeast (153° from true north). The sides were steeply sloping and the base flat. Its filling was a cream loam with small chalk lumps. As surviving, the grave was cut just 0.18m into the chalk but it seemed clear that the natural surface here had been considerably lowered and that the grave was originally dug some 0.35–0.40m into the chalk, perhaps 0.80m from the ground surface overall.

The grave contained the moderately well-preserved skeleton of a male aged about 30–35, of fairly slight stature (see below, p. 116–17). There was no evidence that the body had been placed in a coffin, although it was lying in an extended, supine position overall, with the head at the southeastern end of the grave. The long bones survived largely complete, as did the hands and feet. The legs were straight, as was the right arm, which lay along the side of the body. The left arm was slightly bent, across the left pelvis; its radius and ulna had separated during the decay of the body and fallen on either side of the pelvis, so that the ulna lay on top of the ilium and the radius underneath it. It seemed clear that the deceased had been buried with a shield over the left side of the body; presumably the arm bones were able to move within the void below it. The pelvis and vertebral column survived reasonably intact, although the ribs were partially decayed. The skull was pushed forward, resting on the end of the grave and facing towards the right. The top of the skull had been broken and damaged by later activity in this area and part of it was already missing when excavated.

Accompanying the body was an impressive assemblage of mainly bronze grave-goods. A bronze headband (f), still around the skull seemed to form part of some kind of crown or headdress (pl. III; fig. 3, no. 3). Originally, it had had a plain cross-band running over the top of the skull from side to side but later disturbances had damaged it and it was not recovered complete. Resting over the right arm was an iron sword (b), in a decorated bronze scabbard (c) and (d) closed at the lower end by a bronze chape (a) (fig. 3, no.1). Perhaps significantly the sword, within its decorated scabbard, had been buried face down. The pommel of the sword was level with the right shoulder and near the top of the scabbard was a circular cast bronze suspension ring (e), also buried face down but decorated with coral beads and a cast design (fig. 3, no. 5). It seemed clear that the warrior was not buried wearing his sword, which had been laid in the grave after the body.

Resting on the left shin, again face down, was a small bronze brooch (j) also decorated with coral beads and a raised design (fig. 3, no. 4). Its unusual position suggests that the brooch did not secure clothing being worn by the deceased, but it may well have been pinned to a cloak draped over the legs.

A scatter of sheet bronze edge bindings and fittings were recorded over the body, down the left side of the grave, (g) to (i) and (l) to (gg). The fragments covering a roughly oval area, some 1.19m (NW–SE) by 0.33m (NE–SW), had discoloured the underlying bones. Seemingly unrelated to the other items was a triangular strap-fitting of bronze, decorated with a small coral bead in each corner (k) which lay above the left lower arm and presumably related to a belt connected with the sword (fig. 3, no. 6). It seems clear that the concentration of bronze fragments in this area, including many pieces of decorative mountings, together with a considerable quantity of bronze binding of U-shaped cross-section, represented the remains of a decayed shield (fig. 3, no. 2).

Of particular significance were three V-shaped corner bindings, each having one almost straight arm and the other markedly concave, (g), (h) and (i), with a knobbed terminal at their junction. One (g) occurred at the upper limit of the bronze scatter above the left shoulder, with one end of the concave arm resting upon the side of the skull above the headband. A complementary pair lay one (h) above the other (i) at the lower limit of the scatter, just below knee-level: in section they were separated by some 65mm of soil at their southwest end but touched at the northeast.

All three corner bindings lay with their straight edges towards the outside of the grave and fragments of edge binding scattered between them suggested that they had once been joined, although the intermediate edging fragments were somewhat disjointed when found. Due to its relatively thin construction much of the edge binding was in a fragmentary state when excavated, and some was so corroded that it could not be lifted at all. Edge binding pieces totalling some 963mm in length were recovered, but other small fragments, perhaps amounting to a further 150mm, were too corroded to save.

Almost all the edge binding was along the left margin of the grave, mostly concentrated in the lower three-quarters of the shield area. It occurred in two discrete levels. The upper level fragments were between 0.03m and 0.08m below the surviving chalk surface and generally lay a little to the southwest of the lower level bindings which occurred between 0.08m and 0.15m below the surviving chalk surface. The general rarity of binding at the top end of the shield area was presumably due to later disturbances. This implies that the shield when laid in the grave was not horizontal but was higher at the upper end, perhaps because it was resting partially on the skull. It seems fairly certain that there was originally a second corner binding at the upper end of the burial, removed when the Roman gully was cut through the grave.

The arrangement of the two lower corner bindings, one above the other, together with the occurrence of virtually all of the straight-edge binding fragments along the outside of the grave, suggest that the shield had, in fact, been placed over the body broken and folded in half longitudinally, with its two edges towards the outside of the grave. There seems to be only one other possible explanation for the position of the bindings: if the shield had been originally buried in an upright position, leaning against the edge of the grave pit, the weight of the chalk and soil filling might have caused it to bend. However, it is difficult to see how the shield could have been so completely compressed by the overlying soil, bearing in mind the relatively shallow depth of the grave. Deliberate breakage seems far more likely.

The Central Cemetery

(Graves 15, 20, 24, 26, 28, 30, 31, 41–44, 110, 130–132; fig. 4)

An Anglo-Saxon cemetery was focused on the prehistoric barrow and consisted of two distinct burial areas situated upon the northeast and southwestern sides of the monument (fig. 2; pl. IV). The burials on the northeast (plot A) were well laid out and yielded ample evidence for their sixth-century date but the layout of the graves on the southwest side of the barrow (plot B) was very different. At least three separate phases of partially superimposed graves were located here, suggesting that the plot had been intensively used. However, detailed examination and recording of the sequence on this part of the site was greatly hampered by the presence of an extensive complex of shallow pits and hollows, apparently representing ancient chalk quarries. The upper levels of these quarries were filled with an almost uniform deposit of brown loam containing a considerable quantity of Roman pottery dating from the later first to the early third century AD. Colour changes within this deposit were impossible to distinguish and many of the graves were not revealed until the quarry fill had been largely removed, by which time details of the original stratification were less than certain. The problem was compounded by the keen pace at which the excavations needed to be conducted and it was not possible to establish confidently the exact site sequence here.

Of the three phases of graves identified in plot B, the most numerous were the middle phase burials, which produced many characteristic grave-goods to demonstrate their contemporaneity with the sixth-century Anglo-Saxon burials of plot A. The latest phase of interments, although on a different axis, was also clearly Saxon from the evidence of the grave-goods. Several earlier graves, cut by the middle-phase Saxon burials, represented the first burials in the area. They were quite different in form, being moderately deep and narrow, and frequently contained a comparatively well-preserved skeleton. In marked contrast to the later burials, they were either completely unfurnished or contained only one or two grave objects. Although clearly of a different character to the later burials, these early inhumations were also assumed to be Anglo-Saxon when first discovered.

Of the few grave-goods within the early burials none was recognisable as a familiar Anglo-Saxon type. The only readily dateable objects were an unworn coin of the Iron Age king Eppillus (*c.* AD 1–10) from Grave 30 and broken late Iron Age grog-tempered pottery vessels from Graves 15 and 30. Subsequently, as excavation work proceeded elsewhere on the site the general form of these early graves appeared remarkably similar to those of the nearby South-West Cemetery, more securely dated to the late Iron Age. The unlikely notion that the Anglo-Saxon graves on the southwestern side of the barrow circle had been placed partially across the site of an earlier Iron Age inhumation cemetery, with many of its graves set upon very similar axes, increased in strength as the excavation work proceeded.

Including Grave 30 with the coin, 12 inhumations exhibited stratigraphic and/or structural characteristics to suggest that they were of pre-Saxon age. Bone samples from five (Graves 15, 20, 31, 44 and 110) were submitted for carbon–14 dating at Oxford (Accelerator lab) and the British Museum in order to test the inferred dating. The calibrated results (p. 153) amply confirm a pre-Saxon date for all these burials and, combined with the Eppillus coin and pottery finds and the characteristic form of the graves, there can now be no doubt that a series of late Iron Age and early Roman inhumation burials lay in the same area as the graves of Anglo-Saxon cemetery plot B. These pre-Saxon graves constitute an early cemetery (here designated the Central Cemetery) quite separate from the larger but broadly contemporary South-West Cemetery (see below); they form another key element within the burial sequence upon the site, although the precise number of graves to be included within the group remains difficult to define.

The identification of two overlapping sets of graves of significantly different ages, refocuses attention on their relationship with the complex of quarry pits here. From the evidence of their filling and the pottery they contained, it would seem that the quarries silted up gradually during the first half of the Roman period. This implies a post-Conquest date for their excavation, although it is not impossible that some were originally dug during the late Iron Age. Either way they appear not to be very far removed in time from the date of the early-phase burials. It seems likely that the early graves were cut by the quarries, but it is just possible that they were dug into the base of the open pits. The Saxon burials of the middle and late phases must have been dug through the in-filled quarries and, on site, a few Saxon grave cuts were visible in the top of the quarry filling. The full extent of the burials, however, did not become clear until the quarries had been excavated.

Two late Iron Age cremation burials (Graves 130

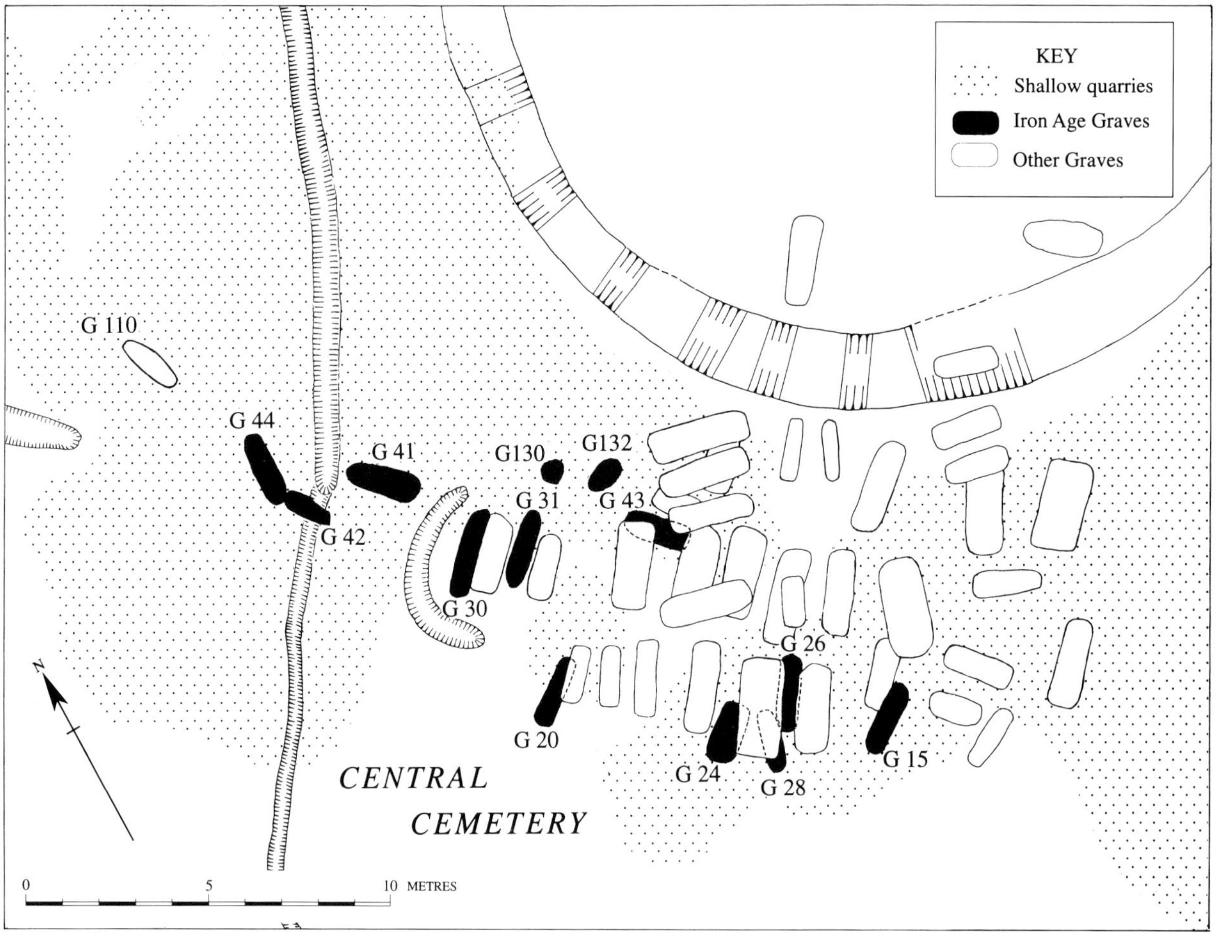

Figure 4. Plan of the Central Cemetery. The shaded and numbered graves are Iron Age and Roman; other graves are Anglo-Saxon; the large ring-ditch (Feature 200) is Bronze Age.

and 132) lay within the area of the Central Cemetery, although they seem to have been redeposited during the Roman period. A third, in situ cremation, Grave 131, lay well to the north of the main cemetery area.

The Inhumation Burials

A total of 12 inhumations has been assigned to the pre-Saxon Central Cemetery (Graves 15, 20, 24, 26, 28, 30, 31, 41, 42, 43, 44 and 110). These were fairly randomly scattered over a narrow strip of ground measuring some 23.5m (N–S) by 6.5m (E–W). Four undated outlying inhumations, Graves 11, 109 and 111 to the northwest and Grave 56 to the southeast, are probably of Roman date but as they lie well beyond the main cemetery area they have not been included in the present report.

The individual grave axes were variable. Six were aligned roughly northeast by southwest with the head at the southern end in every instance. Interestingly, this orientation and head positioning was the same as in the adjacent middle-phase Saxon graves but the axes were slightly more easterly than the majority of graves in the Iron Age South-West Cemetery. Graves 41 and 43 were aligned northwest by southeast, the head being at the southern end in both cases. A further four graves were aligned almost north–south (including Grave 110 of Roman date), with the head at the south end in just one instance (Grave 44). The majority of skeletons were extended and supine but two bodies had been laid on their sides (Graves 24 and 26), whilst Grave 42, probably disturbed by a Roman field ditch (Feature 211), was apparently crouched. In most extended supine burials the arms were straight, though some were bent across the pelvis. Both the burials placed on their sides had the arms bent double and the legs slightly bent. In contrast with the South–West Cemetery no graves contained children under 14 years old.

Despite the stratigraphic problems caused by the extensive quarry pits, reasonably clear dating evidence is available for six graves: the radiocarbon date from Grave 31 is Iron Age, and those from Graves 15, 20 and 44 leave little doubt that they belong to the late Iron Age or very early Roman period; whilst the coin and pottery evidence from Grave 30 demonstrates a similar date. The result of the carbon–14 date for Grave 110 indicates that it is a little later, belonging more probably to the Roman period.

Less certain stratigraphic evidence is available for dating the other graves assigned to this early phase. Graves 28 and 43 were definitely cut by middle-phase Saxon graves. Graves 15, 20, 24 and 26 all appeared to be cut by sixth-century inhumations but definite relationships were difficult to show during excavation. Grave 42 seemed to be cut by a Roman field boundary ditch. Grave 41 has been dated principally by its shape and positioning in relation to the other early burials.

It is possible that one or two graves included in the early cemetery are actually Saxon and it is also possible that a few other Iron Age and Roman graves have not been recognised. Moreover, some other early graves may have been completely destroyed by the later burials, as was almost the case with Grave 28. However, it does seem clear that the Central Cemetery was never as large as the South-West Cemetery, its full extent being contained within the present excavated area. The radiocarbon date from Grave 110 helps to confirm that the cemetery continued to be used well into the Roman period.

Although very similar in form to the graves of the South-West Cemetery, the graves of the Central Cemetery were generally slightly wider, but still markedly narrower than the bulk of adult Saxon graves excavated. The general lack of space within the grave pits was never such a prominent feature here as in the burials of the South-West Cemetery (see p. 24).

The Cremation Burials

Three late Iron Age cremation burials (Graves 130, 131 and 132, figs 2, 4) found in the area of the inhumation burials have been included here as part of the Central Cemetery, although they do not seem to be closely related to the inhumation graves. All three had been disturbed by subsequent Roman activity in the area. Indeed, Graves 130 and 132, only 0.7m apart, had apparently been reburied in Roman times, within the partially-filled quarry pit complex (similar redeposited cremation deposits have recently been recorded at Baldock, Burleigh 1993).

Grave 131 was isolated some 20m to the north of Grave 110. It was found in situ but had been partly cut away by the later quarry pits. A Pedestal Jar (fig. 58, 131, b), of which less than half survived on the southern side of the burial pit, had acted as the cinerary urn. It had been damaged by the quarrying and the upper part had been removed but a quantity of cremated bone survived within it. The missing base of this vessel cannot be explained by the later activity: it would seem that an old, bottomless pot was used in the original burial. A small jar (fig. 58, 131, a) was the only other object contained in this burial.

The South-West Cemetery

(Graves 46–55, 107–108, and 113–128; fig. 5)

A group of 28 graves, excavated in two phases during the winters of 1987 and 1988, was situated at the extreme western end of the site, along the northwest edge of the South-West Quarry and about 35m to the west of the Central Cemetery. The graves occupied an almost flat piece of ground at an elevation of about 35m OD, just off the highest part of the ridge. All were inhumations and clearly formed part of a larger cemetery, partially destroyed by the quarry (fig. 1). The grave-goods show that this cemetery was of later Iron Age date.

The surviving part of the cemetery covered an area some 22m (N–S) by 19m (E–W). Its northern and western limits were certainly located during the present excavations but the eastern and southern sides had been previously destroyed. It is not clear how much of the cemetery has been dug away but at least two related inhumations exposed during the quarrying, including the well-known burial with a pair of bronze 'spoons' beside the head (Grave X2), can still be identified in the early site records (see p. 172). A number of late first- to second-century Roman cremations also recovered during the quarrying seem to have been found to the east of the Iron Age burials (Woodruff 1904).

Few other archaeological features were located in the area of the excavated cemetery, although an undated (possibly Roman) straight gully (Feature 503) ran across its southwest side and two small pits (Feature 265 and Feature 428), one dated to the later Neolithic period, were located on its northeastern margin. Recent activity in the area was represented by a group of structures relating to the adjacent chalk quarry, in particular two sub-surface lime kilns situated immediately to the southwest. Prior to the initial excavations in 1987 the central part of the cemetery area was occupied by a substantial nineteenth-century brick-built outhouse and an extensive series of sub-rectangular post pits revealed in the same area must relate to one or more of its timber predecessors. Fortunately, damage to the archaeological remains had not been too severe beyond the quarry edges, although there had been some disturbance of a few graves.

The Burials

From the beginning there was a marked contrast between the graves of the South-West Cemetery and the more frequent pagan Anglo-Saxon burials previously excavated. Their general size, shape, axis, less ordered layout and comparative lack of grave-goods clearly set them apart from those of the Saxon cemetery, although it was not until the end of 1988 that sufficient dateable material had been recognised to confirm their pre-Saxon age. Indeed, only one quarter of the burials within the present cemetery contained grave-goods and none was richly furnished. However, six of the graves (Graves 47, 50, 108, 122, 123 and 127) yielded brooches of La Tène II or III type dating from the mid-second to mid-first century BC. Bones of two animals were also recovered. The disturbed skeleton of a small lap dog found above the body of Grave 47 must have been thrown into the grave as it was being back-filled. Grave 53 yielded a complete horse burial.

The graves were fairly irregularly laid out. Graves 46, 114, 123 and 127 occupied isolated positions in relation to their neighbours which could suggest that they were originally covered by barrows. An enclosing ring-gully around Grave 123 helps to reinforce this view. Possible clusterings of the other graves around these burials are apparent from the plan (fig. 5).

Most graves were broadly aligned north-northeast by south-southwest, with the heads at the northern or southern end of the grave in almost equal numbers. In depth, the graves ranged from 0.07m to 0.80m and none produced certain evidence for a coffin. Nine short graves (Graves 52, 55, 107, 113, 116, 117, 118, 122 and 128) appeared to be of small children but the skeletal remains were very poorly preserved and in three no bone whatever had survived; where bone did remain children aged from 1–11 were identified. The majority of the graves for adults had skeletons in fairly good to moderate condition.

All the graves contained extended inhumations but in comparison with the adjacent Anglo-Saxon cemetery they were very small and narrow: 14 graves may be regarded, from the size and positioning of the body, as being too small for the occupant (five of the adult-sized graves were less than 0.50m in maximum width). A number of minor variations in body posture and positioning appeared to be directly connected with this lack of space. In at least five burials (Graves 46, 54, 113, 122 and 126) the legs had been bent at the knee, towards one side of the grave, effectively shortening the overall length of the body in the ground. The same result was achieved in Grave 51 by bending the body to one side at the waist. In at least ten graves (Graves 46, 47, 50, 108, 115, 119, 121, 123, 124 and 125) the skull was pushed forward hard against the end wall, and in Grave 50 the end of the grave had actually been undercut to accommodate the head. In two other graves within this group (Graves 119 and 123) the feet also rested hard upon the opposite end wall.

With the exception of the five bodies bent to save space, the position of the legs was generally straight, although in Graves 51, 119 and 124 the legs had been crossed at the ankle and in Grave 123, crossed at the knee.

The width of the grave tended to dictate the position of the arms. In four exceedingly narrow graves (Graves 46, 47, 54 and 115) either one or both of the arms rested on the side walls rather than the base of the grave. Usually arms were placed either straight at the sides or bent slightly across the pelvis but in Graves 46 and 108 they had been bent across the chest.

Excluding the horse burial (Grave 53) and the ditched grave (Grave 123), only Graves 114 and 127 were comparatively large, perhaps indicating individuals of a higher status. Grave 114, a probable male aged 35 to 45, was on the eastern side of the excavated area, close to the quarry edge. It had no grave-goods but the overall cemetery plan suggests that it was an early grave with a cluster of subsequent burials around it. Indeed, from the spacings of the other burials it seems quite possible that a small barrow, of which no trace had survived, once covered the grave. Moreover, the 'spoon burial' (Grave X2) found in the vicinity at the beginning of the century could have been within this cluster.

Grave 127, a male aged 22 to 27, isolated on the western limit of the cemetery, close to the horse burial,

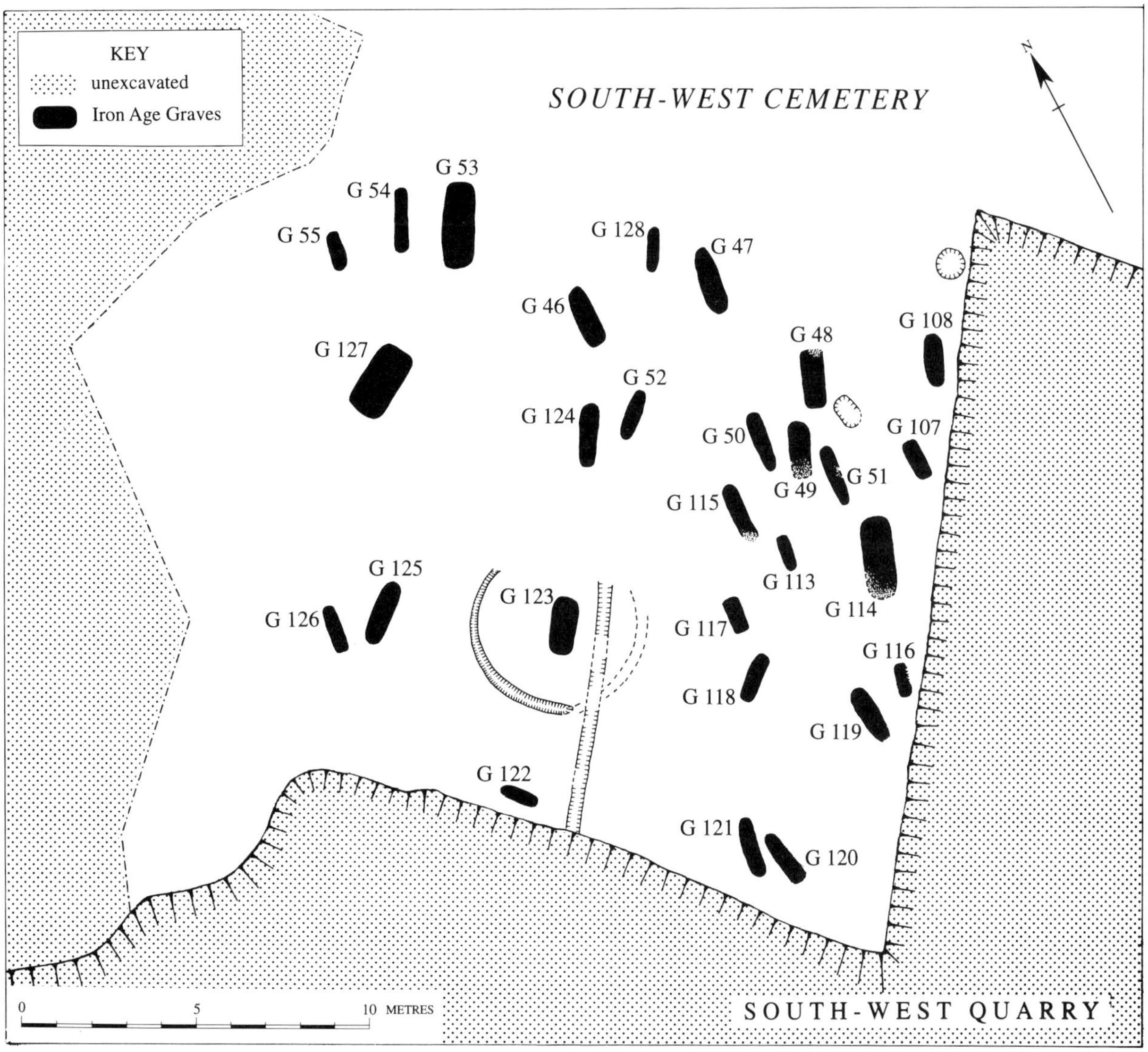

Figure 5. Plan of the South-West Cemetery.

was orientated on a more westerly axis (250°) than all but one other grave. It produced an iron involuted brooch of the mid-second century BC, suggesting that it is one of the earliest graves in the cemetery. It seems that a number of the other graves were grouped around this burial, including Grave 53 with the horse. The space between Grave 127 and the other burials would allow it, also, to have been covered by a barrow which has not survived.

Three further graves are of special interest:

Grave 48, The Prone Burial

Situated on the northeastern edge of the surviving cemetery, it is one of the graves which seemed to cluster around the larger Grave 114. Initially, there was nothing to distinguish it from the majority of the other burials. The grave contained a moderately well-preserved skeleton of a 13–15 year-old juvenile: unfortunately the upper body and skull at the northern end of the grave were missing. A modern post pit had cut its northeast corner and caused some disturbance, but it did not itself appear to have been sufficiently deep to account for the missing bones. From the position of the bones which did survive it was clear that the individual had been buried face down. The body had been laid out flat on the base of the grave in an extended position, with the head towards the northern end. The lower legs, however, were bent back at the knee and lay upon a wedge of chalk-rubble fill in the end of the grave. The arms were straight by the sides and the hand bones lay under the pelvis and femurs. There were no grave-goods.

Grave 53, The Horse Burial (fig. 6)

Located at the northern corner of the cemetery, it was one of the largest graves discovered. Orientated on the same general axis as the other burials (37°) there seems no doubt that it was contemporary with them. The point is amplified by the close proximity of Grave 54, only 1m to the west, on almost exactly the same axis (31°) and aligned with the northern end of this grave (pl. V). Indeed, Graves 53, 54 and 55 (a child's grave without bone) seem to constitute a single row of contemporary burials along the northern edge of the cemetery, perhaps grouped around Grave 127.

Grave 53 contained the complete skeleton of a horse (see p. 146), well preserved and lying on its left side, with the head to the northeast (fig. 6). Although a comparatively large grave, the animal barely fitted it and the forelegs had been bent, resting hard against the southeastern side of the grave, whilst the straight hind legs had been carefully angled into the south corner to make maximum use of the available space. Curiously, the skeleton did not lie on the base of the 0.6m deep grave, but was about halfway down its filling. Below the skeleton was a sterile layer of pure, loose small chalk rubble up to 0.23m thick, representing direct backfilling of the original upcast, rather than weathered silt. Its upper surface was slightly dished in cross-section possibly because of the weight of the dead animal. The bones of the horse were between 0.2m and 0.4m below the top of the grave. Immediately around and above the skeleton was a thin deposit of dark loam, presumably representing decayed flesh. The general filling of the grave over the skeleton, however, consisted of a uniform layer of cream-brown clay loam with small chalk lumps in which were two small, flint-tempered potsherds of indeterminate prehistoric date and a few struck flints, all probably residual. There were no other finds from the grave.

It seems clear that the dead horse had been placed in a

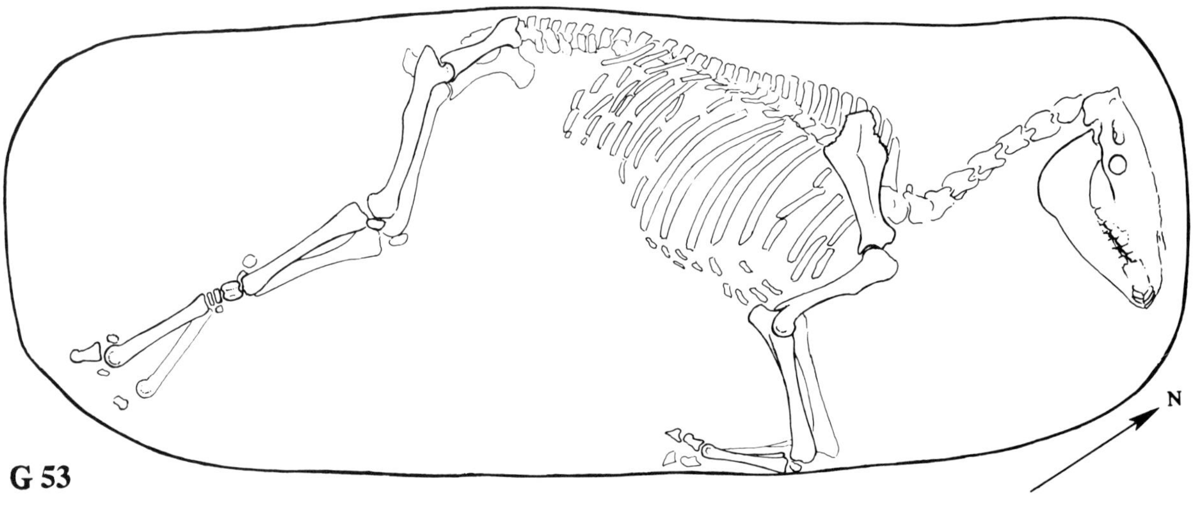

Figure 6. Plan of the Horse burial (Grave 53). (Scale 1/15)

partially backfilled, but otherwise empty grave. There was no indication of any human interment and the well-preserved state of the horse skeleton shows that a human body would not have disappeared without trace. The reason for the unusual position of the horse burial within the filling is obscure: perhaps the simplest explanation is that the grave, as originally dug, was deemed too deep and was reduced by partially backfilling the pit. Perhaps the adjacent Grave 54, a probable male aged 27–32, could be interpreted as the horse's owner buried next to his mount.

Grave 123, The Ditched Burial (fig. 5)

This comparatively wide and deep grave, almost central within the excavated cemetery area had been enclosed by a shallow ring-ditch or -gully (Feature 513). Only the western half of the gully had survived, from 0.15m to 0.38m wide and no more than 0.05m deep. The sides were sloping and the base slightly rounded, with a filling of brown clay loam and chalk, devoid of finds. It seems fairly certain that the gully once fully encircled Grave 123, with an internal diameter of about 4.5m; its upcast was doubtless used to raise a small barrow over the burial, suggesting that the deceased, a probable female aged 20 to 25, was someone of relatively high status. This grave provides the most convincing evidence for the presence of barrow burials in the South-West Cemetery.

The number of artefacts recovered sets this burial apart from the other graves in the cemetery. Two groups of iron joiner's dogs, one in the area of the skull and the other around the feet were initially thought to represent coffin fittings. But the grave was so short that both the feet and the skull rested upon its sloping end walls, leaving the body in a bowed posture and no room for a coffin. The location of the objects, away from the corners of the grave, also seems inconsistent with their interpretation as coffin fittings, but they must relate to a single large wooden object, perhaps a board over the body, forming a lid. The chalky filling of the grave did not preserve any evidence of this arrangement.

In addition to the iron fittings, there were two other iron fragments, part of a brooch and part of a pin. The general filling of the grave produced six small potsherds, three of prehistoric flint-tempered ware and three of probable Neolithic Grooved Ware.

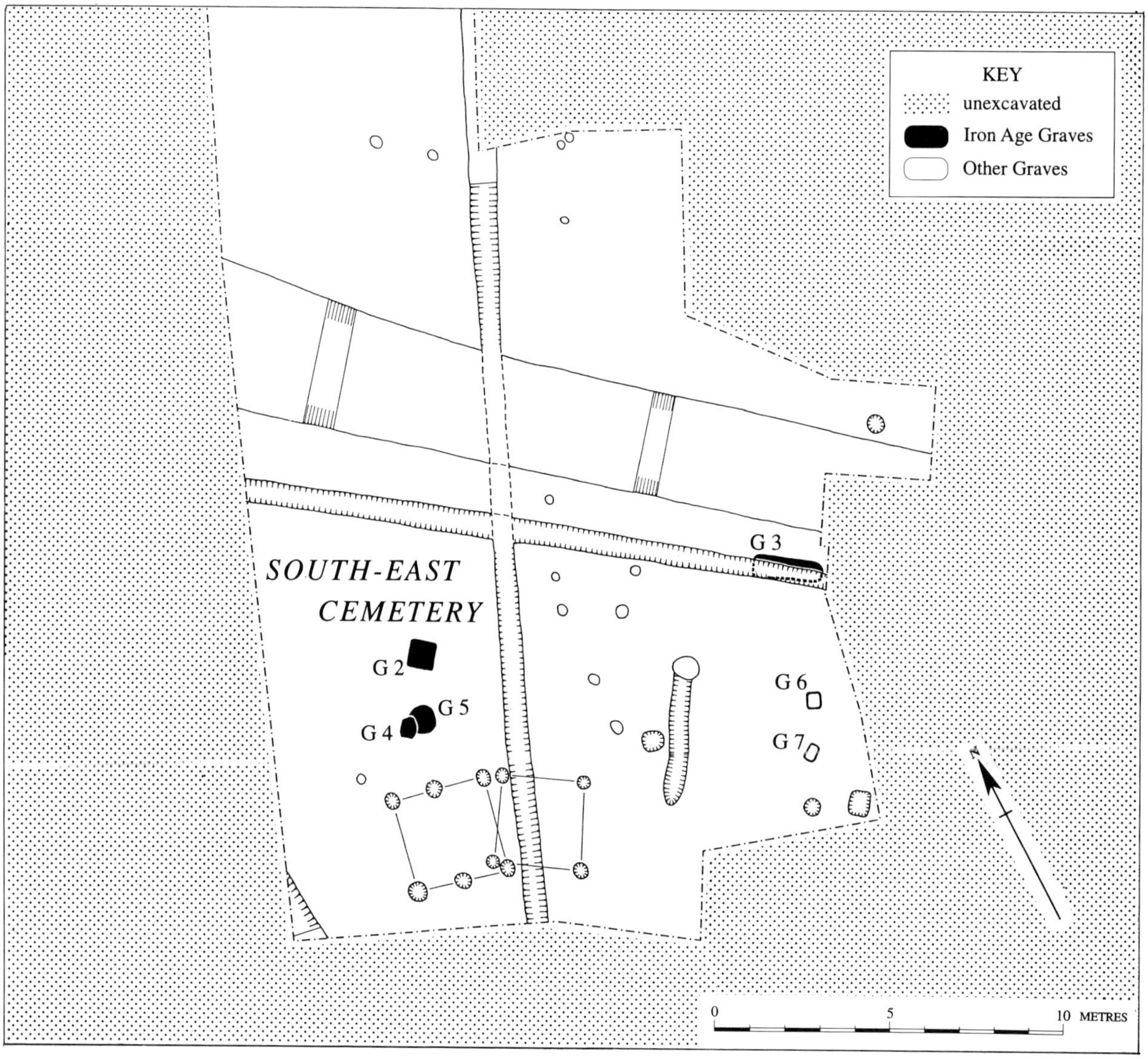

7. Plan of the South-East Cemetery (Graves 6 and 7 are Romano-British cremations).

The South-East Cemetery

(Graves 2, 3, 4, 5, 6 and 7; fig. 7)

The small South-East Cemetery consisting of four Iron Age graves, two cremations (Graves 2 and 4) and two inhumations (Graves 3 and 5), together with two second century Roman cremations (Graves 6 and 7, not described here), was discovered in 1984 under the turning circle of the new Walmer Way estate road in the southeastern corner of the site (fig. 1). Two of the Iron Age graves (Graves 2 and 4) were cremations of classic Aylesford type both with imported pottery, whilst Grave 5, cut by Grave 4, was a crouched inhumation representing the earliest burial discovered on the site. Grave 3 consisted of an extended inhumation, undated except by the observation that it was cut by a Roman field boundary ditch probably of first- or second-century date.

Of the Aylesford Culture cremations, Grave 2 had been thoroughly disturbed, if not partially robbed, in antiquity. It seems clear that none of the vessels recovered was a cinerary urn and it is probable that the cremated bone was originally placed in an organic container that had decayed. Such a practice was more clearly seen in Grave 4, just 2m to the southwest, where a bronze brooch on top of a loose pile of cremated human bone adjacent to the pots may have been used to close the top of a leather or cloth bag containing the ashes of the deceased. An identical arrangement seems to have occurred in Grave X11 found in 1909. Both 1984 cremations also contained a quantity of unburnt animal bone, identified as fowl and pig (see p. 000) and clearly representing food offerings.

Grave 3, located some 12m to the east of Grave 4, was an extended inhumation of a male, aged 25 to 30 years, aligned southeast by northwest, with the head at the southeast end (fig. 62). There were no grave-goods or other dateable material but it was clear that the burial predated the Roman field boundary ditch (Feature 76) which cut its upper filling. The general form of the burial was similar to many of those in the Central and South-West Cemeteries and a similar date has been inferred; nevertheless, the grave was not especially narrow (0.55m–0.65m) and its axis was roughly at right angles to most of the graves in the main cemeteries.

Grave 5 is one of only two crouched inhumations discovered on the site. The body, probably a juvenile female, lay on its left side with the head to the south. Finds were limited to a single burnt flint nodule which appears to have become accidentally mixed with the general backfilling. The lower legs of the burial were missing and must have been removed when Grave 4 was later cut through it. The bones which had survived were so tightly packed that the body could have been trussed up to allow it to be fitted into the pit.

Undated crouched inhumations of this general form are often assumed to be of early Bronze Age date, but since there was no reason to accept this at Mill Hill it was decided to submit the bones for carbon–14 dating, generously financed by the Kent Archaeological Society. The results, calibrated to 765–385 BC (two sigma, HAR–8444) shows that it belongs to the early or middle Iron Age period (p. 153).

This otherwise isolated early grave had been cut by Grave 4 which may imply that it was originally marked in some way, perhaps by a small barrow that had left no trace for the archaeologist. That the site of Grave 5 was clear to later people is strongly suggested by the second Aylesford type cremation placed nearby (Grave 2), the probable late Iron Age extended inhumation (Grave 3) a little further to the east and the two Roman cremations (Graves 6 and 7) a short distance to the southeast. Any barrow erected over Grave 5 could have formed a satellite to the main Bronze Age barrow some 62m to the north, and acted as a more local focus for the five later burials discovered within its immediate area.

Situated some 2m to the south of Grave 5 were a four-post and a six-post structure. Such timber structures are usually regarded as being characteristic of the late Bronze Age and Iron Age periods. There is no precise dating evidence here, but it seems clear from their overlapping position that one was a replacement of the other. The six-post structure, about 2.75m by 2.7m, was only slightly larger than the four-post structure. Although such small timber buildings are generally believed to have been connected with grain storage it has been suggested that some were exposure platforms for the dead (Ellison and Drewett 1971), so that their occurrence adjacent to the South-East Cemetery could possibly be significant.

2

EARLIER DISCOVERIES AND EXCAVATIONS

During the nineteenth century several large chalk quarries were developed by local builders, notably Messrs G. H. Denne and Messrs Cottew, on Mill Hill at Deal. Denne's quarries were opposite the Waterworks and immediately adjacent to the present excavations (fig. 1). The larger of the two (the North-East Quarry) fronted onto St Richard's Road and was very roughly oval in plan with maximum dimensions of 120m (NE–SW) by 140m (NW–SE). It was in existence and indeed, almost fully developed when the Tithe Map was drawn in 1839 (fig. 10). Ownership details recorded in the Tithe Awards suggest that the North-East Quarry began as two separate pits, the southeastern one then being owned by Mr William Bushell and the northwestern by Mr Samuel Welland and others.

From a schedule of previous title to the land occupied by the North-East Quarry, dated 1929 and kindly provided by Kent County Council (a subsequent owner), it would seem that the division in the ownership of the quarry continued well into the twentieth century. Bushell's old pit was sold by a Mr A. H. Lascelles to the owners of Deal Waterworks in 1895. It remained in the ownership of the water companies until 1966 when it passed to Deal Borough Council, thence to Kent County Council in 1974 until 1987, when the land was sold off for building. The former Welland pit, on the evidence of the same schedule, was sold by a Mr W. Watt to the Denne family in 1858 in whose possession it remained until 1922. The area was acquired by the water company in 1929 and remained in their ownership until 1966 when it passed to Deal Council, then to the County Council in 1974.

The first large-scale (1:2500) Ordnance Survey map, published in 1872, shows only a slight expansion in the size of the North-East Quarry since the drawing of the Tithe Map in 1839 (fig. 10). The 1898 edition of the same OS map shows the quarry almost at its maximum extent. The bulk of the chalk digging between 1839 and 1898 took place on the southern side of the old Welland pit and it seems clear that this occurred during the ownership of the Dennes. The 25inch OS maps for 1905 and 1938 show that the quarry finally reached its greatest extent sometime between these dates and by 1938 it lay abandoned, full of bushes and in the initial stages of being backfilled. By the start of the present excavations in 1984 the North-East Quarry had been almost completely infilled. According to Rhodes writing in 1923 (Rhodes MS) the quarry was 'dug some 50 years ago [i.e. in the 1870s] to build the sea wall at Deal'. However, it seems clear that this does not account for the total extent of the quarry workings.

The smaller chalk quarry (the South-West Quarry) lay a short distance to the southwest of the North-East Quarry. It was sub-rectangular in shape, measuring between 30m and 40m in width (NE–SW) and 55m in length (NW–SE). Still open in 1984, access was by means of a long-established track leading in from Cross Road, on the western side. A pair of brick lime kilns, enclosed by a lean-to cover building, were built into the face of the pit adjacent to this trackway. The development of the pit can again be traced through the 25inch OS maps of the area and also through a series of title deeds still in the possession of a recent owner. From the deeds it seems clear that the pit lay within a parcel of land of about 2 acres (0.8 hectares) in extent which was formerly known, significantly, as 'The White Barrow'. The land was purchased for £146 by William Denne in 1855. Chalk digging began some time later.

The OS map shows no quarry in 1872 but by 1898 the west end had been started and the two lime kilns constructed. The pit had been extended eastwards by 1905 and by 1938 it had reached its full extent. The deeds indicate that it passed from the ownership of the Denne family in 1929. In 1984 the vertical-sided quarry was still up to 7m in depth, although some low-level backfilling had already occurred. During 1988 it was completely backfilled.

When the Denne pits were being worked many archaeological finds were exposed by the quarrymen (pl. VI). The bulk of the known finds were discovered between 1900 and 1915 but it seems certain that much went unrecorded. The material that was recovered consists mainly of brooches and complete pots from a series of Iron Age and Roman burials. That some of these remains were recorded was due to the efforts of three local archaeologists, C. H. Woodruff, S. Manser and C. F. Newington, all apparently working with the active encouragement of Mr G. H. Denne himself. The extent to which the three antiquaries collaborated is not entirely clear; however, Woodruff's published paper of 1904, a series of recently discovered letters written by Manser between 1903 and 1909 and Newington's field notebook covering the period 1910 to 1915, now provide the bulk of the surviving information regarding the early discoveries at the site. From these accounts it would seem that no formal archaeological excavations were ever carried out and activities were confined solely to collecting items recovered by the workmen. Thus, individual grave-groups were not always distinguished, although Newington was able to record a number of cremation groups in situ.

Some of the earliest discoveries were published by Woodruff in 1904. Cumberland Henry Woodruff, FSA, (1847-1904) was a barrister, antiquary and collector who lived at Folkestone and was a member of the Kent Archaeological Society for 35 years (there is an obituary, with photograph, in *Arch. Cant.*, 27, 1905, lxii). He seems to have visited the site just once, during or immediately prior to 1904. The following extracts from his report are of particular interest here:

'The graves most recently discovered were cut into and removed in digging out the chalk for lime-burning' (Woodruff 1904, 9). 'On visiting the site I found from the traces of graves not yet wholly removed, that they appeared to have been arranged in a semi-circular position, and so near one another that it is difficult to believe that any long period of time divided the several interments. The great majority are clearly of Romano-British origin, the bodies having been cremated, and three at least of the vases were filled with calcined bones' (ibid. 10). 'Within a few feet of these remains an interment was uncovered which would seem to indicate an earlier period. A skeleton was found lying at full length about north-east and south-west, and on each side of the skull the curious spoon-shaped objects of cast bronze, shewn in the accompanying illustration, had been placed' (ibid. 11). 'A long bow-shaped fibula found in the same locality, but whether in connection with sepulchral remains I have not been able to ascertain, for it had been thrown out with the chalk and removed to some distance, must also be referred to the period of Late Celtic art' (ibid. 13). Woodruff did not publish a plan, and there is no direct indication whether his finds came from the North-East or the South-West Quarry.

Stephen Manser of Deal (listed as a Kent Archaeological Society member between 1898 and 1926, and local secretary for Deal, Sandwich and Walmer) took a great interest in the site but published nothing (though Chapman 1921, 129-34, included a description by Manser of finds in Deal Town Hall dated June, 1916). He may have been the first to hear of archaeological finds at the Mill Hill quarries. He assisted in the preparation of Woodruff's 1904 paper and between 1903 and 1909 corresponded with Reginald Smith at the British Museum. At some time before January, 1903 Smith seems to have visited the Mill Hill site with Manser. Manser's letters, including sketches and photographs, survive in departmental archives at the British Museum. In his paper on Anglo-Saxon antiquities in Kent, Smith (1908, 363 and no. 3) acknowledges information from Manser and also from a Mr H. Dunn of Deal, but no correspondence with Dunn survives (though he did have contact with Newington, see below). Manser's other contribution was in rescuing and assembling many of the artefacts and ensuring their display in a showcase at Deal Town Hall (pl. VII).

Manser's last letter to Smith about finds from Denne's chalkpit is dated September, 1909, although he wrote on other matters in 1913. Meanwhile, the rescuing of finds in the chalk-pit was being undertaken by Captain Charles Newington who was not a member of the Kent Archaeological Society and published nothing, but kept a MS notebook (Newington N.B.) that is currently with the Stebbing archive at Dover Castle. It seems that Newington's interest in archaeology started with flint collecting, for his notebook, begun in 1910, records finds and purchases of flints from 1907. In 1908 he recorded a pit with early Neolithic pottery in the nearby Mill Road brickfields (cf. Dunning 1966a, 1) and three years later George Payne published a series of miscellaneous archaeological finds communicated by 'my friend Mr Charles Newington, of Upper Deal' (Payne 1911, lxxxiii). Newington's notebook, which ends in 1915, records several artefacts and graves from Denne's chalkpit (see Graves X13 and X14; Artefacts X15 and X16). He also purchased artefacts found around Deal including Saxon material from Mr Dunn.

Between them, Woodruff, Manser and Newington recorded more than 70 pottery vessels relating to, at the very least, 15–20 cremations from one or more cemeteries dating from the first century BC to the second century AD. Several inhumations were also noted; some appear to have been of Saxon date but others were certainly or probably Iron Age.

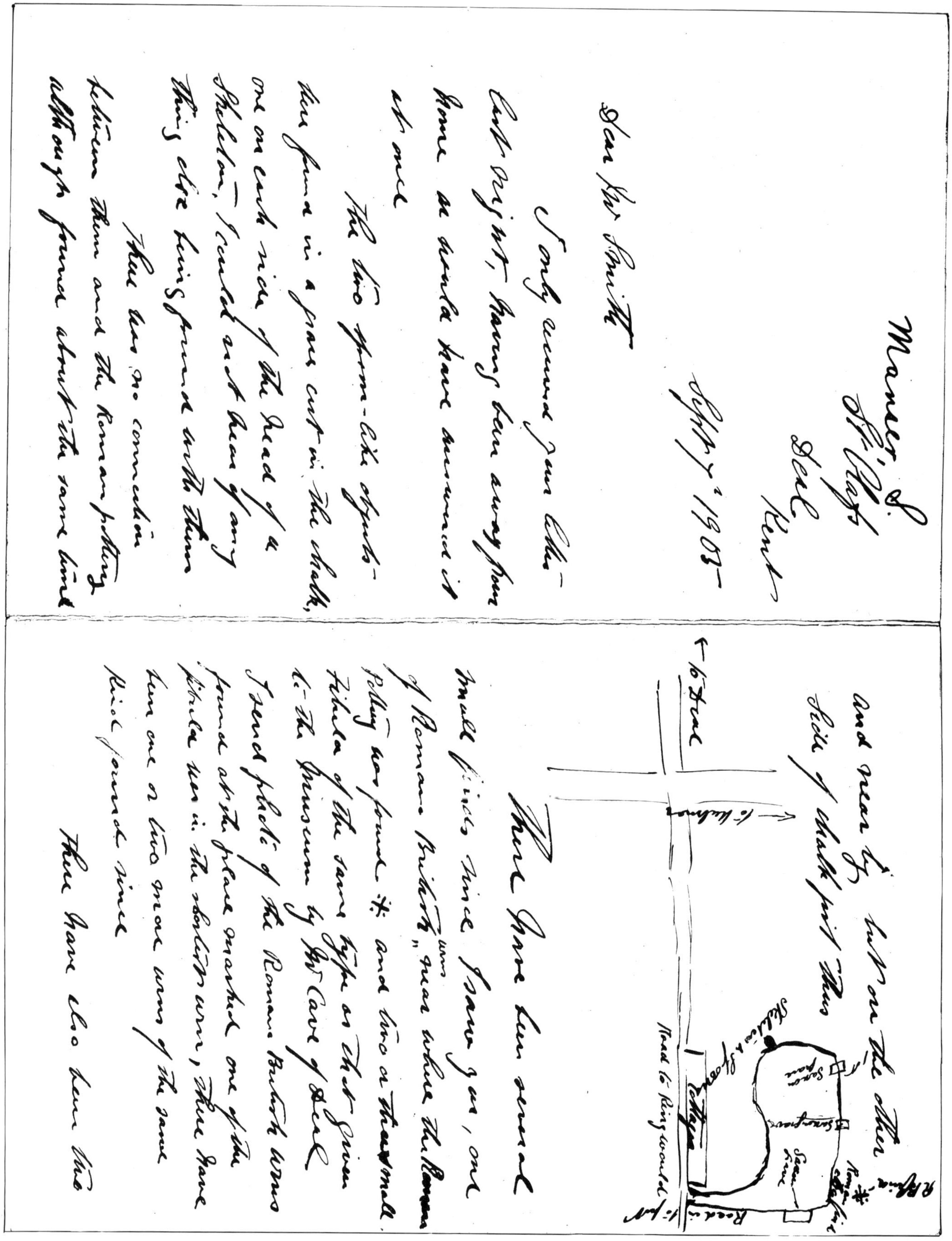
Manser, S.
St Olafs
Deal
Kent

Sept 7th 1905

Dear Mr Smith

I only received your letter last night, having been away from home or would have answered it at once

The two spoon-like objects were found in a grave cut in the chalk, one on each side of the head of a Skeleton, I could not hear of any thing else being found with them

There was no connection between them and the Roman pottery although found about the same time and near by but on the other side of chalk pit thus

There have been several small finds since I saw you, one of Roman British urns near where the Roman pottery was found ✱ and two or three small Fibula of the same type as that given to the Museum by Mr Cave of Deal

I send photo of the Roman British urns found at the place marked one of the fibula was in the shortest urn, there have been one or two more urns of the same kind found since

There have also been two

Figure 8. Letter from Stephen Manser to Reginald Smith giving a sketch of the South-West Quarry and the location of several graves (see fig. 9).

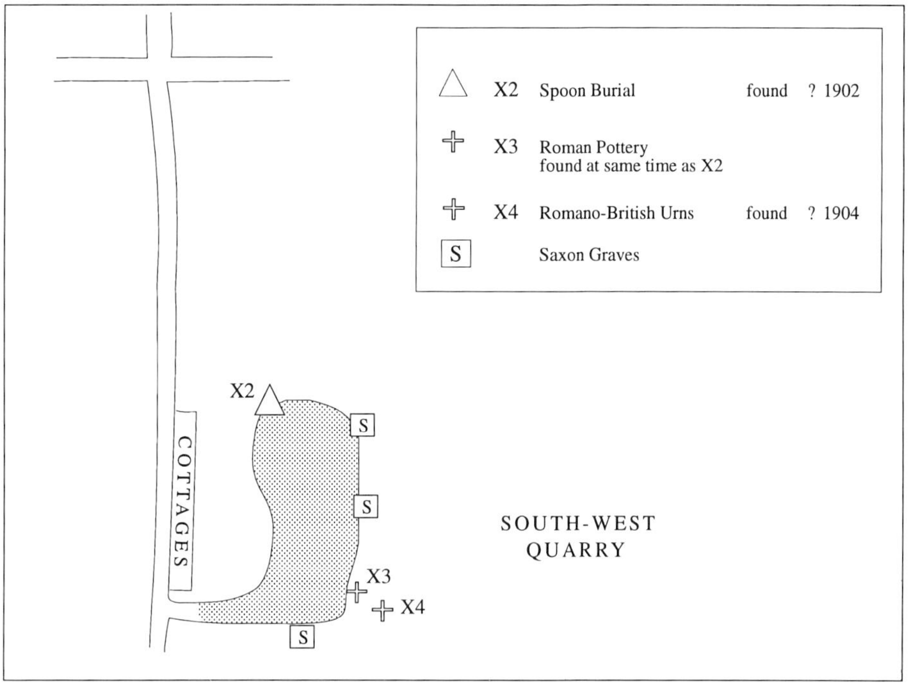

Figure 9. Clarification of Manser's sketch showing the location of several graves (see fig. 8).

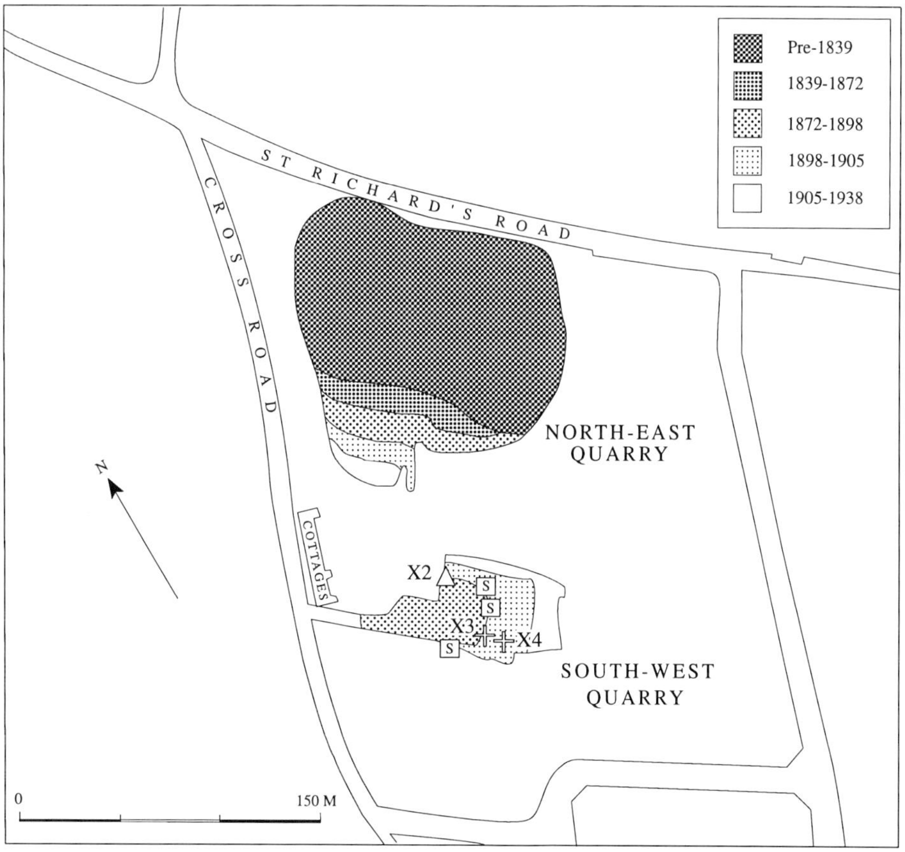

Figure 10. Plan showing stages in the development of the two quarries at Mill Hill, and locating the graves from Manser's sketch (see also the key to fig. 9).

Finds from the Mill Hill site were marked on the 25inch Ordnance Survey map published in 1938: in the North-East Quarry 'Belgic Urn Field found AD 1898' and in the South-West Quarry 'Pre-Roman Graves and Pottery found AD 1925'. Most of the recorded finds from Denne's pit were recovered after 1900 and it has been shown that the bulk of the North-East Quarry was worked out by the end of the nineteenth century (see fig. 10), so it seems highly probable that the majority of them came from the smaller, South-West Quarry developed at a slightly later date. Indeed, Newington specifically records in his notebook: 'In the smaller chalk pit near the waterworks, Walmer both Roman and Celtic pots and bronze brooches etc [have been found]', and an outline sketch plan of the South-West Quarry drawn by Manser in 1905 and sent to Reginald Smith confirms that a number of significant finds were made as this pit was extended (figs 8, 9). In particular, Manser's plan locates the Iron Age inhumation with bronze spoons (Grave X2) at the northern corner of the South-West Quarry, where it would have been in the destroyed part of the present South-West Cemetery.

Manser's 1905 sketch plan also firmly locates three graves of Saxon date and two groups of Romano-British pottery (probably the cremation vessels described by Woodruff) within the South-West Quarry. A bronze and iron object (Context X3) recorded by Woodruff (1904, 16), must also fairly certainly have come from this pit. Valuable details about the context of some other important early finds are also contained within Manser's letters. From these it is now clear that at least one of the La Tène III brooches was certainly associated with a cremation pot (Context X4) found in 1904–5. A fine, bronze coral-mounted La Tène I brooch (Artefact X6) found in or shortly before 1905 (Hawkes 1940; Hull and Hawkes 1987, no. 4991) was located in the immediate neighbourhood of Denne's pit but Manser could not identify the exact place. A rare bronze ring-headed pin (Artefact X10) was found in the topsoil by Mr Denne adjacent to the quarries in, or before, 1909. It is by no means impossible that one or both of these items originally came from other burials in the immediate area of the chalkpits.

It may be that the first archaeological discoveries were made in 1898, as the Ordnance Survey map records: in that year George Dowker wrote 'shortly before reading this Paper [in July, 1898] I made every enquiry at Deal about finds of Roman or Saxon relics, and no one seemed at all interested in the matter or could tell me of any recent finds; but my enquiry has already borne fruit in the finding of Saxon graves near Upper Deal; and pottery has been likewise found there...' (Dowker 1900, 112). The first recorded Iron Age artefact from the site is a brooch registered in the British Museum in July, 1900. But the Ordnance Survey's reference to finds in 1925 is not supported by any other source and is perhaps based on the date of the publication of some of the earlier finds in that year (Bushe-Fox 1925, 18–19). The only relevant records now available from the Ordnance Survey are cards produced in 1964: they include several mistakes and refer to a MS sketch plan in the Stebbing Collection, once in Deal Library, that cannot now be found.

The only formal archaeological excavation to be undertaken on the Mill Hill site prior to the present work was conducted by Messrs A. Du Cros and C. K. Rhodes in 1923. Their results have never been published but a draft report is held in the British Museum archives (Rhodes MS). The investigations consisted of a small area excavation carried out on a plot of land on the eastern side of Cross Road, immediately adjoining the western edge of the North-East Quarry. Ten features, pits and ditches, produced finds predominately of late Iron Age and Roman date. No definite burials were revealed. A photograph appended to the report shows the cremation group found in Denne's pit in 1908 (Grave X8) and the text notes that it was 'found while digging out another chalk pit some hundred yards from the present site'. This again clearly refers to the smaller South-West Quarry.

A total of 31 pottery vessels from probable Iron Age burials can now be identified amongst the early finds from the Mill Hill site. Of these, the cremations found in 1908 (Grave X8) and 1909 (Grave X11) account for 11 of the vessels. From Manser's letters to Smith it would seem that another 11 vessels can be attributed to a minimum of three more cremations (Context X4, 1904–5; Grave X12, 1909 and Grave X13, 1913), although only vessel D26 still contains cremated bone (Context X4, pot no. 3). The contexts of the remaining nine pots is not known; their state of completeness implies that they came from burials which are most likely to have been cremations, although Aylesford style pottery has been found in two of the more recently excavated inhumations. Manser's letters refer to at least one, unaccompanied, inhumation found at the same time as some of the pots in 1909 (Context X9).

Most of the artefacts were assembled by Manser for display in a showcase at the Town Hall, Deal, in the early years of this century, subsequently being loaned to the Ministry of Public Buildings and Works and moved in 1963 for display at Deal Castle (cf. Dunning 1966a and b), and then moved to Deal Public Library where they formed part of the Kent County Museum Service Collection. The display was dismantled in 1992 and currently (1994), the material is in store at Dover Museum and Dover Castle.

3

FINDS

With the exception of the finds from Grave 112, which are in the British Museum, all of the material described below has been placed in store at Dover Museum together with a copy of the relevant site notes and archive reports.

The Pottery

The study includes a catalogue of 40 vessels from the Iron Age cemetery at Mill Hill (MHC), 14 pots excavated between 1984 and 1989, and 26 rescued during quarrying operations between 1900 and 1913 (figs 58, 62–6). Stephen Manser recorded the discovery of 21 pots in MHC; it has been possible to identify all likely candidates, and locate all but one. Three are published for the first time (X4,2, X5,1, X20), while records of one of the best known grave-groups (X8) have been shown to be incomplete (p. 174). Published three times with a single Pedestal Jar, an original photograph taken by Manser at the time of acquisition shows that this particular burial group included two. Moreover, it transpires that while the smaller of the two is in the photograph published by J.P. Bushe-Fox, the larger was drawn by Ann Birchall and listed by Isobel Thompson (Bushe-Fox 1925, pl.iv, fig. 1; Birchall 1965, fig. 11, 88; Thompson 1982, 691). One early Roman group of four pots recorded by Captain Newington has been added because one of the pots parallels exactly an urn found at Folkestone (Grave X14). Finally, three pots without detailed provenances are included because they have always been part of the Deal Town Hall Collection and are therefore almost certainly from Deal, probably MHC (X17,21–2). A Necked Jar previously considered as a likely candidate for inclusion as Iron Age and which was recorded as being from a Saxon grave by Captain Newington has been excluded (Thompson 1982, 816).

For the purposes of this report, the pots have been divided into two categories, imports from Gaul and Italy (fig. 11), and the remainder which is presumed to comprise local products (figs. 12–13). Where vessels have already been catalogued and discussed in Thompson 1982, the relevant classification is given. The summary typological title of each pot is listed in the Inventory of Graves and Grave-goods (pp. 159–170), while the detailed description is appended to the relevant section of the typological discussion (pp. 39–57).

To place MHC in context, a gazetteer of early Gaulish imports, found in cremation burials in the South-East, i.e. Kent, Surrey and East Sussex, which are certainly pre-Flavian and could predate the Roman invasion, has been compiled (figs 67–70). The range of forms and fabrics recorded in this regional survey has been limited to that represented in the King Harry Lane Cemetery (KHL), Verulamium, and so comprises Arretine and Gallo-Belgic Wares, and Central Gaulish Lead-glazed Vessels (Stead and Rigby 1989).

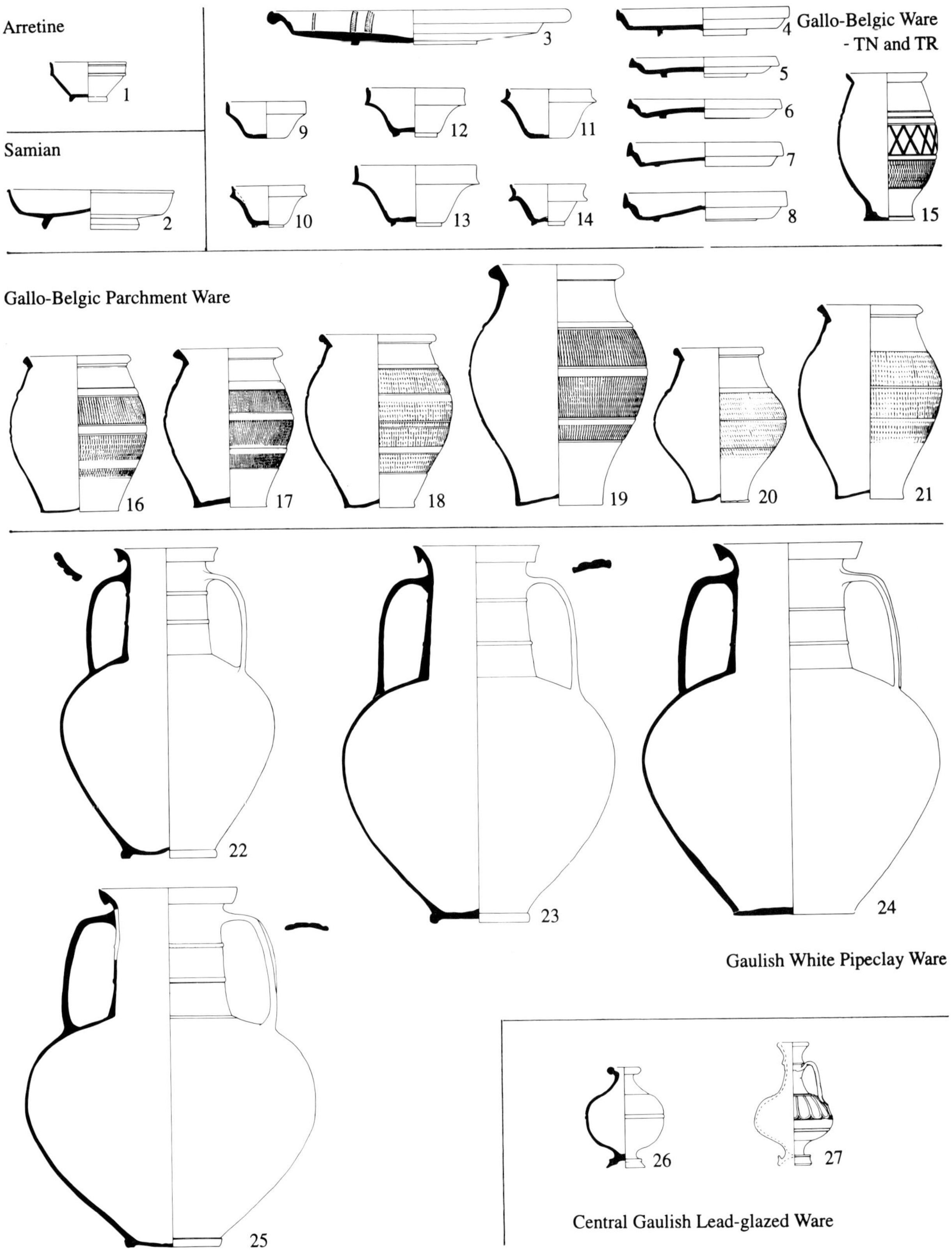

Figure 11. The typology of imported pottery in the Mill Hill Cemetery and the Gazetteer: 1. Ritterling 8; 2. Dragendorf 18–South Gaulish samian; 3. Cam 5; 4. Cam 7; 5–8. Cam 8; 9. Cam 56A; 10–11. Cam 56B; 12–14. Cam 56C; 15. Cam 112; 16. Cam 113 Variant 1A1; 17. Variant 1B1; 18. Variant 1C2; 19. Variant 2B2; 20. Variant 6D2; 21. Variant 2E2; 22–5. Cam 161 Variant GL6; 26. cf. Greene form 2; 27. Greene form 2. (Scale 1/6)

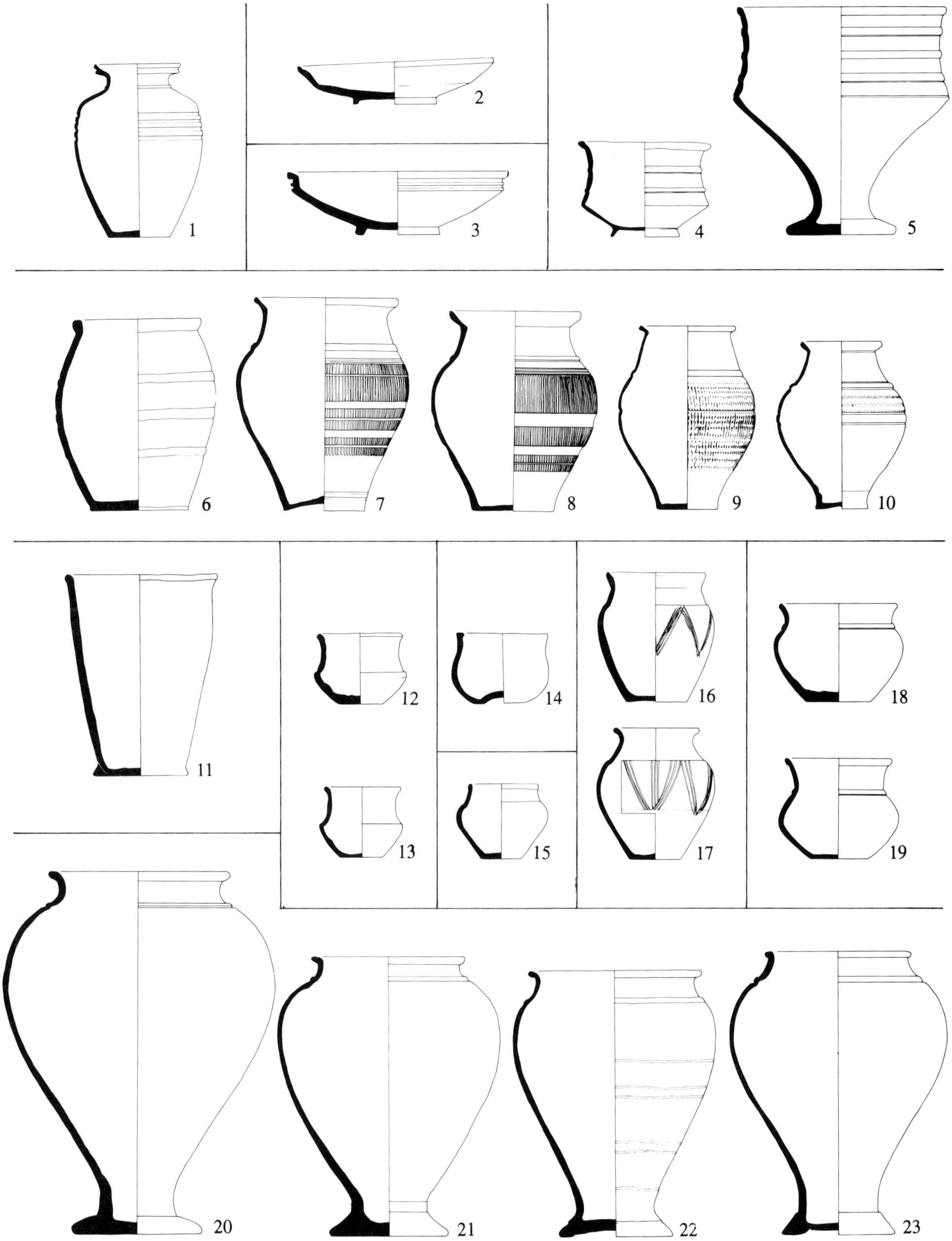

Figure 12. The typology of local products in the Mill Hill Cemetery: 1. flask; 2. foot-ring platter; 3. ribbed open bowl; 4. tazza; 5. pedestal tazza; 6. barrel beaker copy; 7–10. butt beaker copies; 11. conical jar; 12–13. waisted carinated bowls; 14. shapeless bowl; 15. necked bowl; 16–17. long-necked jars; 18–19. cordoned necked bowls; 20–23. pedestal jars. (Scale 1/6)

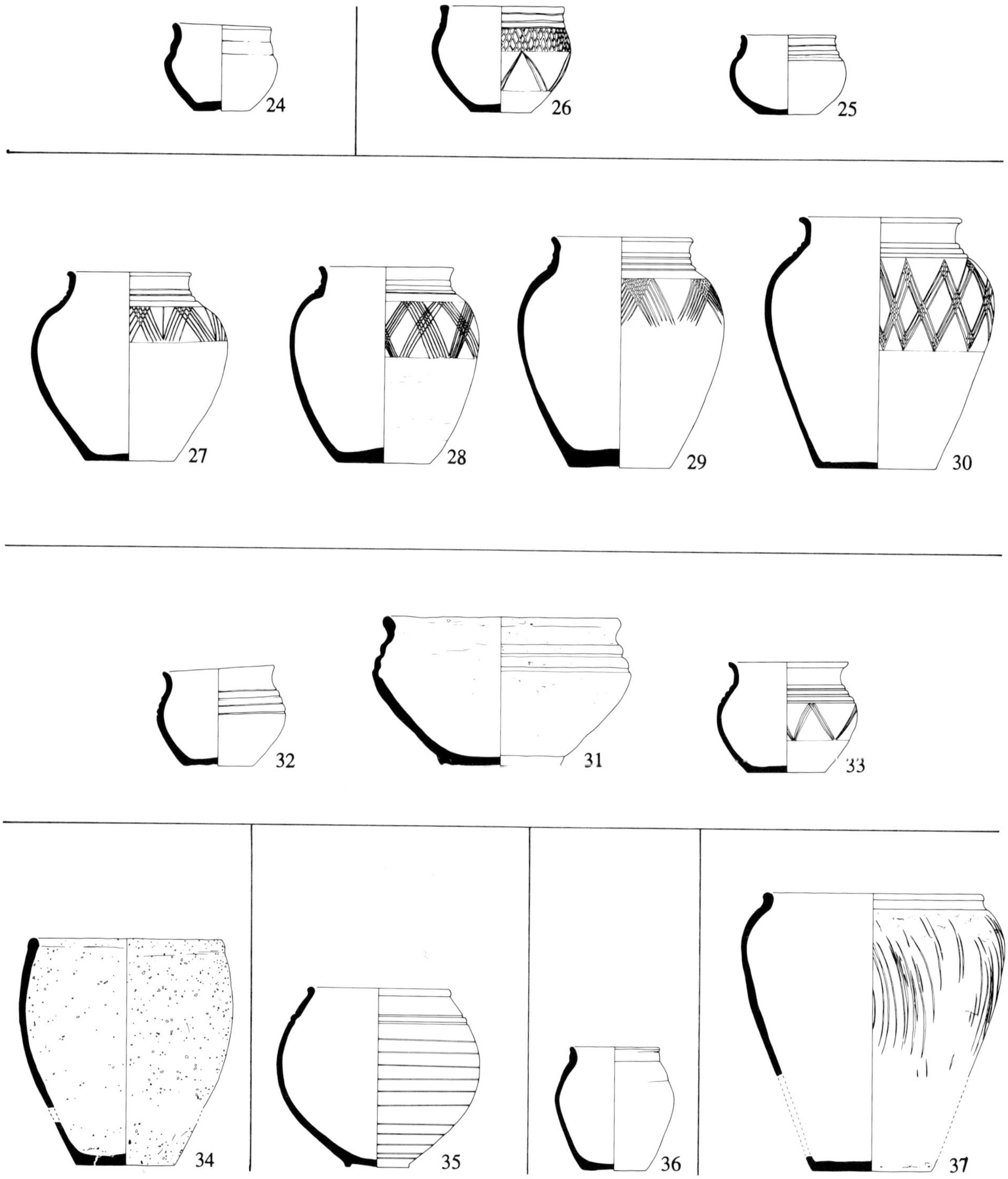

Figure 13. The typology of local products in the Mill Hill Cemetery (continued): 24. cordoned bowl; 25–26. ripple-necked bowls; 27–30. ripple-necked jars; 31–33. ripple-shouldered bowls; 34. lipped jar; 35. bead-rimmed bowl; 36. collar-rimmed jar; 37. wide-shouldered combed jar. (Scale 1/6)

Imports

The classification and discussion of imported vessels recorded in the Gazetteer are included with those from MHC. The range comprises platters, cups, beakers and lagenae (flagons with two handles), with narrowly specific functions for serving and consuming food and drink in the approved Roman manner. The concept of functionally specific shapes and fabrics was introduced to Britain in the first century BC. Although Britons may not have used imports in the intended way, they were rapidly adopted as grave-goods with the result that they figure frequently in cremations of the late Iron Age and early Roman period and, for example, account for over a quarter of the vessels in the KHL cemetery. No other cemetery of comparable size and date to KHL has been systematically excavated, but finds in the Lexden and Stanway areas of Colchester imply the presence of large and important cemeteries there. Early imports have been recorded in at least 70 burials elsewhere in southern Britain, suggesting their wide acceptance as suitable grave-goods.

Imports have initially been classified by fabric-type and then by form. Detailed parallels are confined to examples from cremation burials or cemeteries in southern Britain with comparanda summarised in Tables 1–7.

The quality of the sample is poor, the finds are mainly sporadic so that only 11 vessels have reasonably securely recorded provenances. There is just one definite instance where two imports are associated and that is in MHC Grave 2.

Arretine Wares

Arretine is defined here as forms and fabrics produced in both Italian and Gaulish workshops in the pre-Claudian and early Claudian periods; the plain wares can be distinguished with certainty only by reference to potter's dies and chemical analysis. Pre-Claudian Terra Sigillata, whether from Italy or Gaul, is rare in cremation burials of the late Iron Age and has been recorded in only seven graves in Britain (Table 1). While more has been recovered from settlements, the amount is not large when compared to the quantity of samian imported from La Graufesenque in the Claudio-Neronian period. In the pre-Conquest period supplies from Italy were not readily available even in the environs of major oppida like Camulodunum and Verulamium. They arrived in Britain as the few survivors of a long and involved process of transportation from Italy across Gaul by water and land. Most of the original cargo probably remained at various disembarkation points in Gaul, and was replaced by Gaulish products of regions through which the trading route passed. If pre-Claudian Arretine was scarce, then even one plain cup could represent a major offering in a grave, while a decorated vessel like that in the Foxton burial was a flamboyant sacrifice.

No Arretine has been recorded from MHC, but a plain cup, Loeschcke 8, was found at East Hall (Murston) (fig. 68, no. 8, pp. 184–5). Base and body sherds from a Crater Drag.11 were found at Tong at the same time as imported lagenae containing cremated bone; it is a South Gaulish product, not Italian, and like other plain vessels found in the same area, has not been included in the Gazetteer (Whiting 1926). Two South Gaulish samian vessels were recorded in MHC Grave X14 but only one, the Drag.18 platter from La Graufesenque, can be found (p. 176).

In addition to the cups and craters listed in Table 1, Arretine platters have also been found in the KHL Cemetery, Grave 346, with late Augustan G.-B. imports, and with imports which postdate AD20, at Heybridge, Essex and in the vicinity of Camulodunum, in the rich burial found at Lexden in 1940 and in recently excavated graves at Stanway (Birchall 1965, fig. 16, 139; Hull 1942; Crummy 1992).

Gallo-Belgic Imports

The forms and fabrics have been classified according to Camulodunum (Hawkes and Hull 1947, 202–4) and the KHL Cemetery, Verulamium (Stead and Rigby 1989, 121–45). Since Gallo-Belgic imports have been defined and discussed in detail elsewhere, only a summary is included (Rigby 1981, 1985 and 1986).

The range of functional forms recorded in the South-East extends to cups, platters, beakers and lagenae from various sources in Gallia Belgica; together they easily outnumber imports from other regions of Gaul and Italy. Most are isolated or ungrouped finds rescued in the main from brick-earth digging or chalkpits; there are 11 more or less recorded and surviving burials. The largest and most varied group of imports occurred in the East Hall Cemetery (Murston), but unfortunately no associations can be reconstructed from the surviving records.

Cups and platters in Terra Rubra and Terra Nigra

Terra Rubra

TR 1(A) – not recorded in burials in the South-East
TR 1(B) – not recorded in burials in the South-East
TR 1(C) – fine-grained orange matrix; darker slip, with polished finish confined to upper, visible surface.
TR2 – not recorded in burials in the South-East

No pedestal cups in TR 1 have been recorded in burials in the South-East. Besides the obvious cemeteries, Lexden and KHL, they occur only at Snailwell, Cambs and Owslebury, Hants. A varied range of shapes and sizes was produced, but the quantity from British settlements is too sporadic for any pattern to emerge.

Terra Nigra

TN – matrix variable in texture and colour, white to grey, brown and orange, but typically lighter in shade than the surfaces; surfaces variable in colour, dove grey to blue-black, with a polished finish.

There are 13 cups and platters in TN and TR which comprises the largest group of related imported fine table wares in the South-East (Table 2). A cup and a platter, both TN, were found in a grave in MHC, and two TR platters and one TN cup in the East Hall Cemetery, Murston, otherwise single finds have been recorded.

Twelve stamps are recorded in the Gazetteer. The stamp list differs markedly from that of the KHL Cemetery; the dies are mutually exclusive and stamps of the Ben(t)ios group provide the only recognised overlap. Two major producers, Assin(n)os and Jul(l)ios, each with three examples, comprise half the total, yet neither is represented in KHL where the absence of Jul(l)ios is particularly notable since it is the most common and long-lasting name-group of the G.-B. pottery industry. Both are well represented in the Camulodunum list. Only two dies cannot be paralleled. The early TR cup from Canterbury is unique (fig. 70, 29): the TN cup from Oare (fig. 67, 4), appears closely related to a die used in a workshop at Courmelois (Marne), and may be a second, less common version of the St Andrew's cross motif. There seems to have been no significant difference in supply between the north and south banks of the Thames between AD25 and 60, so that the marked difference between the Gazetteer and the KHL Cemetery is presumably explained by the small size of the sample.

There are no late Augustan products from burials: the TN platter from Cherry Orchard Way, Maidstone, and the TR cup from Kent, possibly Canterbury, qualify chronologically, but are from uncertain contexts. A wide range of late Augustan TR has been found in settlement material at Canterbury on the Marlowe sites, but it has been recorded at only two other sites in the region, Springhead and in settlement material from the Mill Hill site itself. Such scarcity is surely the result of an inadequate archaeological sample, and it is presumably only a matter of time before burials containing some late Augustan TR is found.

Three vessel-forms have been identified, two platters and a cup. A large platter Cam.5/GB 6 in TN, Grave 2, is the only example from a burial found outside the KHL Cemetery, despite the popularity of the form in settlement assemblages. There are five examples of the small platter Cam.8/GB 13, three in TN and two in TR. Cam.8 was standardised about AD20 and continued to be produced until AD65. In the pre-Flavian period it was the most widely distributed platter-form in Britain reaching settlements beyond the area under direct Roman occupation. It is also the most common platter-form in the KHL Cemetery, likewise in late Iron Age and early Roman cremations in southern Britain, presence in the South-East is predictable. Examples in TR are comparatively rare; two were found in the East Hall Cemetery (Murston), the only other recorded examples in burials are at Stanway and Owslebury (Crummy 1992; Collis 1977).

There are six cups Cam.56, four in TN and two in TR. Early variants had been standardised by 10BC but production continued until AD65, and for most of this period it was the only cup-form being made. The TR version in Canterbury Museum is a pre-Conquest product and the earliest in the Gazetteer, but unfortunately it has a dubious provenance. The small version in TN found in MHC Grave 2 is Tiberio-Claudian and may not be a pre-Conquest import (below). After AD20, several potters made both Cam. 56 and Cam.8, even stamping them with the same dies, and presumably distributing them together as a set.

The latest cup- and platter-forms in TN which were widely distributed in the Nero-Flavian period, more particularly to military sites lying north and west of the line of the Fosse Way, are absent from the Gazetteer. A few examples have been recorded in burials at Winchester, Hants, Poundbury and the Jordan Hill Cemetery, Dorset, Duston, Northants, and the KHL Cemetery, but they remain rare, suggesting that by the early Flavian period other imported fine wares were available and preferred.

The limited form-range recorded in the South-East mirrors finds from cremation burials in Britain, generally the most common forms are represented in the greatest numbers and mainly in TN.

Cup Cam. 56C/GB 17

1. Grave 2, a. Small version; one lightly incised circle. TN – patchy light grey surfaces; highly polished interior and rim, less glossy outer surface finish. Condition – restored to complete.

TOR – Central stamp.

The reading is uncertain; it is a short legend of only three letters. While the central O is large and clear, the letters on either side are small and faintly impressed but it appears to be an abbreviation TOR for Tornos since stamps reading TORNOS have been found at Camulodunum (Hawkes and Hull 1947, nos.147–8, two examples). The die has been recorded at Camulodunum where the impression is even less distinct, with only the central letter visible. The workshop was probably in the

Marne-Vesle potteries, and the date of manufacture between AD30 and 60.

Platter Cam. 5/GB 6
1. Grave 2, b. Large version; two lightly incised, bordered rouletted wreaths, with a double incised circle outside. TN – bluish white fine-grained matrix, darker blue-grey surfaces; upper surface polished but flaked in patches; poorly finished and less glossy lower surface. Condition: more than three-quarters of the circuit survives.
IVL:IOS bordered – three radial stamps.

Jul(l)ios Die 2H1 – stamps from this die, on TN platters Cam.8: Crookham House, Thatcham, Berks and Wederath-Belginium Cemetery, Grave 1049; on large TN platters: Camulodunum and Canterbury; on Cam.56 cup: Camulodunum. It may be significant that the same die was used to stamp different items in a 'place-setting': cup, small and large platters.

Stamps from related dies on TN: Camulodunum (five examples); Louvercy Kilns (Marne), Lebach Cemetery, Grave 45 (Gerlach 1976, fig. 39, 2); On TR: Hunnerberg Cemetery, Grave 5 (Vermeulen 1932, stamp 22).

The source was probably Louvercy in the Marne-Vesle potteries. In the absence of late Augustan forms and fabrics, and the dating evidence from Wederath and Lebach, the date of manufacture lies between AD25 and 60 .

Beakers in Terra Rubra

Terra Rubra
TR 3: fine-grained, dense and smooth matrix varying in colour from white to dark red; self-coloured outer surface varies according to firing conditions from clear matrix colour through thin grey 'haze' to black, depending on the degree and intensity of 'fuming' during the final stages.

No beaker in TR3 was identified in MHC. An Ovoid Beaker Cam.112/GB 25A is illustrated amongst the vessels from Elms Vale, Dover (Payne 1889, 203–4). In antiquity it had been broken and repaired with riveted bronze plates. The published illustration is indistinct, but it appears to be a large, pre-Claudian variant, decorated with combed stripes in the upper and rouletting in the lower zone. It is recorded as containing cremated bone and a fibula, but the group was apparently lost due to war damage.

Later variants, Cam.112/GB 25B, are smaller and more curvaceous. There is one virtually complete typical example with a Canterbury provenance which may be from an unrecorded burial. A second may have been recorded by C. Roach Smith and Payne amongst finds recovered from the cemetery at Shorne (Crafter 1849, 406, second from left; and below p. 186).

Standardised about AD10, production continued until *c.*AD60; it is the most common and widely found TR3 beaker in Britain.

Barrel and Butt Beakers in Fine Parchment Ware

Fine Parchment Ware
FPW: fine-grained matrix with fine quartz sand inclusions and variable amounts of grog; the fired fabric varies from white to pale shades of yellow, pink or grey depending upon the quality of the clay matrix and the firing conditions.

The size of the sample in the KHL Cemetery allowed the chronological evolution of the form to be studied (Stead and Rigby 1989, 137–41). Three criteria were isolated as critical, overall body shape (1–6), division of the decorative zone (A-F) and the specific rim-shape (1–6).

The earliest version, introduced in the late Augustan period, had a simple, tubby shape (1) divided by three or four broad, hollow cordons (A-C). The rim was narrow, with an external cordon and a sharply angled, internal cornice (1). To distinguish it from later versions, it is termed a Barrel Beaker. There are two examples in the MHC and a third in the Elms Vale Cemetery, Dover, and they are the earliest imported Gaulish vessels yet found in cremation graves in the South-East.

Taller and more curvaceous shapes were developed, with longer concave neck and base profiles (2–6); offsets and grooves gradually replaced the broad, hollow cordons (C-F). A deeper and heavier rim-shape, retaining the external cordon and internal cornice, was evolved in the Tiberian period, but by the Claudian period it was simplified, so that either the cordon or cornice, or both, were omitted (2–6). Variants of this group are termed Butt Beakers.

Four Butt Beakers have been recorded in burials in the South-East, at Aylesford, East Hall (Murston), Radnor Park (Folkestone) and Herstmonceux. Unlike some imports in the Gazetteer, they have secure provenances and are known to be from burials and cemeteries. The variants are identical to those found elsewhere in Britain suggesting that they were supplied by the same workshops of northern Gaul.

Barrel/Butt Beakers Cam.113 in FPW have been recorded on 20 sites, and are the most common functionally specific imported vessels in cremation burials dating to the early and middle first century AD in Britain. With 65 examples from 63 burials, and at least 20 different variants represented, it was easily the most popular import in the KHL Cemetery (Table 4). The overall distribution area is much greater than that of the cremation rite in the late Iron Age, extending south and east of a line from the River Tees in the north to the Severn Estuary in the west, but excluding Wales and the Cornish peninsula. Given their comparatively large size and fragility, their widespread distribution in Britain is a tribute to the packing and transportation methods used. The number of repaired examples in the KHL Cemetery implies that they were sufficiently prized for imperfect versions to be acceptable; similarly, the Herstmonceux example had undergone very extensive repairs at some time before deposition.

Barrel Beaker Cam. 113/KHL *variant* 1A1

1. Grave X11, 1. Typical Fine Parchment Ware, pinky buff, with occasional red grog inclusions; smoothly burnished rim, neck, cordons and base. Decoration: typical rouletting. A slight 'second'. Condition: repaired to complete.

KHL variant 1B1.

1. Grave 4, c. Typical Fine Parchment Ware: grey core at the rim, otherwise cream at base shading to smoky pink at the rim, probably the result of stacking during the firing process; burnished rim, neck, cordons and base. Decoration – typical fine chattered rouletting. Condition – complete, but with a small chip out of the rim; probably in this condition when deposited.

Lagenae in White Pipeclay

White Pipeclay: fine-grained, smooth and dense white matrix with occasional red grog inclusions: a pure kaolinite clay.

There are two basic lagena types with collared rims. The first has a plain sharply angled and undercut collar and from one to four narrow raised cordons on the neck (Cam.161/KHL GL 6–8), the second has a series of narrow grooves encircling the collar (a reeded rim) and broad, hollow cordons on the neck (Cam.163/KHL GL 9–12); both have broad, strap handles with four or five ribs (Stead and Rigby 1989, 141–3). Some, at least, were manufactured in Cologne in the Tiberian period (La Baume 1963, 12–22).

The single most common variant in the KHL Cemetery proved to be Cam.161/GL 6 with two narrow raised cordons on the neck and four-ribbed handles. It is also the most common variant in burials elsewhere in Britain, and in the assemblages from Camulodunum, so it is predictable that the six examples recorded in the Gazetteer are of this variant. All have fairly secure provenances, and those found at Tong had contained cremated bone. No matching single-handled flagons have been found in burials.

Continental military sites provide a *terminus post quem* of AD10 for the production of lagenae in white pipeclay, and supporting evidence is provided by the KHL Cemetery where none occurred in the earliest burials. The distribution pattern is similar to that of Butt Beakers, with both markedly absent from military sites north and west of the Fosse Way, although present on some native settlements. None has been recorded in Londinium nor the bridgehead settlement south of the river at Southwark, suggesting that import ceased before AD50, the conventional date for the founding of Londinium.

Central Gaulish Imports

Lead-glazed Wares

The fabrics vary in appearance but are typically fine-grained and smooth in texture, white or cream, micaceous or non-micaceous, with lime green or yellowish green glazes.

No vessel in Lead-glazed Ware was found in MHC and there are only five recorded cremation graves in Britain which include at least one example. Two are at Camulodunum, the first, Joslin Grave 3, was found in Lexden Road in the nineteenth century, while the other was recently excavated in a secondary grave in the main enclosure at Stanway (Crummy 1992). Single finds are recorded in the KHL Cemetery, Grave 136, West Wickham, Grave E, and Sanderstead, Grave 5. The recovery of a complete flagon, at Bapchild, Sittingbourne, may indicate a sixth, but disturbed burial.

The West Wickham and Sanderstead vessels are flasks of similar and hitherto unrecorded form, with a markedly recessed rim, possibly to take a stopper, but they are decorated with different motifs. They were found less than 15km apart in an area not known for the richness of its early Roman finds.

Lead-glazed Wares from the Allier valley of the Massif Central in Central Gaul are usually easy to identify due to their fabrics and idiosyncratic forms. The form range is limited to small cups and bowls, narrow-necked flasks and flagons, but also includes a wide variety of bird and animal shapes with the tail folded back to the head to act as the strap handle. Decoration is in relief, with potters using barbotine, moulded and applied motifs. Examples first appear in Britain in the pre-Flavian period, mainly on military sites but glazed wares never achieved the popularity of contemporary colour-coated vessels imported from the same region of Gaul (Greene 1978). Trade apparently continued into the mid-second century AD.

The Joslin group at Colchester is in a class of its own and warrants a brief note. It consists of three flagons and six animal flasks in Lead-glazed Wares accompanied by a menagerie of human and animal figures in White Pipeclay, and a rich array of bronze and glass vessels (May 1930, 251, pl.lxxv). Finally, twenty-five coins of Claudius give a rather early *terminus post quem* for the group. Altogether it is an interesting assemblage for what is claimed to be a child's grave.

Local Products

Thirty-six vessels in the burials had been made within the region using native late Iron Age techniques to produce a range of different functional shapes and sizes. All but seven pots are complete, or restored to complete, so that no systematic fabric analysis has been possible, although opportunistic study occurred where sherds were missing or edges chipped and abraded.

The Fabrics

Temper and Inclusions

Two basic temper-types, crushed grog and calcined flint, were used either separately or mixed to produce three basic fabrics; Grog-tempered Ware is predominant, there is only one example of Flint- and one of mixed Grog- and Flint-tempered Ware. It may be significant that both exceptions are handmade vessels found together with a third, in Grave 132, which on typological grounds, is considered to be amongst the earliest cremations in MHC, and may date to the early first century BC (fig. 58, a-c; p. 51).

Five pots appear to have been fabricated with glauconitic clays because a dense stipple of black argillaceous inclusions is visible where the matrix is exposed by abrasion or fracture. Glauconite occurs in clay as evenly-sized pellets which function as a natural tempering agent and turn black when fired, so closely resembling grog. There is no clay rich in glauconite in the immediate vicinity of Deal, but there are two different sources in the South-East.

Thin-sectioning analysis of Iron Age sherds from Aylesford, Farningham, Squerryes, Sturry, Margate and Worth has demonstrated that glauconitic clay was widely used for domestic pottery (analysis undertaken by Dr I.C. Freestone of the Department of Scientific Research, British Museum). Highly glauconitic clay occurs in the Upper Greensand of the Cretaceous series which outcrops south of the North Downs about 20 km from Deal. When fired, the pellets produce a dense stipple which can be identified in the hand specimen of fabrics with light grey, brown or oxidised matrixes.

The alternative source is the Thanet Beds of the Tertiary Series which include sparse to moderate fragmented glauconite that can only be securely identified by thin-section analysis. There are sources within the 16 miles (26 km approx.) radius of Deal which is usually used to define 'local products', because in historical times the return journey could be accomplished by a horse and cart in a single day. Sherds of domestic pottery from Mill Hill have been analysed and were shown to contain sparse glauconite comparable to fabrics at Margate, Sturry and Worth, where sources in the Thanet Beds are probable. Since this glauconite is not obvious in the hand specimen, if it has been correctly recognised in five complete pots from MHC, the Upper Greensand seems the more likely source for the clay.

In the hand specimen, the majority of fabrics do not contain appreciable amounts of glauconite, nor of any other type of readily identifiable natural inclusion, however, clay from more than one source, including the Thanet Beds, could still have been used.

Fabrication Techniques

Three different fabrication techniques have been identified:

i. entirely handmade
ii. hand-shaped and wheel-finished
iii. entirely wheel-thrown

Over 80% of vessels had been handmade or hand-shaped, and the vessel-forms tend to be idiosyncratically local in their typological characteristics (Table 7). Forms typically found widely throughout southern Britain from the mid-first century BC showed considerably more variation in fabrication technique, for example, all three techniques were used for Pedestal Jars, Cordoned Necked Bowls had been hand-shaped and wheel-thrown, while all three Tazza-variants had been wheel-thrown. The unique Ribbed Open Bowl with its matching Narrow-necked Jar which may be direct copies of contemporary imports were wheel-thrown. The results differ markedly from the KHL Cemetery, where over 95% of locally made pots were wheel-thrown; here too there was at least one handmade Pedestal Jar (Stead and Rigby 1989, Burial 472,1).

The date of the introduction of the potter's wheel can only be deduced. The earliest burials of the Aylesford-Swarling culture have been identified by the presence of two brooch types which were current on the continent before the mid-first century BC (Stead 1976). They occur in sixteen burials, only six of which contained pots and they are: the Bucket Grave at Aylesford, although only one pot can be identified with certainty from the record, Burial 13 at Swarling, two graves at East Wear Bay Villa (Folkestone) found during the 1924 excavations, Borough Green (Plaxtol) Kent, and Burial 5 at Guilden Morden, Cambs (Stead 1976). Others can now be added: Grave 28, Waldon Hall Farm (Maldon) Essex, is a recent find, while at least one pot in MHC, Context X4, pot no. 3, also qualifies for inclusion because of the Manser caption to Photograph J in the British Museum archive, with other probabilities from Contexts X4 and X5.

Only 20 pots were found in the eight listed burials. Four had been hand-fabricated, the remainder were wheel-thrown. There are single, hand-made cremation urns, which on typological grounds appear to belong to the late second or early first century BC at Borough Green, Folkestone and Deal, Kent (Warhurst 1953, fig. 4; Winbolt 1925, fig. 2,2; figs 12,13). They may represent a transitional period, when the cremation rite was being adopted and new brooch types produced, but the fast wheel had not been introduced and no radical changes had occurred in the vessel shape, proportions, decoration and fabric ranges. However, Graves 2, 4, X8 and X12 in MHC demonstrate the surviving popularity of handmade pots into the mid-first century AD with the consequent effect of preserving vessel forms which predate the introduction of the potter's wheel. Moreover, groups found with similarly dated brooches, Swarling Grave 13 and Waldon Hall Farm Grave 28, consist mainly of fully evolved wheel-thrown 'new' types, specifically seven Pedestal Jars, four Necked and Cordoned Bowls and one Tazza-bowl, with only a single hand-fabricated 'survival'. It seems that the introduction of the cremation rite, new brooch types and a new ceramic technology are enmeshed.

Wheel-thrown techniques favour the rapid output of large numbers of pots of standardised shape and size far in excess of the requirements of the potter's immediate family unit: the use of such techniques indicates an increased demand for pots coupled with the reorganisation of production and distribution.

When the fast wheel was introduced north of the Alps in the early fourth century BC, it was initially used for luxury 'display' vessels like the painted Pedestal Jars found in graves at Prunay and Puisieulx (Marne), and Pedestal Jars, Flasks and Bowls with stamped decoration in burials at the Dürrnberg (Duval 1977, pls 60–1; Penninger 1972, graves 16/1 and 2, 46/2). The technology spread to such an extent that by the end of the third century BC a wide range of plain burnished and decorated 'fine wares' were wheel-thrown. The vessel shapes changed because wheel-throwing favoured sinuous S-shaped vessel-forms with cordons and grooves for emphasis rather than complex angled and carinated shapes. There is evidence of regional distribution.

Hand fabrication remained usual for basic utilitarian vessels for cooking and storage. Different fabrics were used which were much more heavily tempered with grog, shell or coarse sand so they could withstand cooking processes: forms also differed from the wheel-thrown range. It appears that until the third century, the demand for pottery in Gaul could be satisfied by hand fabrication techniques, while in southern Britain, no change was needed until the first century BC.

Surface Finishing and Decoration

With the exception of the Flint-tempered cooking pot, all have an overall or partially burnished exterior finish. The wheel-thrown pots were left unfinished inside, while the handmade and hand-shaped pots had been more or less carefully wiped or smoothed to a glossy finish.

About half of the pots are decorated. Eight have a broad zone of pattern burnishing around the shoulder; the design is either lattice or chevrons, on a matt or deliberately rilled background. They are typologically related bowls and jars with ripple cordoning on the neck or shoulder, the local speciality. On one bowl a shoulder zone of chevrons was combined with an upper zone of simple burnished lattice. The chevron or zigzag motif is characteristic of the locality, and survived into the second half of the second century (Parfitt 1989, fig. 2, 1).

The Bead-rimmed Bowl was finished with a continuous burnished spiral forming horizontal bands over the body (fig. 66, X20). A combination of horizontal grooves and banded burnishing had been used to give one Pedestal Jar a textured finish (fig. 63, X4, no. 2).

Combed or grooved decoration occurs on three vessels at MHC. The Butt Beaker Copies in Grave X14 and Radnor Park Grave 1, have a broad band of even vertical combing which was then divided into three zones with horizontal burnished lines drawn freehand. The Narrow-necked Jar from Grave X8 has a broad band of horizontal grooving or combing below the shoulder. Finally, one of the cooking pots in Grave 132 was treated in the standard way for such vessels with overlapped combed swathes forming a broad zone from the shoulder to the base.

Firing

In most cases nothing more elaborate than a simple bonfire or clamp was required for firing. Two pots had been deliberately oxidised to a fairly clear orange-red, the Flagon or Lagena Copy and the Bead-rimmed Bowl; either the fire died down exposing the pots to the oxygen in the atmosphere, or alternatively, they were pulled from the fire and allowed to cool in the open. The remainder were fired in smoky conditions to produce rather patchy black, dark brown or grey surfaces.

Two Butt Beaker Copies, from Grave X14 and West Wickham Grave E, are the only vessels of British manufacture in the Gazetteer which required the comparatively controlled conditions of a kiln, in the first case to exclude oxygen, but in the second to ensure good oxidation.

Stylistic Associations

Five different potters or workshops have been distinguished using the evidence of the fabric, fabrication techniques, finishing and form.

Potter/Workshop Style A

Long-necked Carinated Bowls Grave X11,3
Grave 4, d

The potter appears to have been working in the late Augustan period but using conservative hand-shaping fabrication techniques to produce a form which was widely found in southern Britain both north and south of the Thames, but elsewhere was more typically wheel-thrown (Thompson 1982, 368–9).

Potter/Workshop Style B

Shapeless Omphalos Bowl Grave X8, 2
Ripple-necked Bowl Grave X12,1
Barrel-beaker Copy Artefact X16

All three vessels share a similar rim configuration regardless of size and form. Two appear to have a glauconitic matrix, but the third may just be in Grog-tempered Ware. Again the potter was using hand-shaping fabrication techniques to produce two conservative vessel-forms akin to those current in the early first century BC as well as copying a later imported form.

Potter/Workshop Style C

Ripple-necked Jars Grave 4,b
Context X4,3
Grave X12,2
Artefact X19

Like A and B, a conservative potting tradition was used and the result was an individualistic decorated jar-form which became typical of East Kent and also of the Thanet region. The basic form can be paralleled in assemblages from settlements on the coast of northwestern France, opposite Thanet (p. 44)

Potter/Workshop Style D

Butt Beaker Copy Grave X14,3
Grave 1, Radnor Park (Folkestone)

Although they differ slightly in proportions, the fabric, fabrication and decorative techniques are identical and they must have been made by the same potter who was working after AD50. Despite copying a typologically late Butt Beaker prototype which was not imported until the post-Conquest period, the potter still employed traditional hand-shaping techniques like those used for regionally specialised vessels.

Potter/Workshop Style E

Ribbed Open Bowl Grave X8,1
Narrow-necked Jar Grave X8,5

The forms are unique and are most likely copies of Gaulish imports. Unlike the vessels produced by A-C, they were wheel-thrown and the same glauconitic clay appears to have been used for both. The clay suggests that the source was not in the vicinity of Thanet, but to the south where the Upper Greensand outcrops along the southern edge of the North Downs.

The Forms

Flagon or Lagena Copies

No more than five sherds survive of the only locally-produced copy of a lagena or flagon made in Grog-tempered Ware so far found in a burial in the South-East. It was a large variant and hence most probably wide-mouthed, but insufficient survives to determine if it had one or two three-ribbed handles. Unlike examples in typical Grog-tempered Ware from the Welwyn Garden City Burial or the KHL Cemetery, Herts, which are entirely wheel-thrown, this version has a handmade body at least, and is yet another example of conservative potting techniques in the area. It was allowed to oxidise during the final stages of firing and so conforms to the majority of examples found north of the Thames where orange-buff or red were the preferred colours.

1. Grave X11, 2 (Fig. 65)

Flagon or Lagena Copy. Handmade body, at least. Grog-tempered Ware: dark grey core, patchy oxidised orange-buff exterior, with smoothed finish; dark red-brown interior, unfinished. Condition: only a few base and handle sherds survive. The presence of the handle suggests that the vessel was more or less complete at the time of deposition. (Thompson G6).

Narrow-necked Jars

If Narrow-necked Jars are defined by the criterion that the diameter of the rim is less than that of the base, then there is one example. The shape generally, and particularly the double lip to the rim are so unusual that a continental prototype must be sought. In clay and fabrication technique it resembles the Ribbed Open Bowl found in the same grave and they may have been made by the same potter (see above E). Since they are in the same grave, they can be considered as exactly contemporary.

1. Grave X8, 5 (Fig. 64)

Narrow-necked jar. Wheel-thrown. Glauconitic matrix (like Grave X8,1), with sandy texture: red-brown core; variegated grey-brown surfaces; burnished exterior. Decoration: four broad girth grooves. Condition: complete and standing. (Thompson B3–8).

Foot-ring Platters

There is one foot-ring platter which was probably found in the MHC, but no details survive about the date and provenance (fig. 66, X22). It is a copy of a form in the Central Gaulish rather than the Gallo-Belgic product-ranges, and the prototype could have been available in Britain as early as 15BC. Close parallels have also been recorded in burials at Westbere and Tassell's Quarry, Allington, and a regional production centre may be indicated (Payne 1883; Thompson 1978, fig. 2, 20).

One hundred foot-ring platters were found in the KHL Cemetery, 40 imports and 60 local products, and together they form one of the largest functionally specialised groups represented there. Locally made foot-ring platters are comparatively scarce in burials in the South-East; there are examples at Faversham, Julliberries Grave (three examples) and East Hall (Murston). Even when flat-based versions are added the number is still small – 'Hermitage Farm' (Allington), Aylesford (two examples), East Hall (three examples) and Swarling. None has been found in a grave with imported fine table wares.

Three platters in the East Hall Cemetery are in Grog-tempered Wares but are likely to be post-Conquest in date. The foot-ring platter is of a type which is found elsewhere in East Kent at Julliberries Grave, Ramsgate, Reculver, Sittingbourne, and Canterbury and suggests distribution from a single production centre (Thompson 1982, G1–6, 458–61).

1. Artefact X22 (Fig. 66)
Platter. Wheel-thrown. Glauconitic clay; variable grey and brown surfaces; burnished lower surface, upper surface heavily abraded so that no finish survives. Condition: complete. (Thompson G1–1 or G1–4).

Ribbed Open Bowl

The bowl with deeply cut horizontal ribbing, is unique. The carinated shape with applied foot-ring suggests a continental prototype, and the basic form is represented in the range produced in northwestern Gaul and Armorica in the first century AD (Menez 1985, forms 53–56). It also resembles certain Campanian bowls which is where the origins of the Gaulish versions lay (Morel 1965, type 27c). The fabrication technique is the same as that used for the Narrow-necked Jar in the same burial group, and they may have been made by the same potter.

1. Grave X8, 1 (Fig. 64)
Ribbed Open Bowl. Wheel-thrown. Glauconitic matrix: sooty black inner surface finish, outer surface brown with sooty black patches. Condition: complete and standing. (Thompson L5).

Tazze

Tazze are open bowls with a sharply carinated base angle, one or more raised cordons on the exterior and applied hollow foot-ring or pedestal bases. Their typological characteristics imply that they were originally made in wood, then shale and ceramic, for the latter retain skeuomorphs of woodworking techniques as typological features with no function, for example, wall overhangs to accommodate the base, dowel circles at the centre of the base and raised cordons representing metal hoops.

In ceramic, they are typically wheel-thrown, and the form is amongst the earliest to be copied by potters using the fast wheel in southern Britain to produce pots for inclusion as grave-goods for late Iron Age cremations. There are small drinking-cup sizes in both rich cremations at Welwyn, and large bowl-sized and small drinking-cup versions at Welwyn Garden City, Herts, burials dated to the second half of the first century BC (Stead 1967, figs 7, 10–11, and 8, 18). Numbers from any site are never great, but the wide range of different variants and sizes so far discovered suggest widespread popularity over an extended period. Three different versions have been found in burials in the Deal area – Tazza, Tazza-bowl and Pedestal Tazza.

Tazza

The only Tazza from MHC is in Grave 4 where it was associated with an imported Barrel Beaker of late Augustan date (fig. 62). It is the most typical version from Deal, but with a shallow foot-ring instead of a tall pedestal; the closest parallel is from the disturbed cremation cemetery at Stone (Cotton and Richardson 1941, fig. 2, 5). It is worth noting that none occurs in either the Aylesford or Swarling Cemeteries suggesting that the form was more at home north of the Thames and was a later introduction to the South-East. A Tazza-bowl, with flat base replacing the foot-ring was found in the Sholden burial (Ogilvie and Dunning 1967).

1. Grave 4, a (Fig. 62)
Tazza. Wheel-thrown. Grog-tempered Ware: brown core, orange-brown under-surface, dark brown surfaces; smoothly burnished outer surface, except within foot-ring, unfinished inner surface. Condition: restored to complete, but with a small chip out of the rim.

Pedestal Tazza

The tall Pedestal Tazza is a unique hybrid combining a tazza rim with the typical lower body-shape of a Pedestal Jar. It is entirely wheel-thrown. Unfortunately the circumstances of the find were not recorded although it can now be assumed to have been found in the MHC before 1905 (p. 172).

1. Context X5, 2 (Fig. 63)
Wheel-thrown. Grog-tempered Ware: grey core, brown

surfaces, with grey patches; evenly burnished exterior, unfinished interior. Condition: restored to complete; fractured down full length of the body. (Thompson F3–4).

Barrel and Butt Beaker Copies

The imported prototypes first appear in late Augustan graves in southern Britain. The form was quickly adopted by indigenous potters who made close copies using traditional fabrics on a large scale; as the imports evolved with time, becoming more sinuous in shape and with grooves replacing cordons, so did the copies (p. 41–2). The basic shape was very popular north of the Thames and over 100 Barrel and Butt Beakers Copies were found in the KHL Cemetery in contexts spanning the entire period of its use and occurring in some of the richest graves (Stead and Rigby 1989, 164–9, table 43). When imports and local copies are added together it is easily the most popular functionally specialised vessel-form with 174 examples.

The popularity of the type south of the Thames remains unresolved. There are 11 examples in Grog-tempered Wares from seven sites, two almost identical, the remainder extremely varied and certainly made by different potters. The sites are: Aylesford (three examples), Cheriton and Radnor Park (Folkestone), Sholden, Stone and Swarling (two examples).

Only two, X16 from MHC and one from Grave Group iv at Cheriton, satisfy the criteria for classification as Barrel Beakers; they are handmade, typologically similar and could be from the same source (fig. 66; Tester and Bing 1949, figs 1, 10). The latter was found with an unusual handmade Pedestal Jar and a pair of Colchester brooches: a pre-Claudian date is probable (Tester and Bing 1949, figs 1, 11 and 6,4). The embossed examples from Cheriton, Grave vii, and Elms Vale, Dover, are also barrel-shaped, but their special applied decoration was derived from other Gaulish prototypes (Tester and Bing 1949, fig. 2, 19; Payne 1889, opp. p. 204; Stead and Rigby 1989, Burial 312, 2).

The remaining examples imitate imported Butt Beakers of the Tiberio-Claudian period. Two from Aylesford and the example from Sholden have at least three raised cordons dividing the decorative zone, a characteristic first introduced on Barrel Beaker Copies, but which continued in use on the earliest, pre-Claudian Butt Beaker Copies. Post-Conquest variants, with grooves replacing raised cordons to define the decorative zone occur in Grave B of the Family Circle at Aylesford, Swarling Grave 5, and at Stone.

The latest Butt Beaker Copies from Grave X14 and West Wickham Grave E were made using Roman fabrication techniques (fig. 66, X14, no. 4; fig. 70, no. 21). A fine-grained clay matrix tempered with grog was used to produce thin-walled vessels which required the controlled rise in temperature of a kiln. Both have raised cordons at the neck base and rouletted decoration, and should be contemporary.

1. Artefact X16 (Fig. 66)
Barrel Beaker Copy. Handmade. Glauconitic clay: grey core, red-brown undersurfaces, variegated grey and brown surfaces with sooty patches; abraded exterior, no finish survives. Condition: complete (Thompson G5–1).

2. Grave X14, 3 (Fig. 66)
Butt Beaker Copy. Probably handmade. Sandy textured ware with some grog inclusions: grey core, red-brown under-surfaces, dark grey-brown surfaces; burnished rim and neck, faceted tooling at the base, roughly smoothed interior. Decoration: evenly spaced vertical combing divided into three zones with roughly burnished horizontal bands, and then further sub-divided. This vessel was made by the same potter as one found in the Radnor Park Cemetery at Folkestone (see below p. 183). Condition: complete but for chipped rim.

3. Grave X14, 4 (Fig. 66)
Butt Beaker Copy. Wheel-thrown. Fine Grog-tempered Ware: fine-grained, dense blue-grey matrix, with moderate dark grey grog, abraded darker surfaces; burnished rim, neck and base. Decoration: fine rouletted zone on the shoulder.

Conical Jars

There is one simple handmade Conical Jar from Mill Hill, Context X4, 1, and if the caption on the back of Photo J is correct, it contained one or more early brooches and could therefore date to the mid-first century BC (fig. 63). It was handmade in Grog-tempered Ware, was burnished vertically on the exterior and horizontally inside; it was fired in a clamp or bonfire. In shape and technique it appears earlier than the remaining vessels from the cremation cemetery primarily because it resembles Saucepan Pots which are so typical of settlements in Wessex in the third and second centuries BC (Cunliffe 1984, 254–6, figs 6.70–77). Compared to Saucepan Pots, however, it is conical rather than cylindrical and has a splayed base, so that other influences need to be sought, perhaps even in northern Gaul where both conical and cylindrical versions were placed in burials in the fifth and fourth centuries BC.

There is a second plain example in a large group of typical late Iron Age pottery from the Belgic Ditch of the Rose Lane Site in Canterbury. The group includes sherds from several Gallo-Belgic imports including a TN platter and may have been deposited as late as the Claudian period; typologically earlier vessels are present in the group, and the Conical Jar should also be one (Frere 1954, fig. 5, 26).

1. Context X4, 1 (Fig. 63)
Handmade. Grog-tempered Ware: grey-brown surfaces; vertically burnished outer surface, smoothed interior. Condition: almost complete. (Thompson E3–1).

Waisted Carinated Bowls
Two very similar handmade examples with concave neck and carinated shoulder occur in cremations containing other similar artefacts, suggesting that they can be considered as exact contemporaries and were probably made by the same potter (fig. 65, X11, no. 3, fig. 62, G4, d). Rather different wheel-thrown variants in Grog-tempered Ware have been found in the East Hall Cemetery (Murston) and an unrecorded site in Kent, possibly Canterbury or Oare (Faversham) (Canterbury Museum 981).

The form occurs north and south of the Thames, and unlike many of the vessels at Mill Hill, is not regionally specific (Thompson 1982, 368–9).

1. Grave 4, d (Fig. 62)
Handmade. Grog-tempered Ware: grey core, brown surfaces; burnished outer, unfinished inner surfaces; glossy, black sooty patches. Condition: complete, with chip missing from the rim and a large spall missing from the body.

2. Grave X11, 3 (Fig. 65)
Probably handmade. Grog-tempered Ware; grey; burnished exterior; unfinished interior; sooty black patches. Condition: complete. (Thompson E1–4).

Shapeless Bowl with omphalos base
The omphalos base combined with its fabrication techniques imply that the bowl dates to a period in the second or early first century BC, yet it was recorded in the same burial as a typical wheel-thrown Pedestal Jar and Simple Gallic Brooches which cannot have been deposited before the late Augustan period. Both decorated and plain cremation urns in Graves 1 and 2 at Hothfield Common, Kent, have omphalos bases; it is clear, therefore, that the typological trait survived in the region until the introduction of the cremation rite in the first century BC (Thompson 1982, 738–9, nos 1011–2).

1. Grave X8, 2 (Fig. 64)
Handmade. Grog-tempered ware: light brown surfaces; burnished exterior, unfinished matt interior. Condition: complete and standing (Thompson E2–4).

Necked Bowls
A high-shouldered bowl with an offset at the base of the rim.

1. Artefact X17 (Fig. 66)
Wheel-thrown. Grog-tempered Ware: grey-brown with buff patches; burnished exterior, unfinished interior. Condition: restored to complete.

Long-necked Jars
Both handmade and wheel-thrown versions of this form have similar burnished chevron decoration in a broad band around the shoulder. The handmade jar was in an inhumation grave with a British coin of Eppillus dated to AD1–10. It seems yet another example of the technological conservatism of local potters and survival of the inhumation rite. The wheel-thrown example demonstrates the effect that fabrication technique has on vessel shape, allowing the profile to be greatly exaggerated. Its fabric is harder fired and light grey in colour so that a post-Conquest date is likely. An even later version was found elsewhere in Deal in a cremation with samian dating to the early second century AD demonstrating the staying power of the chevron motif in the locality (Parfitt 1989).

1. Grave 30 (Fig. 58)
Handmade. Grog-tempered Ware: uncontrolled firing conditions, variegated grey and brown surfaces with sooty patches; burnished from rim to offset, lower body matt. Decoration: burnished chevrons on rilled ground. Condition: complete base circuit decreasing to half at shoulder and quarter at rim.

2. Artefact X21 (Fig. 66)
Wheel-thrown. Grog-tempered Ware: hard-fired; variegated grey to orange surfaces; burnished rim and neck, smoothed lower body. Decoration: burnished chevrons on matt ground. Heavy soot encrustation from offset to underside of base. Condition: restored to complete (Thompson E3–1).

Cordoned Necked Bowls
There are two examples each with a raised cordon at the base of the neck, one was hand-shaped and wheel-finished, the other wheel-thrown. The proportions of the latter are unusual, with the rim about twice the normal depth for a vessel of this size; no close parallel has been found in any other cremation burial. Examples in the Aylesford and Swarling Cemeteries are more typical and so resemble the former more closely.

1. Grave 15 (Fig. 58)
Hand-shaped body, wheel-finished rim. Grog-tempered

ware with black organic inclusions; brown matrix; orange under-surfaces, variegated grey and brown surfaces; burnished finish. Condition: complete base circuit reduced to quarter rim circuit.

2. Grave X11, 4 (Fig. 65)
Wheel-thrown. Grog-tempered Ware: grey-brown surfaces; burnished exterior with sooty black patch from maximum girth to the base, smoothed interior. Condition: complete (Thompson E3–2).

Pedestal Jars

Five Pedestal Jars are recorded; one is now missing but survives in the photographic record, another had been trimmed of its base before burial and then disturbed by a Roman quarry so that only three can be fully classified. Two were wheel-thrown and two handmade. The proportions are similar, all have a wide mouth, with a wider shoulder and a narrow foot. There is a narrow cordon at the base of the neck. The underside of the base is flat, none has the recess typical of quoit-shaped pedestal bases which are common north of the Thames.

Four have an overall plain burnished finish. One, Context X4,2, was decorated with pairs of grooves drawn freehand and very unevenly around the body to divide it into alternating matt and burnished zones. Such treatment is usually considered to be a devolved imitation of the raised cordons of Pedestal Jars like those found in the Aylesford and Swarling cemeteries and hence later in the evolutionery sequence. If the caption on the back of Photo J (pl. VII) is correct, then the grooved Pedestal Jar contained one or more of the early knobbed fibulae (figs 63 and 42, nos 10–14) a type which appears to predate the late Augustan period. The typological argument can therefore be reversed, placing the so-called devolved imitation alongside its early cordoned prototypes, thus making it one of the earliest Pedestal Jars in MHC. Two plain versions were found together in Grave X8 with Simple Gallic Brooches and cannot have been deposited before the late Augustan period. No parallels occur south of the Thames but there is one in the north, from Sandy, Beds (BM 1937, 11–11, 2). The technique of banded burnishing is also a common characteristic of 'plain' versions in the rich burials at Welwyn and Welwyn Garden City, Herts and in domestic contexts at Baldock, Herts (Stead 1967, fig. 7, 3–6; Stead and Rigby 1986, figs 109, 60, and 110, 73).

One Pedestal Jar containing the cremation was found in the East Hall Cemetery (Murston) associated with an imported lagena in White Pipeclay of Tiberio-Claudian date (fig. 68, nos 13 and 14). It is rather small and has an unusually narrow quoit-shaped pedestal base which is markedly recessed on the underside. It is the only example recorded with an import in the South-East. Pedestal Jars were used as cinerary urns and accessory vessels in the KHL Cemetery from the late Augustan to the Claudian period (Stead and Rigby 1989, 175–8). Only two of 16 examples were associated with imported fine wares in burials central to the enclosures, the remainder occurred in single- or two-pot secondary graves, so that by the early first century AD their significance was diminished.

Pedestal Jars also occur at Tassell's Quarry and Hermitage Farm (Allington), Aylesford, East Wear Bay (Folkestone), Stone, Swarling and Dover. One from Rochester, or its vicinity, is similar to examples in Grave X8 and Context X5 in its overall shape and proportions, also the base is flat on the underside (Thompson 1982, fig. 66, no.63, type t). No detailed contextual information survives, but it is one of four complete vessels which can be deduced to be from a cremation burial, or burials, acquired by the British Museum as a result of the sale of the Humphrey Wood Collection in 1904 (Wood also figures in the Gazetteer, p. 185–6). The example from Stone has a similar flat underside to the base and a wide shoulder, but is incomplete and so cannot be classified, and has no recorded association (Cotton and Richardson 1941, fig. 2, 6).

The closest parallel in the Aylesford Cemetery has similar proportions but a hollow conical pedestal foot: it may be from the 'Bucket' grave (BM 1886,11–12,11 but not identifiable in Evans 1890). Plain variants in Grave 4 of the Swarling Cemetery are markedly different in shape and proportion, and also have an additional cordon above the pedestal. Found with a pair of 'Aylesford-type' brooches, they too qualify as early variants made in the mid-first century BC (Bushe-Fox 1925, pl. vi, 3–4).

Variants with multi-cordons on the body outnumber those with a single cordon at the neck base and a plain burnished body in the Aylesford and Swarling Cemeteries, but none was found in MHC.

1. Grave X8, 6 (Fig. 64)
Wheel-thrown. Grog-tempered Ware: burnished exterior. Condition: repaired to complete and standing, upper body fractured (Thompson A1).

2. Context X4, 2 (Fig. 63)
Handmade. Grog-tempered ware: grey matrix, variegated grey and brown surfaces with over-fired orange patches; roughly wiped inside; pairs of burnished grooves drawn freehand around the body to imitate cordons, burnished rim, imitation cordons and base with matt zones between.

3. Context X5, 1 (Fig. 63)
Hand-shaped body, wheel-finished rim. Grog-tempered Ware: brown matrix, variegated grey and brown surfaces,

with over-fired orange patches; roughly wiped interior, burnished exterior.

4. Grave 131, b (Fig. 58)
Wheel-thrown. Grog-tempered Ware: brown core, dark grey-black surfaces; burnished finish outside. Condition: about half of the body circuit, but no base, shoulder or rim sherds. While the upper body sherds appear to have been removed subsequently by the quarry pits, the base appears to have been deliberately removed in antiquity, prior to deposition. Since it contained the cremation, a sherd or stone may have been used to block the hole in the base.

5. Grave X8, 7 – vessel not located (Fig. 63)

Cordoned Bowl

A shallow wide-mouthed necked bowl with a broad cordon on the shoulder which is related to the Ripple-shouldered Bowls discussed below.

1. Grave X8, 3 (Fig. 64)
Handmade. Grog-tempered Ware: light grey-brown surfaces with oxidised orange patches; burnished exterior, unfinished matt interior (Thompson E2–3).

Ripple-necked Bowls

There are two shallow wide-mouthed bowls with undefined raised cordons (ripples) on the neck above the shoulder, a characteristic repeated on taller jar-forms. The distribution of both bowls and jars is concentrated in East Kent, particularly the immediate area of Thanet. A plain variant which was hand-shaped and then wheel-finished, occurs in Grave 2 with Tiberio-Claudian TN (p. 168).

1. Grave 2, c (Fig. 62)
Handmade and wheel-finished. Grog-tempered Ware: grey core, brown under-surface, abraded grey surfaces; highly burnished from lip to maximum girth, less glossy, smoothed lower body, interior roughly smoothed. Condition: restored to complete.

2. Grave X12, 1 (Fig. 66)
Handmade. Glauconitic clay with quartz sand inclusions: grey core, brown surfaces with grey patches; burnished from rim to maximum girth, lower body and underside of base, smoothed inner surface. Decoration: upper zone, burnished lattice on burnished ground; lower zone, burnished chevrons on matt ground. Condition: complete (Thompson E2–3).

Ripple-necked Jars

There are four tall wide-shouldered jars with flat bases, two or more undefined cordons or ripples on the neck and a broad zone of pattern burnishing on the shoulder, either lattice or chevrons. They were either handmade or hand-shaped and wheel-finished, and are so similar it has been argued that they belong to the same workshop style (p. 45). Close parallels have been found at Birchington so that the form appears typical of the Thanet region of East Kent (Thompson 1982, nos 315 and 1515). Related squat bowl versions have been discussed above. The form can also be paralleled on the opposite side of the Channel in assemblages from settlements at Frencq and Wissant (Pas-de-Calais), denoting close cultural and technological ties (Dilly 1978, pl. iii, 1–2; Marriette 1966, figs. 11, 22 and 31, fig. 12, 32–7, fig. 19, 56).

MHC may provide useful dating evidence for the type: Context X4, pot no. 3, contained one of the five early brooches, possibly the smallest and non-paired example (figs. 63 and 42, no. 12), demonstrating that the form was standardised in the early first century BC. Another was in Grave 4 associated with a later brooch-type and a Barrel Beaker of late Augustan date. Two are known to have been used as cremation urns.

1. Grave 4, b (Fig. 62)
Wheel-thrown. Grog-tempered Ware: uncontrolled firing conditions, variegated grey and brown surfaces, with sooty patches; burnished from rim, rilled zone on the shoulder, and lower body matt. Decoration: a band of burnished chevrons on the shoulder. Condition: complete but for a recent chip at the rim.

2. Context X4, 3 (Fig. 63)
Probably handmade. Grog-tempered Ware: grey core, brown under-surface, variegated grey and brown surfaces; burnished neck, smoothed lower body; smooth interior. Sooty haze extends from maximum girth to base. Decoration: burnished chevrons on rilled, matt ground; burnished cross on the underside of the base. Condition: restored to almost complete; small rim and shoulder sherds missing (Thompson B2–4).

3. Grave X12, 2 (Fig. 66)
Handmade body and wheel-finished rim. Sandy textured ware with grog inclusions: brown core, variegated grey and brown surfaces; burnished rim and lower body, smoothed interior. Decoration: burnished lattice on a rilled matt ground. Sooty zones at the rim edge, shoulder and base. Condition: complete except for a chip at the rim and a hole in the shoulder, both with abraded fracture edges (Thompson B2–3).

4. Artefact X19 (Fig. 66)
Hand-shaped body, wheel-finished shoulder and rim.

Grog-tempered Ware: grey matrix, variegated grey and brown surfaces with sooty patches outside; highly burnished rim and cordons, burnished body. Decoration: scribble burnished lattice.

Ripple-shouldered Bowls

There are three squat, wide-mouthed bowls with two or more undefined cordons on the shoulder, below the rim, all apparently handmade.

The variant in Grave 132 is unusually large, and is in a unique fabric tempered with a high proportion of fine calcined flint mixed with grog. It had been severely spalled and distorted by heat so that it is either an overfired waster made more or less on the site, or it was placed too near the funeral pyre and burnt. The combination of its early fabric, fabrication method and size suggest that it is an early example dating to the first century BC. When excavated it was in a heap of sherds, but most of the pot proved to be present, so that although it was broken elsewhere, the sherds were carefully collected up for burial.

The smaller examples are of similar size and typological detail, one is decorated with a broad zone of burnished chevrons on the body. Similarly decorated examples in settlement material at Birchington and Maidstone in a cremation burial containing a Pedestal Jar and an iron brooch, stress the specifically local character of many of the pots in MHC (Thompson 1982, 1041 and 1517; Kelly 1963, 194–5). A late Augustan date is likely for the plain example.

Like Ripple-necked Jars, the form can also be paralleled in northern Gaul at Marck and Wissant (Pas-de-Calais) (Van Es and Wynia 1979, fig. 6, 1–6; Marriette 1966, figs. 10 and 11).

1. Grave 132, a (Fig. 58)
Handmade body, with wheel-finished shoulder and rim. Grog- and Flint-tempered Ware: partially oxidised orange-brown ware shading to grey; overfired to sinter-point, either at the time of firing or during the cremation ceremony, the base has spalled from the lower body where it was luted into place and no finish survives. Condition: a complete shoulder circuit can be restored but base and rim sherds are missing; the pot was already fragmented before it was deposited.

2. Grave X8, 4 (Fig. 64)
Handmade body, wheel-finished rim. Grog-tempered Ware: heavily sooted exterior, well-burnished rim, roughly smoothed lower body; smoothed grey-brown interior. Condition: base spalled and body cracked but still complete and standing (Thompson E2–3).

3. Context X18 (Fig. 66)
Wheel-thrown. Fumed black ware, with quartz sand inclusions and probably also grog: unevenly fired with buff and grey patches; burnished rim, cordons and lower body, unfinished interior. Decoration: burnished chevrons on matt ground. Condition: complete except for chipped rim (Thompson E3– 1).

Lipped Jar

The only example is a tall, wide-mouthed jar with a rounded lip thickened on the inside. The form was typically used for cooking and this is the only example used as a funerary offering. Like one of its associated vessels, it had been overfired or heavily burnt on a subsequent occasion, and broken elsewhere so that only a selection of sherds were found in the pit. The basic shape, both plain and decorated with overlapped combed swathes, can be paralleled in settlement material at sites north of the Thames, like Baldock, Herts and Harrold, Beds. It also occurs in the assemblages from Wissant and Frencq (Pas-de-Calais) (Marriette 1966, figs 15–17, all examples combed; Dilly 1978, pl.1).

1. Grave 132, b (Fig. 58)
Handmade. Flint-tempered Ware, heavily tempered with calcined flint 1–4mm in diameter: overfired, or subsequently burnt and discoloured to light buff with grey patches; no surface finish survives so that the flint protrudes. Condition: medium to small sherds with abraded edges comprising about half of the rim and a quarter of the base circuit, with only a few body sherds. It has suffered the same disturbance as other vessels in the grave.

Bead-rimmed Bowl

The body shape is globular with the maximum girth at about mid-point between the rim and base, unlike the more common combed bead-rimmed jars, which have a wide shoulder tapering to a narrow base. Perhaps the closest parallels, each with a raised cordon below the rim, occur in the Aylesford Cemetery, the first in Grave D of the Family Circle, associated with a Tazza-bowl (see above p. 46), the second, ungrouped (Evans 1890, pl.vii, 3, list no. 27 and 2, list no. 29). A third, found in Grave 9 in the Swarling Cemetery, is rather taller and hence is classed as a jar rather than a bowl; it was associated with two other jars in an unusual grouping confined to bead-rimmed vessels (Bushe-Fox 1925, pl. viii, 17 and 21, ix, 29). None exhibits the narrow burnished spiral on the body, although this does occur in the Stone Cemetery on a matching set of three necked jars (Cotton and Richardson 1941, fig. 2, 5–8).

1. Artefact X20 (Fig. 66)
Wheel-thrown. Grog-tempered Ware: grey matrix; orange surfaces; burnished finish. Decoration: burnished spiral on the body below the cordon and on the underside of the base within the foot-ring.

Collar-rimmed Jar

The only example is small and slim-bodied with a narrow upright collared rim and a plain burnished external finish. It was found with the trimmed body of a Pedestal Jar.

1. Grave 131, a (Fig. 58)
Handmade. Grog-tempered Ware: brown ware with black sooty patches; highly burnished but faceted outer surface, smoothed inner surface. Condition: complete rim and base circuits, but with a few intermediate body sherds missing.

Wide-shouldered Combed Jar

There is one example with a narrow upright neck and a high shoulder below a marked offset. It is a typical handmade cooking pot with deeply scored overlapped combing on the body. The type seems to have been introduced in the early first century BC as a similar jar was used as the container for the cremation and a silver brooch at East Wear Bay (Folkestone). The brooch is of the Aylesford type and the grave was included in the list of the earliest Aylesford-Swarling burials and hence dated to the mid-first century BC (Stead 1976). This is yet another form paralleled at Frencq (Pas-de-Calais) (Dilly 1978, pl.4).

1. Grave 132, c (Fig. 58)
Handmade. Grog-tempered Ware: unevenly fired, or subsequently burnt and discoloured, generally black and sooty with oxidised patches; burnished rim, roughly smoothed inner surface. Decoration: deliberately roughened and deeply combed exterior. Condition: only a few small sherds with abraded edges were found, comprising about half of the rim and base circuits, but only about a quarter of the shoulder; like its associated vessels, it was not complete when placed in the pit.

Pottery and the Burial Rite

There is little information concerning the disposition of the cremation in the original discoveries in MHC (X1–20). Only one pot contains cremated bone, in accordance with its label (X4). The cremation was inurned in Grave 131, but was on the floor of Graves 2 and 4 and no evidence survived of any container. It seems that at least two different methods were used, and this corresponds with the practice in other cremation cemeteries.

All but one late Iron Age pot in the Deal Town Hall Collection is complete, or restorable to complete, the exception being the sherds from a flagon or lagena found in Grave X12 accompanied by two complete pots. Seven pots in Graves 2, 4 and 131, were whole when deposited in the grave, but the large platter in Grave 2 had been broken, deliberately or accidentally, and the base and rim placed in different positions before backfilling. The pedestal jar in Grave 131 had been trimmed of its base before deposition, and since it was used as the urn, some sort of temporary base may have been required. Trimmed and repaired pots proved to be a repeated feature in the KHL Cemetery, although here most were imports, with scarcity value (Stead and Rigby 1989, 203–4). Judging from the number of complete and restorable vessels found in MHC and other cemeteries in the South-East, complete vessels were a common offering. Given the chance nature of most of the discoveries, and that quantities of complete pots were not saved, it is more than likely that few broken pots were saved, so skewing the sample in favour of complete vessels.

Grave 132 may illustrate a different rite, although it could perhaps have been very thoroughly disturbed. Sherds from three pots were scattered in the filling along with a small amount of cremated bone. Two pots had been burnt, possibly the result of exposure to the pyre. A similar rite has been observed on the continent, and may have been identified in the KHL Cemetery, Folly Lane, Verulamium and Stanway, Colchester (Stead and Rigby 1989, Burial 132; Crummy 1992). It is unlikely that fragmented grave-goods from other such burials were rescued during quarrying at Mill Hill, or any other late Iron Age cemetery.

Burial Group Size

The small size of the sample, variability of recovery and quality of recording methods limits the viability of interpretative analysis of the cremations in the MHC. The KHL Cemetery has provided a range of data against which late Iron Age and early Roman cremation burials from other sites can be compared. Results can only be provisional because Swarling is the only excavated and recorded cemetery in the South-East, and it was not fully excavated nor is it of comparable size.

The richest burial in MHC is Grave X9 with seven pots and three brooches, which accords with existing evidence for the late Iron Age. Recorded burials at Aylesford are limited to the 'Family Circle', and they vary between one and three pots, with no other artefacts. In the Swarling cemetery, the richest grave, which may well also be the earliest, contains six pots, an iron-banded bucket and two brooches; otherwise, the range is between one and four pots, occasionally with a brooch (Evans 1890; Bushe-Fox 1923). The range in the KHL Cemetery varies from no grave-goods to a maximum of ten pots with one brooch and seven pots with six metal objects (Stead and Rigby 1989). There appear to be no burials notably rich in grave goods in cemeteries of the late Iron Age.

Functional Range

Functionally specialised vessel-forms were introduced to Britain by imports of fine table wares from the Roman world in the late first century BC. There is no evidence to demonstrate that native Britons used the imports for their intended functions; however, they were quickly adopted as grave-goods, and local potters included the new forms in their repertoire.

Imported Table Wares and Locally Produced Copies

Platters have the most obvious and limited function. They were first imported in the second half of the first century BC apparently from Central Gaul, and then Gallia Belgica. They first appear in the Welwyn Garden City Burial and then the earliest burials in the KHL Cemetery (Stead and Rigby 1989). They were certainly not used for the cremated human bone, but there are rare burials with animal bone *in situ* (for example Westbere, Kent) but if other offerings were preferred, they would have left no trace.

Platters are more consistently represented than almost any other functional type in the KHL Cemetery; they are in approximately one in four burials and all chronological phases, demonstrating that they were common offerings, either in their own right, or for the food they contained. Directly comparable data cannot be established for any other contemporary British site. However, it seems that platters were never as popular as grave-goods in the South-East. Besides 13 imports listed in the Gazetteer, platters are recorded in cemeteries at Allington, Aylesford (2), Dover (2), Murston (2), and Westbere, and also with inhumations at Julliberries Grave (2), but are absent from Stone and Swarling, bringing the total to 23.

Given the general scarcity of platters, the shortage of matching cups is perhaps predictable. There are four imports and no local copies have been identified. Other vessel-forms, or vessels in materials other than ceramic, may have been used for small amounts of liquid: Ripple-necked or Ripple-shouldered Bowls are a possibility in the Thanet area.

Flagons with one handle, and lagenae with two, are presumed to be specialised liquid containers. The earliest versions were imported from Central Gaul, the most common were made in White Pipeclay in northern Gaul and they were widely distributed (Table 5, p. 56). They range in capacity from about 1 litre (2 pints) to 18 litres (four gallons) and usually the lagenae are considerably larger than the flagons; the type of liquid may have varied according to the size of the container rather than its shape. Local copies in grog-tempered wares are generally scarce in the South-East, and Grave X11 contains the only example recorded in a grave in the region.

Flagons and lagenae occurred in roughly one in ten graves in the KHL Cemetery, so that if they had a ritual function or symbolic value, it was not essential to the burial rite. If the KHL Cemetery is representative, then their symbolic value is uncertain. All complete flagons were accessory vessels and could have contained liquid at the time of deposition. The flagons have apertures less than 50mm in diameter; there was, therefore, a practical problem of inserting the cremation, so that the only flagon used as a cinerary urn had been trimmed of its neck. In contrast, six of a total of seven lagenae, variant GL 6, contained cremated bone, so that they only symbolise liquid at the time of burial; in any prior ritual, they could have contained a libation. Flagons continued to play a significant role in the cremation rite in the first and second centuries AD.

Barrel- and Butt-shaped beakers, so named because of their overall shape which was combined with horizontal cordons and grooves to indicate hoops, have long been presumed to be large drinking vessels used for the consumption of the local alcoholic brew. Together, imports and local versions occur in almost half of the burials in the KHL Cemetery: they range in size from large, containing perhaps 2 litres (four pints), to miniature, with capacities of less than a quarter litre, and occur in all chronological phases. The imported versions in FPW form the most common functional group with examples in burials throughout Herts, Essex, Suffolk, Beds, and Northants. Even allowing for the very different nature of the data, Barrel and Butt Beakers were never as popular as grave offerings in the South-East as they were north of the Thames. In all there are seven recorded imports, with local versions at Aylesford, Cheriton, Dover and Folkestone, giving a total of 14. When combined with the apparently different rate of uptake of flagons and lagenae into local pottery production, there appears to be a major regional and tribal distinction between the north and south banks of the Thames which the imports tend to mask.

Local Forms

While several different jar-types were common in the KHL Cemetery, both as cinerary urns and accessory vessels, typical cooking pots (i.e. necked jars with deeply incised horizontal combing on the body, so common in settlement assemblages encrusted with sooty deposits) were absent; they seem to have been unacceptable as grave-goods and so were systematically avoided (Stead and Rigby 1989, 20). In terms of size, shape and availability, they were apparently no different to acceptable vessels, so presumably some other factors were involved. The most obvious causes – function, materials and producer, seem unlikely, because acceptable and unacceptable do not obviously differ; however, the taboo appears to have been strong in the early first century AD though it diminished in the Roman period. The avoidance of storage jars is perhaps understandable for sheer practicality, since they were so large they would have required enormous grave pits. Two cooking-pot forms occur together in Grave 132, otherwise the evidence for MHC and the South-East remains too sparse for comparison.

Abbreviations and references used in Tables 1–6

SITES

Aldbury — Herts. Unpublished, finds in priv. coll.
Ardleigh — Vince's Farm, Ardleigh, Essex, *Col. Mus. Rep.* 1956–62.
Arrington — Cambs. Taylor 1993.
Baldock KBS — Kayser Bondor Site, Baldock 1947, Herts. Unpublished, finds in Letchworth Museum.
Brundon — Brundon, Suffolk. Unpublished, finds in Ipswich Museum.
Burghfield — Cunning Man Site, Burghfield, Berks. Boon and Wymer 1958.
Duston — Northants. Unpublished, finds in Northampton Museum.
Foxton 1855 — Foxton, Cambs. Fox 1923.
Guilden Morden — Cambs. Fox 1926.
Jordan Hill — Jordan Hill Cemetery, Weymouth, Dorset. (Additional plates to Warne 1872).
Joslin Gr.3 — Joslin Collection, grave group 3, Colchester, Essex. May 1930.
KHL — King Harry Lane Cemetery, Verulamium, St Albans, Herts. Stead and Rigby 1989.
Lexden 1924 — Lexden Tumulus, Colchester, Essex. Laver 1927.
Lexden 1931 — Colchester Museum Report 1932, 35.
Lexden 1940 — Hull 1942.
Lexden 1963/73 — Crummy, in preparation.
Litlington — Cambs. Fox 1923.
Lt Waltham — Little Waltham, Essex. Drury 1978.
MHC — Mill Hill Cemetery, Deal, Kent.
Mount Bures — Mount Farm Barrow, Mount Bures, Essex. Roach-Smith 1882, vol. ii, pp. 25–29.
Owslebury — Hants. Collis 1977.
Puckeridge — Station Road, Puckeridge, Herts. Partridge 1979.
Sheepen Gr. 3 — The Sheepen Site, Colchester, Essex, Niblett 1985.
Shefford 1826 — Shefford, Beds. Fox 1923.
Snailwell — Cambs. Lethbridge 1953.
Stanfordbury — Stanfordbury Farm, Southill, Beds. Fox 1923.
Stanway — Stanway, Colchester, Essex. Crummy 1992.
Stevenage — Sish Lane, Stevenage, Herts. Holmes 1956.
Thatcham — Crookham House, Thatcham, Berks. Peake 1930.
Ver. Folly — Folly Lane Site, Verulamium, St Albans, Herts. Niblett, forthcoming.
Ver. Stad. — Stadium Site, Verulamium, St Albans, Herts. Anthony 1968.

ABBREVIATIONS

[ ] — possible burial
? — uncertain provenance
C. — *Conspectus Formarum*. Ettlinger et al., 1990
L. — Loeschcke 1908
Drag. — Dragendorff
FPW — Fine Parchment Ware
WP — White Pipeclay
TN — Terra Nigra
TR — Terra Rubra

TABLE 1: 'ARRETINE WARES' IN BURIALS

TYPE	GAZETTEER SITES	KHL GRAVE NO.	OTHER SITES
Cup L.8/C.22.9	East Hall (Murston)	346 365	Lexden 1940 Stanway 6 Stanfordbury
Crater Drag. 11	[Tong]		Foxton 1855

TABLE 2: PLATTERS AND CUPS IN TN AND TR IN BURIALS

TYPE	FABRIC	GAZETTEER SITES	KHL GRAVE NO.	OTHER SITES
Platter Cam. 5/GB 6	TN	MHC Grave 2,b	27	
Platter Cam.7/GB11	TN	Maidstone	27 280	Lexden 1963/73
Platter Cam.8/GB13	TN	Faversham Rainham Creek, Gr.1 Priory Hill (Dover)	6 52 67 365 423 438 462	Lexden 1940 Lexden 1924 Baldock KBS Burghfield Brundon Duston Foxton 1855 Guilden Morden Litlington Mount Bures Shefford 1826 Stanway 6 [Thatcham]
	TR 1(C)	East Hall (Murston (2 egs))		Stanway 6 Owslebury [Thatcham]
Cup Cam.56(A)/GB 17	TR 1(C)	[Kent,? Canterbury]	149	Lexden 1940
Cup Cam.56(C)/GB 17	TN	MHC Grave 2,a East Hall (Murston) Shorne Oare (Faversham) [Kent,? Canterbury]	9(2egs) 173 217 224 365 470	Lexden 1940 Baldock KBS Lt. Waltham Snailwell [Ardleigh] [Thatcham]

TABLE 3: OVOID BEAKERS IN BURIALS

TYPE	FABRIC	GAZETTEER SITES	KHL GRAVE NO.	OTHER SITES
Beaker Cam.112/GB25a	TR3	Elms Vale (Dover)	305 325	Lexden 1924 Lexden 1940
Beaker Cam.112Cb/GB25b	TR3	[Canterbury] ?Shorne	405 50	

TABLE 4: BARREL AND BUTT BEAKERS IN BURIALS

TYPE	FABRIC	GAZETTEER SITES	KHL GRAVE NO.	OTHER SITES
BARREL BEAKERS				
Cam.113/KHL 1A1	FPW	MHC Grave X11,1	237 241 268	
/KHL 1B1	FPW	MHC Grave 4,c		
/KHL 1C2	FPW	Elms Vale (Dover)		
BUTT BEAKERS				
Cam.113/KHL 2C2	FPW	Radnor Park, Gr. 3 (Folkestone) Herstmonceux, Gr.5	14 egs	Ardleigh Burghfield Owslebury Aldbury
/KHL 6D2	FPW	Aylesford	12	
/KHL 2E2	FPW	East Hall (Murston)	77 373	Lexden 1924 Puckeridge Ver. Folly Sheepen Gr. 3

TABLE 5: LAGENAE IN BURIALS

TYPE	FABRIC	GAZETTEER SITES	KHL GRAVE NO.	OTHER SITES
Cam.161/KHL GL 6	WP	Allington (Maidstone) East Hall (Murston) Tong (3 egs.) Herstmonceux	24 42 67 173 197 282	Braughing Lexden 1931 Lexden 1940 Stevenage Ver.Stad.Gr.5

TABLE 6: LEAD-GLAZED VESSELS IMPORTED FROM CENTRAL GAUL IN BURIALS

TYPE	FABRIC	GAZETTEER SITES	KHL GRAVE NO.	OTHER SITES
Flasks	CGLG	West Wickham, Gr.E Sanderstead Gr.5		
Flagons Greene 3	CGLG	[Bapchild (Sittingbourne)]	136	Joslin Gr.3 Stanway Arrington

TABLE 7: FABRICATION TECHNIQUES AND FORMS

	HANDMADE	HAND-SHAPED AND WHEEL-FINISHED	WHEEL-THROWN
Copies of Imported Fine Table Wares			
	Flagons/Lagenae		
	Barrel Beakers		
	Butt Beakers		Butt Beakers
			Foot-ring Platters
Forms Paralleled in Southern Britain			
	Waisted Carinated Bowl (A)		
	— — — — — — — — — —	— — — — — Pedestal Jars — — — —	— — — — — — — — — —
		— — — — — —	Cordoned Necked Bowls — — — — — —
			Tazze
East Kent Forms Paralleled in North-western France			
	Lipless Jar		
	Wide-shouldered Combed Jar		
	— — — — — Ripple-necked Bowls	— — — — —	
	— — — — — Ripple-necked Jars (C)	— — — —	
		Ripple-shouldered Bowls — — —	— — — — — — — — — — —
Other East Kent Forms			
	Conical Jar		
	Cordoned Bowl		
	Long-necked Jar		Long-necked Jar
Other Forms			
	Collared Jar		
	Shapeless Omphalos Bowl		
			Ribbed Open Bowl (D)
			Narrow-necked Jar (D)
			Bead-rimmed Bowl
			Necked Bowl

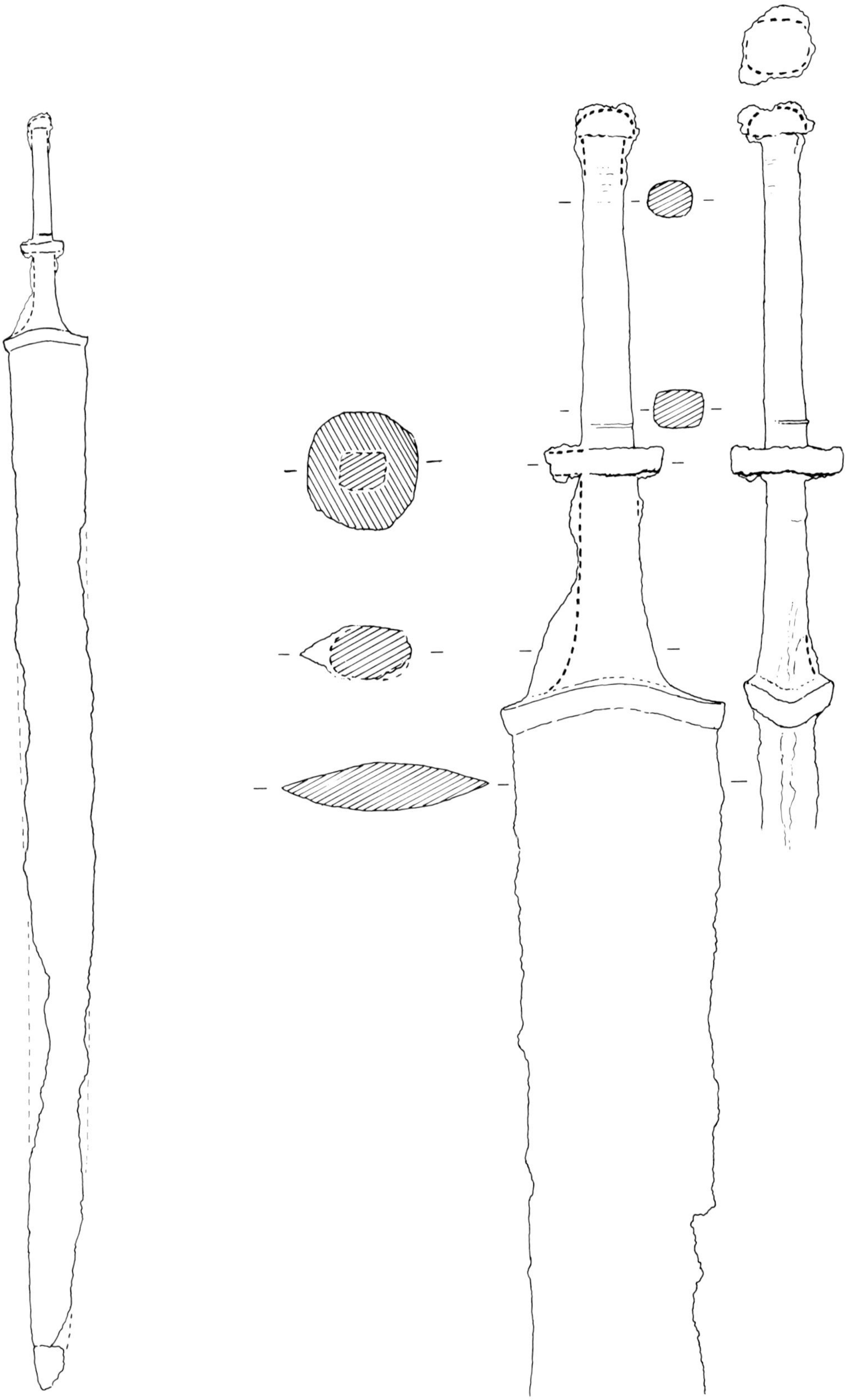

Figure 14. Iron Sword. (Scale 1/4, detail 2/3)

The Metalwork

Warrior burial (Grave 112)

1. Sword and scabbard (Figs. 14, 15)

A corroded iron sword 786mm long, of which the blade is 643mm long. On discovery it was badly damaged in a length between 370 and 500mm from the top of the blade, and below that it is slightly distorted. The blade is thickened in the centre (12mm at the top) but without an obvious median ridge. Its taper is not easy to assess because of corrosion at the edges: from a width of 49mm at the top there seems to be little decrease to the damaged area, below which it tapers markedly to a point. It seems likely to have tapered for the final 190mm, between 1/4 and 1/3 of the length of the blade. Doubtless the tang has been rectangular in section, but much of it is obscured by mineral preserved organics. The handle had been made of bone (unidentified to taxon: a small sample was removed and thin-sectioned by Caroline Cartwright, Department of Scientific Research, British Museum), and constructed in two lengths divided by a fairly thick (5mm) iron washer (cf. Stead 1991a, 70, fig. 54, for two-part handles). The upper length is now 72mm, but a line in the corrosion parallel with and 7mm above the washer suggests that once it may have been shorter. At the top corrosion products from the tang have extended into vertical cracks in the bone handle. The bottom of the lower length of the handle may have been cracked too, because there is a very marked but narrow expansion of the corrosion products on one side. At the top of the tang, above the mineral preserved organics, is a pronounced but corroded knob, and at the bottom of the handle a separate iron hilt-end with a very low curve – only 5mm high on one face and 7mm on the other.

The scabbard, made of leather or wood with bronze fittings, had been about 660mm long. There is a bronze panel at the top, on the front, 95mm long and 59mm wide at the top (expanding to 61mm wide at the bottom), with a high campanulate mouth – much higher than the iron hilt-end of the sword (16mm as opposed to 5–7mm) which suggests that sword and scabbard were not originally intended for one another (pl. VIII; fig. 15, a). About 11mm below the mouth on the inside of the front panel is the impression of part of another curve, shallower and more in keeping with the shape of the present hilt-end. The panel is very slightly down-curved at the bottom and has broad overlaps deeply rounded to clasp the presumed leather scabbard and cover the edges of a bronze back panel; the rounded edges continue to the front where each is bordered by a notched rib. Similar notched ribs define a central vertical panel decorated with an overall repoussé design (p. 93). The bronze back-panel is 315mm long, much longer than the front panel, and 53mm wide with a campanulate mouth as high as that on the front panel (fig. 15,c). Its bottom end is straight, with no hint of rivets or any other form of attachment to the presumed leather scabbard. The cast bronze suspension loop is 31mm long and 15mm wide, with slight raised flanges; its long narrow loop-plates, the upper shorter than the lower, have been attached to the back plate by iron rivets, and the entire piece is 110mm long. On the underside the lower half of the back plate has two or three shallow grooves down the centre, reflected on the surface by a very slight median ridge and a couple of cracks.

The chape, 160mm long, is lacking a length of binding on one side, and most of one clamp (fig. 15, b). The binding, bridge and clamps have been cut from metal sheet, and the chape-end is cast on. The bridge is bordered top and bottom by notched ribs; the clamps are open rings, wider in the centre than at the side, decorated with repoussé dots in very high relief (almost vertical sides) rather like some of those in the repoussé ornament on the front panel (cf. similar dotted rings on the shield, fig. 22, and suspension ring, fig. 32, no. 5). The chape-end, surmounted by moulded 'finishes' decorated with dots, is ornamented front and back with circular settings (? for coral or enamel) surrounded by rings in high relief. Below each ring on the front is a lobed bird-head device in a tapering panel (cf. p. 93); the pattern on the left is worn, and its lower part is obscured by corrosion (possibly where the casting has been modified in construction, cf. also the assymetry of the two sides of the chape-end). At the bottom is a worn moulding.

The Deal sword has a typical La Tène I blade, tapering between 1/4 and 1/3 of its length to a sharp point (de Navarro 1972, 21 and 40). Its scabbard is more unusual, made of either leather or wood (no trace of organics in the corrosion products of the metal), but with a decorated bronze panel at the top – an arrangement that can be matched on three other British scabbards, from Shepperton, Standlake and the River Witham (for references see p. 63, nos 2, 3 and 26). The lower edge of the Shepperton and Witham panels follow the complex shapes of their repoussé ornament, crossing the scabbards diagonally. Each has a short iron panel on the back, overlapped by the bronze front panel. But the Standlake panel is square, serrated at the bottom, has no overlaps (it

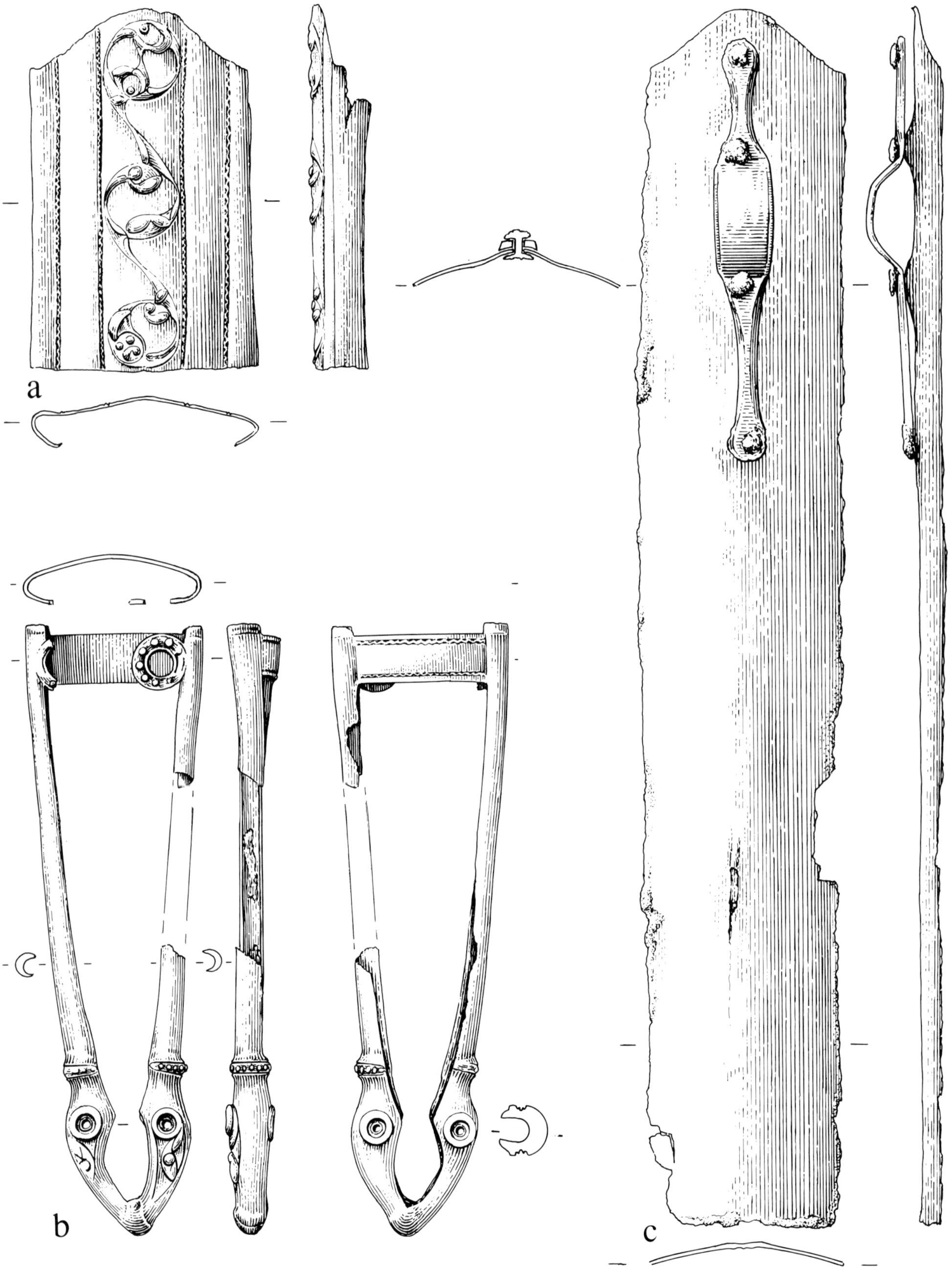

Figure 15. Bronze scabbard fittings. (Scale 2/3)

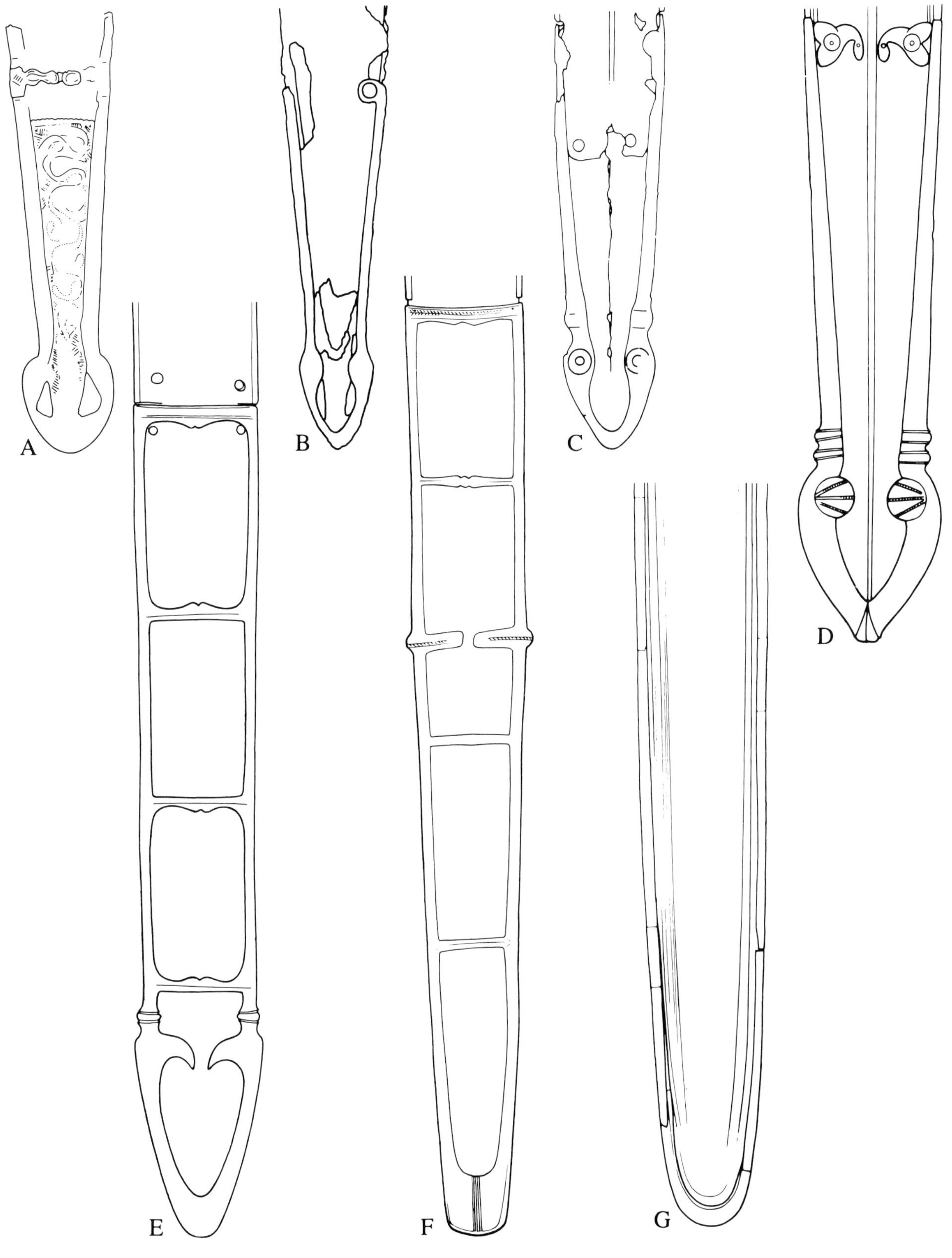

Figure 16. Typology of British Iron Age scabbard-chapes: A. Standlake, no. 3; B. London, no. 4; C. Fovant, no. 6; D. Hunsbury, no. 11; E. London, no. 16 (back view); F. Abingdon, no. 17 (back view); G. Battersea, no. 19. For numbers, see fig. 18; drawings by Robert Pengelly. (Scale 1/2)

may have had a separate metal binding), and no surviving metal back panel. Of these scabbards only Shepperton now has a suspension loop (Witham has a rivet hole from a loop-plate), which is long, narrow and band-shaped with rounded loop-plates – a typical La Tène I form (see de Navarro 1972, type Ia). The Deal suspension loop is also long and narrow, but the loop-plates are elongated, and it is attached to a bronze back plate which is far longer than its iron counterparts on the Shepperton and Witham scabbards.

The contrast between Deal on the one hand and Shepperton and Standlake on the other, is much more marked when the chapes are compared. Shepperton and Standlake are similar, with iron chapes bridged front and back, and rounded open chape-ends. Within are bronze panels, each decorated to correspond with the ornamented panel at the top. Unfortunately the Witham chape is now lost: an early illustration (Willson 1852) shows some bronze that may have been the remains of a panel within the chape or perhaps the chape itself. With rounded open chape-ends and chapes bridged front and back, Shepperton and Standlake are La Tène I pieces. The Deal chape is very different: it is made of bronze, not iron; bridged on the back but clamped on the front; it lacks the decorated panel and its chape-end is heart-shaped. These features relate Deal to another group of scabbards, typologically later than the trio discussed above.

Iron chapes bridged on the back and clamped on the front are typical of La Tène I and II scabbards on the continent, and they also occur on La Tène I scabbards in Britain (e.g. from London, no. 4, and the River Witham, no. 5). One from Fovant (no. 6) has similar bridge and clamps, but the chape-end is closed, so it should be classified as a La Tène II form (de Navarro 1972, 33, fig. 12, no. 6, type Bi). The chape from Deal is a bronze version resembling Fovant, but with more elaborate details and designed for a slightly more tapering blade. A chape from Little Wittenham (no. 9; fig. 17) is similar but without the details, and with the addition of decoration on the back – an openwork design, resembling in technique the decoration on the boss of the Deal shield (p. 93). Otherwise the closest British chapes are from Spettisbury (Piggott 1950, fig. 3, 6) and a very crude example from Hunsbury (no. 8) both designed for blades with very little taper.

The Deal sword and scabbard may be compared with others from Britain by establishing a typology of scabbards and relating them by plotting the measurements of the sword-blades they enclose. The typology of scabbards relies very much on the form of the chape (fig. 16): A, iron, with rounded open ends; B, iron, narrower and more pointed than A, but still open; C, iron or bronze, close-fitting and heart-shaped; D, bronze, larger and more developed than C, the 'chape-clamps' separate and purely decorative; E, bronze, elongated heart-shaped chape-ends, most on laddered chapes; F, bronze laddered chapes with thickened rounded ends; G, bronze scabbards with wrapped rounded ends that have no need for chapes.

Figure 17. The back of a bronze chape from Little Wittenham. Drawn by Robert Pengelly. (Full size)

In the diagram (fig. 18) the seven groups of scabbards are distinguished and plotted according to the length and top width of the sword-blades they held. The importance of blade and scabbard measurements has been demon-

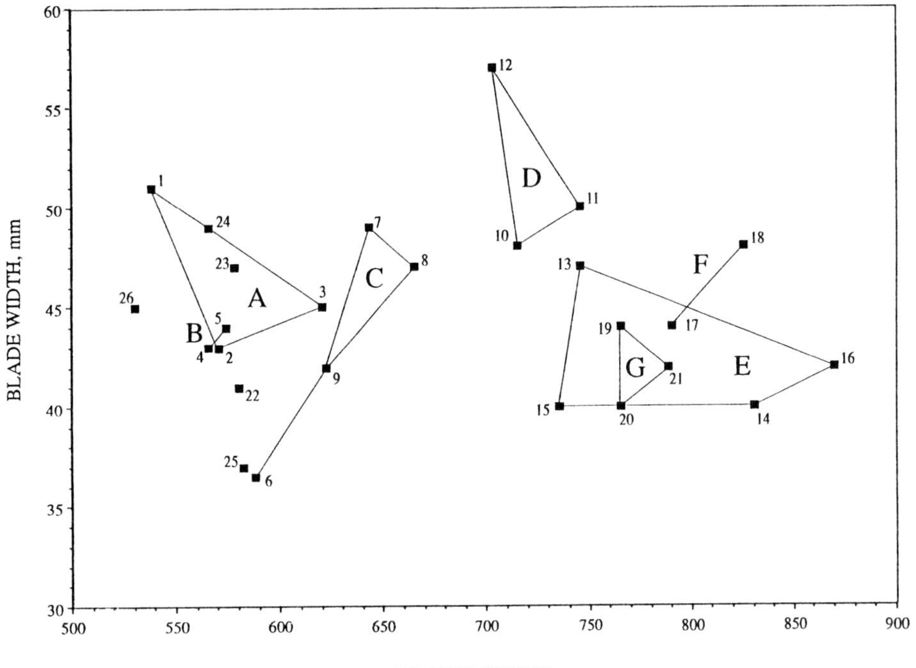

Figure 18. Diagram, plotting the length and width of some British Iron Age sword-blades distinguished by the typology of their scabbards (for the typology of the scabbards see fig. 16): A. 1. Orton Meadows, Peterborough, Cambridgeshire (538×51mm) Stead 1984a, 49; 2. Shepperton, Surrey (570×43mm) unpublished (Poulton forthcoming); 3. Standlake, Oxon (620×45mm) Case 1949; Fox 1958, pl. 22a; B. 4. London (566×43mm) unpublished (BM 56 7–1 1402); 5. River Witham (574×44mm) Petch 1957, 9; C. 6. Fovant, Wilts (588×36.5mm) not yet published in detail; scabbard-mouth decoration, Stead 1985b, pl 23, right; chape-end, Stead 1985a, fig. 10c; 7. Deal, Kent (643×49mm); 8. Hunsbury, Northants (665×47mm) Fell 1936, 65, pl. 3, nos. 2 and 2a; 9. Little Wittenham, Oxon (622×42mm) fig. 17; Harding 1972, 173, pls 78B and 79D; D. 10. Henley, Oxon (715×48mm) Rutland 1972; chape-end, Stead 1985a, fig. 10, f; 11. Hunsbury, Northants (745×50mm) Fell 1936, pl. 3, nos. 1 and 1a; Piggott 1950, fig. 3, 1; 12. Little Wittenham, Oxon (703×57mm) Sherratt 1983; Stead 1985b, fig. 66 (top of scabbard), 1985a, fig. 10, g (chape-end); E. 13. Meare Heath, Somerset (745×47mm) Piggott 1950, fig. 3, 3; 14. Amerden, Bucks (830×40mm) Piggott 1950, fig. 3, 4; 15. Lakenheath, Suffolk (735×40mm) Fox 1923, 107, pl. xviii, 1; Piggott 1950, fig. 2, 3; 16. London (870×42mm) Smith 1854, 67–72; Smith 1905, 95, pl. vi, 4; F. 17. Abingdon, Berks (790×44mm) unpublished (Reading Museum 118.69, TCB 330); 18. Orton Meadows, Peterborough, Cambs (825×48mm) unpublished (Mackreth forthcoming); G. 19. Battersea, London (765×44mm) Piggott 1950, fig. 10, 6; 20, Isleham, Cambs (765×40mm) Stead et al. 1981; 21. River Witham, Lincs (788×42mm) Fox 1958, pl. 49b; some other scabbards, lacking chapes: 22. Battersea, London (580×41mm) Stead 1984b, 269; 23. Hammersmith Bridge, London (578×47mm) ibid. 269–71; 24. Fiskerton, Lincs (565×49mm) unpublished (Field forthcoming); 25. Sutton, Notts (582×37mm) Fox 1958, pl. 21; 26, River Witham, Lincs (530×45mm) Kendrick 1939; Fox 1958, pl. 22b.

strated for the site of La Tène (de Navarro 1972), has some validity in Champagne (Stead 1983), and seems equally significant in southern England. A sequence of the typological groups can be distinguished on fig. 18, with A and B followed by C on the left, then D, and finally E, F and G together on the right. Scabbards on the left (A and B) have typical La Tène I chapes, whilst those on the right are typical of La Tène III, including both laddered chapes (E and F) and scabbards rounded at the ends (F and G). Those in the middle of the diagram (C and D) have measurements that compare favourably with those of La Tène II swords from La Tène.

Four other swords and a scabbard-plate, that cannot be grouped because the scabbards lack chapes, have been plotted on fig. 18. Within or near the La Tène I Groups A and B are swords from Battersea and Hammersmith Bridge (nos. 22 and 23), in scabbards decorated with dragon pairs, and one from Fiskerton (no. 24) the same site as artefacts with Waldalgesheim Style decoration. The Sutton scabbard-plate (no. 25), whose decoration is discussed below, has measurements very similar to the Group C Fovant scabbard. But the Duke of Northumberland's Witham sword (no. 26) appears to be an anomaly: it is the shortest of the swords plotted here, whereas its decoration would be more in keeping with a length around 600mm. However, apart from that one example all the swords and scabbards plotted in fig. 18 seem to occur in a chronological sequence consistent with both typology and the development of La Tène art in Britain. Swords and scabbards found north of the Humber have been omitted from this exercise because they do not increase in length as the Iron Age progresses (Stead 1991a, 64). The La Tène I scabbards from Wetwang Slack and Kirkburn would fall in their expected positions in the diagram, grouped at the bottom left, but the much more developed scabbards from Grimthorpe and Bugthorpe held swords of very similar length, well within the Group A range.

The Deal sword, then, has a blade of La Tène I shape, its scabbard has features comparable with La Tène I scabbards from Shepperton and Standlake (Group A), but its chape is more like La Tène II forms (Group C). The measurements of the sword-blade (fig. 18, no. 7) are consistent with a date early in La Tène II, perhaps 200 BC.

2. *Shield* (figs. 19–24)

The bronze bindings of three corners of a shield were found with the incurved edges at the ends of the grave and the straighter binding along the side. Many pieces of bronze sheet (several with openwork ornament), nails, lengths of binding and clamps were scattered between the two ends of the shield, mainly in the middle of the southwest side of the grave (fig. 19). From one extreme to the other the corner pieces were 1.19m apart, and it seems reasonable to suppose that that was the length of the shield. But the distribution of fragments in the grave gives no indication of its width, because the two bottom corners (2 and 3) were found immediately above one another. The lower corner (3) was flat and about 50mm above the floor of the grave; the upper piece (2) was slightly angled with its curved end almost touching the comparable part of 3 whereas the two knobbed corners were 65mm apart (fig. 20, b). Perhaps (as the excavator suggests, p. 20) the shield had been broken along its length and folded in two, but the deliberate breaking of metalwork is not a feature of British Iron Age burials. Alternatively, it could have been on its edge between the corpse and the side of the grave; it is much wider than the depth of the grave when excavated (fig. 20, c and d) but there is no knowing how it might have collapsed and settled as the organics in the grave rotted. The way in which the two bones of the left forearm were separated by the pelvis shows considerable scope for movement within the filling of this side of the grave.

The total length of binding recovered (as measured on site by the excavator) amounts to less than 1m, i.e. less than was needed to bind one side. If the entire circuit had been bound then much would have been destroyed before the excavation. Some of the damage may have been caused by levelling in connection with the quarry, because the grave was only 0.13 to 0.18m deep when excavated; other damage must have occurred when the Roman gully (Feature 504) was cut across the southeast end of the grave. Within the shallow grave the excavators recorded the shield binding and other bronze fragments in two levels, upper and lower, but it may be that the situation was complicated because the remains of the shield were higher at the southeast than at the northwest end of the grave. At the northwest end there were two layers of fragments and two superimposed corners, but at the other end the one layer and one corner were in the upper part of the surviving filling (figs 19, 20). The missing corner and associated binding must have been even higher in the grave and long since lost. Hence at the southeast end fragments recorded in the upper level might have been from the lower edge of the shield (fig. 20, c).

All the metal fittings of the shield are bronze; the letter after the measurements, (a), etc, was assigned in the field:

A. Binding survives from three corners (fig. 21). Each piece has a straight and a concave length meeting at a globular knob. The knob is hollow and seems to have been worked from sheet, not cast.

(1) L 126mm (straight), 102mm (curve), (g). The binding has secured the edge of organics 4mm thick on the curved side, increasing on the straight side from 4mm near the corner to 6mm. The curved end is broken, but when found it was covered by clamp 5 – increasing its length to 139mm as shown in fig. 21 (cf. pl. II).

(2) L 102mm (straight), 101mm (curve), (h). Organics have been 4mm thick at the binding, increasing slightly away from the corner on the straight side to 4.5mm. The curved end is unbroken, and a change in the patina suggests that it was covered by the clamp 4 (as shown in fig. 21).

(3) L 164mm (straight), 111mm (curve), (i). The curved length of binding terminates (an original unbroken end) halfway under clamp 4. The end of the straight length is slightly angled and not obviously unbroken, but when excavated it was within clamp 10.

The binding has been secured by clamps of three different types (B–D):

B. Four clamps each shaped in four segments (no. 7 has five segments), the outer two convex and the inner two concave in profile (fig. 22). Each clamp seems to have covered a join in the binding, and they reduced the thickness of the organics from 4mm to 2–3mm where clamped.

(4) L 15mm. On the curved length of binding of corner 3.

(5) L 16mm. On a curved length of binding. When found this was part of the corner 1 (cf. pl. II), and the impression of the end of 1 can still be seen in the patina on the underside of the clamp. There had been a gap of about 6mm between the ends of the two lengths of binding covered by this clamp.

(6) L 14.5mm. On a straight but fragmented length of binding (ff).

(7) L 16.5mm. Five segments (an additional convex-profile segment in the middle). On a straight but fragmented length of binding (o).

C. Three segmented clamps, 15 to 17mm long, each with an asymmetric ring on one side – i.e. a circle with an

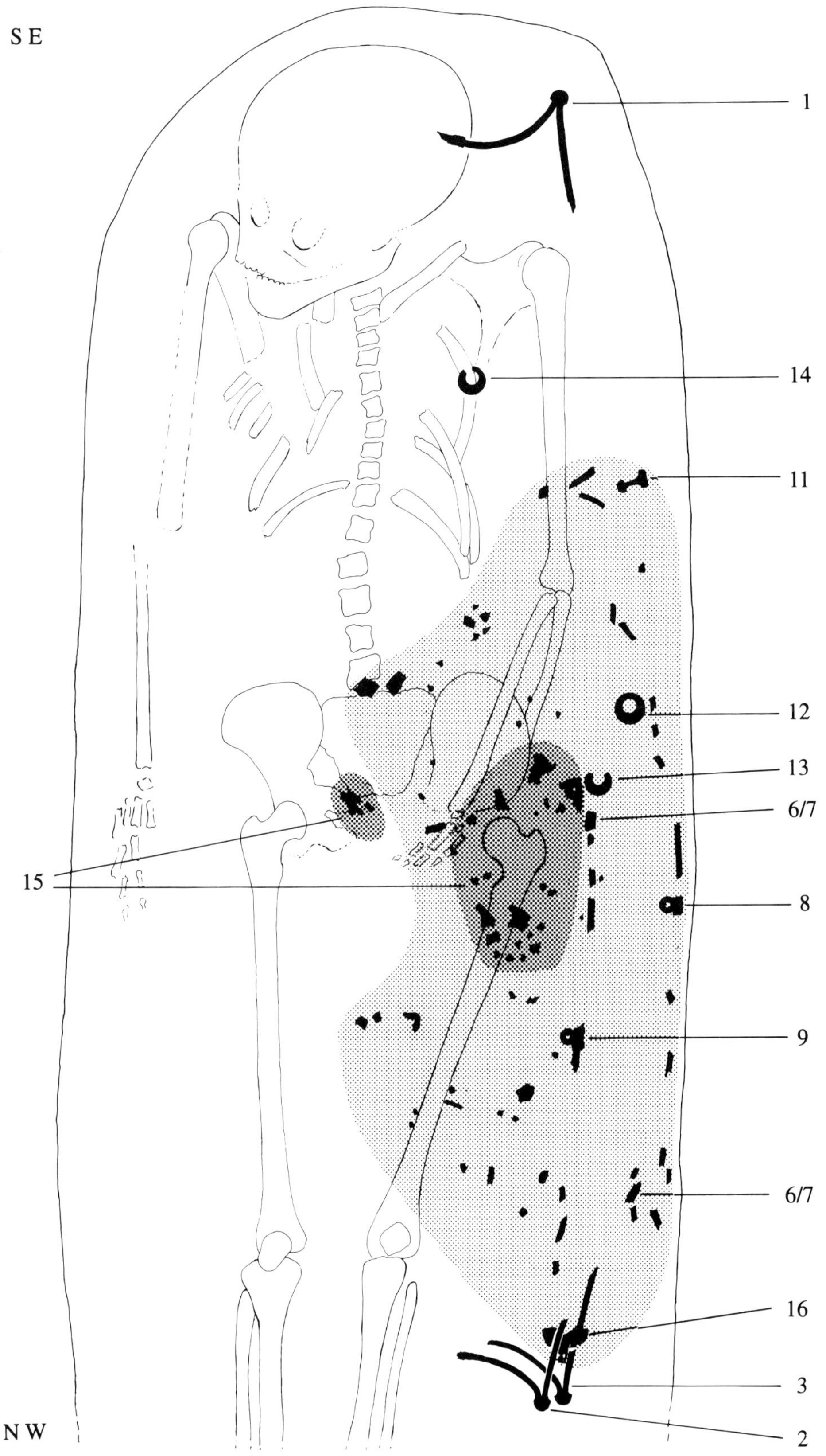

Figure 19. Plan showing the distribution of bronze fittings of the shield within Grave 112. The main shaded area shows the limits of the distribution of decorated sheet bronze fragments; the shaded areas numbered 15 show where fragments from the cover of the boss were found. (Scale 1/6)

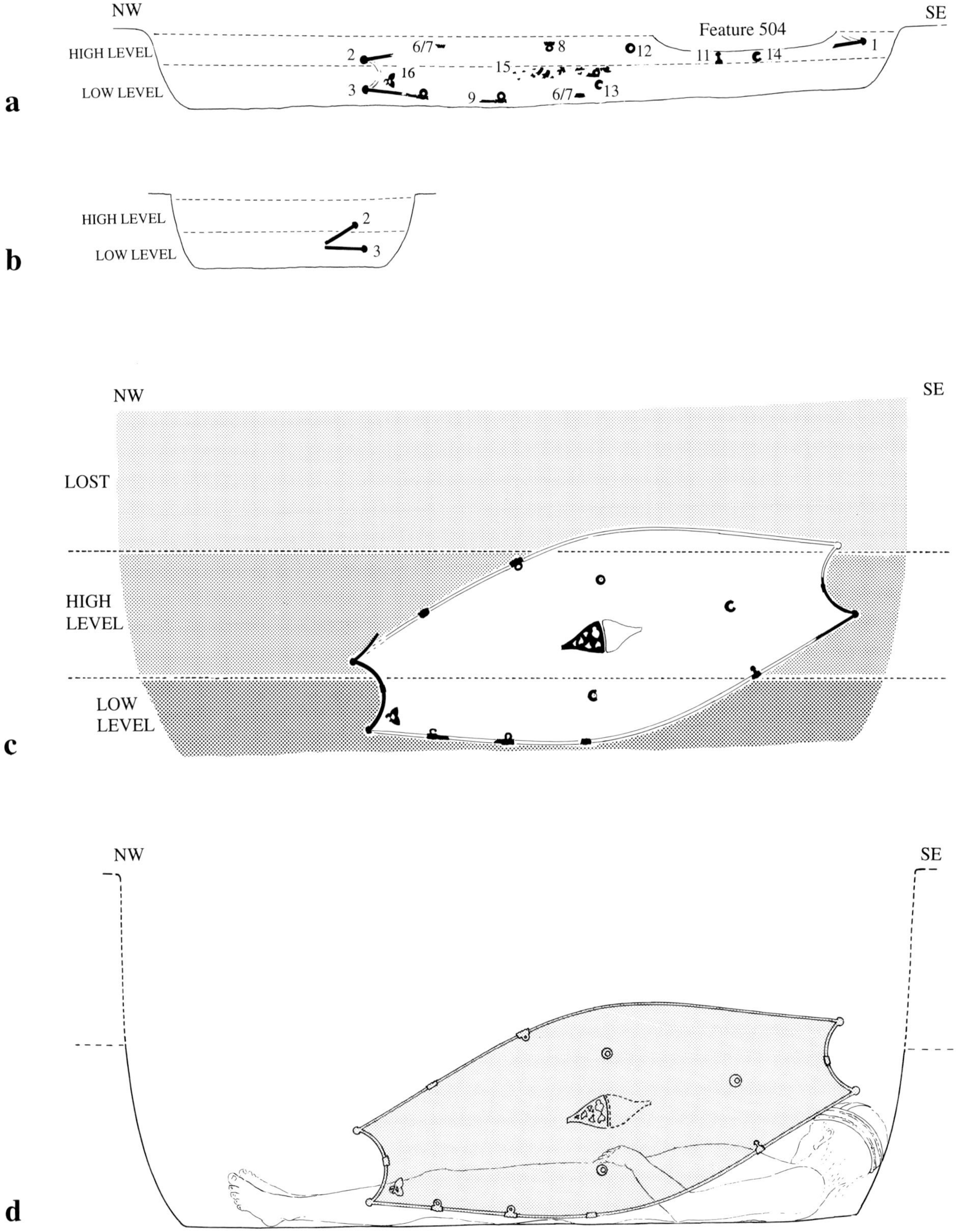

Figure 20. The shield from Grave 112: (a) and (b) diagrams showing the distribution of bronze fittings in section, as excavated in two levels; (c) and (d) a hypothetical reconstruction of the shield as deposited – indicating in (c) the two levels as excavated and the grave filling lost before excavation.

Figure 21. Bronze bindings from three corners of the shield. (Scale 1/2)

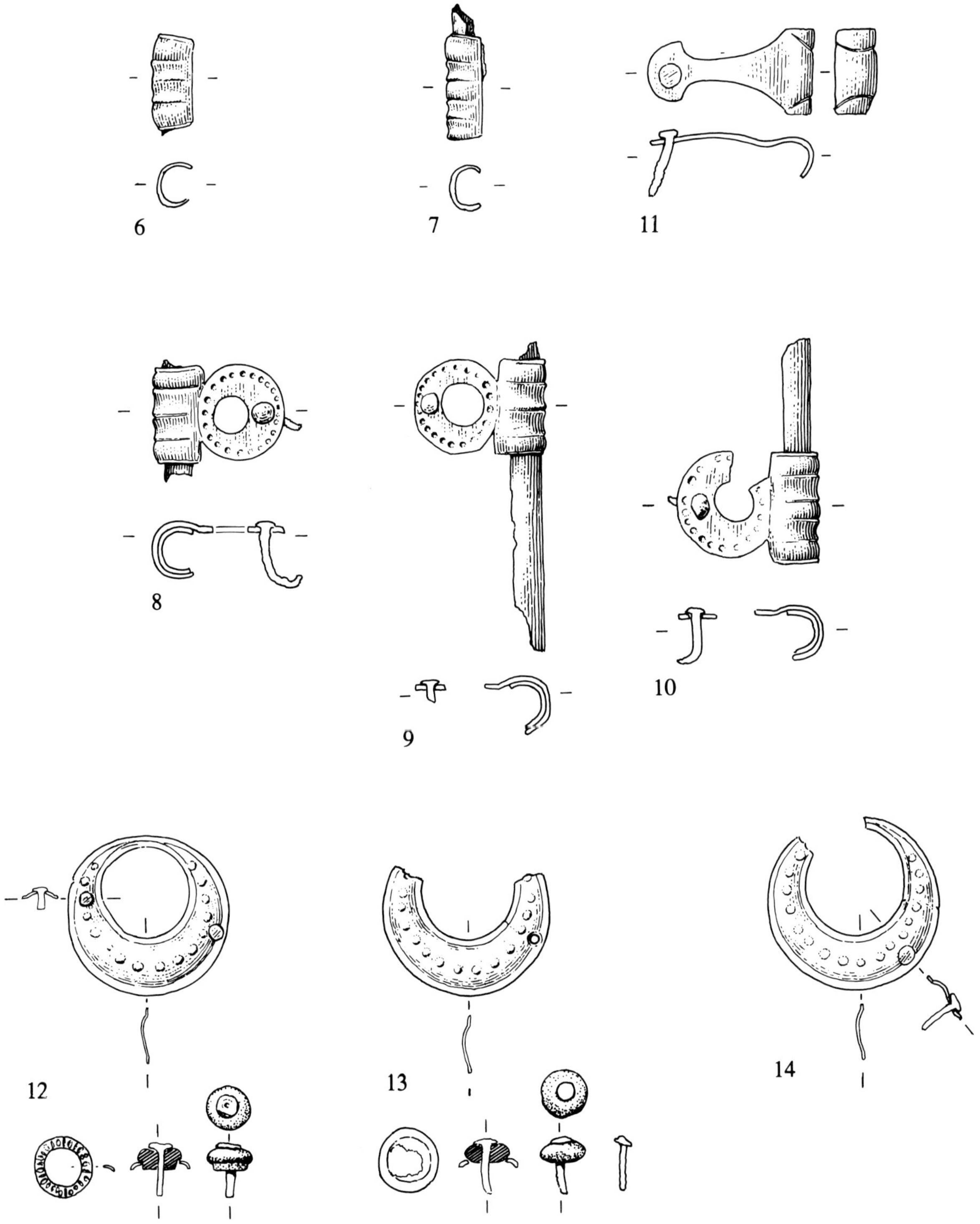

Figure 22. Bronze clamps and other fittings from the shield. (Full size)

off-centre perforation forming a ring with narrow side adjoining the clamp and broad side away from the clamp (fig. 22). Each ring has a bronze nail through its broad side, and is bordered by a ring of punched dots. These clamps, 8–10, are much more open than 4–7. Whereas 4–7 compressed the binding and organics, 8–10 acted as hooks, relying on the nail to secure them to the board of the shield.

(8) L 15.5mm, ring 14–15mm diam, (q). Bent nail shows that organics were 7mm thick; 4.5mm thick where clamped. A continuous length of binding under the clamp, broken at both ends.

(9) L 15mm, ring 13.5–14.5mm diam, (x). Broken nail; edge of organics 5mm thick where clamped. A continuous length of binding under the clamp, extending 32mm beyond, straight.

(10) L 17mm (additional segment, central, convex-profile), ring 15–16mm diam, (i). Bent nail through organics 6mm thick; 5.5mm thick where clamped. The clamp seems to have covered a straight break in the binding: one length survives and extends 17mm beyond the clamp, the other is the end of the straight length of corner 3, see fig. 21 – its position was recorded in the field.

D. A unique clamp, (11), L 13mm, decorated over the binding with two curved incised lines; a long narrow appendage, L 26mm from the edge of the shield, with D-shaped terminal through which a nail 7mm long (broken point) has secured it to the shield (fig. 22).

E. Three asymmetric rings, similar to but larger than those attached to 8–10, were found in the same vicinity and may have ornamented the shield (fig. 22). Each is decorated with a ring of repoussé dots and has been attached to an organic base by two nails. Associated with two of them were decorative knobs of polished coral that may have fitted within the central perforations of the rings. The coral knobs are shaped underneath and set in thin bronze rings decorated with radiating grooves; they have been secured by central bronze nails.

(12) 26–7mm diam, (n). Both nails broken. Coral knob 7–8mm diam; central nail with large head, overall L 9mm (point broken).

(13) 27.5mm diam, incomplete (gg). One nail separate, overall L 9mm (point broken); thin bronze ring includes a black adhesive (? resin, cf. p. 86).

(14) 28.5mm diam, incomplete (l). One nail, broken. No coral knob.

F. Openwork ornament was found amongst the binding and other fittings, and one major piece (fig. 23, 15) certainly belonged to the shield. Its fragments (aa, bb, dd, ee and v) were scattered over a length of 0.17m, mainly within 0.1m of one another but one piece 0.15m away from the rest (fig. 19, shaded area). All were within the lower half of the shield, but none was more than 0.18m from the centre. These pieces join to form a triangular plaque, 80×99mm as bent. It has sharp corners at the ends of the shorter side, but the third corner has an elongated projection with a 7mm wide squared end. The projection has been secured to a presumed wooden base by two nails, now broken; there is a nail through each of the other corners, one unbroken, straight and projecting 14mm from the metal sheet and the other 9mm but lacking its point; and two other nails, broken, in the middle (perhaps there would have been a third in the short length now missing). The triangular plaque has bordering grooves along two edges and openwork ornament that is discussed below (p. 88).

Despite the distortion, it is obvious that the triangular plaque was not originally flat. Its convexity, overall shape and position in the grave suggests that it covered the lower part of a spindle-shaped boss. The one complete nail shows that it had been attached to organics much thicker than the board of the shield, and a carved wooden umbo would seem a strong possibility. Some miniature shields have short spindle-shaped bosses with markedly squared ends (cf. especially Stead 1991b, nos 2 and 11).

The other pieces of openwork bronze are from flat sheet, and include positive cut out designs as well as the negative shapes like those on the triangular plaque; the outline of the design is sometimes in the form of projecting lobes rather than a straight edge. Only a very few fragments can be joined and the overall design cannot be reconstructed. There are at least 45 nails and it may be that the fragments belonged to several isolated motifs rather than a relatively large panel. Most of the nails are broken but several have been deliberately bent, showing that they have pierced organics 7–9mm thick – presumably the board of the shield. One of the largest surviving fragments (fig. 23, 16) was found in three pieces between the two superimposed corners of the shield (2 and 3, see fig. 20, a) suggesting a decorative motif near one corner (cf. Stead 1991b, no. 4); others were nearer the centre of the shield, but there were none at the southeast end of the grave (fig. 19). Only two small fragments seem to have straight edges, and both are grooved (their rarity may suggest that a lot has been lost). Several of the larger pieces are illustrated in fig. 23, 17.

A considerable amount of time was spent, especially by Ruth Goldstraw, in trying to establish joins between the many fragments, but apart from the openwork boss (fig. 23, 15) success was limited. Susan LaNiece, British Museum Research Laboratory, who attempted to simplify the problem, reports: ‘The pieces were analysed by XRF on the uncleaned surface to see if any grouping could be done by composition. The fragments of sheet are too

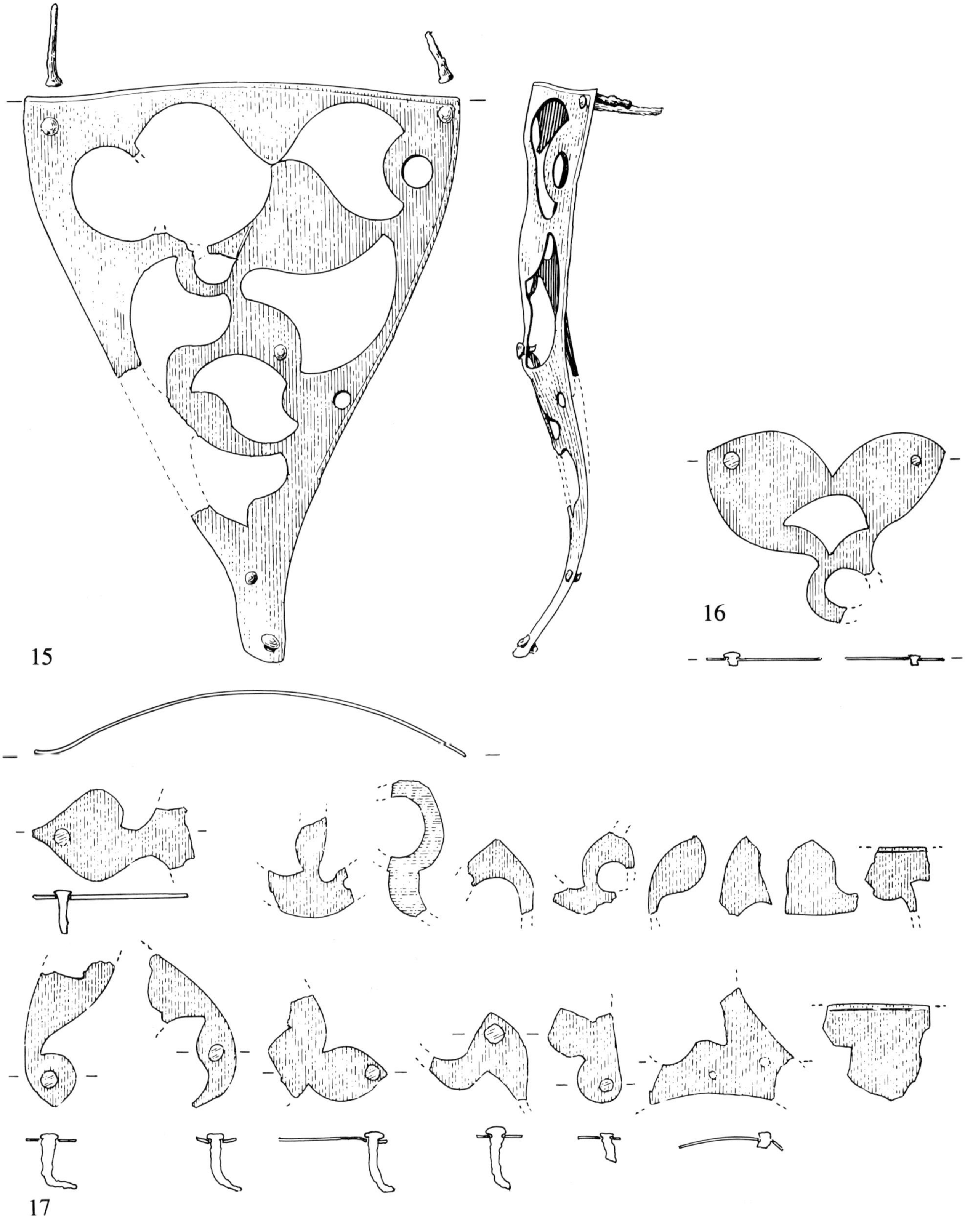

Figure 23. Sheet bronze cut-out ornament from the shield: 15. from the boss; 16. from near a corner; 17. from the main area shaded on fig. 19. (Full size)

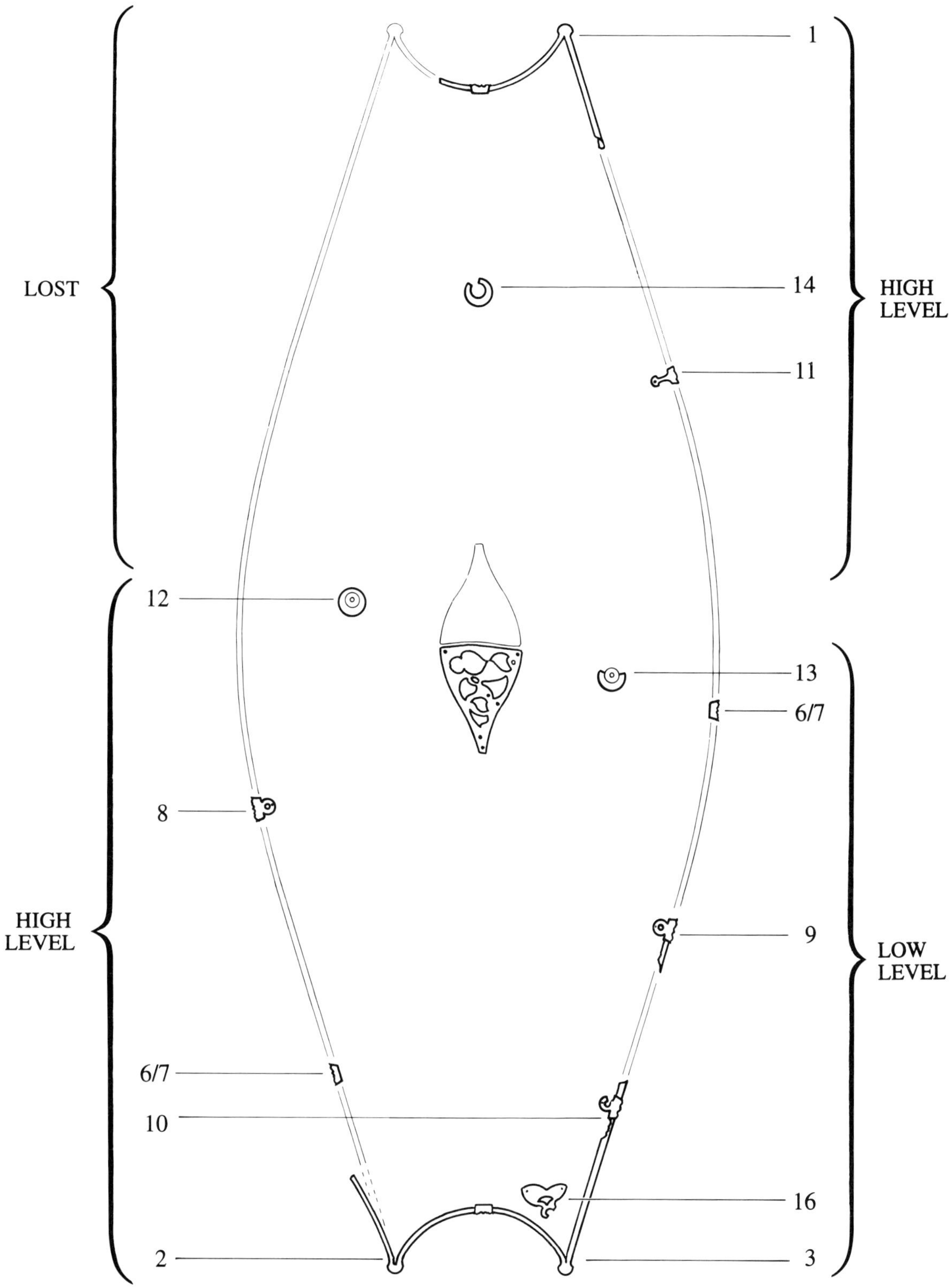

Figure 24. Reconstruction of the shield from Grave 112; for the high and low level, as excavated, see the section, fig. 20. (Scale 1/6)

fragile to allow cleaning for quantitative analysis. All the pieces have a surface composition of approximately 83% Cu, 3% Pb, 15% Sn and 0.4% As. No zinc was detected in any of the fragments. On more heavily patinated fragments the figures for tin and arsenic were higher, but this is a corrosion phenomenon and is unlikely to reflect any real difference in metal composition. Unfortunately the fragments of sheet bronze are too similar in composition to allow grouping.'

The shield belongs to a common British type, but curiously it was unknown to scholars until five months before the Deal grave was excavated. The key to the identification of the type was the discovery of a collection of miniature shields, found near Salisbury, that surfaced in July 1988 (Stead 1991b). That discovery allowed the distinctive bindings of full-scale shields to be correctly identified, and the hide-shaped shield promptly became a common type, known from 12 sites. In December 1988 the excavation of Burial 112 at Deal provided the first example of a hide-shaped shield in a grave and confirmation (five months earlier it would have been 'recognition') of the new type.

Apart from Deal full-size hide-shaped shields are known only from isolated corner-bindings and some possible fittings from Bredon Hill (Hencken 1938, 68–71, fig. 4, nos 2-5, and perhaps also nos 10, 15 and 18). Other sites have produced fittings that can be matched on the Deal shield, but not associated with shield bindings, e.g. Hod Hill, Richmond 1968, 41, Pit 15C, no. 1, fig. 32, bottom right. Deal provides the only length for a hide-shaped shield, 1.19m, but because of its position in the grave the width of the shield is not obvious – though there are some clues.

A change in the patina suggests that the end of corner 2 slotted within clamp 4 which is attached to corner 3 (fig. 21), thus relating the two corners at the northwest end and having the clamp midway between them. The two corners were found together (fig. 20, a and b) and there were no other curved lengths of binding in the vicinity. At the opposite end, clamp 5 is in a comparable position relative to corner 1 and it too could have been midway between two corners. The ends thus restored are extremely narrow (0.17m between the centres of the corner knobs) relative to the length of the shield. The Deal shield is seven times longer than the distance between its terminals; the comparable figures for the miniatures range from 3.2 to 6.3, with a mean of 4.6.

The overall width on the suggested reconstruction (fig. 24) was established by projecting the straight sides from the corners: corners 1 and 3 have comparable angles, but 2 is different and would suggest a wider shield (but there is a split at its corner knob, so it may be distorted). Projecting from corners 1 and 3 produces a narrow shield, some 0.45m wide; its width is $^3/_8$ of its length. The miniature hide-shaped shields have widths on average almost $^1/_2$ of their lengths, so they represent relatively wide shields (though Stead 1991b, no. 6, has similar proportions to Deal, and no. 14 is even narrower relative to its length).

The remaining fittings have been distributed as they occurred in the grave (figs 19, 24): there seems no symmetry about the arrangement of clamps 6–10, and the three rings (12–14) need not have been placed as symmetrically as the reconstruction suggests. It seems likely that the openwork ornament (15) covered the lower half of the boss.

One feature missing from the Deal shield is a handle. As only two British shields, Battersea and Chertsey, are known to have had metal components in the handles (Stead 1991b) this might occasion no surprise, but all the Salisbury miniatures have riveted handles.

Those hide-shaped shields that can be dated seem to belong to the second or first centuries BC (ibid. 24).

3. *Crown*

Found on the skull, the crown is a decorated bronze band worn round the head with an attached plain bronze strip over the top of the head (Frontispiece; pl. III; fig. 25). The decorated band, 38mm wide, has two raised cordons bordered by plain flanges, with the decoration in the 15mm width between the cordons. It was made from two unequal lengths (380 and 245mm) that overlap by 12–14 and 15–17mm respectively, each joint being secured by two rivets, one in each flange. The decoration does not run smoothly from one length to the other, suggesting that it was executed before they were riveted together. The bronze strip over the head is 25–26mm wide, undecorated but for two grooves near the edges and two others that define 5–6mm wide borders. Its ends (for 10–11mm) are covered by the decorated band and each is secured by two rivets (one now missing) through the upper flange. On each side one of these rivets goes through the border of the strip whilst the other penetrates the central area. The crown was damaged in the ground, doubtless when the burial was disturbed by a Roman gully (Feature 504): the strip over the head suffered most and a substantial piece is missing, but the decorated band was also broken and some fragments of the flanges have been lost. The decoration (p. 93), consisting of engraved, chased or incised lines, with some rows of punched dots alongside, is quite worn.

Traces of mineralised fibres on the inside of the crown were recorded and plotted in the course of conservation (cf. fig. 26). They were concentrated at the junctions of the strap with the band, and at the back of the band (note that the strap is slightly forward of the midpoint of the crown). The mineralised fibres were examined by

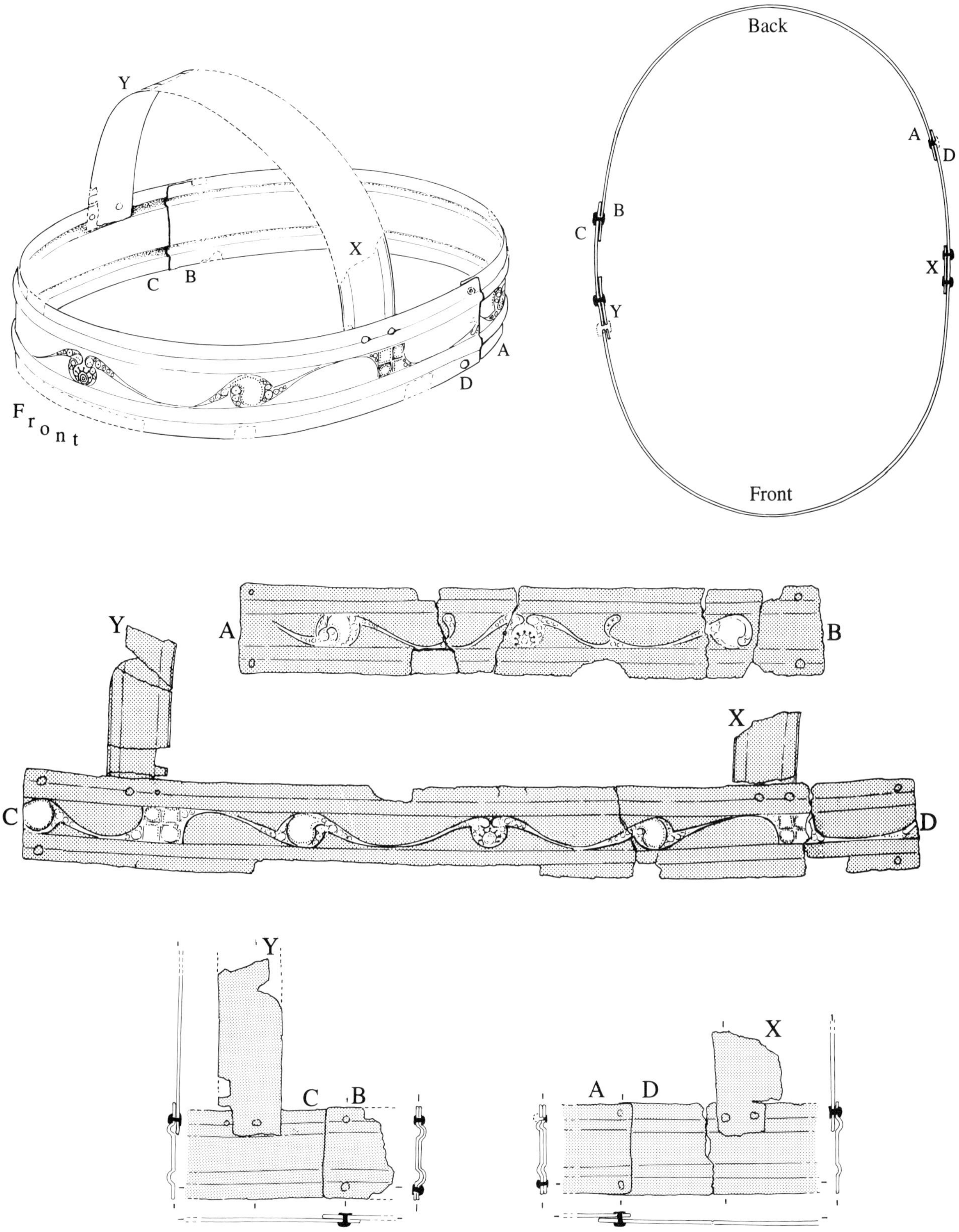

Figure 25. Crown from Grave 112: drawings to illustrate its construction. (Scale 2/5)

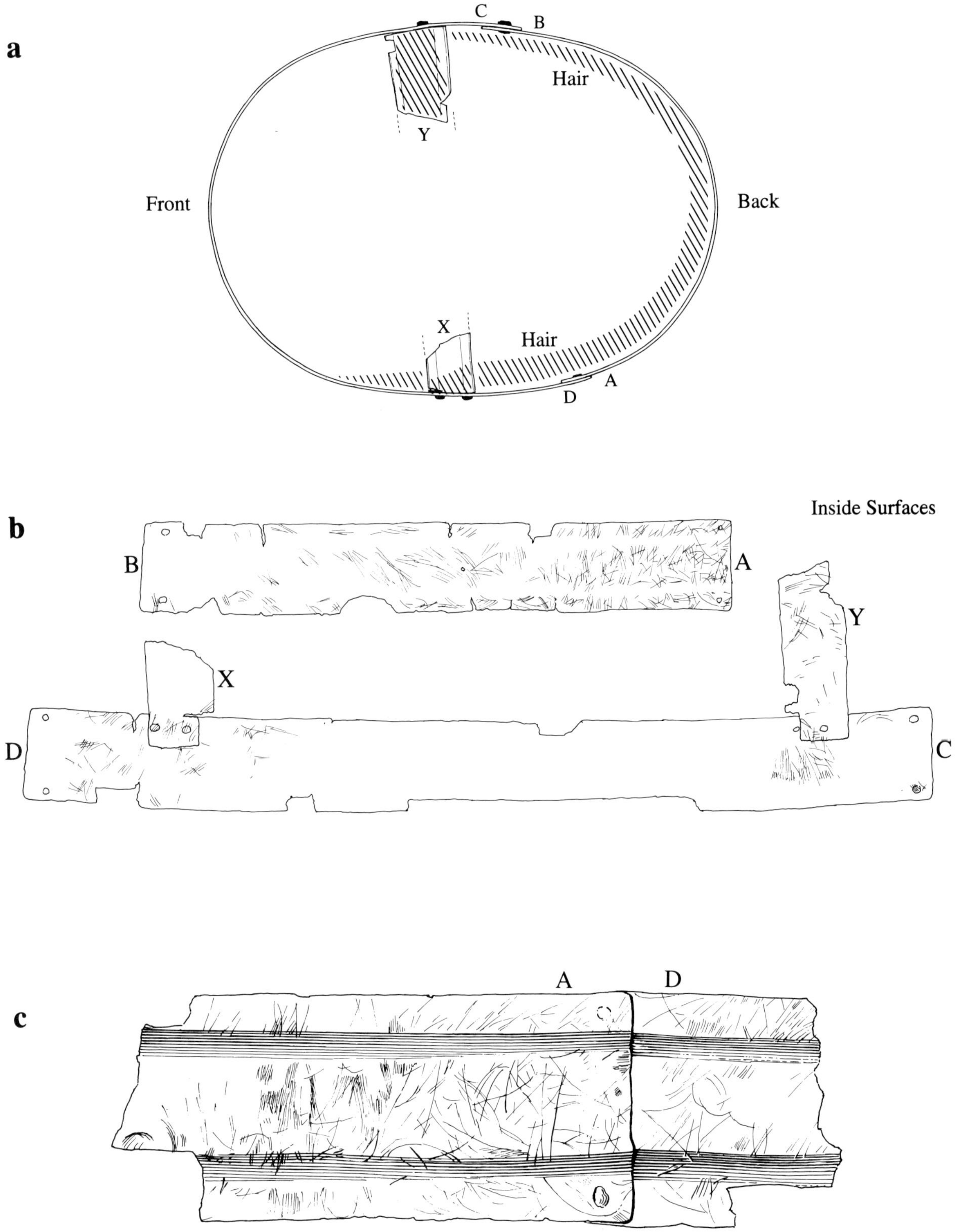

Figure 26. The distribution of mineral-replaced hair on the inner surface of the crown (b), its limits indicated by shading in (a); and a detail of the mineral-replaced hair (c). (Scales, (a) and (b), 2/5; (c), full size)

Caroline Cartwright, Department of Scientific Research, British Museum, and 'identified as human hair. The possibility of the presence of a fur lining (particularly kid) was investigated, but none of the fibres examined could be securely attributed to anything other than human hair'. So it seems that the metal sat directly on the head (pl. IX).

The best surviving parallel for the Deal crown comes not from an Iron Age context but from Roman Britain. Found at Hockwold, Norfolk, in 1957 but not yet fully published, it has a headband with two bronze strips that cross one another at right angles over the head where they are surmounted by a projecting knob (fig. 31, a; Toynbee 1962, 178, no. 128, pl. 139; sometimes known as the Wilton crown – the parish is Hockwold-cum-Wilton). There has been a decorated roundel on the band at the junction with each strip (one of the four roundels has not survived). The Hockwold crown was found in the course of ploughing, along with a simpler crown consisting of a band with an upright feature at the front (usually known as a diadem). In the same field three more diadems had been discovered the previous year. A subsequent excavation located a rammed chalk floor cut by two pits, and in one of the pits was a fifth diadem. The excavators also recovered possible votive deposits, including an unusual collection of brooches and a surprisingly large number of coins with a distinctive pattern of coin-loss, suggesting that the site was related to a temple. It may have been a ritual storehouse. The floor seems to have been constructed *c.* AD200, although associated finds continued to the end of the fourth century (Gurney 1986).

Another complete bronze crown was found with a burial at Leckhampton, Gloucestershire, but its present whereabouts are unknown (fig. 31, b; Demmin 1870, 137, is incorrect in ascribing it to the British Museum). Some scholars have accepted it as an Anglo-Saxon helmet, a view decisively rejected by Bruce-Mitford and Luscombe (1974, 243–5) who compared it with the Hockwold crown. The Leckhampton crown was found in 1844 when labourers digging for gravel discovered a well-preserved skeleton 'doubled up about 3 feet under the surface ... On the skull, fitting as closely as if moulded to it, was the frame of a cap ... When first found, there was a complete chin chain, of this only three links remain, those next the cap very much worn. The skull is tinged at the top with green, from the pressure of the metal, and in other parts blackened, as though the main material of the cap had been felt, and the bars added to stiffen it ... Nothing else whatever was found' (Larking 1845). Subsequently W. H. Gomonde provided further details, including a sketch from which an engraving was published (Anon 1846, 352; a slightly different illustration was published by C. Roach Smith, 1852, 238). Gomonde also recorded the discovery of another skeleton 'near the same spot ... the clay surrounding the skull ... was full of iron studs ... indicating that the head had been protected by a cap of singular construction, having been covered all over with these iron studs' (Anon 1846, 353).

The Leckhampton crown was published and illustrated in more detail a decade later, after it had been sent for exhibition to a meeting of the Archaeological Institute (Way 1855). The ribbed bronze band was perfectly circular, $7^1/_2''$ (190mm) in diameter and $^1/_{24}''$ (1mm) thick and seems to have been constructed in two halves, riveted together at the junction with the ends of one of the strips over the head. Each end of this strip was attached to the band by a single rivet on either side of which two more rivets secured the ends of a suspended bronze loop. The 1855 illustration shows one of the loops complete and the other broken ('worn away by friction', Way 1855, 15); only one loop can be distinguished clearly in the 1846 illustration and two links of a chain are attached to it (Larking 1845 recorded the complete chain; Way 1855, 14, saw and illustrated a single separate ring but no chain links). The second strip, also fixed by one rivet at each end, was broken: one half was intact but only the terminal of the other half survived. At the top the two strips were riveted to a knob terminating in a ring with another linked ring. Way (ibid. 13) recorded that 'one of the plates forming (the band) had become unsoldered, and has been re-united since the discovery'. The two strips did not cross at right angles to one another but were 'placed so that the moiety of the frame, which would probably form the fore-part of the cap, is considerably larger than the hind-part, the effect being to throw the apex with its knob and ring backwards; the knob itself is likewise so shaped as to incline slightly in the same direction' (ibid.).

The skeleton wearing the Leckhampton crown was found at the side of the road from Cheltenham to Bath; 'a Roman camp (= Leckhampton hillfort) rises immediately over the spot where this relic was found, and large traces of Roman interment are found within a hundred yards of it' (Larking 1845). A barrow to the east of the hillfort (the crown was found to the west of the hillfort) is defined by a square banked enclosure and may perhaps have been Iron Age (Stead 1961, 52; but see O'Neil and Grinsell 1960, 121, suggesting that the square might have been eighteenth-century). Certainly inhumation was practised in the area in Iron Age times, for the Birdlip mirror was found with one of a group of inhumations less than 4km to the southwest (Green 1949).

There seems to be no other record of a skeleton wearing a crown of this type (a supposed example from Souldern, Oxfordshire, sometimes mentioned in the

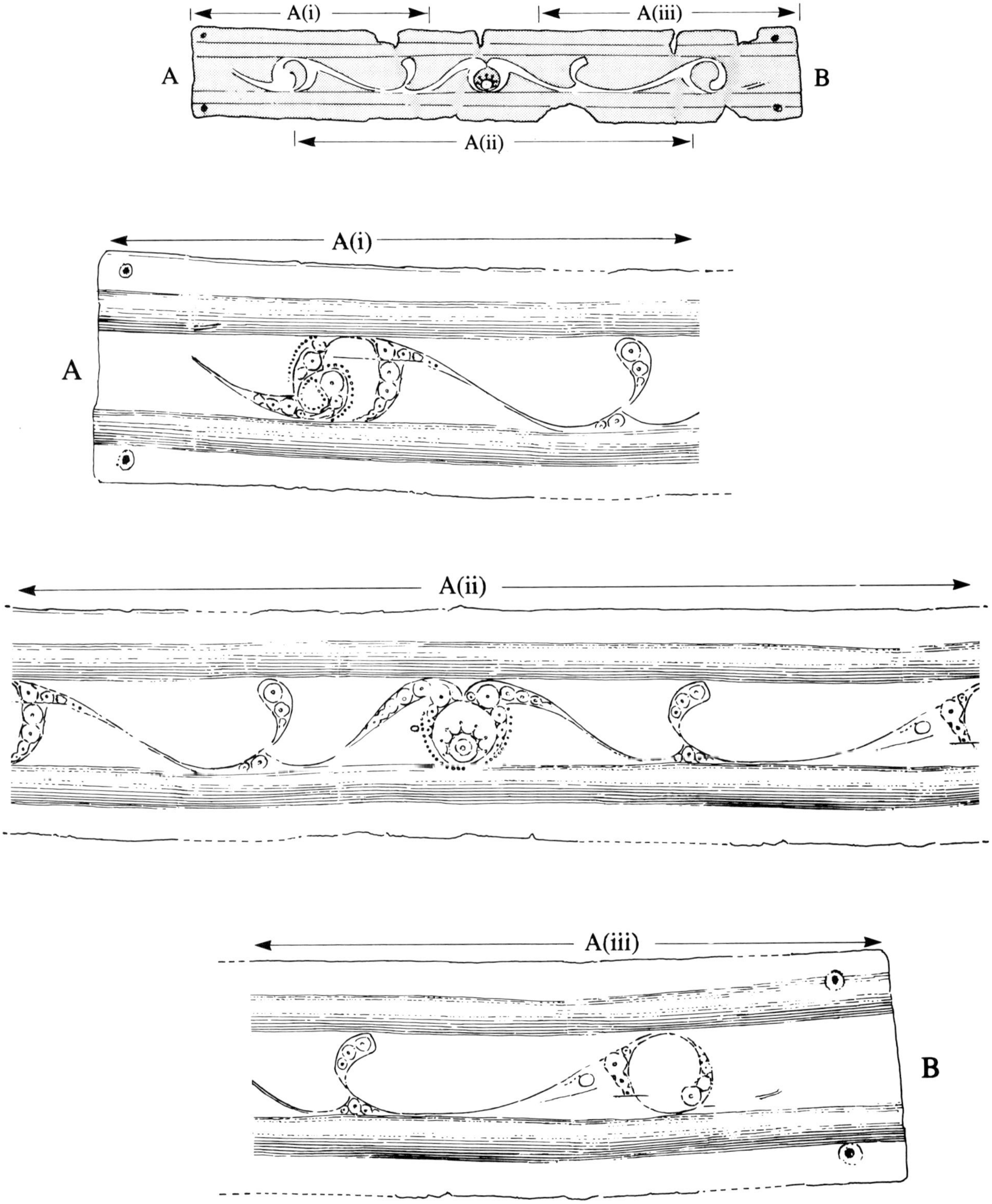

Figure 27. The decoration on the band of the crown. (Full size, apart from the diagram at the top)

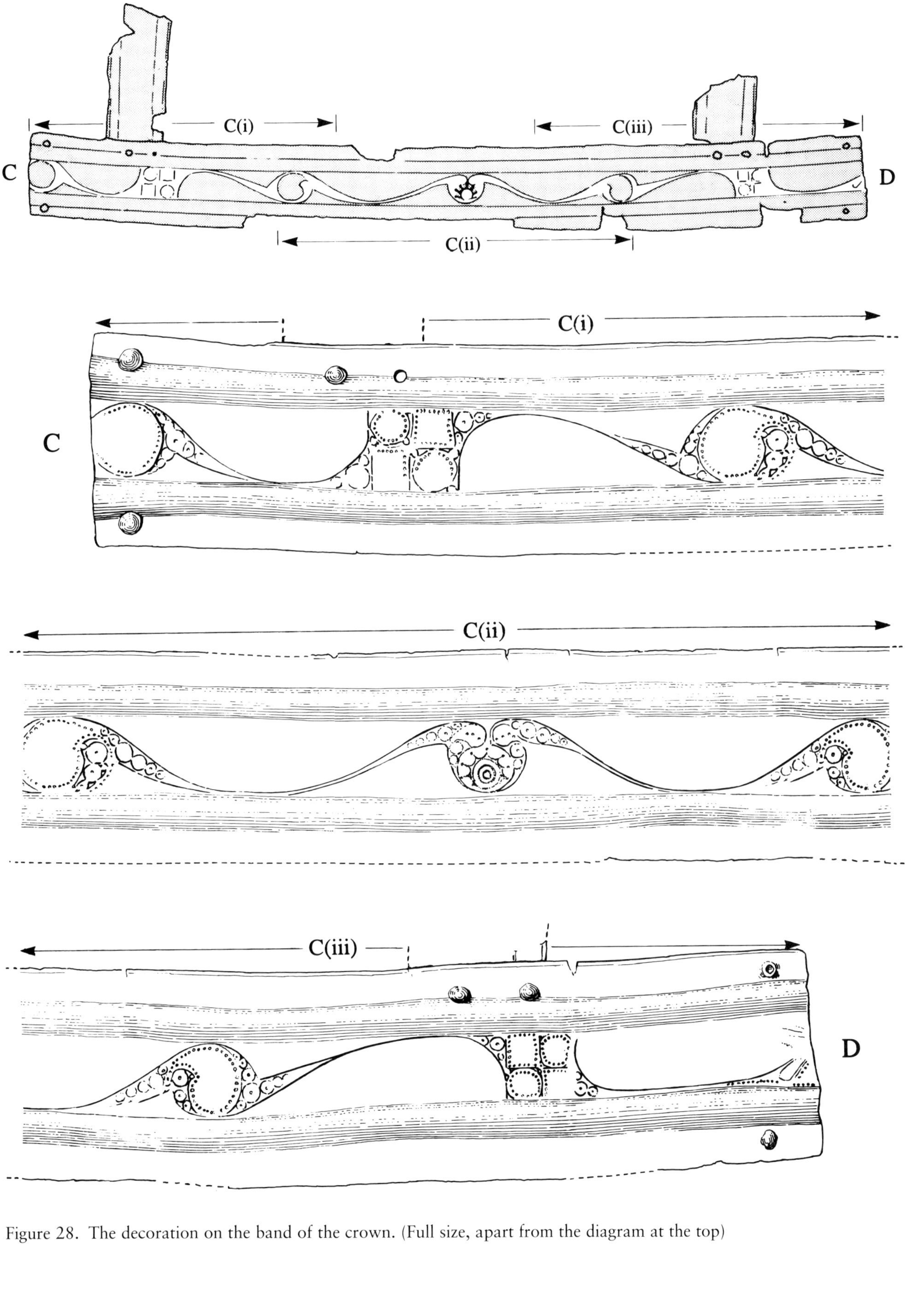

Figure 28. The decoration on the band of the crown. (Full size, apart from the diagram at the top)

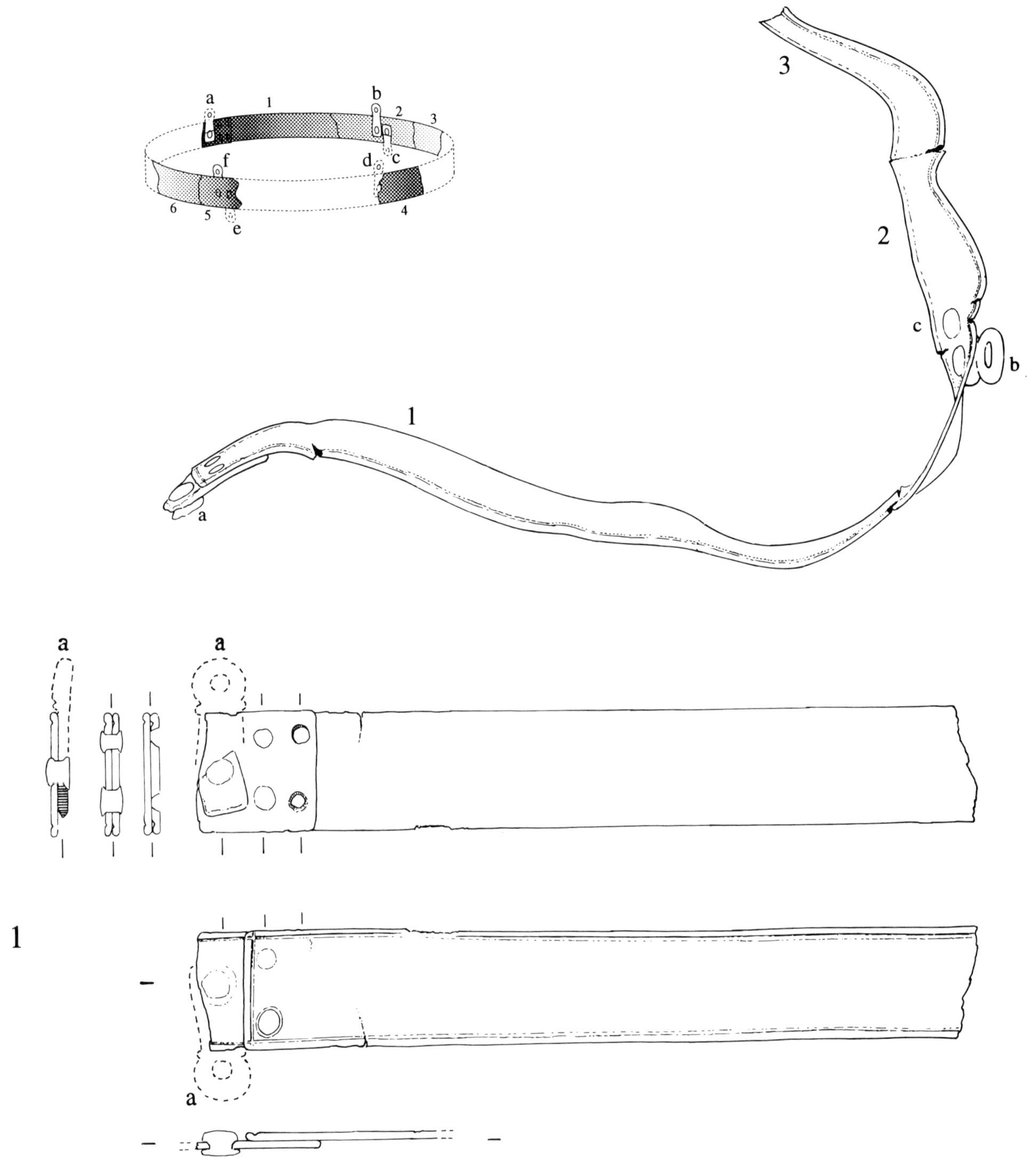

Figure 29. The remains of a crown from Hounslow. (Full size; reconstruction, about 1/4).

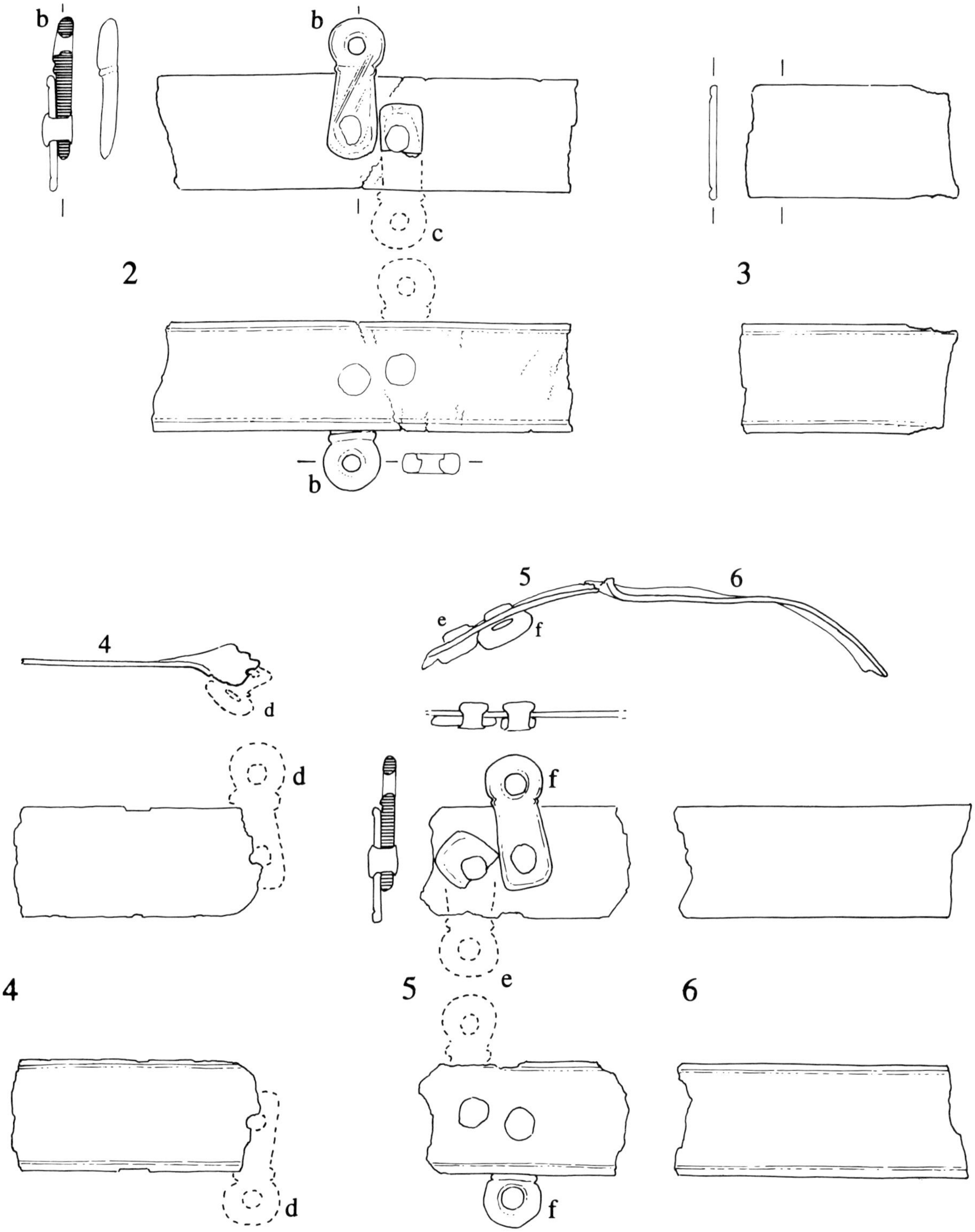

Figure 30. Fragments of the Hounslow crown, see fig. 29. (Full size)

context of the Leckhampton crown was an Anglo-Saxon bucket, Bruce-Mitford and Luscombe 1974, 245–6), and no complete example has survived from any other context. But other such crowns might be represented by fragmentary bands, and two examples from hoards are especially serious contenders. The first was found at Felmingham Hall, Norfolk, in a hoard of mainly ritual artefacts buried some time after AD255 and found in 1844, the same year as the discovery of the Leckhampton crown (Gilbert 1978). There are several lengths of bronze band of three different widths, and some of them terminate in hooks (ibid. 181–3, fig. 9). They might well relate to three triple-looped masks, perhaps the survivors of four that could have been linked by the bands (or leather straps) to form a headband with two cross-strips over the head (ibid. 170–2, fig. 4 A–C, pl. viiia). But there were already two crowns in this hoard, each represented by a four-looped top-piece, one surmounted by a bronze bird (ibid. 172–4, fig. 5A and B).

The second hoard with a possible crown also has religious connotations. Fragments of a band were included in the collection of Bronze Age and Iron Age bronzes found by labourers in a field at Hounslow, London, in 1864 (fig. 29). The discovery was recorded by Franks (1865) who was told that all the antiquities were found together, but on further enquiry it was said that two groups of artefacts (one Bronze Age and the other Iron Age) came from different parts of the field. The British Museum acquired the collection in two lots, with Bronze Age and Iron Age antiquities in both lots; some seventy years later the Register was annotated by C. F. C. Hawkes to distinguish two 'hoards', A and B. The Iron Age 'hoard' B comprises five animal figurines (ibid. figs pp. 90 and 91; registration nos 64 5–1 8–10, 64 5–2 16 and 17) a wheel ornament (Smith 1925, fig. 172, centre; 64 5–1 11) and two lengths of the bronze band (64 5–2 15).

The Hounslow bronze band is fairly substantial (1mm thick), 18–19mm deep, with bordering grooves on the outside; there are now six fragments, with three joins to produce three lengths:

(i) Distorted, but apparently 220mm long (in three pieces, figs. 29 and 30, nos. 1–3). Towards one end (fig. 29, no. 1) is an original join, with a 13mm overlap secured by two rivets (and two unused rivet holes, neatly countersunk, in the underlying end). Near the broken end, just beyond the joint, a bronze tab (a) has been attached to the underside of the middle of the band by a single rivet, and has broken at the side of the rivet. Further along (fig. 30, no. 2) two other tabs (b and c) have been riveted to the middle of the underside of the band, side by side but facing in opposite directions. One is complete, neatly shaped, 22mm long and terminates in a loop (b); the other (c) is broken at the rivet and faces in the opposite direction to the broken tab (a). The rivets for (b) and (c) are 9mm apart between centres, and approximately 154mm and 163mm from the riveted tab (a). All the breaks in this band seem to be deliberate: it had been repeatedly bent in both directions until it snapped.

(ii) (fig. 30, no. 4). Distorted, 40mm long; the edge of a rivet-hole at one end suggests the position of another tab (d).

(iii) Distorted, but about 80mm long (in two pieces, fig. 30, nos 5 and 6). Like fig. 30, no. 2, it has a pair of adjoining riveted tabs on the underside, facing in opposite directions. One (f) is complete, and like the complete tab (b) it is neat, has a looped terminal, and is 21mm long. The other (e) is angled, and broken at the rivet. The two rivets are 8mm apart between centres.

The fragments could be reconstructed to form parts of a complete band with two looped tabs (b and f) and the end of another (a) projecting in one direction, and the ends of two others (c and e) projecting in the opposite direction. The presumed sixth tab (d) could have projected in either direction. This reconstruction is consistent with a crown: loops in tabs a, b, d and f could have connected with chains crossing over the head, whereas c and e could have secured a chin-chain. The distance between the centres of a and b is 154mm, so if the tabs had been evenly spaced the circumference of the crown would have been 616mm (but the strips on the Deal and Leckhampton crowns were not evenly spaced). The band is more likely to have belonged to a crown than a bucket (Spratling 1972, no. 418, suggested that it was from a bucket containing the figurines) in view of the relative thickness of the band, the delicacy of its fittings which are attached only to the band and not to any underlying wood, and indeed the absence of nail holes to fix the band to wood.

The animal figurines from Hounslow, including three boars (Foster 1977, 10–13, 29–30), and a wheel ornament (cf. Green 1979, 352 – there was also a model wheel in the Felmingham Hall hoard, ibid.) suggest that the site had some religious significance in the Iron Age and provide a fascinating context for the bronze band. The Bronze Age 'hoard' A has implements that 'cover a considerable chronological range with Early, Middle and Late Bronze Age types present (Needham 1983, ii, 156; the Bronze Age component was the subject of an unpublished dissertation by Alexandra Tittensor, University College of North Wales, Bangor, 1981). Perhaps Franks, followed by Hawkes, unwittingly simplified the evidence when he distinguished two hoards. The entire find recalls the 'Salisbury' hoard, where Iron Age votive artefacts were allegedly found with antiquities spanning the length of the Bronze Age (Stead 1991b). The suggestion that the Hounslow boars were helmet crests (e.g. Smith 1905, 136; Fox 1958, 76; cf. a scene on the Gundestrup Cauldron) might seem more feasible now that a crown has been identified among the associated bronzes, but the animal figurines presumably shared the same function (though only one has a suspension ring) and there is insufficient bronze band for more than one crown.

Other forms of crowns and related headdresses have been found in Romano-British and perhaps Iron Age contexts, and it is convenient to classify them in types. Type I has now been discussed and includes the Deal, Hockwold and Leckhampton crowns with bronze head-bands and one or two bronze strips over the head.

Type II crowns, with a single band (sometimes adjustable) round the head and an upstanding decorative feature at the front, are usually called diadems (fig. 31, c). In addition to the five examples from Hockwold, there are two from Cavenham Heath, Suffolk, part of another from Lydney, Gloucestershire (Toynbee 1962, 337–9), and fragments of three more from Deeping St James, Lincolnshire (Painter 1971). A rather different bronze diadem was found on the skull of a skeleton near Dover, briefly recorded by a Dr Astley (1867) but now apparently lost. Unlike the others it was round in section, and had at the front terminals in the form of small knobs. It was thicker at the front than at the back, where there was a joint, the two ends tapering and overlapping, with two ?rivet holes in each. That might equally describe a torque, but the account leaves no doubt that the 'circlet' rested on the brow. The grave is undated, but there were Roman finds in the vicinity, including coins and cremation urns; Philp (1981, 11, and fig. 2, B5) identified the site as Elms Vale, in the western suburbs of Dover.

In the Cavenham Heath hoard the Type II crowns were associated with another item of headgear that presumably served a similar purpose (Type III), and was formed of five roundels linked by chains (fig. 31, d; Layard 1925). The roundels are the equivalent of the top-piece and roundels of the Hockwold crown, whilst the chains take the place of the encircling band and the strips over the head. Other Type III chain-linked crowns are known from Stony Stratford, Bucks (fig. 31, e; ibid. pl. xxviii, fig. 2), Wanborough, Surrey (four examples, each with a chin-chain and three of them with a top-piece surmounted by a wheel, Bird 1989), Farley Heath, Surrey (Bird 1987, fig. 7, 17), Ogmore Down, Mid Glamorgan (Francis 1871, pl. xxxvi, figs 3 and 4; see also below) and possibly Lydney Park, Gloucestershire (Wheeler and Wheeler 1932, 91, pl. xxxB). There may have been another, once in the collection of William Walter. It came from the vicinity of the Medway Marshes and is illustrated (a knobbed cap, two broken roundels and three lengths of chain) by Payne (1893, pl. xxii) but the accompanying text pays more attention to praising Walter's hospitality than to describing his collection of antiquities. Most of the Type III top-pieces are perforated for the chains, but Farley Heath has loops like the top-pieces from Felmingham Hall and Ogmore Down. At least one of the Felmingham Hall top-pieces was designed for a leather strap or metal band rather than a chain (Gilbert 1978, 172, fig. 5A), and no chain was found in that hoard. Jope (1960, 82, note 87) has suggested that some bosses from Peterborough were perhaps the fittings of a helmet, but they are neither looped nor perforated for chains and their function and means of attachment is not obvious. The largest of the Peterborough bosses is illustrated by Brailsford (1953, fig. 25, no. 2) but they do not feature in R. A. Smith's Guides (1905, 1925) which suggests that he was not confident about classifying them.

In her publication of the Felmingham Hall hoard, Gilbert (1978, 172–4) compared the top-pieces with an enigmatic artefact from Newnham Croft, Cambridgeshire, that might well have been yet another Type III crown. If so, it is particularly interesting in the present context because it came from an Iron Age grave more or less contemporary with grave 112 at Deal. Discovered in a drainage trench in May 1903, the burial was recorded but not published by Baron von Hügel. The first published reference seems to have been a mention by Greenwell (1906, 268, note a) and the finds were first illustrated in the Annual Report of the Cambridge University Museum of Archaeology and Ethnology, 1909, pl. iii. More details, with photographs, were given by Fox (1923, 81 and pls xv, 5 and xviii, 2x); the best-known drawing of the finds first appeared in Clark 1938, fig. 26; and eventually von Hügel's original note was published by Cra'ster (1973). This prime source refers to a skeleton in 'very bad state of preservation' orientated NNE/SSW 'in a somewhat contracted attitude, but owing to decay rather difficult to locate': an accompanying sketch shows the skeleton crouched or flexed, on its left side, with the hands in front of the skull. Greenwell (1906, 268, note a) had stated that it was the skeleton of a woman; Fox (1923, 81) recorded Duckworth's opinion that the skull was 'that of a middle-aged individual'; Clarke (1926, 176) followed Fox but changed 'individual' to 'man', as did Clark (1938, 293) and subsequent writers. But the only authoritative view is Duckworth's 'individual'.

A bow brooch and two penannular brooches were found on the chest of the Newnham Croft skeleton; a bracelet 'on the right lower arm (above wrist)'; a bronze '(?) lamp' near the feet; and three small bronze rings had been taken off the skeleton before von Hügel saw it (Cra'ster 1973). Fox (1923, 81) varied the position of von Hügel's (?)lamp to 'under the vertebral column of the skeleton', and identified it as 'almost certainly a harness mounting'. As he also compared the bow brooch with

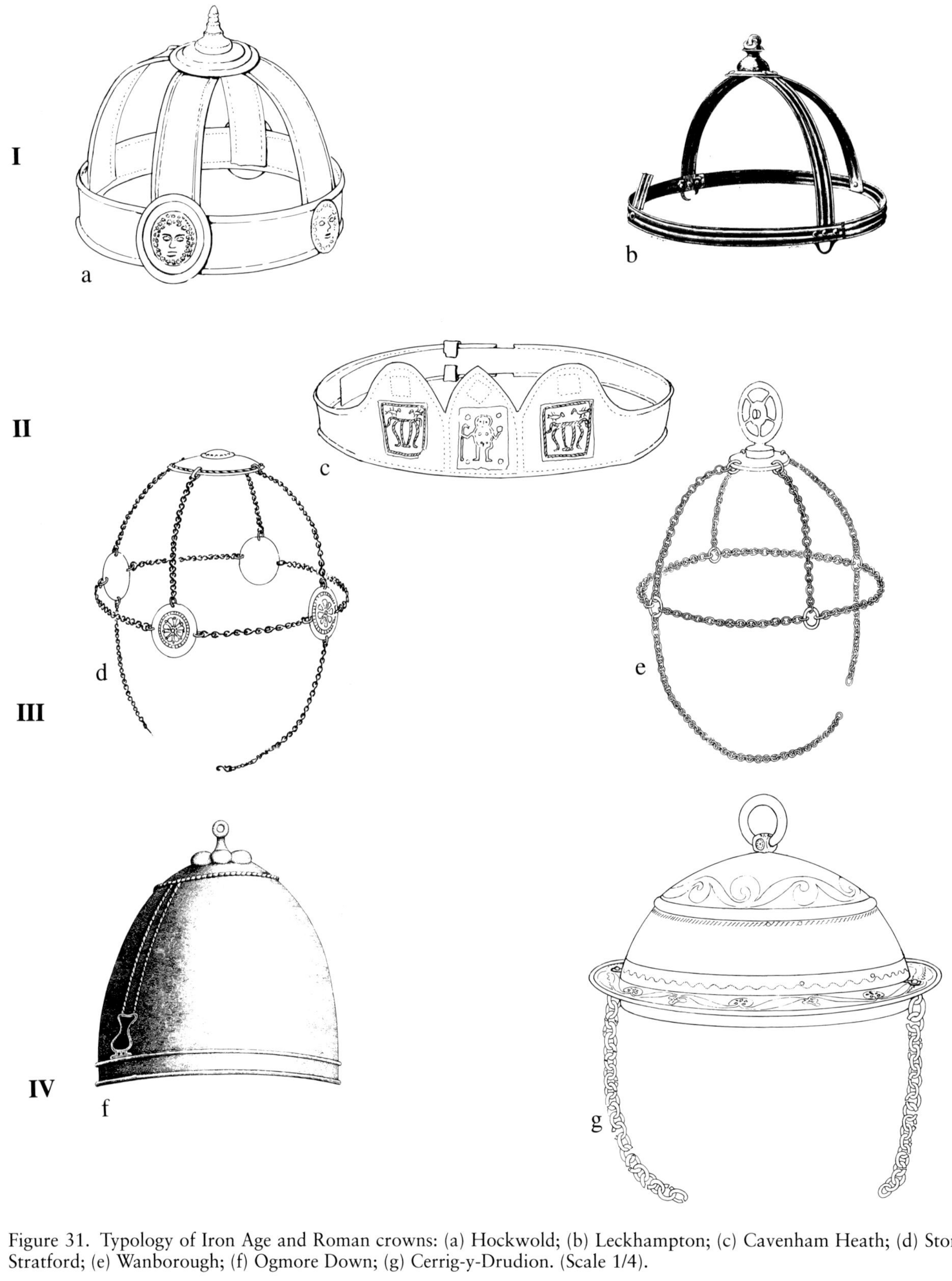

Figure 31. Typology of Iron Age and Roman crowns: (a) Hockwold; (b) Leckhampton; (c) Cavenham Heath; (d) Stony Stratford; (e) Wanborough; (f) Ogmore Down; (g) Cerrig-y-Drudion. (Scale 1/4).

'several found in the chariot burials at Arras', Newnham Croft was allowed to enter the literature as a possible chariot-burial (e.g. Clarke 1926, 177). Stead (1965, 9) rejected it as a chariot-burial because no iron tyres had been found, and there was no parallel for the 'harness mounting', but the myth has survived (cf. 'a possible chariot burial', Megaw and Megaw 1989, 192). The so-called 'harness mounting' is a cast bronze roundel with a knob in the centre, and its flange is perforated for the attachment of four chains (all but one of the original perforations have been renewed, one of them twice renewed). Gilbert's suggestion that it was the top of a chain-linked headdress like that from Cavenham Heath is far more convincing than any attempt to match it as a harness mounting. It might be argued that its position in the grave does not support this identification: whether it was at the feet or under the vertebral column is open to doubt, but it was certainly not on the skull (nor was it found on a horse). However several undoubted helmets in continental La Tène I graves were found at or near the feet of the skeleton (e.g. Berru, Châlons-sur-Marne and Somme-Tourbe, Marne, and Dürrnberg bei Hallein, Austria: Schaaf 1973, pls 12–15).

One further type of related headgear (Type IV), with the entire cap fashioned from bronze, includes the two lost 'helmets' from Ogmore Down, found with skeletons and a looped top-piece from a Type III crown in the parish of St Bride's Major (Mid Glamorgan) in 1818 (fig. 31, f; RCAHMW 1976, 6). They were despatched to London for exhibition to the Society of Antiquaries, but seem to have fallen off the back of the waggon – 'the package containing them was unfortunately lost on the road and the helmets have never since re-appeared' (Francis 1871, 553). However they had been drawn before they left Wales, and the drawings did eventually reach London for exhibition to the Society in 1865. Since then they, too, have gone astray but not before engravings based on them were published, along with notes made by W. W. Young and Charles Redwood who were on the scene very soon after the discovery and organised excavations on Ogmore Down (ibid.). The contemporary account was written by Charles Redwood, who recorded that on 29 September 1818 labourers digging for limestone 'discovered a couple of antique helmets, together with many human bones and pieces of iron ... neither of the helmets was preserved whole, but some ornamental parts ... remained in excellent preservation'. The surviving ornaments were (1) a silver top-piece [cf. that on the helmet, ibid, pl. xxxvi, fig. 2] 'about the size of a common tea saucer, or perhaps a little larger'; and (2) a piece 'supposed to have come from the side of the helmet [cf. the side-pieces shown in ibid. pl. xxxvi, figs 1 and 2] ... composed of gold with a considerable quantity of alloy in it ... inlaid with a composition of wax and vermillion. It was fastened to the helmet by a sort of hinge at the lower end, by which it could be turned up or down. There were wires attached to the two holes at the upper end, composed of silver and copper twisted together, and these appeared to have been attached to the silver top-piece. There was only one of the side-pieces found, but no doubt there was originally one on each side' (ibid. 554–5, quoting Redwood's manuscript dated 1818). A few weeks later, at the same place, Redwood found the 'copper helmet' (= looped top-piece, cf. ibid. pl. xxxvi, fig. 3) and 'many heads of spears ... interred upon a bed of small coal'.

Apart from the looped top-piece, this first account of the Ogmore Down find mentions two complete helmets of which only two fragments (one top-piece and one side-piece) survived intact. On 11 May 1865 Major Francis exhibited to the Society of Antiquiaries 'a series of sketches, made at the time of the find, 1818': they are described by the editor of Archaeologia, and were engraved to illustrate the note (ibid. pl. xxxvi). There were three drawings: A, showing a 'dagger' (= spearhead), helmet and 'skull cap' (= looped top-piece); B, helmet with skull in position (skull omitted from the engraving) and 'skull cap'; C, full size drawing of helmet. The editor pointed out that the two drawings of 'skull caps' were different, so both were engraved, although only one such object was recorded in the note; he assumed that the helmets in A and B were the two helmets recorded, and that the helmet in B was the same as that in C. Alternatively, it seems possible that the helmets depicted in A, B and C are different versions of the same object - this interpretation would be quite consistent with the two different drawings of the one recorded 'skull cap'. It is also consistent with the second memorandum quoted by Francis, written by Young in 1836: referring to the illustrations, Young lists no.1, a dagger (= spearhead); no. 2, a helmet; and no. 3 a 'skull cap'. Young (in Francis, ibid.) confirms that the two helmets were broken by the workmen, but (writing eighteen years after their discovery and loss) he adds that 'the parts were afterwards put together ... The body of these helmets was of very good brass, very little oxydated, about one line in thickness; the ornament on the top was silver, and weighed about an ounce; the small bands were gold and silver wire twisted; the side or ear-piece moved on a hinge; it was of brass, and the hollow that was in it filled with a composition of wax and vermillion; the lower rim had two bands of brass, with a blue enamel between, laid on the brass'. Subsequent finds included 'several pieces of iron much decayed, some bones, and one or two pieces of small brass chain, about the size of jack-chain'. Later still, the 'skull-cap' was found by Redwood. 'I believe Mr Redwood has the skull-cap and some chain, but I know nothing of the other things' (ibid.).

From these accounts it would seem that one bronze looped top-piece was found: one drawing (pl. xxxvi, fig. 4) shows a single small loop on the lower edge and the other (fig. 3) has three larger loops on the lower edge and a ring on top. It is conceivable that both drawings show the same object from different angles, with the ring on fig. 3 intended to represent the fourth loop on the lower edge. Redwood compared the looped top-piece with the silver ornament on top of the helmets (which do have rings on top) and Young described it as 'very much oxydated, but near a quarter of an inch thick'. The top-piece of one of the Type III crowns from Felmingham Hall has very similar loops (Gilbert 1978, fig. 5B); no other Type III crown seems to have had a ring on top, but those from Wanborough are each surmounted by a wheel. It seems likely that Redwood's chain belonged to the same headdress.

Two solid metal crowns were found, and 'the skulls were in them!' (Young, quoted by Francis 1871, 554). The reliability of the published engravings may be questioned, because the crowns were broken and restored and it may be that the published drawings show alternative restorations of one helmet. It had a top-piece, said to have been silver, surmounted by a ring; a band round the bottom, defined by two cordons, and inlaid in blue enamel (according to Young); and a pair (Redwood records only one) of hinged side-pieces with red enamel inlay ('a composition of wax and vermillion'). The top-piece recalls cast knobs on other crowns, and that from Leckhampton also has a ring on top. The band round the bottom also features on Type I crowns, though never made in one with a solid bronze cap. The hinged side-pieces are more curious, and as illustrated it is difficult to see how they functioned. They are shown hinged above the upper cordon and fixed by wires to the top of the crown; Wheeler (1925, 206) suggested that the wires held the 'cheek-guards' when not in use, but that would leave extremely short 'cheek-guards' with the enamel facing inwards. It would seem more reasonable to have the side-pieces suspended below the lower cordon, with the wires corresponding to the chin-chains on Type III crowns. But it is impossible now to judge the limitations of the evidence on which the reconstructions were based.

Francis and his contemporaries dated the Ogmore Down find to the later Roman period, though previously it had been regarded as Anglo-Saxon (Francis 1871, 553); Wheeler (1925, 205–8) suggested that it was Late Celtic but no earlier than the first century AD because of the blue enamel; Ashbee (1960, 103–4, 143 and fig. 52) identified it as Bronze Age; Hogg (1965, 128) included it in the later phases of the Iron Age; Ritchie (1968, 131–5) in a detailed discussion, argued for an Iron Age or early Roman date; and Savory (1984, 271–2) put it not long before the Roman conquest. The blue enamel mentioned by Young in his 1836 note is one clue to chronology, but its presence in such a deep and very long band is without parallel so the reliability of his account may be questioned (RCAHMW 1976, 6, wondered if the blue colour might have been vivianite or some product of corrosion); the red enamel ('wax and vermillion') seems more reasonable. But a second clue is provided by the associated top-piece whose loops recall the top-pieces in the Felmingham Hall hoard.

If, as seems likely, the Ogmore Down helmets belonged to the tradition of Iron Age and Romano-British crowns, then another Welsh find must be considered in the same context. The Cerrig-y-Drudion 'hanging bowl' was discovered in a stone cist in 1924; presumably it was with a burial, but there was no trace of human bones. Its identification as a hanging bowl (Smith 1926) has now been demolished, but no satisfactory alternative has been substituted (Stead 1982). It seems that the object was some kind of lid, decorated over the top and on the top of the projecting flange, with a chain suspended from the flange on each side. The cist produced no other vessel for this 'lid' to have covered, and the idea that it might have been a helmet was too readily dismissed (ibid. 231; fig. 31, g). It resembles the Ogmore Down helmets in that it is completely fashioned from sheet bronze. The long chain suspended from two points on the flange recalls the chin-chains on crowns at Leckhampton (also with excessive wear on the suspension loops), Stony Stratford and Wanborough. The frieze of Celtic art can now be compared with the decorated band on the Deal crown (though in the opposite plane), and both Deal and Newnham Croft take the tradition of 'priestly crowns' to within a century of the deposit at Cerrig-y-Drudion. The search for a context for the Deal crown seems to have provided an explanation for Cerrig-y-Drudion far more satisfactory than either a hanging bowl or a lid. The main objection to accepting it as a crown is its rather large size. Its remains are too distorted to allow an accurate diameter to be measured, but a 'best-fit' reconstruction of the design suggested an internal diameter of 650mm (ibid. 228) which is greater than any of the crowns listed in Table 8. But in detail the design is far from symmetrical (ibid. 230) so the crown could have been smaller.

Before leaving Type IV crowns, the two surviving Iron Age helmets from Britain should also be considered. One, unprovenanced and formerly in the Meyrick Collection, can be dismissed because it is a native version of a Roman military helmet (Brailsford 1975, 40–8; MacGregor 1976, 89-90, no. 189). But the other, found in the River Thames near Waterloo Bridge some time before 1866, is unique (Fox 1958, 49-51; Brailsford 1975, 32–9). Made from sheet bronze, decorated in repoussé, it is the only horned helmet to survive from the Celtic world, though others are known from representations. The overall domed shape of its cap, and the loops for a chin-strap (or chin-chain) are reminiscent of an Early La Tène iron helmet from Böckweiler, Saarland (Schaaf 1974, 194–5). When found the Thames helmet was apparently identified as a jester's cap, but Franks (1866, 343) recognised it as a Late Celtic military helmet. It seems that its purpose was not questioned during the next century, until Ritchie (1968, 140, 146) argued that its unparalleled shape, thin bronze and presumed votive deposition in the Thames might suggest that it was intended not for the battlefield, but for the parade ground or even for a temple where it might have adorned a deity. He was followed by Megaw (1970, 170) as far as the parade ground and by Brailsford (1975, 39) almost into the temple - 'it was surely intended as a ritual article'. Ritchie (1968, 144–6) also introduced the Cork Horns and the Petrie Crown into the discussion (cf. also O'Kelly 1961; Raftery 1983, 259–61 and 1984, 268–75), and it may well be that these Irish pieces served the same purpose as the Thames helmet.

Measurements of several prehistoric and Roman helmets and crowns are recorded in Table 8, and the opportunity has been taken to measure them with a standard English hat gauge (kindly lent by Messrs James Lock & Co.). For comparison, according to Messrs Lock the average hat size of a modern English male is 7 1/4. The two crowns (nos. 2 and 9) and the Thames helmet (no. 3) are significantly smaller than the rest, and the Roman helmets are the largest in the sample. It is likely that the larger Roman helmets were padded (Robinson 1975, 144) but the small size of the crowns, consistent with the mineralised remains of hair on the inside of the Deal crown, suggests that they were worn without a lining (fig. 26 and pl. ix).

Another potential source of information is the representation of crowns on British coins, but there are few headdresses other than wreathed heads copied from Greek or Roman prototypes (information from Andrew Burnett). However, it does seem reasonable to compare the Deal crown with the decorated head band depicted on rare Icenian silver coins of 'Bury' type (May 1991, 266), and there is an obvious representation of a crown with a wheel-crest on a unique silver coin from Petersfield, Hants (Boon 1982, interpreting the crown as a band round the head and a single strap over the head, but from front to back, unlike Deal).

Various headdresses have now been discussed, mainly from burials, temples and hoards, ranging in date from perhaps the fourth century BC to the fourth century AD. Of the four types distinguished, I and II are associated at Hockwold, II and III at Cavenham Heath, III and IV at Ogmore Down; and there are looped top-pieces from Farley Heath and Ogmore Down (Type III) as well as Felmingham Hall (Type I). These links allow the possibility that the four types served the same function

TABLE 8: MEASUREMENTS OF SOME IRON AGE AND ROMANO-BRITISH HELMETS AND CROWNS IN THE BRITISH MUSEUM COLLECTIONS

		Internal measurements at the rim (mm)				
		LENGTH	WIDTH	CIRCUMFERENCE	HAT SIZE	REFERENCES
1.	ex Watney Collection P1982 10–2 1	210	172	603	7 5/8	Unpublished; for the type see Schaaf 1981, 221, no. 6
2.	Deal	210	163	595	7 1/2	pp. 72–5
3.	River Thames P 1988 10–4 1	195	175	585	7 3/8	Brailsford 1975, 32–9
4.	ex Meyrick Collection 72 12–13 2	208	165	605	7 5/8	Brailsford 1975, 40–43
5.	Coolus, Marne ML 1734	210	172	618	7 3/4	Robinson, 1975, 26, pl. 37, fig. 35
6.	Berkhamsted 13 3–13 1	212	193	640	8 1/8	Robinson 1975, 27, pl. 55, fig. 41
7.	London 1950 7–6 1	210	182	628	7 7/8	Robinson 1975, 33, pl. 54, fig. 42
8.	Guisborough 78 9–10 1	216	160	640	8 1/8	Robinson 1975, 109, pls 391–3
9.	Hockwold 1957 2–7 15	208	163	585	7 3/8	Toynbee 1962, 178, no. 128

(Table 9). Types I and III seem to have been used during much of the Iron Age and throughout the Roman period, whereas type IV may be exclusively Iron Age and Type II only Roman. The earlier crowns have been found with burials, whereas the later examples are from temples or hoards. The later finds are generally accepted as priestly regalia, so perhaps that is the explanation for the earlier finds, too. But deposition in a grave suggests a personal possession, for if a crown were a symbol of religious office it would be needed for the next incumbent. Perhaps the significance of crowns changed over the years. At Deal and Ogmore Down the burials were also accompanied by weapons, so the crowns might be interpreted as military helmets. But the thin bronze strips of the Deal crown would have given no protection to the head, and there were no weapons with the burials at Cerrig-y-Drudion, Leckhampton and Newnham Croft. It seems that crowns were symbols of status worn by military or religious leaders in the Iron Age, whilst in Roman times their significance became wholly religious.

TABLE 9: TYPOLOGY, CHRONOLOGY AND CONTEXTS OF IRON AGE AND ROMANO-BRITISH CROWNS

SITE	CROWN TYPE				APPROXIMATE DATE (centuries)	PROVENANCE
Cerrig-y-Drudion				IV	4 BC	Cist
Newnham Croft			III		2 BC	Inhumation
Deal	I				2 BC	Inhumation
Hounslow	I				? 1 BC	Hoard
Thames Helmet				IV	? 1 BC	River
Cork Horns				IV	? AD 1	River
Petrie Crown				IV	? AD 1	?
Leckhampton	I				?	Inhumation
Ogmore Down			III	IV	?	Inhumation
Medway Marshes			III		?	?
Deeping St James		II			AD 2/3	Hoard
Stony Stratford			III		AD 2/3	Hoard
Cavenham Heath		II	III		AD 2/4	Hoard
Wanborough			III		AD 2/4	Temple
Farley Heath			III		AD 2/4	Temple
Felmingham Hall	I				AD 3/4	Hoard
Hockwold	I	II			AD 4	Temple store
Lydney		II	? III		AD 4	Temple

4. Brooch (fig. 32, 4; pl. X, right)

A cast bronze brooch, L 51mm, elongated in the form of a central oval shape with trefoil appendages at the head and foot. The construction of the hinged pin is unusual: instead of a pin between two projecting tabs, there is only one tab and the end of the pin is divided to accommodate it, hinged on a short rod or rivet with large neatly rounded ends. The pin is down-curved and its tip broken. Under the foot is a short solid catch-plate. The centre of the brooch is ornamented with a large rounded knob of coral (11mm in diameter) attached by a bronze rivet; there are three similar but smaller coral settings supported on the trefoil head and three others, smaller still (6mm) on the foot (one lost). Under one of the knobs (top left, as drawn) is some original black adhesive that has been identified as a resin; Vincent Daniels (Conservation Research Section, British Museum) reports: 'The sample was a resin, i.e. a terpenoid such as might be derived from the exudate from a tree, e.g. pine resin, etc.'

The cast decoration around the central coral knob is quite simple: at the head is a device of two attached triangular shapes each with a tendril springing from opposed corners, the one terminating in a keeled tendril, the other more rounded. There are two dots in the fields defined by the tendrils and two beyond. At the foot is an elongated hourglass shape with a lip-motif in higher relief at the top: on either side of the lip-motif, on the bow, is a raised dot.

This hinged plate brooch would be assigned to type 2B in the Hull/Hawkes typology: 'decorative forms, peculiar to Britain' (Hull and Hawkes 1987, 143). In particular, the large circular feature in the centre of the bow combined with a triangular arrangement of decoration on the foot invites comparison with brooches from Newnham Croft (ibid. 147–8, no. 4283), Red Hill (ibid. 152-3, no. 6912) and Beckford (unpublished, inf. D F Mackreth). It also shares features with brooches of Hattatt's Upavon type – especially one from Bledlow, Bucks (Hattatt 1989, 7, fig. 2, no. 721). In a European context the circular device on the bow is extremely rare, but it does occur on two more conventional brooches from Kent – a La Tène I form from Deal (p. 95) and a La Tène III brooch from Lenham (Kelly 1988, 298–300).

Chronologically the most useful comparison for the brooch from Grave 112 is probably that from Newnham Croft, whose equally unusual design must have been inspired in part by a La Tène II form with foot attached to the bow by a collar. Indeed the foot of the Newnham Croft brooch has been cast in one with the bow, a feature of La Tène III brooches, but these elaborately decorated British brooches are so far removed from the continental tradition that this detail need not be so significant (cf. the Queen's Barrow brooch, from Arras, and a comparable piece from the Harborough Cave, Hull and Hawkes 1987, 144–6, nos. 3693 and 2248). But the skeuomorphic collar is surely significant, so that the Newnham Croft brooch cannot date earlier than La Tène II. Another clue to chronology is provided by the Wetwang Slack cemetery, where coral-decorated plate-brooches belong to the earlier part of the cemetery, preceding the development of involuted brooches (Dent 1982, 441–4). A date early in the second century BC seems to be indicated.

The brooch was found in a curious position in the grave, by the lower part of the left leg. Most brooches in

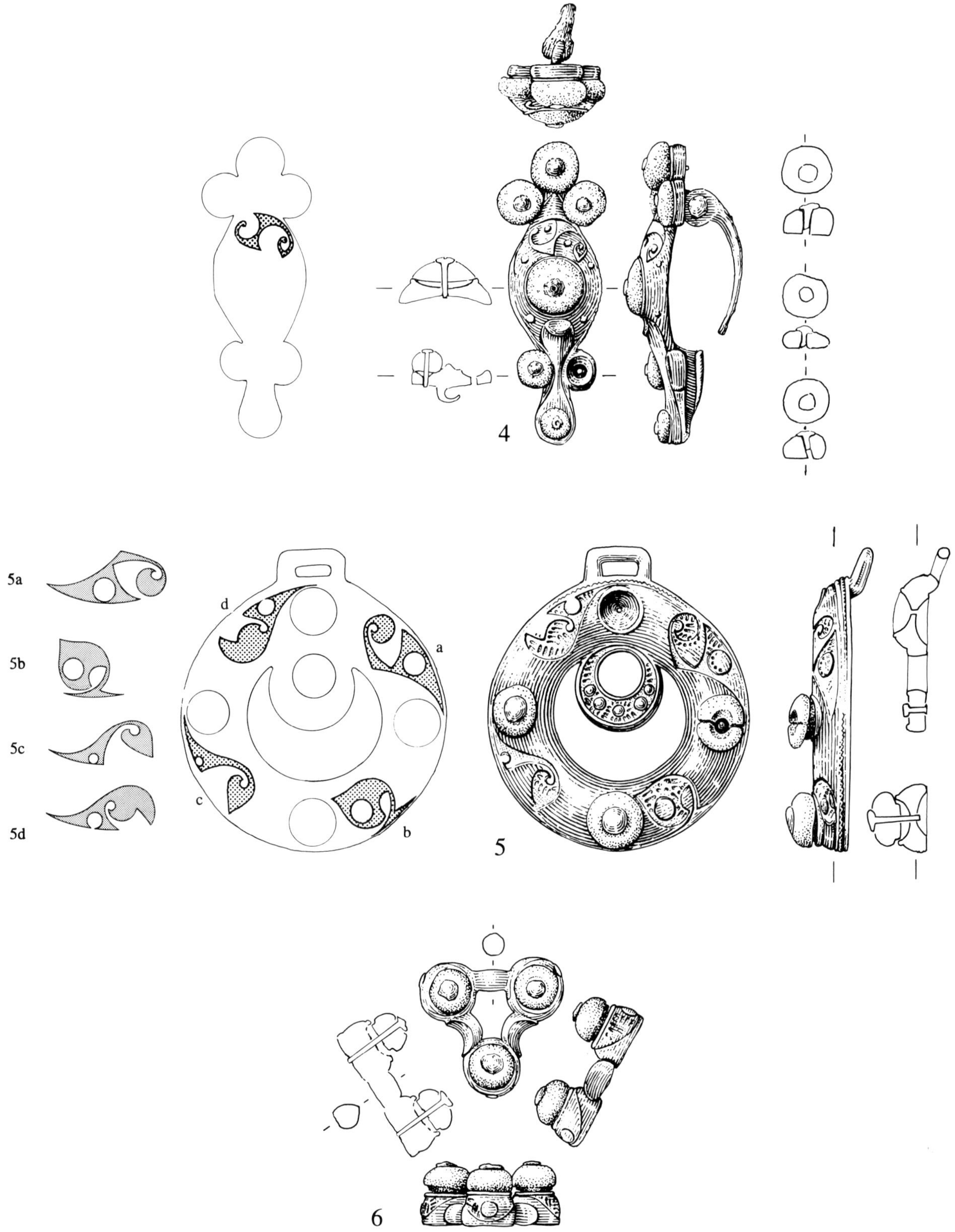

Figure 32. Bronze artefacts from Grave 112: 4. brooch; 5. suspension ring; 6. strap-link. (Full size)

Iron Age graves occur near the head or shoulders, where they are assumed to have fastened a cloak (Stead 1991a, 90; but in two of the Yorkshire graves, R140 and BF4, brooches were found over the leg bones). Perhaps it had been in a cloak placed over the corpse, in the same way as at Kirkburn a mail tunic was found on top of the skeleton, its shoulder-flaps covering the leg bones (ibid. 54–6, fig. 127).

5. *Suspension-ring* (fig. 32, 5; pl. X, left)

A decorated bronze ring, diam. 45–6mm, with a rectangular loop (6.5mm across on the inside) for suspension; L 52mm, including loop. The ring is half-round in section and decorated in low relief; it is a lost-wax casting and the decoration would have been executed in the wax (for the designs see p. 90). There are four circular settings for round knobs of coral; each knob is perforated and attached by a rivet with a large head (only two intact, another has lost the head of the rivet, and the fourth lacks the coral and the rivet). The back is slightly concave. Within the ring, on one side, a much smaller ring with offset circular hole bordered by a hatched crescent with five raised dots. Radiographs suggest that these raised dots are the heads of separate rods inserted in perforations in the ring. This distinctive motif has already been noted on the scabbard and shield, which suggests that the suspension ring was made to match.

The suspension ring was found face down near the suspension loop of the scabbard (which was also face down), so it may have belonged to an attached belt, although the ring's loop is very narrow. In Britain little is known about the suspension of the scabbard. Four burials have produced pairs of rings or roundels immediately adjoining the suspension loops of scabbards: Wetwang Slack (East Yorkshire) Cart-burials 1 (two coral-ornamented bronze discs) and 3 (two coral-ornamented rings) – Dent 1985, 88, fig. 2; 91, fig. 4; Owslebury (Hants), Burial 39 (two bronze rings near the iron suspension loop of a leather bound wooden scabbard) – Collis 1973, 126, fig. 3, no. 3 and fig. 4, nos 3 and 4; and Whitcombe (Dorset) Burial 9 (two iron rings adjoining the top of the sword; only slight traces of the wooden scabbard and no suspension loop) – Aitken and Aitken 1990, 73, fig. 10, nos 3 and 4 (cf. fig. 9 and pl. 10). The Wetwang Slack examples were found with scabbards whose suspension loops were towards the middle, whereas at Owslebury and Whitcombe they had been at the top. But the Deal suspension ring was a single piece, not one of a pair, so perhaps it is more comparable with the 'baldric rings' from Owslebury and Whitcombe (Collis 1973, 126–7, fig. 3, no. 4 and fig. 4, no. 5; Aitken and Aitken 1990, 73, fig. 10, no. 5).

6. *Strap-end* (fig. 32, 6; pl. X, centre)

A cast bronze open triangular shape, L 23mm, flat on the back, formed by three linked circular settings, each ornamented with a knob of coral. One of the links is a rounded bar, presumably to take the end of a narrow strap (no more than 6mm wide), and the other two are curved and unworn. Each of the settings is decorated on the outside with cross-hatching and a raised central dot within a lunate frame (the decoration executed in wax for the casting). One of the coral knobs is loose, so its fixing can be examined: the circular setting has a black filling (? resin, cf. p. 86) which is penetrated by the rivet (its end is visible in the base of the setting) that secures the coral knob.

The strap-end was found by the left forearm near remains from the shield and, perhaps more significantly, not far from the waist. It could have belonged to the same narrow strap that attached the suspension loop, though the two metal fittings were some distance apart. Perhaps this strap-end should be regarded as a variety of the button-and-loop fastener (Wild 1970; Stead 1991a, 56).

Another Kentish find is worth noting here: an open parallelogram shape with four linked circular settings each with a knob of (presumed) coral (Brent 1864, 176–7, pl. vi, fig. 9; in Maidstone Museum). It was found in Grave 126 in the Anglo-Saxon cemetery at Sarre, but it is not an Anglo-Saxon artefact (White 1988, 143 and 221, suggests that it is Iron Age and the Deal grave provides better parallels than those he quotes).

7. *The decoration on the artefacts in Grave 112*

Grave 112 has one of the largest and most important collections of metal artefacts from any Iron Age burial in Britain. It is only the second grave-group with a brooch and a sword associated – and the other, a much later grave at Whitcombe, Dorset (Aitken and Aitken 1990) had scant remains of the scabbard. But even more significant is the association of so many decorated artefacts: the crown, shield, scabbard, brooch and suspension ring are all ornamented with examples of Celtic art and no other British burial can compare with that. The range of decorative techniques is equally impressive: casting (brooch, suspension ring, strap-end and chape), repoussé (scabbard), 'engraving' (crown), and positive and negative openwork designs cut from sheet (shield), as well as the application of knobs of coral (brooch, suspension ring, strap-end and shield). The range of designs is extensive: the decoration of the brooch and suspension ring is related, but different from that at the mouth of the scabbard which instead is linked to the design on the crown and perhaps the motif on the chape; the openwork ornament on the shield-boss is different again. Such variety might suggest that pieces had been accumulated over the years, but at least one element – the ring with

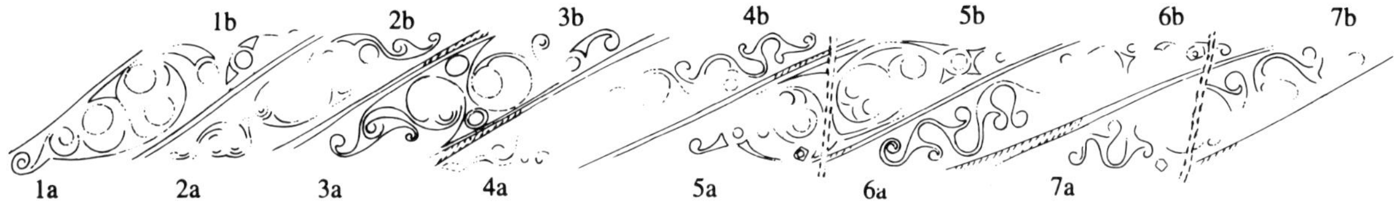

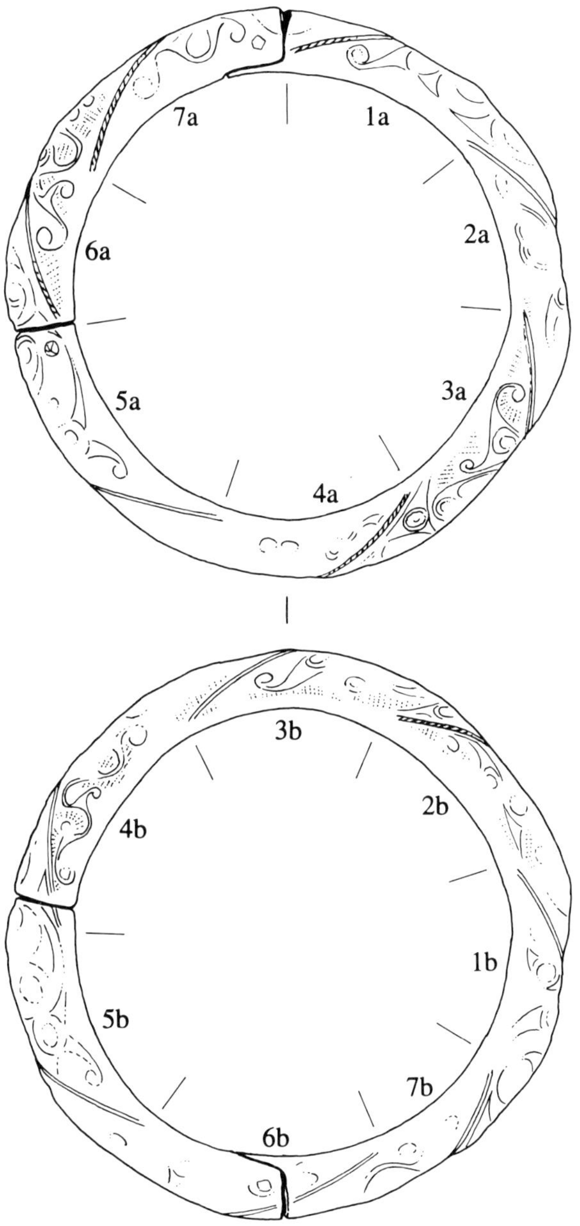

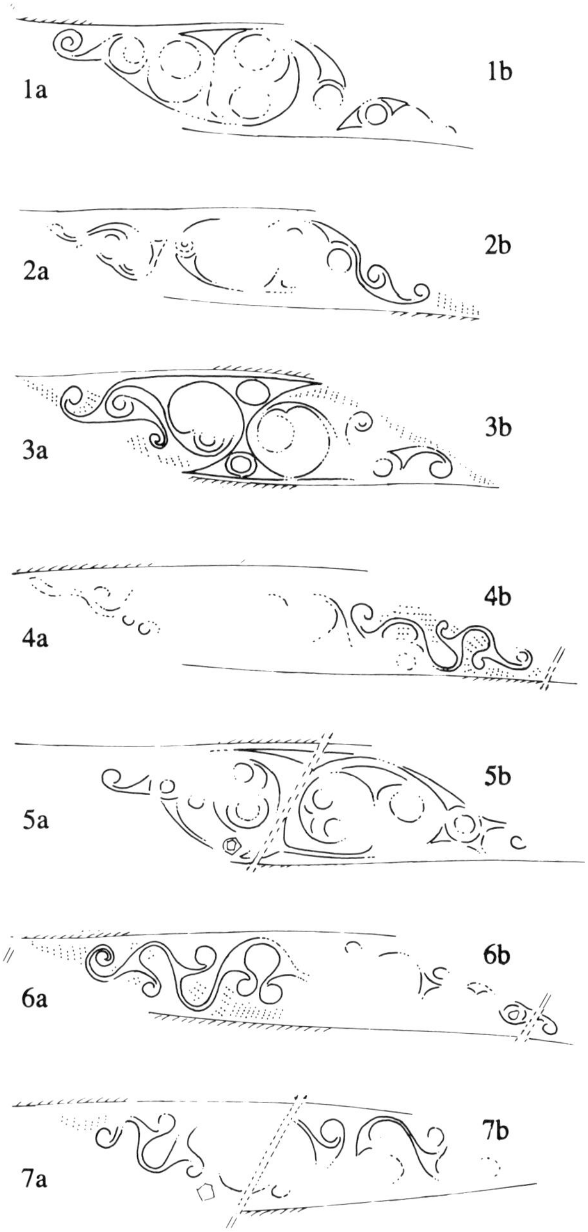

Figure 33. The Newnham Croft bracelet, with details of surviving ornament. (Full size; the diagram at the top is approximately 2/3)

off-centre perforation – links the scabbard with the suspension ring and the shield, suggesting that all the warrior's equipment could have been made and used at the same time.

The suspension ring has four panels of ornament – three of them pear-shaped (or tear-drop) and the fourth similar but with one concave side (fig. 32, 5). The three more elongated panels (a, c and d, lettered clockwise, starting from the loop) each enclose a curved triangular shape sprouting a single knobbed tendril, with a large circle in the field beyond. The fourth panel (b), relatively squat, has two large circles (perhaps one is a knobbed tendril). These motifs are shown against a background of basketry hatching, the decoration having been executed in the wax before casting. The brooch, also a lost-wax casting, has similar ornament with two linked triangular shapes, from two of whose diagonally opposite corners springs a knobbed circular tendril. On either side of the triangles, and in the field beyond, there are circular dots but no basketry hatching.

The pear shapes framing the ornament of the suspension ring can be matched at Waldalgesheim and Comacchio, but with different fillings (Jacobsthal 1944, pp. 457, 459 and 460). The fillings of the Deal frames, triangular shapes with knobbed tendrils (fig. 32, a–d), may be regarded as fragments of the motifs on the bridge of a chape from Little Wittenham (fig. 17, p. 63, no. 9), where they are also associated with a circle and basketry hatched background (though 'engraved', not cast). Two of them (a and c) can also be interpreted as fragments from a flowing tendril design such as that on the Newnham Croft bracelet – another lost-wax casting with a background of basketry hatching. Unfortunately the bracelet is extremely worn: the hatching is at best faint (cf. Megaw 1970, pl. 131) and much of the tendril design is now lost. The frequently reproduced drawing (originally in Clark 1938, fig. 26) includes a large element of imaginative reconstruction – some of which has found its way into grammars of ornament (Atkinson and Piggott 1955, fig. 3, 11, left; Fox 1958, fig. 82, C16, 18 and 19; and Duval 1977, fig. 440, X, right, are examples of motifs that seem to derive from the illustration rather than the object). An excursus to analyse the surviving decoration on this important bracelet is worthwhile not only to set the record straight but also to draw attention to another motif shared with Deal.

The Newnham Croft bracelet has seven decorated bands, twisted rope-wise round the outside, but in only two halves of two bands is the ornament sufficiently well preserved to be recorded with confidence. Band 6 (for the numbering see fig. 33) starts with a standard Waldalgesheim tendril (Verger 1987, type B) whose fourth triangle seems to swing the wrong way (certainly there are two adjoining terminals) and thereafter the layout is obscure. Bands 4 and 7 are less well preserved, but can be reconstructed as standard type B tendrils (fig. 34); Band 2 is worn and flawed and the design cannot be distinguished. The other reasonably preserved design, on Band 3, is different. In the centre two linked triangles each have an elaborate tendril springing from opposing corners. The terminals are very clear but the central part, curling back towards the triangles, is rather worn. Bands 1 and 5 may have had somewhat similar designs, but are too abraded to allow reconstruction.

In essence the design on Band 3 of the Newnham Croft bracelet (fig. 35, f) is a more complex version of the motif on the Deal brooch (fig. 35, a). It also appears in a simplified form on a sword-handle from Fiskerton (fig. 35, b), and features on the Sutton scabbard-plate (fig. 35, d). Diagonally balanced tendril designs centred on opposed triangles are rare on the continent, though there is an example on a torque from the vicinity of the Camp de Châlons (fig. 35, c, from Duval 1977, fig. 280; for further details see Kruta 1974, 25, note 1 = MAN 11353 and Jacobsthal 1944, no. 213). Diagonally balanced designs based on S motifs are much more common in continental La Tène art, cf. ibid. pp. 453 and 435. Kruta (1974) illustrates examples ('symétrie par rotation') of S and reversed-S motifs linked in continuous waves (ibid. figs 3, 5 and 6) and in pairs (Kruta and Roualet 1982). Diagonally balanced designs are an important component in the Irish Scabbard Style, especially on the Lisnacrogher 1 and Toome 1 scabbard-plates (Raftery 1984, 81) where they can be read either as triangular based (fig. 35, e) or S-based, because the triangles are at the junction of adjoining S motifs (Lisnacrogher 1) or reversed-S motifs (Toome 1).

Figure 34. The Newnham Croft bracelet: suggested reconstructions of the designs on bands 3, 4 and 7. (Full size)

Figure 35. Diagonally balanced designs centred on opposed triangles: (a) Deal brooch; (b) Fiskerton sword handle; (c) Camp de Châlons torque; (d) Sutton scabbard-plate; (e) Toome scabbard; (f) Newnham Croft bracelet. (Not to scale)

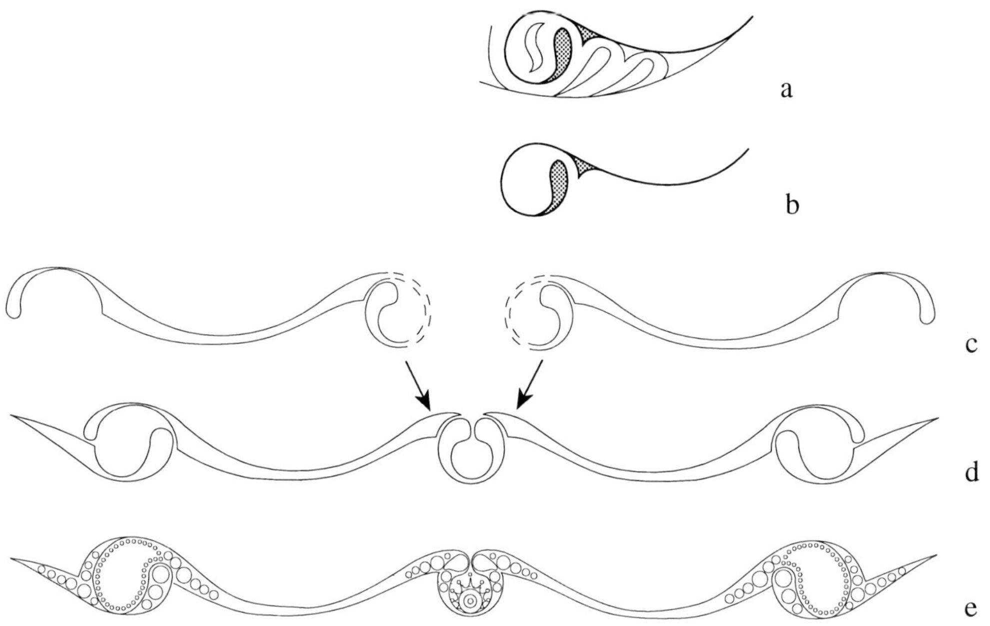

Figure 36. Showing how the design on the Deal crown (e) is constructed from lobe and cusp motifs (b) derived from a palmette ((a) = a half-palmette, Saulces-Champenoises).

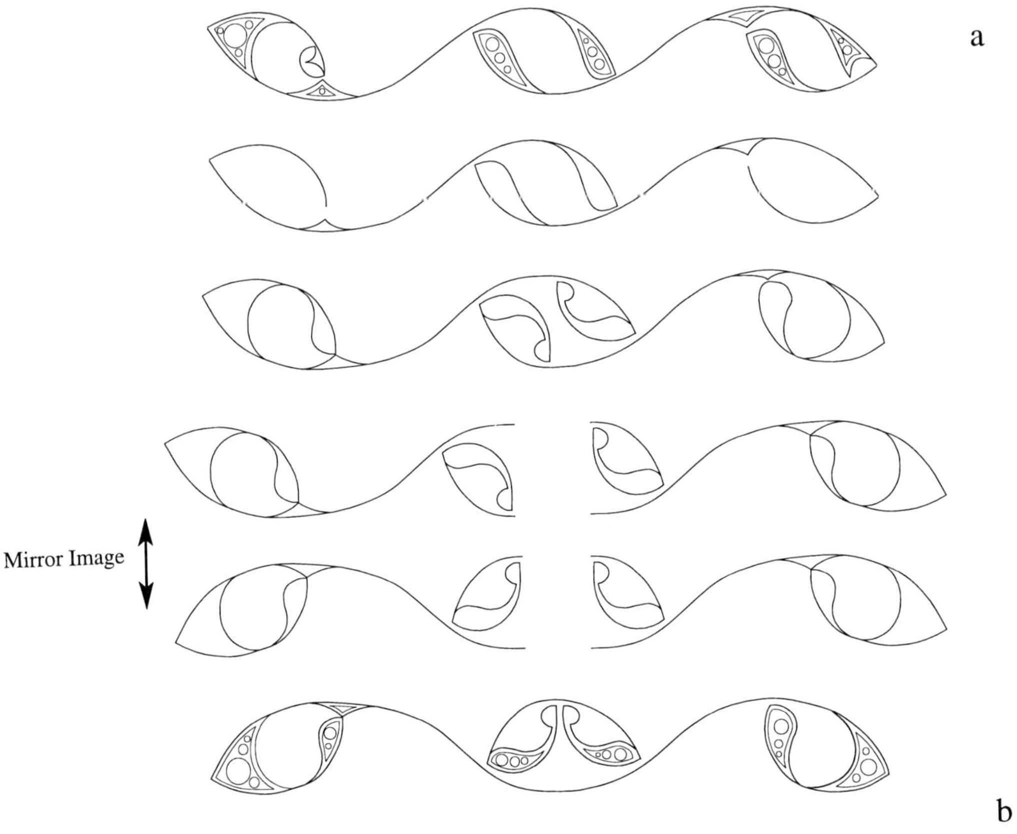

Figure 37. Showing the relationship between two designs on the Sutton scabbard-plate (a) and (b) and the derivation of the central double-lobe motif.

The band round the Deal crown is formed of two unequal lengths each with a symmetrical wave pattern with a circular motif under the central crest. On the longer piece (fig. 28; the central part of the design is shown on fig. 36, e) the circle is flanked equidistantly on each side by a nodule with a central dotted comma motif and beyond that a crossed square framing the dotted outlines of two circles and two squares. The shorter piece (fig. 27) has the same central motif and similar comma-centred nodules, but between the two is another device – a triangle on the stem with a thickening tendril springing from its free corner. The pattern is probably based on a lobe and triangular cusp – a motif derived from the palmette and used as the basis of designs in the Yorkshire Scabbard Style (Stead 1991a, 181–2, and fig. 99; see also fig. 36, a and b). On the Deal crown the comma-centred nodules are the junctions of two of these motifs interlocking, with each lobe merging into the opposing triangular cusp; the lobe and cusp combined have a filling of graded circles with central dots. At first sight the central circle is an oddity, in a position where a palmette might have been expected. But it, too, may perhaps be explained in terms of the lobe and cusp device with the design abbreviated by cutting the final curve and then repeated as a fold-over (fig. 36, c, d). Again the merged fillings have graded circles, terminating on one piece in a comma-leaf with dotted line. There are somewhat similar split and inverted designs on the related Sutton scabbard-plate (fig. 37; see also Frey 1974, 142 and fig. 1, 1–3). The decoration on the Deal crown is not precisely symmetrical, the main exception being the nodule at the left (fig. 27, Ai) of the shorter length which has two dotted commas: there the main lobe is itself composed of a lobe touching a triangular cusp. The simple graded circles filling motifs on the Deal crown contrast with the varied fillings of Irish and Yorkshire Scabbard Style designs, but can be matched closely on the Sutton scabbard-plate (fig. 37). Circles with a central dot also occur on the Little Wittenham chape (fig. 17), but usually in terminals or central to swellings where they are accompanied by hatched lines.

The bronze panel at the top of the Deal scabbard has a repoussé design whose basic layout (fig. 38, a) is very similar to that on the crown, with two interlocked S-shapes; the central nodule is a pair of linked lobe and cusp motifs with each lobe touching the opposite cusp. Each stem has a second cusp beyond, facing the opposite way and touched by quite complex circular terminals (fig. 38, b). Some of the repoussé shapes have additional relief recalling the fillings of engraved Scabbard Style and related designs (fig. 38, c, is shaded to emphasise these features): thus the innermost cusps have a pair of lobes meeting at the point of the triangle as on the Wetwang Slack scabbard-plates and 'bean-can' (Dent 1990, fig. 3); and the outer cusps have central oval shapes like those on the Fovant and Bann scabbards (Stead 1985, 20, pl. 23 shows the two together), and the Sawdon brooch (Stead 1979, 66, fig. 24, no. 2).

The circular terminals of the Deal scabbard-plate design may have been based on lobes touching the triangular cusp on the stem, but they have been elaborated in detail and are not closely similar to one another. The design of the upper terminal may have started with a 'bird-head' lobe but if so it was then linked with another similar motif facing the opposite way, creating a trumpet-shaped void at either side (shaded in fig. 38, d) and completely filling the circle. The design of the lower terminal seems more closely based on a yin-yang motif (the upper design could be interpreted in the same way) and the main feature of the right half is another trumpet void (fig. 38, d). There is a fourth trumpet void in the central node (fig. 38, d).

The cast lobe and circle ornament on the Deal chape-end (fig. 15, b) is a simple motif with elements resembling those on the repoussé panel. Similar cast designs are associated with Yorkshire Scabbard Style ornament at Kirkburn (Stead 1991a, 183 and fig. 99 g).

The triangular plaque that covered the lower half of the shield-boss has an openwork design, a technique used, for instance, on the back of the Little Wittenham chape (fig. 17) and on an object from Meare found in fragments (Gray and Bulleid 1953, 225, no. E168). The decoration can be described in terms of the pieces that have been cut away, for it seems to be a fairly random arrangement of trumpet-shaped voids (fig. 39). Each void has three sides: one concave, the second convex, and the third concavo-convex (S-shaped). Allowing for the suggested reconstruction of a piece missing from the top left of the design, there are six trumpet shapes, the top pair flanked by open-work circles (one much larger than the other), with a small central lobe to complete the pattern. Two sides of the plaque are bordered by grooves and a further short groove springs from the point of the central lobe.

The trumpet void is a typically British motif that seems to develop as a negative shape within tendrils - especially within a tendril terminating in a 'bird-head' (Fox 1946, 49; Stead 1985, 22, fig. 26). Usually it seems to be a significant but secondary element in the design, and as such it appears on the Kirkburn scabbard (Stead 1991a, 181–2, fig. 99c) as well as on the panel at the top of the Deal scabbard (fig. 38, d). But on the shield-boss there are no tendrils and no bird-heads: the trumpet voids are the only recognisable elements. Their dominance recalls the design on the Old Warden mirror (Fox 1958, 94, pl. 60, a; Spratling 1970) where a mass of trumpet voids interlink, leaving narrow hatched ribbons between them.

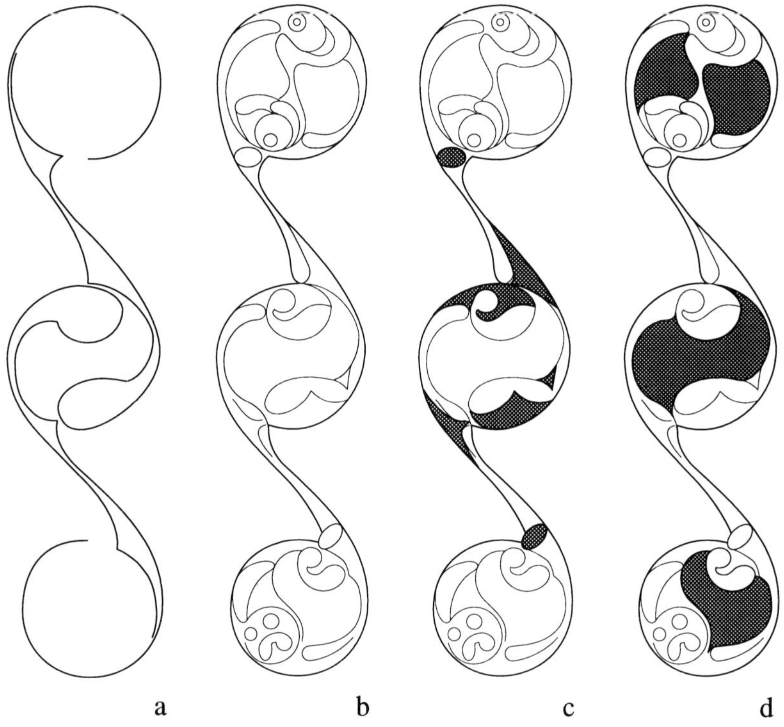

Figure 38. The design on the Deal scabbard: (a) simplified version to emphasise the lobes and cusps; (b) detailed design; (c) emphasising the infilling of the lobes and cusps; (d) trumpet voids in the circular terminals and central node.

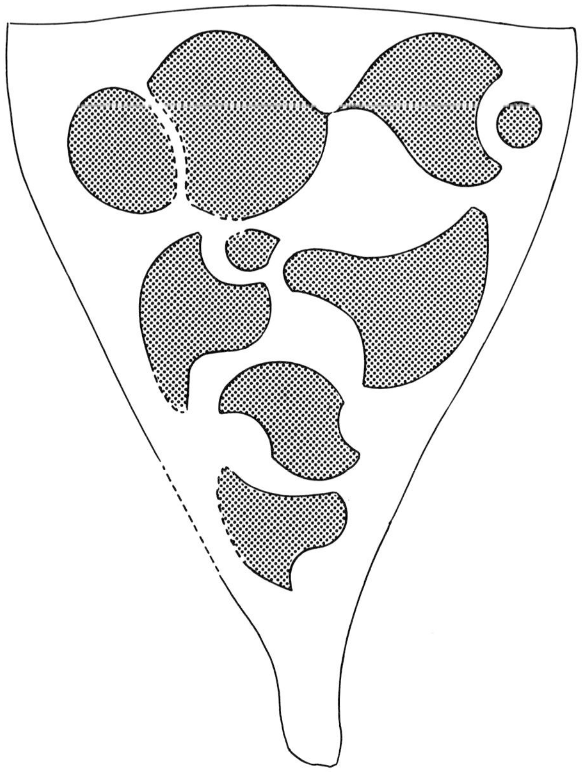

Figure 39. Trumpet voids on the open-work plaque that covered half of the shield-boss. (Full size)

On the Deal plaque the voids are more scattered, with broader divisions, one of which is itself almost in the form of a trumpet void. The design on the Old Warden mirror is generally regarded as late in the typological sequence of British Celtic art - 'it is a late piece ... the craftsman is surely building up a new "diffusive" style, in which the voids are intended to please the eye as much as the pattern' (Fox 1958, 94–5). On the Deal plaque the voids are the pattern. Spratling (1970, 14–15) was cautious about Old Warden's position in the typology of British Iron Age mirrors, but argued that the entire sequence belonged to the century after Caesar's incursions, with the Old Warden mirror 'more probably later than earlier in that period'. Subsequent discoveries suggest that some of the decorated mirrors might be slightly earlier than Spratling thought, but there is still no evidence for one earlier than the middle of the first century BC (Stead and Rigby 1989, 103). If it had been a chance find there is little doubt that the Deal plaque would have been given a post-Caesarian date, but the other items in Grave 112 suggest that it should be much earlier.

A recent detailed attempt to classify La Tène art in Britain (Stead 1985a, 27–36; 1985b, 15–23) reverted to de Navarro's (1952) numbered styles (I to IV), adding Style V to complete the sequence. The attempt was rightly criticised for simplification but some such classification is needed to attempt to explain the development and chronology of La Tène designs in Britain (cf. its adoption in Cunliffe's textbook, 1991, 470–9). Discoveries since the 1985 publications can be accommodated reasonably within the scheme of development, but they have made notable changes to its chronology. Decorated artefacts from Yorkshire cart-burials and associated graves have led to the recognition of a Yorkshire Scabbard Style (Stead 1991a, 183) which belongs to de Navarro's Style IV, is associated with Group A scabbards of La Tène I form (two at Wetwang Slack and another at Kirkburn), and should be dated no later than the third century BC. On the Kirkburn scabbard the fan-shaped or trumpet-shaped void figures prominently, but that motif had been taken as diagnostic of Style V (Stead 1985a, 27) 'which seems to coincide with the first century BC' (Stead 1985b, 23). Grave 112 at Deal confirms its early appearance for it occurs not only in the design at the top of the scabbard but also as an independent motif on the shield-boss (figs 38 and 39). If Style V is to be defined by the trumpet void, then it starts not in the first but in the third century BC.

Metal artefacts from other burials and other contexts

1. Brooches

Nos. 1–25 are from the Mill Hill site, and most are from burials; for Artefact, Context or Grave X1 to X23 see pp. 171–8, and for the excavated finds, Grave 1, etc, see pp. 159–70. Unless otherwise stated the brooches are bronze (none has been analysed, so 'bronze' refers to all copper alloys).

I. LA TÈNE I (fig. 40)

1. Artefact X6. (D58) L 86.5mm. A La Tène I brooch with four-coil spring and external chord. There is a solid bronze rivet through the coils, but the spring has been properly functional; one of the outer coils has broken, and the rivet may have been needed to hold the spring together. The chord has squarish ends, and slight ornamental grooves where the original surface survives (the outer part is eroded). The bow has a central circular feature with a knob of worn coral secured by a ?bronze pin (on the underside the surface has broken away, which might suggest that the pin had been iron). Much of the surface ringing the coral is decorated with punched dots. On either side of the central circle is a moulding with a shallow pear-shaped hollow bordered by a line of dots. The foot has a circular element drilled and perforated for a knob of ornament (now lost), presumably of coral, and a tapering finial beyond. There is a slight decorative moulding at the junction of the bow and the back of the catch-plate. Most of the pin is missing.

Hawkes (1940, 277, and in Hull and Hawkes 1987, 117–19) suggested that this brooch had been imported from Switzerland; Jacobsthal (1944, 211) regarded it as 'a coarse copy of a Swiss brooch'. The Swiss brooch with which they compared it, from Münsingen t. 49 (ibid. no. 340; Hodson 1968, pl. 22, no. 798) is not the only one with a circular setting in the middle of the bow, cf. Champ du Moulin, Neuchâtel (Jacobsthal 1944, no. 293). See also the comments on the brooch from Grave 112, p. 86.

II. LA TÈNE II (fig.40)

2. Grave 112, see p. 86.

3. Grave 127. Complete but badly corroded iron involuted brooch, L 56mm (including 'external chord' corrosion, or 53mm omitting that corrosion). Foot flat (no sign of applied knob of 'enamel'), 12mm wide, its end wrapped onto the bow. Hint of a cylinder rivet in the head, possibly a 'stop', and on one side only a lump of corrosion that may represent part of an 'external chord'. Too corroded to distinguish the precise details of the head (for the range of 'mock-spring' constructions see Stead 1979, 68, fig. 25, and 1991a, 80).

In the Hull and Hawkes (1987) typology it falls between 2Ca and 2Cb (e.g. between pl. 45, no. 1016 and pl. 48, no 3194): the series (i.e. type 2C) 'runs from within the middle third into the second century'. At

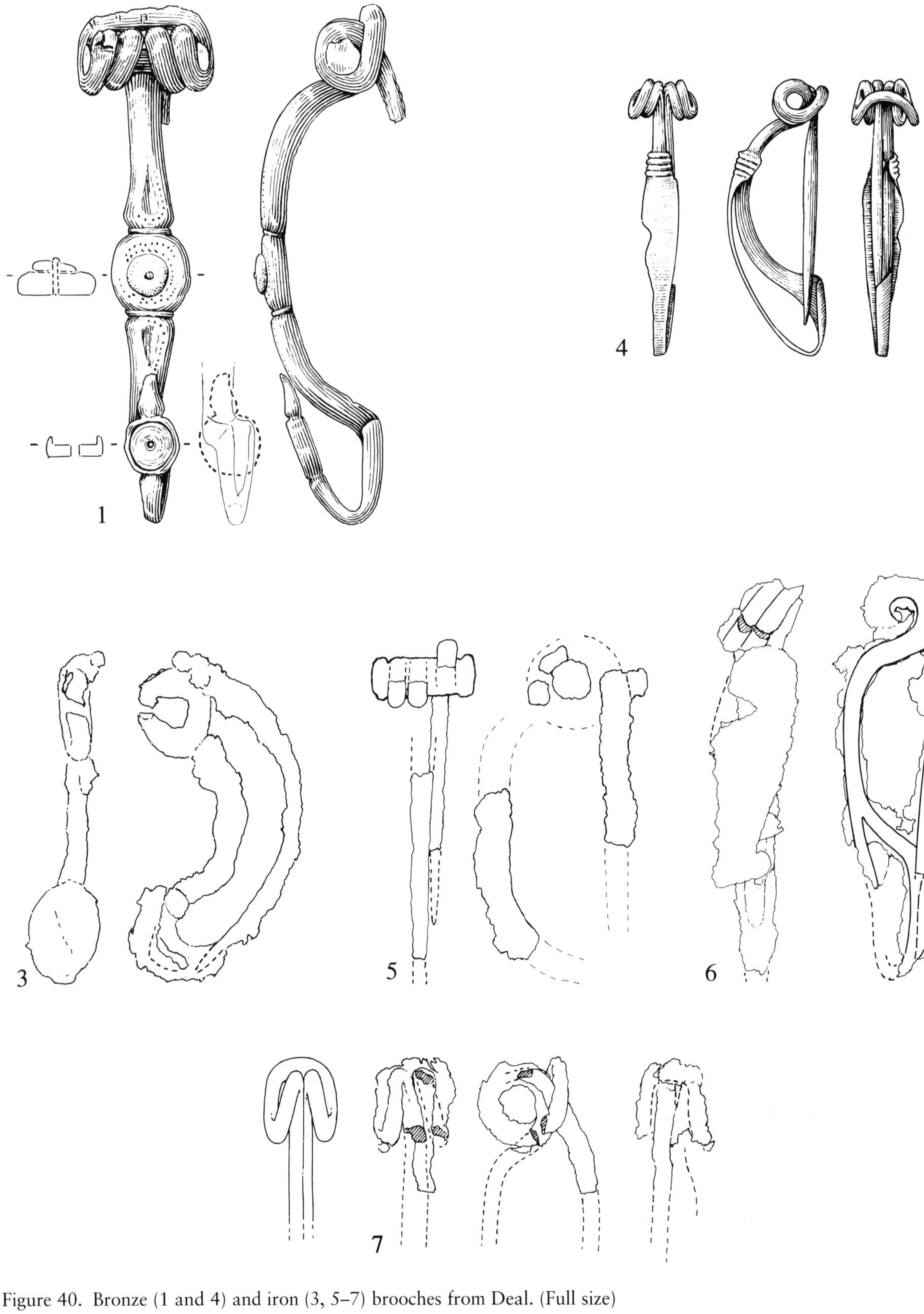

Figure 40. Bronze (1 and 4) and iron (3, 5–7) brooches from Deal. (Full size)

Rudston a more developed brooch was associated with a pot 'tentatively dated to the late second or early first century BC' (Rigby, in Stead 1991a, 110, Burial R143). So the brooch from Deal 127 seems likely to date from the second century BC. In length and overall shape it resembles type E in the Yorkshire cemeteries (Stead 1991a, 85–7) though the examples from Rudston and Burton Fleming have applied knobs of 'enamel'; F5 (ibid. 87) is comparable but has a wider foot. It is midway between the long and short involuted brooches at Wetwang Slack (Dent 1982, 441 – e.g. between nos. 233 and 312 on fig. 4).

The distribution of involuted brooches has changed significantly since they were last mapped (Stead 1979, fig. 35; see now fig. 41). The number of sites has increased from 15 to 24 and eight of the new sites are south of the Humber: one more in the Welsh Marches, three in the southwest, one in East Anglia and three in the southeast. There is now an overall, if thin, distribution over southern England. The vast majority of involuted brooches (74) are from graves in Yorkshire, but not one has been found on a settlement there. Of the 31 brooches found south of the Humber only four are from burials, the others being from settlements or chance finds. At Shoreham, Sussex, one involuted brooch was found with a burial in a pit on a settlement site and there were two others with domestic debris. The Deal involuted brooch is the sole example from the southeast found in a cemetery; the only other cemetery in the south with an involuted brooch is Trethellan Farm, near Newquay, Cornwall (the Trevone brooch was with an isolated burial). The Trethellan Farm burials are crouched or contracted inhumations like those in Yorkshire and unlike the extended burials at Deal, but their brooches have more in common with Deal for two others are generally related to nos. 4 and 6 from Deal.

4. Grave 47. L 46mm. Four-coil spring, external chord; the long flat foot is ribbed at the end where it clasps the bow.

This is a variant of Hull and Hawkes (1987, 173–8, pl. S1) type 3B, which usually has a longer spring and a collar to secure the foot to the bow. A type 3B variant from Lydney (ibid. 177, no. 2768) has the four-coil spring and wrapped foot of the Deal brooch. Type 3B is distributed mainly in southwest England where it is followed by a La Tène III version (ibid. 193–6, pl. S5, type 6), but there are now three examples from Kent. The first, from Maidstone (ibid. 175, no. 2251) is typical of type 3B, whilst the second, from the Medway Marshes (BM P1981 10–2 1) has the typical long spring but a ribbed and wrapped foot similar to the third – the Deal brooch from Grave 47.

5. Grave 108. Iron fragments, apparently from a brooch:

(i) L 19mm. A solid length, circular in section, unbroken at the ends. Perhaps a solid rivet that would have passed through the coils of a brooch-spring (and a separate tiny fragment might be parts of two adjoining coils). Alternatively this length of iron might be a long and very compact spring, but no coils are visible on X-rays.

(ii) L 28mm. A length perhaps from a brooch pin, with a shorter piece corroded at right angles at one end. The shorter piece is unlikely to have been part of the catch-plate (unless this length of pin was within the catch-plate) but may have been part of an external chord, or spring-coil.

(iii) L 29mm. A slightly curved length, possibly from the bow of a brooch.

The only diagnostic piece is the ?solid rivet, which is more likely to have been from a La Tène I or II than from a La Tène III brooch. Bronze versions of these solid rivets are more obvious than iron, with La Tène I examples from Deal (above, no. 1), Hammersmith and 'Thames at London' (Hodson 1971, pl. xiii, b and d) – these and several others are in the Hull and Hawkes (1987) corpus; for a good La Tène II example see Wetwang Slack (ibid. 136, pl. 39, no. 7869).

III. LA TÈNE III

a) Iron brooches, (fig. 40):

6. Grave 50. An iron La Tène III brooch with open catch-plate, flat bow broad at the head and tapering to the foot, and probably a four-coil spring with external chord. It lacks the foot of the bow, part of the spring and all of the chord. There are two surviving coils in the spring, the outer coil turning to either another coil or, more likely, an external chord. Surviving L 70mm.

The flat bow and open foot are features of the Nauheim brooch, but that has a four-coil spring with internal, not external, chord. Furthermore the proportions are not consistent with those of a Nauheim brooch, for the Deal brooch is relatively short and its bow is relatively high; most Nauheim brooches are made of bronze. For the true Nauheim brooch see Werner 1955; Hull and Hawkes 1987, 197 and pl. S6, no. 1 – it will feature in Type 9 in the next volume of the Hull corpus; Ettlinger 1973, type 1 (pl. I, nos 1–6); Riha 1979, type 1.1; Feugère 1985, type 5a; Gebhard 1991, groups 7 and 27; for British examples, Stead 1984, 54, fig. 20, no. 4.

7. Grave 122 (a). Head of an iron brooch, two-coil spring with external chord. L 25mm. The fragment comprises one complete coil, part of the other, the complete external chord, and a length of the pin.

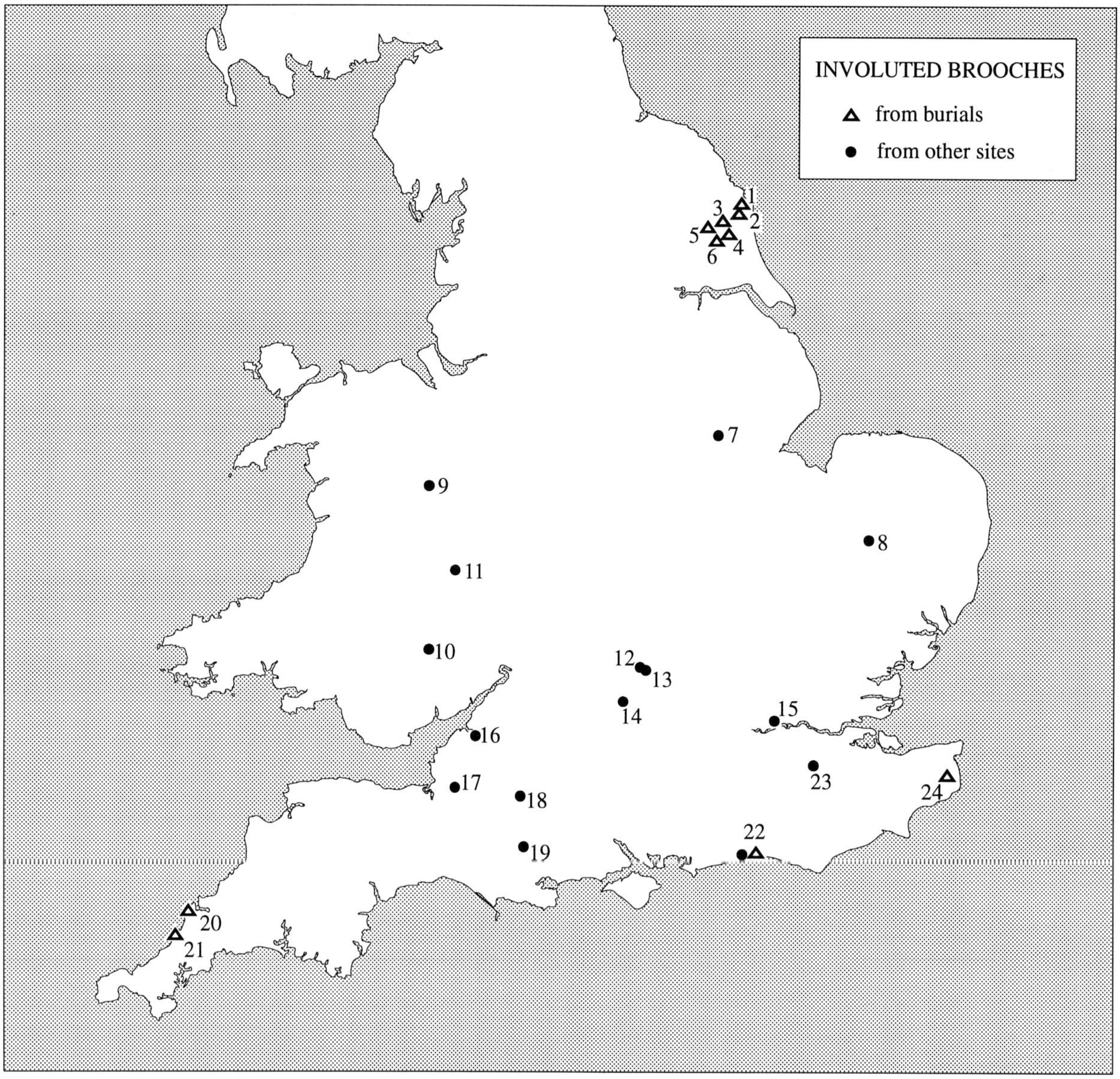

Figure 41. Distribution of involuted brooches: 1. Burton Fleming, Humberside (Stead 1991a, 87); 2. Rudston, Humberside (ibid. 83–9); 3. Danes Graves, Humberside (Stead 1979, 68–9); 4. Eastburn, Humberside (ibid. 68); 5. Garton Slack, Humberside (Hull and Hawkes 1987, 159 and 161, nos. 1527 and 1599 – the same brooch illustrated twice; Dent 1983, 11, fig. 8, A–D); 6. Wetwang Slack, Humberside (Dent 1982, 441–4); 7. Ancaster, Lincolnshire (Hull and Hawkes 1987, 161, no. 9220); 8. Thetford, Norfolk (Gregory 1991, 123–4, no. 27); 9. The Breiddin, Powys (Musson 1991, 142–4); 10. Twyn-y-Gaer, Gwent (Probert 1976, 115); 11. Croft Ambrey, Hereford and Worcester (Stanford 1974, 162–4); 12. Wood Eaton, Oxon (Hull and Hawkes 1987, 163 and 164, nos. 3070 and 4281); 13. Beckley, Oxon (ibid. 163, no. 2244); 14. Frilford, Oxon (ibid. 158, no. 3071); 15. London (ibid. 166, no. 2242); 16. Stokeleigh Camp, Avon (Haldane 1975, 59, fig. 19, M49); 17. Meare East, Somerset (Coles 1987, 75, no. EE15; 77, no.EE 66.56; 127, no. 184); 18. Cold Kitchen Hill, Wiltshire (Hull and Hawkes 1987, 160, no. 2247; 162, nos. 5475 and 5477; 165, nos. 3194 and 5476 [?the same brooch]; 166, no. 2246); 19. Hod Hill, Dorset (ibid. 158, no. 3071); 20. Trevone, Cornwall (ibid. 158, no. 6889); 21. Trethellan Farm, Newquay, Cornwall (Nowakowski 1991, 222, fig. 84, no. 205); 22. Shoreham, Sussex (Hartridge 1978, 99, nos. 7–9); 23. Farningham Hill, Kent (Philp 1984, 35, no. 6); 24. Deal, Kent (Grave 127).

8. Grave 123 (d). (fig. 60, no. 6). Part of an iron brooch: a single piece comprising one coil with a short length of pin and the start of an external chord, maximum L 22mm. Also a short (11mm) length probably from the same brooch. Perhaps a two-coil spring like no. 7.

Although La Tène I and II brooches with two-coil springs and external chords are known in Britain, this form of construction seems to be more common in La Tène III (see Hull and Hawkes 1987, 125, no. 4280, La Tène I, and 139, no. 3157, La Tène II; some others with supposed two-coil springs have three-coil mock springs. For La Tène III brooches with two-coil springs and external chords see no. 9, Artefact X1, below; and others from burials at Folkestone and Great Chesterford, Stead 1976, figs. 2, no. 6; 3, no. 3; and 4, no. 2).

b) Knotenfibeln (fig. 42)

La Tène III brooches with a moulding on the bow, derived from the La Tène II brooch whose foot is clasped to the bow by a collar. Often loosely classified as Knotenfibeln or Almgren 65; Ettlinger 1973, type 8; Feugère 1985, type 8; Gebhard 1991, groups 11, 12, 33 and 34. La Tène III brooches with collars or mouldings on the bow will be included in the second volume of the Hull corpus, as types 18-20 (Hull and Hawkes 1987, 198). The overall type belongs to the second half of the first century BC: it occurs at Manching by or soon after 50BC (Gebhard 1991), and Le Câtillon in the third quarter of the first century BC (Fitzpatrick and Megaw 1987, 434–8). Iron examples, but not bronze, were still used at the time of the King Harry Lane cemetery, i.e. after AD1; indeed one was buried *c.* AD50 but that must have been exceptionally late (Stead and Rigby 1989, 96).

(i) Two-coil spring, external chord; moulded collar on the bow; open catch-plate.

9. Artefact X1. (BM 1900 7–25 1). L. 111mm. A fine cross-hatched moulding on the bow, from which a line to the open catch-plate, down the sides of the bow, is a reminder of the distinction between foot and bow on a La Tène II brooch. Woodruff 1904, 12–13, pl. iv, no. 2; Smith 1925, 95, fig. 100; Stead 1976, 404, fig. 1, no. 3.

The four silver brooches from Great Chesterford share some features with this Deal brooch: two-coiled spring with external chord, collar central to the bow, and two of them have a groove at the side of the bow below the collar – but the only surviving foot is sub-divided (Krämer 1971, pl. 24; Stead 1976, 406, fig. 3, no. 3); four of the five Le Câtillon brooches have similar features – the fifth lacks the spring; a silver brooch from Folkestone is comparable, though lacking the groove between collar and catch-plate (Stead 1976, fig. 2, no. 6).

(ii) Four-coiled spring, internal chord; moulding on the bow; open catch-plate.

Feugère classifies simpler versions of this with his type 5b (the wire-bow version of the Nauheim brooch), e.g. his nos 751, 752, 755, 763 and 764.

10. Context X4. L 75mm. Bushe-Fox 1925, 19, 44, pl. xv, 16, top left; Stead 1976, 404, fig. 2, no. 2.

11. Context X4. L 70mm. Bushe-Fox 1925, 19, 44, pl. xv, 16, bottom right; Stead 1976, 404, fig. 2, no. 3.

(iii) Four-coil spring, internal chord; moulding on the bow; catch-plate with four perforations.

cf. Feugère 1985, no. 890, which has only two perforations in the catch-plate = Feugère 1985, type 6b, which includes brooches of very different appearance.

12. Context X4. L 47mm. Bushe-Fox 1925, 19, 44, pl. xv, 16, centre; Stead 1976, 404, fig. 2, no. 4.

(iv) Four-coil spring, internal chord, expanded trumpet-shaped head; elaborate moulding on the bow, and the bow is flat from the moulding to the foot; open catch-plate.

Feugère 1985, type 8a2, distinguished by the flattening of the bow between moulding and foot.

13. Context X4. L 105mm. Bushe-Fox 1925, 19, 44, pl. xv, 16, bottom left (shows the catch-plate complete); Dunning 1966, pl. vi, no. 1; Stead 1976, 404, fig. 1, no. 4.

14. Context X4. L 94mm. Bushe-Fox 1925, 19, 44, pl. xv, 16, top right; Stead 1976, 404, fig. 2, no. 1.

(v) Four-coil spring, external chord.

15. Grave X8. (D134). L 87mm. Only the pin and two coils with the start of an external chord. Not illustrated.

c) Kragenfibel (fig. 43)

Ettlinger 1973, type 19; Feugère 1985, type 10a. The type is very rare in Britain, where the only published example seems to be Hawkes and Hull 1947, 313, no. 67. It is absent from Manching (Gebhard 1991), but occurs at Basel-Münsterhügel (Furger-Gunti 1979) and in Haffner's Horizont 5 (Haffner 1974, fig. 4, nos. 49–50). Site evidence suggests a date in the final third of the first century BC, but a Kragenfibel seems to be depicted on Criciru's gold staters dated nearer 60 than 50BC (Allen 1972).

16. Context X7. L *c.*53mm. Not located, but recorded in two of Manser's photographs (Photos Qa and Qb) – fig. 43, no. 16 has been drawn from the photographs. It

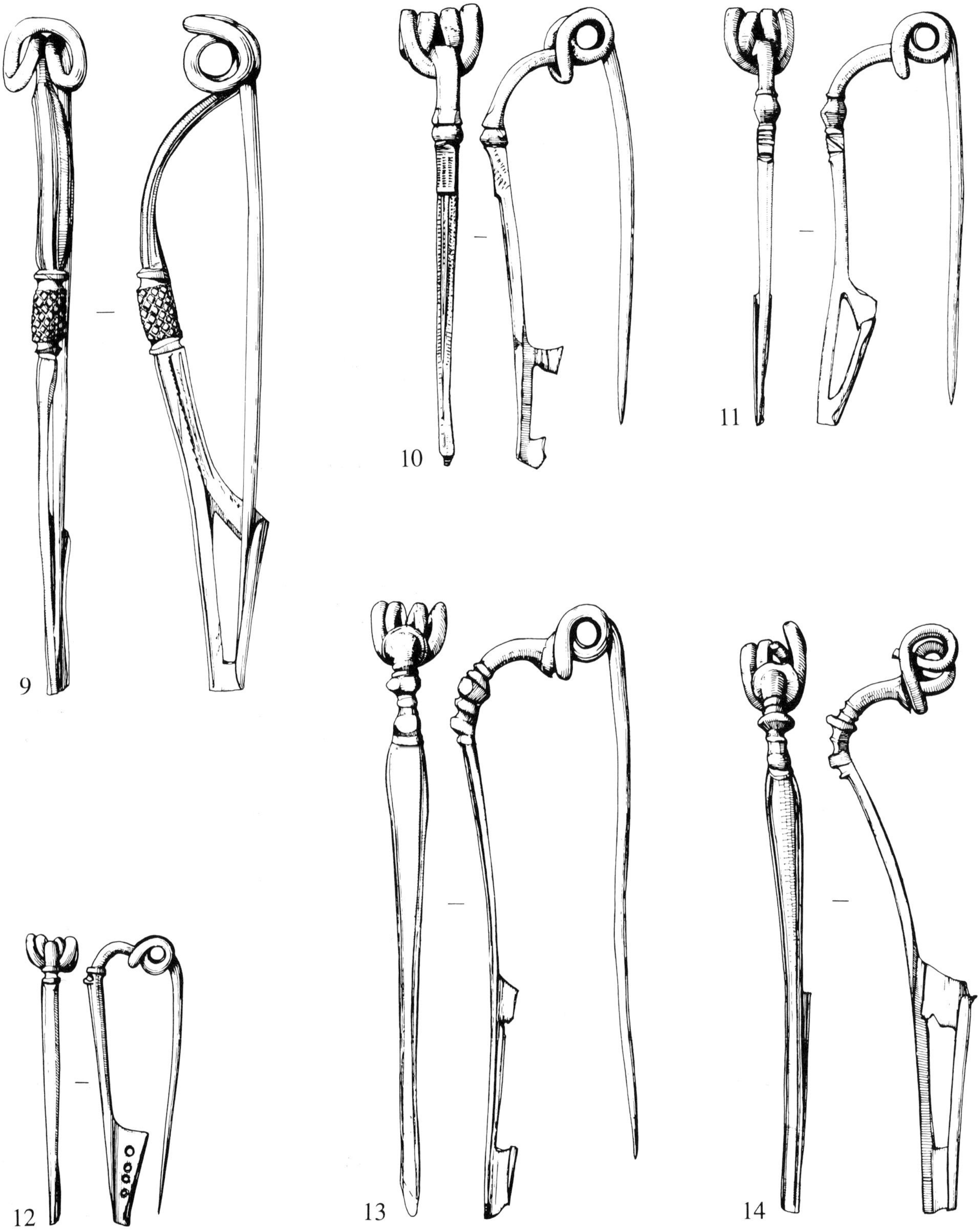

Figure 42. Bronze brooches from Deal; drawn by Frank Gardiner. (Full size)

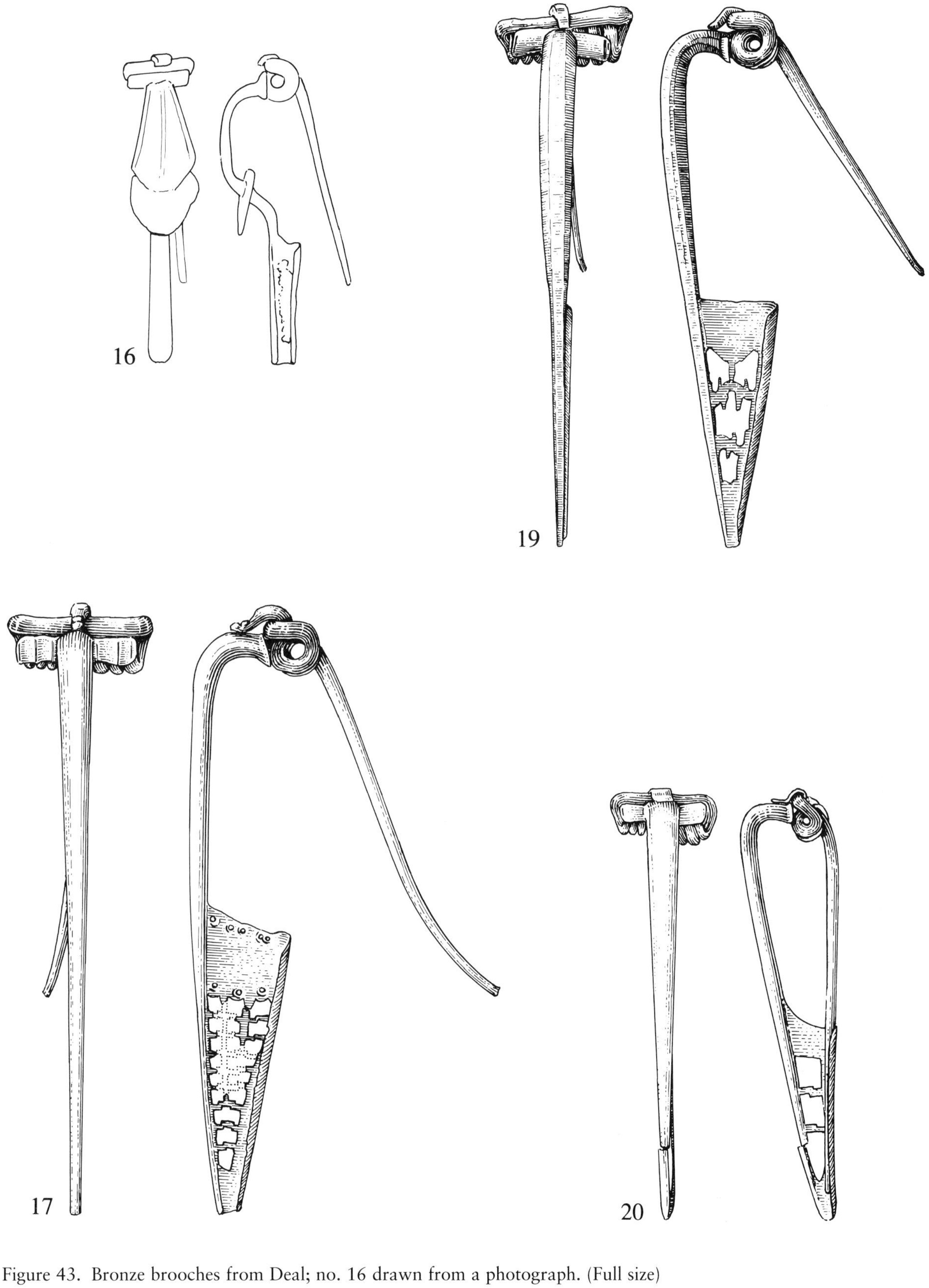

Figure 43. Bronze brooches from Deal; no. 16 drawn from a photograph. (Full size)

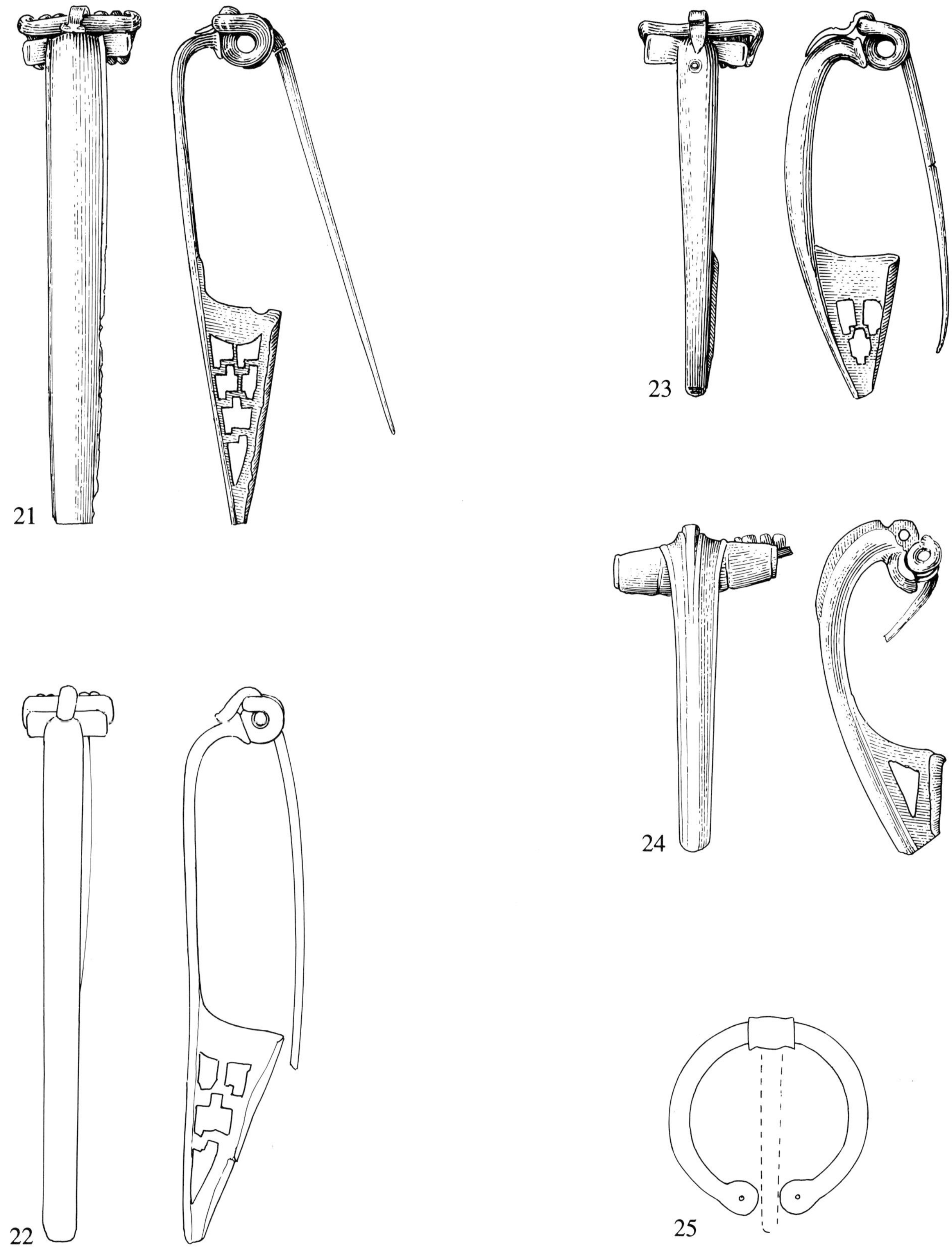

Figure 44. Bronze brooches from Deal; no. 22 drawn from a photograph and no. 25 from a sketch by Newington. (Full size)

has a large disc or collar threaded onto the bow: above the collar the bow is flat, narrow at the head but expanding markedly to about the width of the collar, then contracting sharply to allow the collar to be fixed. Long shallow catch-plate (possibly with perforations), six- or eight-coil spring, external chord, hook and wings.

d) Simple Gallic brooches
(i) tapering bow (fig. 43)
Ettlinger 1973, type 9; Riha 1979, type 2.2 (the Deal examples resemble Riha's nos 182-4, classified within her type 2.2.4); Feugère 1985, type 14a. At King Harry Lane it occurred throughout the first half of the first century AD (Stead and Rigby, 1989, type B), and on the continent it is found slightly earlier (e.g. the Augustan fort at Dangstetten, 15–10BC, Fingerlin, 1971, fig. 9, no. 7).

17. Grave X11. (D54) L 106mm. Slightly faceted bow; ribbed and grooved wings; eight-coil spring with external chord; hook with neatly modelled terminal; elaborately pierced catch-plate (broken) with two lines of punched rings (cf. Stead and Rigby 1989, 89, type Bb). Bushe-Fox 1925, 43, pl. xiii, no. 9; Birchall 1965, 305, fig. 12, no. 100.

18. Grave X11. (D133). L 71mm (lacking much of the catch-plate). Not illustrated. The pair to no. 17, differing only in the hook which is forked. The pin is broken and distorted; the catch-plate is broken but with remains of the first two partitions for the perforations. Recorded on Manser's Photo W which shows more of the catch-plate, including punched rings. Not published by Bushe-Fox (1925) or Birchall (1965).

19. Grave 4. L 93mm. Similar, but markedly faceted bow with little taper until just before the catch-plate. Wings grooved at each end; six-coil spring; broken pin; four elaborate perforations in the catch-plate.

20. Grave X8. (D53) L 75mm. Tapering bow, rounded in section, sharply angled under the head, wings grooved at each end. Eight-coil spring with external chord secured by a broad hook. Three perforations in the long narrow catch-plate. Bushe-Fox 1925, 43, pl. xiii, no. 8; Birchall 1965, 305, fig. 11, no. 95.

(ii) broad untapered bow (fig.44)
Feugère (1985) includes two comparable examples in his type 14a (nos 1173 and 1178, both shorter than the Deal brooches), but there are none similar in the typologies published by Ettlinger (1973) and Riha (1979), nor in the King Harry Lane cemetery (Stead and Rigby 1989). The nearest approach from Camulodunum (but with a bow more rounded in profile and a single triangular perforation in the catch-plate) was classified as 'type III, continental form' (Hawkes and Hull 1947, 310, pl. xci, no. 34). There is another Kent example from Lenham (Kelly 1990, 281–2).

21. Grave X8. (D53) L 89mm. Broad flattish bow with a slight median ridge and slightly raised edges each defined by a groove. Six-coil spring with external chord secured by a hook that terminates in a pair of circles each crudely defined by a groove; wings with a groove at each end. Elaborately pierced catch-plate (six perforations); broken pin recently repaired. Bushe-Fox 1925, 43, pl. xiii, no. 7; Birchall 1965, 305, fig. 11, no. 94.

22. Context X7. Brooch similar to no. 21, not located but recorded in two of Manser's photographs (Photos Qa and Qb) – fig. 44, no. 22 has been drawn from the photographs. It was longer than no. 21 (*c.* 95mm) with a rather narrower bow (*c.* 5–6mm) and only four perforations in the catch-plate. Six-coil spring, external chord, hook and wings.

e) Colchester Brooch (fig.44)
Hawkes and Hull 1947, type III; Stead and Rigby 1989, type C (the following piece would have been classified as Cd but for the single circular stamp on the bow). First half of the first century AD.

23. Artefact X23. (D52) L 66mm. Short rounded slightly tapering bow with two grooves across the end. Eight-coil spring, external chord, long pointed hook; a single circular stamp on the bow just beyond the tip of the hook; a groove at the end of each wing. Three perforations in the catch-plate; broken pin.

f) Colchester-derivative brooch (fig.44)
24. Context X3. (D48) L 56mm. Triangular perforation in the catch-plate. Broken spring (five coils on one side, four on the other, central bronze rod), separate length of pin with part of one coil. Woodruff 1904, 13 and 16, no. 22, pl. I, back row, centre. The Colchester-derivative brooch is a post-Conquest type, and this one is similar to, but smaller than, one from Baldock, Stead and Rigby 1986, fig. 44, no. 79, found in a Neronian context.

g) Penannular brooch (fig.44)
25. Artefact X15. Newington (MS notebook, 18 November 1913, no. 108) lists a bronze ring 1 7/20" (= 34mm) across. His sketch shows a penannular brooch with broken pin whose ring is still in position on the arc of the brooch opposite the terminals. The terminals are circular, one with a rivet through the centre and the other

perforated for a corresponding rivet. Doubtless the terminals were flat, and the rivets may well have secured knobs of coral like those on the (much smaller, diam. *c.* 22mm) penannular brooches from Newnham Croft (only one of those coral knobs survives, Fox 1958, fig. 6c). The Deal penannular brooch has not been located, and fig. 44, no. 25, is based on Newington's sketch.

Overall, seven inhumations were buried with brooches, three (perhaps four) in the second century BC and one (perhaps three) in the first half of the first century BC (Table 10). The majority of inhumations were buried without brooches and cannot be dated closely. Six brooches (nos 15, 17–21) were found with three cremations dating from the last decade of the first century BC and the first quarter of the first century AD. Two others (nos 22 and 23) date from the first half of the first century AD, and one (no. 24) is post-Conquest; they may well have been found with burials (and even cremations) because there are pots from cremations of that date. One of the Knotenfibeln from Context X4 (probably no. 12) is said by Manser to have been inside a pot (Smith's annotation of a photograph seems to contradict this, but Manser's statement is quite clear): a brooch in a pot implies a cremation, and this type of brooch indicates a cremation in the second half of the first century BC. The evidence of the brooches suggests a continuous tradition of burial at Mill Hill from about 200BC to AD70 (and the pottery extends the range to AD150 or even later), with a change from inhumation to cremation at some time in the middle of the first century BC. But that interpretation is too simple, because no brooches were found with the 14 skeletons in the Central Cemetery where the coin from Burial 30 shows that inhumation was still practised in the first decade of the first century AD. If brooch no. 1 came from a burial then the funerary tradition at Mill Hill started even earlier than 200BC.

	INHUMATION	?	CREMATION
400			
300		1	
200	2		
	3		
	4		
	(5)		
100			
	6		
	(7, 8)		
BC		9-11, 13,14,16	12 ?
AD		22	15, 17-21
		23	
		24	
100			

Table 10. Showing brooches (numbered as in the brooch report) associated with inhumations and cremations in the Mill Hill cemetery, and their approximate chronology. Numbers in brackets indicate a doubt about classification or chronology because the remains are incomplete; no. 12 was probably but not certainly with a cremation.

2. *Pins*

1. Artefact X10. (D59) (fig. 45) L 75mm. A cast bronze involuted pin with a heavy circular head, flat on the back, rounded and with a bordering groove. The head is in the opposite plane to the long and rather squared bend in the shank. There is a neatly-moulded finial on the point.

The involuted pin was defined and discussed by Gerald Dunning (1934, 278–80) who knew five examples; at that time he was unaware of this rather longer pin from Deal.

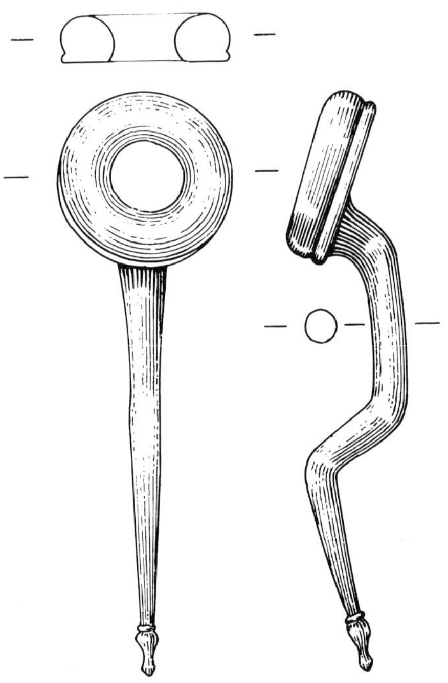

Figure 45. Bronze pin. (Full size)

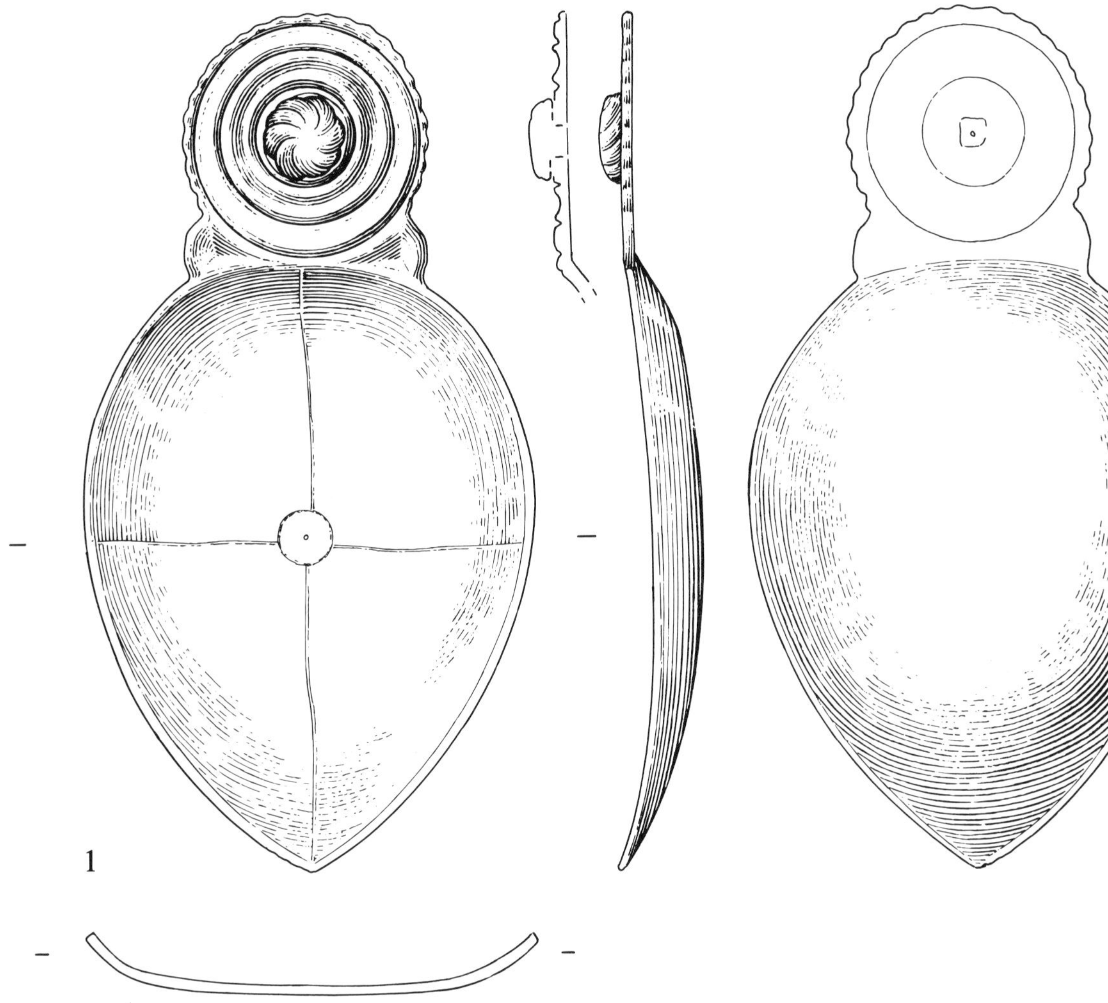

1

Figure 46. Bronze spoon. (Full size)

The moulded finial may be compared with pins from Cold Kitchen Hill (ibid. fig. 5, no. 2) and Danebury (Cunliffe and Poole 1991, fig. 7.6, no. 1.119), and the pin on a penannular brooch from Huntow (Stead 1979, fig. 26, 9). An iron involuted pin from Wetwang Slack (Dent 1982, 444–5, fig. 6, 145) was buried subsequent to a grave with a long involuted brooch, and that is the nearest approach to dating for the type (?second century BC). If the Deal pin did come from a burial then it is more likely to have been an inhumation than a cremation; ring-headed and involuted pins are unknown from cremations.

2. Grave 123 (e) (fig. 60, no. 7). Iron fragment, L 24mm, apparently from a ring-headed pin. In shape it could be interpreted as part of an involuted brooch, but the diameter of the ring is too great.

Iron ring-headed pins were found in two Iron Age graves in Yorkshire, Burial 64 at Rudston and Burial 286 at Wetwang Slack (Stead 1991a, 91–2; Dent 1982, fig. 6, 286b). The Deal pin was associated with an iron brooch, perhaps La Tène III.

3. Spoons (figs 46 and 47)

A pair of bronze spoons from Grave X2:

1. (D57) (fig. 46) L 114. The handle is circular and its junction with the bowl is strengthened with rounded 'gussets'. On the front it has a series of deep concentric grooves, and the edge is notched; at the centre is a domed whirl, presumably solid, made separately and riveted to the handle; its shank on the back is almost square in plan, 3.5mm across. There are two slight concentric grooves on the back, and a central dot on the end of the rivet. The heart-shaped bowl has slight bordering grooves front and back; its concave surface is crudely quartered and has a

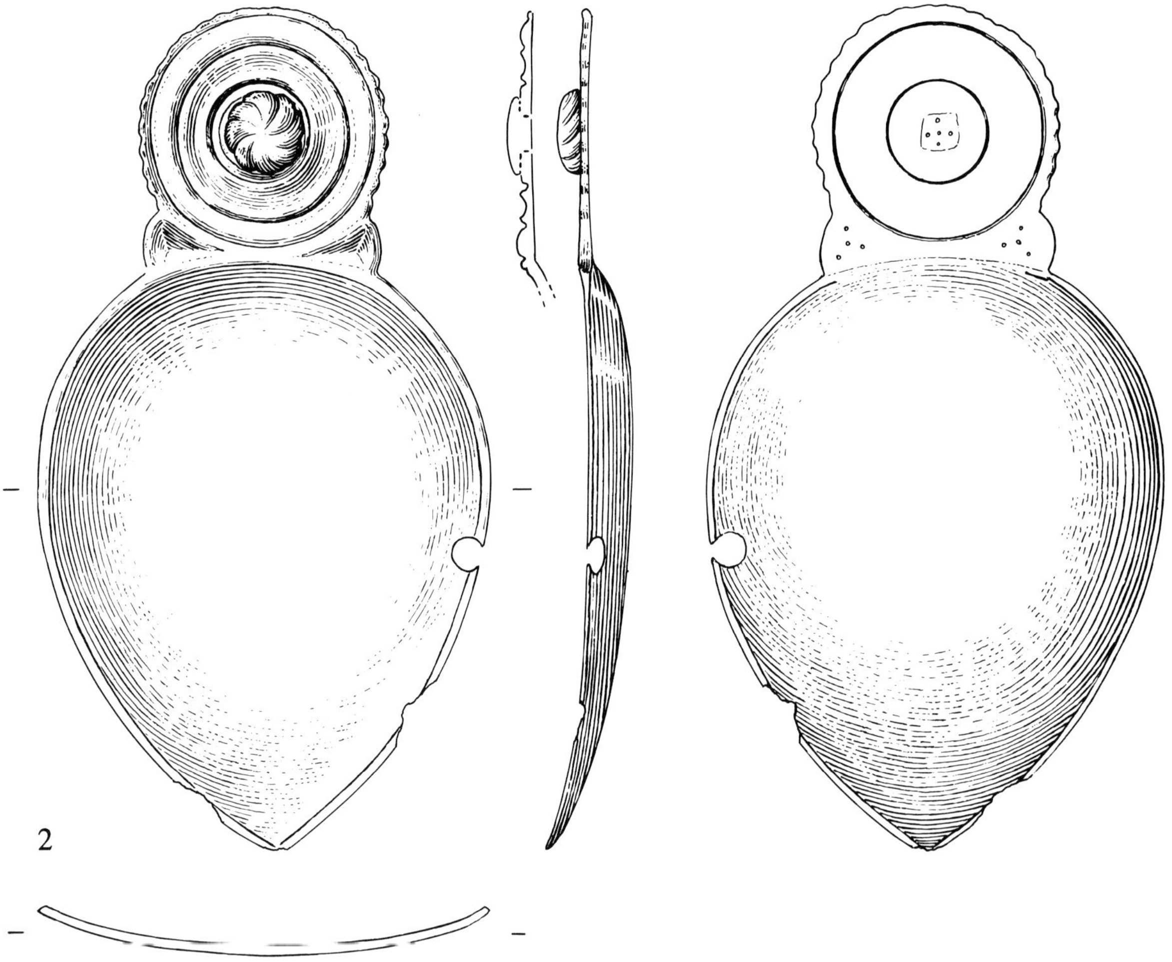

Figure 47. Bronze spoon. (Full size)

circle and dot approximately (not accurately) central to the crossing of the quartering lines. Although the metal is quite thick (slightly more than 1mm) it may have been worked from a sheet rather than cast. Certainly there are tool marks in the grooves front and back, and if it had been cast there would have been no need for a separate riveted whirl.

2. (D57) (fig. 47) L 111.5mm. Similar, but in slightly better condition; the tool marks in the grooves are clearer, especially on the back. The back of the handle has some additional dots: four more, arranged cross-wise on the end of the rivet, and a group of four on the back of each 'gusset'. Apart from bordering grooves the bowl is undecorated; a circular perforation, 4.5mm in diameter, clips the edge.
Woodruff 1904, 11–12, pl. IV, 1; Craw 1924, fig. 4, nos. 6 and 7.

The Deal spoons belong to a type of Iron Age artefact remarkable on two scores: (1) its function is unknown, and (2) its corpus (twenty-three examples) has not increased in recent years. The discovery of a pair in a grave at Burnmouth, near Berwick, in 1923, prompted J. H. Craw to publish an admirable survey of the type including a tabulation and a complete set of sketches drawn to a standard scale (Craw 1924). Only two spoons have been published subsequently, one from Andover (Smith 1933) and the other from Ireland (J. Raftery 1951, 196, fig. 231; cf. B. Raftery 1983, no. 826).

The Burnmouth spoons were found with an inhumation orientated northeast/southwest (as Deal) on its right side with the legs slightly flexed and the arms bent so that the hands were in front of the chest. Between the hands and the face were the two spoons, an iron knife and some bones of a young pig. Pairs of spoons from Weston, Avon, Penbryn, Dyfed and Llanfair, Clwyd, were found together and could conceivably have been with burials whose bones had not survived or were not recognised; but the spoons from Crosby Ravensworth, Cumbria, are unlikely to have been in a grave – they were found 6 or 7m apart in boggy ground near a spring (Way 1869, 64). Two pairs from Ireland are also unlikely to have been with burials because Iron Age burials are so rare in Ireland (B. Raftery 1981). Of the five single finds, two are from London, two from Ireland and the fifth from Andover.

The only comparable artefacts on the continent were found by Dr Baffet with a burial at Pogny, Marne, and published by Déchelette (1914, 1275–7, fig. 552 – taken from drawings provided by the excavator). There are more details in Baffet's (1911) rather obscure report of a cemetery excavation – so obscure that the name of the site is omitted! (the name of the commune – Pogny – given by Déchelette is confirmed by Schmit 1928, 219, who records the lieudit as 'Le Grand-Mont'). Baffet (1911, 186) declared his intention to deal with this discovery in detail but nothing more was published. However, on 16 February 1910 he read a paper on the subject (again without naming the site) to a meeting of the Société d'Agriculture, Commerce, Sciences et Arts de la Marne and the manuscript survives: M. J.-P. Ravaux, Conservateur of the Museums at Châlons-sur-Marne very kindly provided a photocopy and additional information as well as permitting the study of objects in his care. In his 1911 publication Baffet was particularly interested in the fillings of the graves, which had a layer of 'terre noire' covering the skeletons, then clean chalk in the upper filling. The twelve graves he excavated were surprisingly long and wide: up to 2.96m long (average 2.48m) and 1.5m wide (average 1.22m). Most were orientated north/south (or NNW/SSE) but two were south/north. The spoons were found in Burial 12, an extended inhumation orientated SE/NW, 2.6m long, 1.5m wide and 1.15m deep. The skeleton was that of a woman 40 to 50 years old. The two spoons were on the right humerus, with a bronze bowl inverted over them and a bronze ring nearby. Photographs of the bowl and one of the spoons were illustrated by Baffet (1911, pl. 8) and there is a drawing of the bowl with his manuscript. The bowl and one of the spoons are now in the Musée municipal at Châlons-sur-Marne (registration nos. 922.2.246 and 244) where they were examined by Valery Rigby: the bowl is 130mm in diameter and 35mm deep; the spoon is 90mm long and 54mm wide. The second spoon (decorated, Déchelette 1914, fig. 552, no. 2) was lost when Dr Baffet's collection was looted by the Germans in September 1914, eight years before the remains of the Baffet Collection were acquired by the municipal museum. The lost spoon was decorated with a cross and a central circle: Déchelette (ibid. 1275) calls the circle an 'orifice' but on the analogy of British and Irish examples an engraved ring is more likely. However, Baffet's manuscript leaves no doubt: 'en son centre un orifice circulaire volontairement fait et livrant passage à un grain de plomb no. 4' – i.e. a deliberate perforation through which a piece of no. 4 lead shot could pass (no. 4 measures 3.05mm in diameter, and no. 3, which presumably would not pass through, is 3.25mm). Baffet's published conclusion (1911, 186), that the grave-goods from this cemetery were La Tène III, is presumably a misprint because all the illustrated artefacts (including seven brooches) are La Tène II and that is the date he gives in the manuscript (cf. also Kruta 1985, 29–35).

The Pogny spoons were in a cemetery with La Tène II finds, and those from Deal were with a skeleton from a site that produced La Tène II and La Tène III inhumations. Others have to be dated on typological grounds (cf. Spratling 1972, 244–6; Raftery 1984, 264–7) and recent research has made little advance on Franks' conclusions (in Kemble 1863, 184); he grouped them with his Late Celtic antiquities dated from the second century BC to the first century AD.

Typically the spoons have decorated handles and one of each pair has a plain bowl with a perforation at or near the edge (always the same side, to the left of the handle), whilst the bowl of the other is marked with a cross (and sometimes a central circle). Only the French spoons differ because their handles are not decorated, the plain spoon is not perforated, and the spoon with the cross has a central hole. One of the Irish examples has a 'jagged hole ... likely to be accidental' (Raftery 1983, no. 826) – but it occurs where a deliberate perforation would be expected: if the hole is entirely accidental then this spoon, too, is exceptional.

The three recorded grave-groups provide little clue to the function of the spoons, though their deposition in graves may suggest that they were personal possessions rather than ritual objects for religious ceremonies (nineteenth-century discussions of possible religious functions are summarised in Way 1869, 78–83). Woodruff (1904, 12) thought that they might have been used for fine powder, whose outflow could have been regulated by the perforation; Dèchelette (1914, 1277) wondered if they could have been used for make-up; Craw (1924, 146, no. 2) recorded an experiment showing that oil (but not water) would flow through such a small perforation. Spratling (1972, 247) noting the consistent position of the perforation (first observed by Barnwell 1862, 212), suggested that the spoons had been intended for right-handed people, and speculated that the contents of the perforated spoons might have been poured into those marked with a cross. Unfortunately Craw's conclusion (1924, 146) cannot be bettered: 'further discoveries must be awaited to solve the mystery'.

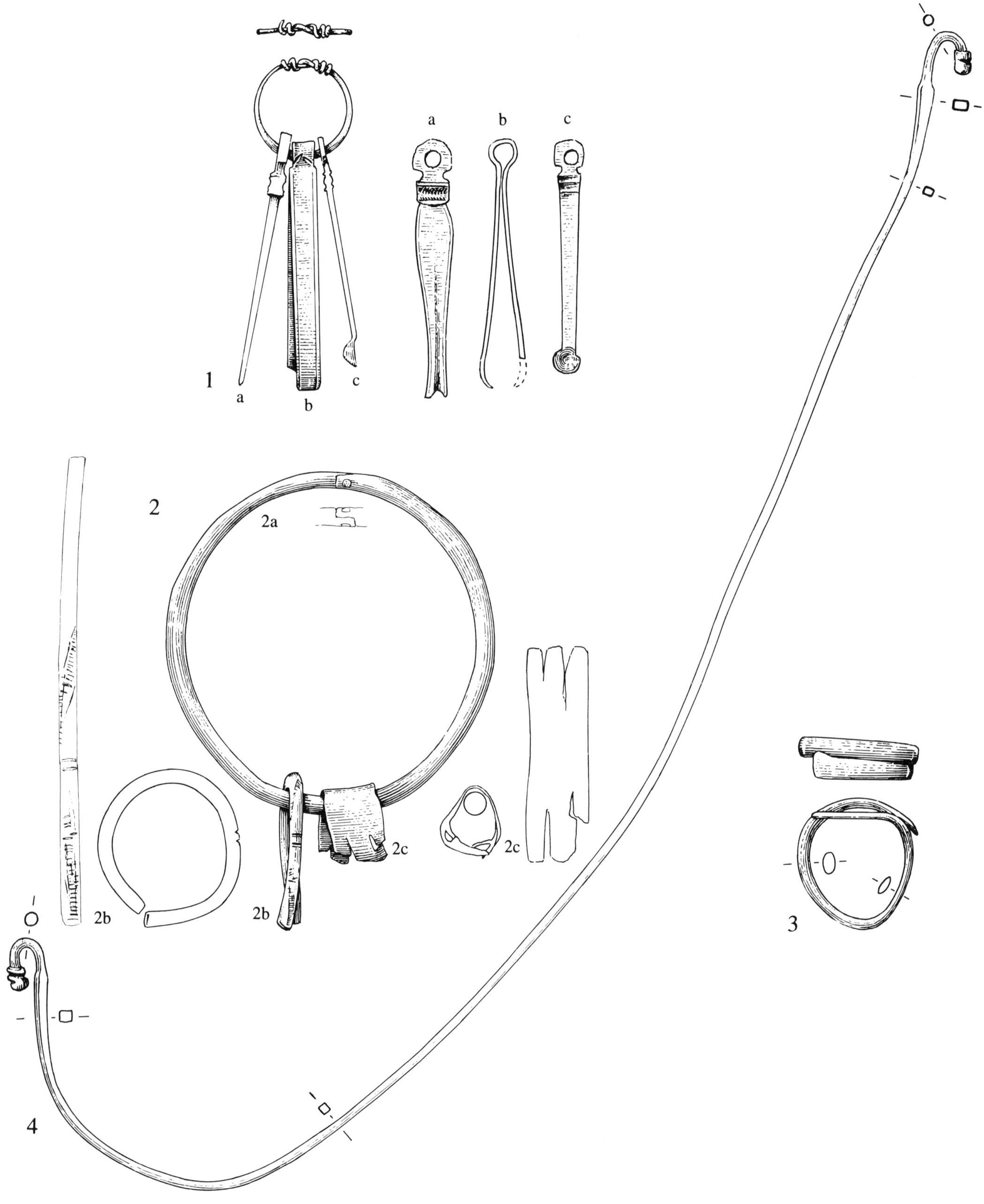

Figure 48. Bronze objects: 1. toilet set; 2. bracelet with suspended rings; 3. finger-ring; 4. handle. (Full size)

4. Other bronze objects

I. TOILET SET

Grave X11. (fig. 48, 1; D55) Three toilet items suspended on a single wire ring with wrapped terminals. Ear-scoop, L 44mm; tweezers, L 46mm, with very slight grooves down the sides and a marked shoulder at the top of the blades; nail cleaner, L 48mm, with elongated tapering groove from the fork on one side only, and 'walked scorper' ornament on both sides of the quite deep collar. Bushe-Fox 1925, 19, pl. iv, no. 3; Birchall 1965, 305, fig. 12, no. 101.

It seems to be the earliest complete bronze toilet set from Britain, though there were two broken items in the much earlier Queen's Barrow at Arras (Stead 1979, 84). At King Harry Lane a single pair of bronze tweezers came from a grave marginally later than Deal X11, and there were iron toilet instruments from four others (Stead and Rigby 1989, 104); bronze toilet instruments do not occur at Baldock before the Roman conquest (Stead and Rigby 1986, 124, fig. 51p, and 130). On the continent there are complete bronze sets (riveted, not on rings) about a century earlier than the Deal example from Manching (van Endert 1991, 60, 126, pl.16, no. 292) and the Basel-Gasfabrik site (Furger-Gunti and Berger 1980, pl. 12, no. 264) but most Iron Age toilet instruments seem to have been made of iron (e.g. Rozoy 1987, 291–4) and the ear-scoop is very rare. A complete set in iron (with bronze suspension rings) from a grave at Aussonce, Ardennes, cannot be dated other than to the La Tène period in general (Déchelette 1914, fig. 548, no. 1; Logeart 1931, 30–32).

II. BRACELET AND RINGS

1. Grave 121 (fig. 48, 2) Bronze bracelet (a), with two bronze rings (b and c) suspended from it. Found on the left forearm of a young adult.

(a) The bracelet, diam. 61–3mm, is quite crudely shaped from a solid rod with a lap-joint secured by a rivet.

(b) The larger ring, diam. 27–8mm, is penannular and crudely decorated with fine grooves – two diagonal bands of decoration separated by two cross-grooves on the outside only. One end of this ring is original – the end adjoining the decoration – but the other has been broken in antiquity. Perhaps it was originally a bracelet (but a thin one); the overall scheme of decoration resembles that on a bracelet from Burton Fleming (Stead 1991a, fig. 117, no. 2).

(c) The smaller ring, diam. *c.* 12–14mm, is a broad penannular strip with split ends – one end split into three roughly equal lengths and the other into three irregular lengths.

2. Grave 44 (fig. 48, 3) Bronze finger-ring, crudely shaped, diam. *c.* 22–4mm, flat with overlapping terminals. Found amongst the finger bones of a man.

Rings with overlapping terminals, sometimes spiralled, are quite common in the British Iron Age (Bulleid and Gray 1911, 209–16; Wheeler 1943, 266–7) but only rarely have they been recorded on skeletons. Some were certainly used as toe-rings, e.g. Burial 49 (P2) in the Maiden Castle War Cemetery (on the big toe of the right foot of a man, ibid. 278, 352 and pl. lvi, b); and two from Yorkshire burials (one on the left foot of a man and the other on the right foot of a woman, Stead 1991a, Burials GS7 and R183). A bronze example with a skeleton at Garton Slack is described as a finger-ring (Dent 1983, 11 and 12, fig. 8J, Burial 14), and one of iron in a grave at Trethellan Farm, Newquay, may also have been worn on a finger (Nowakowski 1991, 226, fig. 84, no. 204), but a bronze ring from a multiple grave at Harlyn Bay was discovered 'amongst teeth and lumbar vertebrae' (Bullen 1912, 53, 95 and pl. 18, fig. 4; Whimster 1977, 75, 85 – Grave 55, and fig. 30, no. 10).

III. DISTORTED HANDLE

Grave 26 (fig. 48, 4) Distorted and broken length of bronze wire, L *c.* 325mm (*c.* 255mm + 36mm + 34mm). Its body is squared in section, 1.8×1.8 mm, expanding slightly and then contracting to a circular section just before the terminal. Each terminal is curved back and neatly knobbed.

The identification of this distorted artefact is not obvious. It could have been a torque, but it is very small, reverted terminals are unusual on Iron Age torques, simple bronze wire torques are extremely rare in England, and it was not on the neck but behind the back of the skeleton (a young adult, possibly male). A vaguely comparable item from Manching was identified as a distorted spiral bracelet (van Endert 1991, 114, pl. 3, no. 26), but it does not have reverted terminals and the section of its body is round, not square. It seems more likely that the Deal object had been a handle: this would explain the reverted terminals (whose knobs can also be matched on handles), and the square section that becomes circular near the ends (e.g. examples from Manching, Jacobi 1974, pl. 36, and van Endert 1991, pl. 24). There was no other metalwork in the Deal grave, so it cannot have been the handle of a metal vessel, or from a wooden vessel with metal fittings (and there is no wear, so it has not constantly rubbed on a metal attachment); but it is sufficiently delicate to have been the handle of a leather or cloth bag, and that explanation would be consistent with its position in the grave. But this Deal artefact is not a distinctive Iron Age piece, and there is

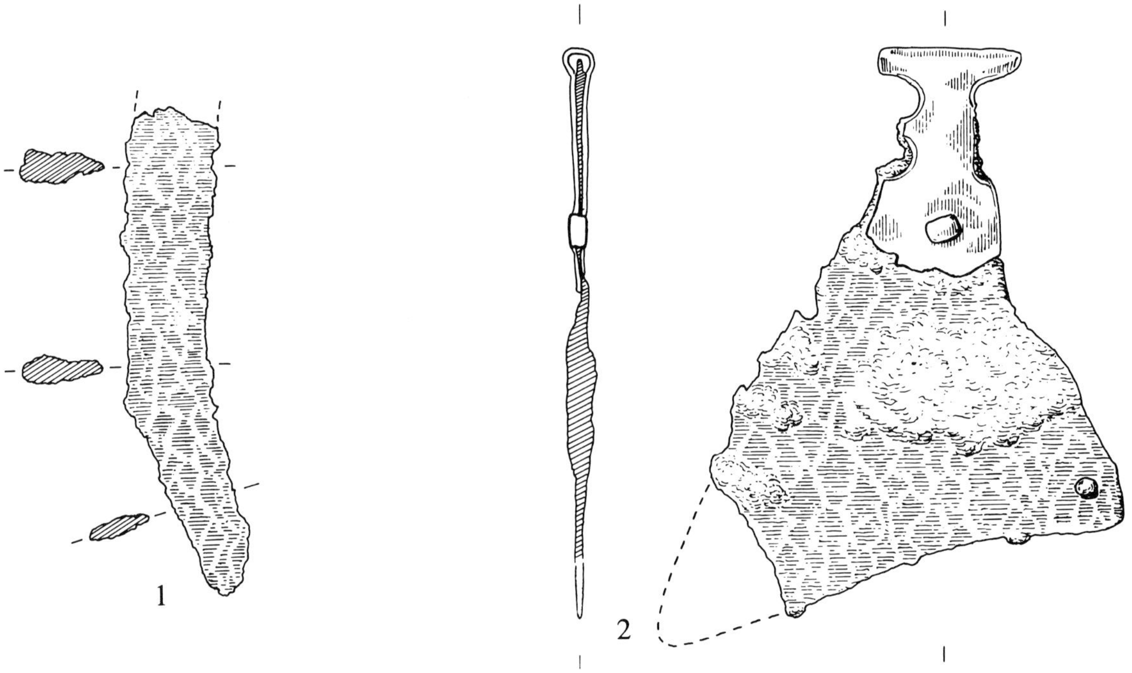

Figure 49. Iron objects: 1. blade of a knife; 2. triangular knife with bronze handle. (Scale 2/3)

doubt about the dating of some of the graves in the Central Cemetery.

Perhaps attention should be drawn to a slightly different length of bronze that might have served a similar purpose, with an Iron Age inhumation at Whitcombe, Dorset (Burial 9, Aitken and Aitken 1990, 73, fig. 10, no. 9, found between the right forearm and the leg, pl. 10).

5. *Other iron objects*

I. KNIFE

Grave 110 (fig. 49, 1) The blade only, lacking the handle or tang, L now 96mm. The back of the blade is initially flat, then sharply angled to the point; the cutting edge is slightly concave. Well-preserved mineral replaced textile on one side only at the tip.

Ralph Jackson identified it as a Roman knife of Manning's (1985) type 7 (lacking the plate-tang and loop-end); subsequently bone from this grave was submitted for carbon-14 dating which confirmed the Roman date.

II. TRIANGULAR BLADE

Context X3 (fig. 49, 2; D129) L 115mm, lacking one corner. The handle (L 47mm) has been cut from sheet bronze, roughly shaped, folded over one corner and secured with a single crude bronze rivet. A considerable amount of mineral replaced wood on the back (as illustrated) of the blade. Woodruff 1904, 16, no. 21, and pl. I (a general photograph of Roman cremation pots), back row, right; Stead 1967, 38, fig. 23, no. 3.

Triangular knives are known from Iron Age and early Roman cremations in England and on the continent. They first occur about the middle of the first century BC, and there are six in the King Harry Lane cemetery (Stead and Rigby 1989, 104–5, with discussion of the type). The Deal example may be Roman rather than Iron Age and certainly the other finds from Context X3 are Roman. Triangular blades are usually regarded as either razor-knives or the tools of a craftsman or cook, but the only clue provided by their contexts is that they are found in men's graves. Boon (1991, 28) is confident that they were razors, and emphasises that their handles 'are really only terminals, and not suited to the application of force, pressure, or leverage'.

III. JOINER'S DOGS (fig. 60)

Grave 123. Five iron dogs, four grouped at the foot of the grave and the fifth about 1.25m away, near the skull. Their arms had been driven into wood, whose traces had survived in the corrosion products of the iron: the grain was aligned (more or less) with the arms, apart from no. 1 where the grain was across the arms.

(1) (= a, as excavated) Lacking the end of one arm, L 82mm; complete arm curved (L 42mm), broken arm now L 40mm. Cross grain at the edge of one arm and inside the other.

(2) (= b) Lacking the end of one arm, L 80mm; arms L 46 and 37mm (broken). Grain vertical on both arms

(only slight traces on broken arm).

(3) (= c) Lacking one arm, L 65mm, the surviving arm L 32mm. Grain at a slight angle along the complete arm, and at the top, inside, of the broken arm.

(4) (= h) L 62mm, arms L 40mm. Grain at a slight angle on both arms (only slight traces on one arm). Recorded with (h) was a separate length of clamp-arm, or nail, L 27mm, with vertical grain.

(5) (= g and f) Two joining pieces, L 73mm, one arm complete (L 49mm) the other (= f) broken (L now 40mm). Grain at a slight angle along the complete arm. The two pieces were found 0.1m apart, (g) at the end of the grave and (f) by the side of the skull.

Five wood samples taken from the inner surfaces of the five joiner's dogs were examined by Caroline Cartwright, Department of Scientific Research, British Museum, who reports: 'The wood samples were thin-sectioned in transverse, radial and tangental planes. Consolidant obscured much of the anatomical detail but sufficient diagnostic features were present to enable these samples to be identified as Tilia sp (Lime).'

Three of the pieces were found amongst the foot bones (nos 1, 2 and 4), a fourth (3) was to the side of the feet, and the fifth (5) in two pieces by the skull. They had been used to join two or more substantial pieces of wood, but the obvious explanation, a wooden coffin, is precluded by the shape of the very short grave in which the skull and feet were resting on the ends and well above the floor. Perhaps there had been a wooden board over the corpse, but why four dogs were needed at one end and only one at the other is a mystery.

The joiner's dog is a common Roman type (Manning 1985, 131) occasionally found on British Iron Age sites (e.g. Danebury, Cunliffe 1984, 370, fig. 7.22, nos 2.156 and 7, Cunliffe and Poole 1991, 353, fig. 7.24, nos 2.332–7; Meare, Gray and Bulleid 1953, 241, nos I 121 and 123) and frequent at Manching (Jacobi 1974, 235–6). Apart from Deal, no British Iron Age inhumation has included joiner's dogs, but a fragment was found with a cremation at King Harry Lane (Burial 457, Stead and Rigby 1989, 107, fig. 179) and there are several from French Iron Age inhumations (e.g. Connantre, Marne, Morel 1898, 142, pl. 31, fig. 8; Châtenay-sur-Seine, Seine-et-Marne, inhumation 3, Bontillot et al. 1975, 445–6).

The Coin

An Iron Age coin (pl. XI) was discovered on the base of Grave 30 in a position which indicates that it had been deliberately buried with the occupant, a probable female aged 20 to 25. Upon cleaning, the coin was found to be a bronze issue of King Eppillus who apparently held power in Kent during the first decade of the first century AD. Details of the coin have been included in the Celtic Coin Index held at Oxford and it has been previously noted in the Coin Register of the *Brit Numismatic J*, 61, 1991, no. 47.

Description:

Reign:	Eppillus
Date:	*c.* AD1–10
Obverse:	Bull charging right, EPPIL above, F below
Reverse:	Eagle standing left with head right and wings spread; pellet-in-ring ornaments in field.
References:	Van Arsdell 1989, VA 451; Mack 1975, M 310
Diameter:	14–15mm.
Weight:	2.60g.
Die Axis:	180°
Notes:	Coin in very good condition although struck off-centre.

The generally unworn condition of this coin suggests that it did not circulate for any great length of time: the writer has seen several other examples of this type recently, found by metal detectorists in Kent but only one has been in as good a state of preservation. The apparent wear on the eagle's feet on the reverse is probably due to mis-striking which resulted in both sides being struck off-centre. As a consequence, the design is incomplete although other examples enable the complete form to be reconstructed.

The obverse is markedly off-centre with only 75% of the design on the flan. Other examples show the letters COF below the bull (Commii filius, i.e. son of Commius). A noticeable feature of the design is that the 'E' and the first 'P' of EPPIL are separated by the bull's tail: this has been the case with most other examples seen. (A different obverse die exists on which the tail curves round behind the bull and does not pass through the legend). This side of the coin has a beaded border. The design is derived from the reverse of a denarius of Augustus dateable to *c.* 14BC – *c.* 9BC (Augustus *RIC* 327, 334 or 338).

The reverse bears an eagle which also appears on another bronze coin of Eppillus (Van Arsdell 1989, VA450; Mack 1975, M309) to which it is die-linked, and is not dissimilar to that on a bronze coin minted by Dubnovellaunus-in-Kent a few years earlier (Van Arsdell 1989, VA180; Mack 1975, M289). The inspiration for this design almost certainly came from a foreign coin, probably from the Mediterranean area. The most likely prototype is a quadrans of Augustus, dateable to *c.* 11BC–*c.* 3BC (Augustus *RIC* 227), the reverse of which shows an almost identical eagle standing right with head left. If this is indeed the prototype it is quite possible that the Eppillus dies were direct copies of the Roman coin, thus producing a mirror image on the Eppillus coins themselves. The pellet-in-ring motifs on either side of the eagle and attached to its tail are commonly found on Iron Age coins in Britain and Gaul and occasionally appear in larger numbers (cf. Van Arsdell 1989, VA171, of Dubnovellaunus-in-Kent, and Scheers 1983, Series 82–4, of the Ambiani tribe of northeast Gaul).

One other possibility for the reverse prototype should, however, not be totally discounted. A recent find from near Deal of an early third-century BC bronze coin from Sicily (*Corpus Nummorum Siculorum*, Mamertini 15) bearing a very similar eagle reverse is worthy of note. Several other late fourth-century BC and early third-century BC coins of Sicilian or Siculo-Punic origin have been found by metal detectorists in east Kent, these being primarily of the *Corpus Nummorum Siculorum*, Kartago 20 series, showing a horse and palm-tree reverse. The presence of two of these coins at Archer's Low Farm, Sandwich (Holman forthcoming), where in excess of 50 Iron Age coins (including a higher than usual percentage of Gaulish types) have been found in addition to imported Terra Nigra and Terra Rubra, suggests that they may have entered Britain through trade with Gaul in the late Iron Age. Being of similar module, they could have circulated freely with the native coinage and the Gaulish imports. Certainly, they are not primary losses as no other finds of the same date as these Sicilian coins (*c.* 320BC) are present at Archer's Low or on other sites where they have been found. Clearly, the late Iron Age 'import through trade' theory is a possible explanation for the appearance of at least some of these coins in Britain, and their presence shows the possibility of Celtic coins being descended from prototypes other than Roman. A securely stratified context for one of these coins would be most welcome.

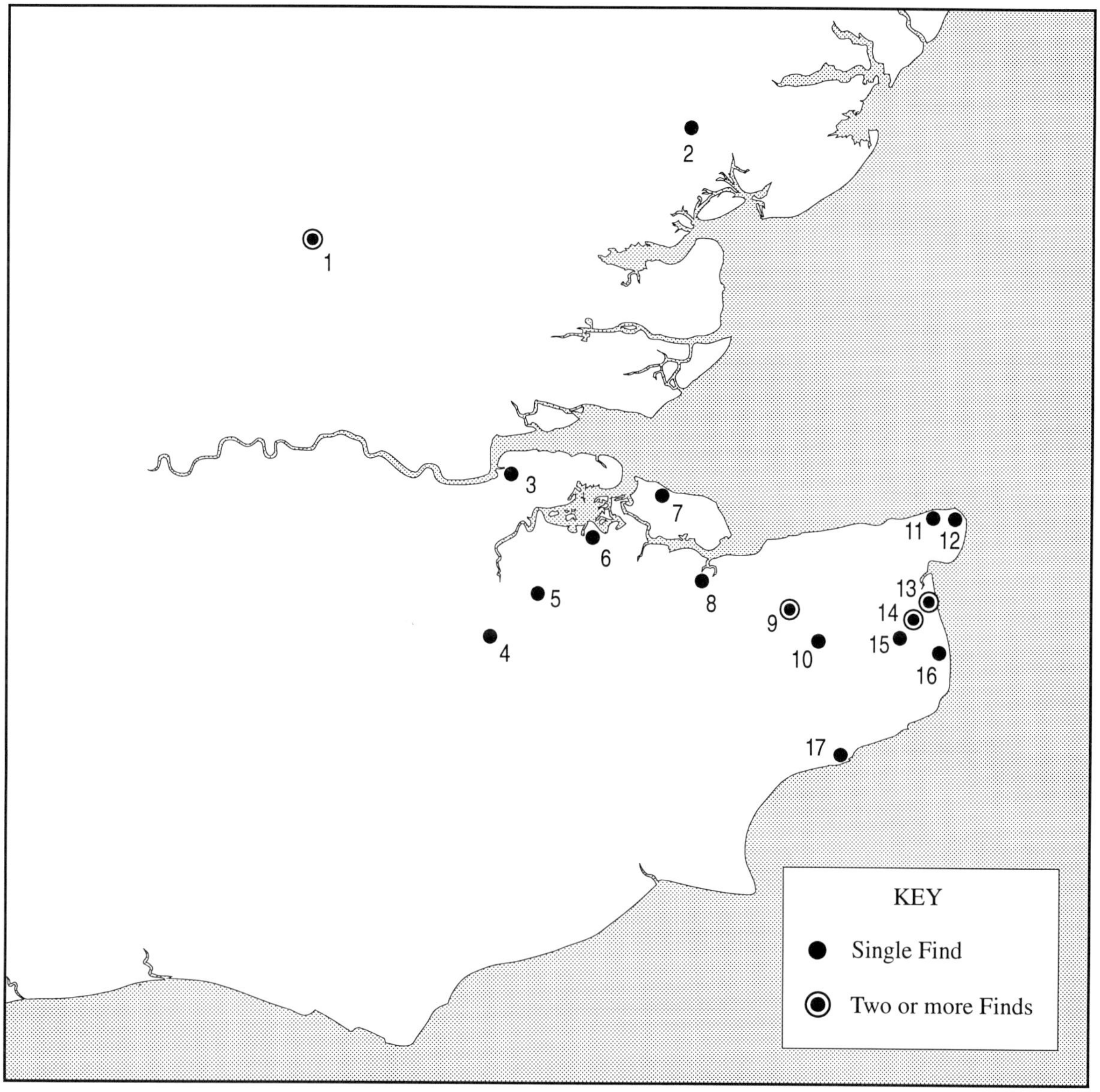

Figure 50. Distribution of bronze coins of Eppillus (VA 451; M 310) in Kent and Essex: 1. Harlow; 2. Colchester; 3. Cliffe; 4. Teston; 5. Boxley; 6. Birdcage Marsh, Lower Halstow; 7. Isle of Sheppey; 8. Faversham; 9. Canterbury; 10. Bishopsbourne; 11. Margate; 12. Broadstairs; 13. Archer's Low, Sandwich; 14. Worth; 15. Ham; 16. Deal; 17. Folkestone.

The distribution of this type of Eppillus coin (Van Arsdell 1989, VA451) is spread across the whole of north and east Kent, with in addition to the Deal coin, examples known from Birdcage Marsh at Lower Halstow, Bishopsbourne, Boxley, Broadstairs, Canterbury (two), Cliffe, Faversham, Folkestone, Ham (Northbourne), the Isle of Sheppey, Margate, Sandwich (Archer's Low, two), Teston and Worth (seven). Examples are also known from Colchester and the Harlow Temple (three) in Essex. More than 30 examples have now been recorded, of which 27 are provenanced (see fig. 50) and several unprovenanced to Kent and Essex. It presently appears to be the commonest type within Eppillus' Kentish series. At least three obverse and two reverse dies are known for this type which is a greater number than has so far been noted for any other type in his Kentish series. Current recording of metal-detector finds may well reveal more examples.

The Human Skeletons

Introduction

Trevor Anderson's detailed report has been placed at Canterbury Archaeological Trust and with the archive in the British Museum and Dover Museum:

Copies of the report may be purchased on request from Trevor Anderson, Canterbury Archaeological Trust Ltd, 92a Broad Street, Canterbury, Kent, CT1 2LU. The tables, summary and the account of the skeleton in Grave 112 are published here in full, together with extracts dealing with the palaeopathology and oral health. For each skeleton the sex, age and code for completeness/condition is included in the inventory of graves and grave-goods, pp. 159–78.

Summary

Note: Tables 11–34 will be found on pp 125–44.

A small group (no. 38) of carefully excavated Iron Age inhumations from St Richard's Road, Deal, Kent were subjected to osteological examination. The rarity of inhumations dated to this period, and the lack of published detailed human bone reports, means that this sample is of great importance for furthering our meagre knowledge of Iron Age skeletal biology. The condition of the bones is rather poor, with the majority of the burials being incomplete and fragmentary; only three skeletons are solid and complete (Table 11). A high percentage of the population failed to reach adulthood (31.6%). In the adult material, sexual dimorphism was not strongly expressed, with several cases of contradictory pelvic and cranial morphology. No children under one year were recovered and the greatest sub-adult mortality (50%) occurred in the juvenile age group (Tables 12 and 13).

Two cemeteries were excavated, the main South-West Cemetery contained 24 skeletons and in the smaller, Central Cemetery 12 Iron Age or early Romano-British burials were recognised. This report also includes two isolated skeletons (SK3 and 112). The Iron Age burials in the Central Cemetery were slightly better preserved, except for being disturbed by later Anglo-Saxon inhumations. In both cemetery samples males and females are equally represented and life expectancy was similar for both sexes. However, in the Central Cemetery there were no children and only two juveniles.

The sample was too small to assess if there was a significant difference in stature between the two cemeteries. However, the mean height of the Deal community is slightly taller than that obtained from most other Iron Age settlements (Tables 14 and 15). Male stature has hardly altered from the Roman period to the later nineteenth century (Kunitz, 1987). Increase in mean stature has mainly occurred during the last 50 years. Consequently, the height of the Deal community is similar to later Victorian mean stature.

Measurement of the crania and calculated indices suggest that the long-headed Deal crania are perhaps morphologically closer to the Yorkshire than the Maiden Castle material (Tables 16–22). The latter are, on average, less long-headed and have a lower vault than found at Yorkshire and at Deal. The areas in which the Deal and Maiden Castle crania display similarities, mainly the facial bones, are thought to be more influenced by external, environmental factors.

Post-cranial metrics and calculated indices have examined the shape of the upper arm and the leg bones (Tables 23–8). There was no evidence that long bone flattening was due to nutritional disorder. Indeed, flattening of the femur (platymeria) appeared to be inversely related to flattening of the tibia (platycnemia). Platycnemia appears to be related to increased antero-posterior bending strain, such as occurs when walking over rough terrain, or when squatting. The degree of tibial flattening is similar in the Deal, Yorkshire and Wetwang Slack samples. In the Deal material, there does appear to be a direct relationship between squatting facets and platycnemia (Table 29).

Cranial and post cranial non-metrics are traditionally utilised as a possible method of separating different population groups (Tables 30 and 31). Unfortunately, their method of inheritance is poorly understood. It appears that many may be influenced by external, environmental factors and consequently, their value for assessing biological distance must be questioned.

The uncertainties of non-metric inheritance patterns coupled with the small sample size at Deal meant that no clear familial groupings could be ascertained. It is necessary to examine the distribution of the different traits in each skeleton since apparently unrelated variants are aetiologically similar. Certain traits, the humeral septal aperture and those of the femoral neck and squatting facets, are environmentally influenced and are of limited value in assessing genetic relationships.

Three rarely reported anatomical variants, absence of mental foramen, cubo-navicular bridging and os metastyloideum, were noted in the same individual (SK 31). It is possible that these congenital anomalies are, in part, related to inbreeding in a small community.

When compared to other Iron Age sites, the Deal material appears relatively healthy, or more precisely, there is little evidence of bone disease in our sample. The most frequently encountered disease process, joint degeneration, is not severe and less than half the available spines displayed degenerative joint disease (DJD). There was no evidence of direct violence or of weapon injury and accidental trauma was uncommon. There was no definite evidence of infection and the only sign of possible iron deficiency was a single orbital lesion. An example of

Scheuermann's disease was identified in a juvenile male (SK 26) which is only the second published British archaeological example.

One definite finding is that disease was much less common in the main South-West Cemetery, than in the central burial ground. In the main cemetery, pathology was limited to joint degeneration and spondylolysis, whereas in the central area traumatic lesions, metabolic disease (iron deficiency), marked spinal degeneration, Scheuermann's disease and possible infection and cystic cavitation were encountered. This may be partially explained by the higher percentage of children (who do not normally present with osseous pathology) and the poorer preservation of the adult bones in the South-West Cemetery.

However it does appear that those buried in the central area were subject to greater stress and harder physical activity. The majority of squatting facets (80%) were found in the Central Cemetery. Also, the only enthesopathy, evidence of muscle strain, came from the central burial ground (SK 42). Thus, it appears that the central burials may have been of lower social status than the inhumations in the South-West Cemetery.

Only one case of multiple pathological involvement was noted. An adult male from the Central Cemetery (SK 44) suffered from 'arthritic' degeneration of the spine, compression fracture of a vertebra, spondylolysis (LV 4), and a possible naso-maxillary infection, as well as poor oral health. The picture painted is one of pain and suffering: difficulty in eating due to loss of many teeth and presence of painful sinuses, probably coupled with constant back pain and hunchback deformity.

Although bone pathology was infrequent at Deal, the standard of oral health was relatively low (Tables 32 and 33), with evidence of periodontal disease almost universal in the adult material. Caries and ante-mortem tooth loss are much more serious than at the Yorkshire sites (Table 34) and only the Beckford material display a similar low level of dental hygiene. The absence of refined carbohydrate in the diet would suggest that caries experience should be quite low. It is possible that the Deal community were eating nuts and gnawing bones which may have lead to fracture of tooth crowns and subsequent carious cavitation. Enamel hypoplasia was infrequent, suggesting a low level of childhood morbidity. Calculus was relatively infrequent, but it appears that several deposits had become detached after burial.

Grave 112

Archaeologically, it is of great interest, since it was buried with weapons (sword, scabbard, shield) and a bronze coronet was in situ, encircling the skull. It was an isolated burial, located in the north-west corner of the excavation. Although most of the skeleton is present nearly all the bones, including the skull, pelvis, spine, ribs and most of the long bones, are badly fragmented.

The bones are rather small and gracile, displaying certain feminine characteristics, but the available evidence from both pelvis and skull point to the remains being male. The dental evidence, the degree of suture closure as well as the morphology of the sacro-iliac articulation favour a young adult, aged *c.* 30–35 years old at death. Based on the length of the right fibula a stature estimate of 1.605m was obtained (Trotter and Gleser, 1958).

The fragmentary skull had been conserved by the British Museum and it was possible to calculate six cranial indices. Four of these (Cranial: 74.6; Height-Length: 75.8; Left Orbital 79.4 and Occipital Curve: 84.6) are similar to the indices generated from the later Iron Age population (Table 19). The nasal and foramen magnum indices, 54.9 and 93.9 respectively are much broader than the mean indices from the later Deal material. The aetiology of the latter index is poorly understood. Nasal morphology, however, appears to be related more to environmental, climatic conditions than genetic influence (Thomson and Buxton 1923).

The skull appears to have suffered a certain amount of post-mortem distortion and the accuracy of the nasal measurements may have been compromised. Even allowing for this, the nasal index is extremely broad. It has been argued that wider noses are related to warm moist conditions (Thomson and Buxton 1923). It is tempting to consider the possibility that the warrior had arrived from a warmer, but quite wet country. It must be stressed that no firm conclusions can be made from a single index, especially on a distorted skull.

Four post-cranial indices (brachic, meric, pilasteric and cnemic) could be calculated. The meric and cnemic indices were broadly similar to the overall figures from later Iron Age Deal (Table 26). The brachic index (83.6) suggests that the left humerus was less flattened than in our sample (the right index could not be calculated). The pilasteric index (R 108.7; L 116.0) shows that both femora, especially the left, were clearly flattened at their mid-shaft diameters. Modern-day femora are more flattened than those at Deal. As such, it is possible that the greater flattening in SK 112 is evidence of a less primitive and less strenuous life style.

Examination of the cranial non-metric variants showed that the skull presented with: large ossicles at the lambda, an unilateral frontal notch (right), bilateral absence of the mastoid foramen, absence of the left zygomatico-facial foramen (right unavailable for study), and bilateral patency of the posterior condylar canals. All of these traits were noted in the Deal material (Table 30). The large ossicles at the lambda, which are considered to represent a partially developed os inca, are worthy of further discussion. Only one other case (SK 54), presented with a large ossicle (53×48mm) in the (right) lambdoid suture. Os incae are an infrequent finding and contain a high genetic component (Hauser and de Stefano 1989, 102). Consequently, it is tempting to consider the possibility that SK 54, a ?rich male, buried next to his horse, may be a descendant of SK 112, the aristocratic warrior.

The fragmentary post-cranial skeleton was examined for non-metric variants. Out of twenty-nine traits, thirteen could be scored; however no variants were recorded as present. The left calcaneus (right incomplete) presented with a discontinuous facet morphology (type B). This is slightly less frequent than a continuous facet (type A: Table 31). However, no significance can be attributed to this finding.

The only evidence for osseous pathology was located on the spine, but interpretation is handicapped by the very fragmentary nature of the vertebrae. Most of the bones are present but consist of broken arches or fragmentary bodies. The involved bones are the two upper lumbar vertebrae. The first lumbar vertebra consists of two joining fragments: spinous process, right lamina and pedicle and right body fragment. The second lumbar vertebra consists of two separate fragments: the arch, with left superior facet pedicle and lamina absent and body fragment with left side and most of the caudal surface eroded.

On the right side both bones display exuberant osteophytic outgrowth which in life had fused the two bones. The bones are too damaged to assess if the left side was also involved. The body of the first lumbar vertebra is too fragmentary to diagnose; it consists of little more than the osteophytic outgrowth. The cranial aspect of the second lumbar vertebra is eroded post-mortem but it also displays pathological involvement (pl. XII). The central area displays an irregular, linear, roughened defect. It runs diagonally from the dorsal aspect to the centre of the body. A larger cavitation (18mm wide, 7mm deep) is present on the ventral aspect of the body (pl. XII, larger arrow). Its surface is roughened and markedly porotic. The broken osteophyte is also visible, in section, on the right side (smaller arrow).

A definite diagnosis is difficult in such fragmentary remains. However, the linear nature of the defect is suggestive of an old fracture. The larger cavitation with its smooth edges is not post-mortem and it may also be related to a healed traumatic incident, although an infective cavitation is a possibility (pl. XII, larger arrow). The extensive new bone growth rules out tuberculosis, in which overall bone quantity would be reduced, leading to pathological kyphosis or Pott's disease. The spine is not a common site for osteomyelitis, accounting for only 2% of all cases (Schmorl and Junghanns 1971, 389) and in many cases it affects the neural arch rather than the vertebral body (Ortner and Putschar 1985, 116).

It must be remembered that the pattern of infective lesions may have changed from prehistoric to modern times. However, on balance the favoured interpretation is a healed traumatic incident, with an infective process as a less likely diagnosis. There is no evidence that the lesion was the cause of death. The smooth-edged nature suggests that the defect occurred some time before death. The lack of vertebral bodies means that it is not possible to assess the degree of kyphosis that may have developed secondary to the vertebral cavitation.

A total of 18 teeth were available for examination. The standard of oral health was no worse than that found in the later Iron Age sample. There was no evidence of caries or hypoplasia on the teeth. Just under half the teeth displayed calculus, the majority of the deposits were minimal. One tooth, the maxillary left first molar presented with an apical abscess.

Anatomical Variants

In addition to the established non-metric traits, three rarer anatomical variants were noted in the Deal material. They occurred in the same skeleton, a tall (1.792m) adult male (SK 31).

Mental Foramen Absence

The absent foramen occurred on the left side, a normal, single foramen was present between the first molar and second premolar on the right side. The foramen transmits the inferior alveolar nerve (Williams and Warwick 1980, 1067) and complete absence is a rare finding (Hauser and De Stefano 1989, 230). In a sample of 1435 mandibles de Freitas et al. (1979) only found mental foramen absent in three cases; little is known about racial, sexual or side differences.

Os metastyloideum

In the normal hand, the third metacarpal is distinguished by its styloid process which, when viewed dorsally, projects proximally between the capitate and trapezoid bones. The styloid process is unique to man, it developed to protect the third metacarpal base from subluxation (Marzke and Marzke 1987) during the newly acquired human manual dexterity. In rare cases, the process may present as a separate ossicle, the os metastyloideum.

Examination of the left hand of SK 31 shows that the styloid process was not fused to the third metacarpal. Although the small os metastyloideum itself was not recovered, its original position can be ascertained from the articulated bones. When the bones are viewed from the dorsal aspect, a space is clearly present between the third metacarpal and the capitate (pl. XIII). The slightly roughened and porous nature of the metacarpal and capitate margins (pl. XIII) confirms the presence of an unfused ossicle, which at this location, must equate with an os metastyloideum.

In the right hand, the styloid process is fused to the third metacarpal. However, the proximal portion of the process displays a roughened and porous surface, evidence that the tip was unfused. The capitate shows a dorso-lateral bony overgrowth on its metacarpal articular surface. These alterations are superficially similar to joint degeneration; however, the normal joint is not affected. This lack of involvement, coupled with the evidence from the left hand, supports a diagnosis of proximal tip of styloid process fused to the capitate.

According to Prescher (1988) the os metastyloideum was first described in 1878 by Gruber. Examination of the literature shows that the variant has been rarely reported since then; Prescher (1988) discovered thirteen cases and added two of his own. In a detailed osteological study of 564 hands, 5.3% (no. 30) displayed evidence of os metastyloideum (Thomson 1893). It was shown that the os metastyloideum may remain as a separate ossicle (no. 9) or it may fuse to the capitate (no. 19), or less frequently fuse to the trapezoid (no. 2) (ibid.).

The true prevalence of os metastyloideum is probably under-represented in modern populations, since only the painful, symptomatic cases will be discovered. In clinical cases, os metastyloideum may be mistaken for fracture. Careful examination of dry bone material suggests that the variant may not be as infrequent as previously thought.

Cubo-Navicular Bridging

In the normal foot the cuboid and navicular are two separate bones. Occasionally, a small, smooth facet is present on the cuboid, which represents contact from the navicular (Williams & Warwick 1980, 413). In SK 31 the articulations are much larger, roughened and extremely porous. These enlarged articulations are atypical and suggest an anomalous articulation: it is evidence of attempted coalition, so-called bridging. Indeed, it is possible that the two bones were joined in life by fibrous tissue.

If two bones are completely joined the term coalition is used, which reflects the aetiology of the anomaly, i.e. failure of mesenchymal cavitation, rather than bony fusion (Calder and Calder 1977). Coalitions are largely genetic and there is clear evidence for a familial inheritance pattern (Anderson 1987, Appendix Q). Cubo-navicular coalitions are distinctly rare (Basu 1963; Cavallaro et al. 1978; Del Sel and Grand 1959; Waugh 1957). However, it must be pointed out that both talo-calcaneal and calcaneo-navicular coalitions can cause symptoms, whereas other coalitions, often sub-clinical, may be under-represented.

In addition, both cuneiform-metatarsal III articulations display a cystic cavitation on the plantar portion of the joint surface. The radiographic appearance is highly suggestive of arthritic degeneration. This is not a normal location for DJD in either modern or archaeological material. Indeed, it has been suggested that a cystic lesion at this joint may be a non-metric variant (Tenney 1991), rather than pathological degeneration.

In our specimen, we suggest that the cystic cavitation represents DJD, developing secondary to the anomalous cubo-navicular bridging. It is possible that the bridging has compromised the movement of the involved metatarsals and the resultant increased mobility of tarso-metatarsal joints is responsible for the anomalous degenerative changes. Based solely on dry bone evidence, it is uncertain if the condition was painful. Although, cubo-navicular coalitions can give rise to painful peroneal spastic flat feet (Waugh 1957) the contour of the arch in SK 31 appeared to be within the bounds of normality.

Examination of dry bones will permit all coalitions and bridges to be recognised. The fact that they are apparently genetically controlled suggests that they are of value in assessing familial relationships. In the Deal material, the case is of interest, but a single example is of no value in establishing familial grouping. As far as I am aware, these three rare anomalies, namely mental foramen absence, os metastyloideum and cubo-navicular bridging have not previously been found in the same individual, either in an archaeological skeleton or in a modern patient.

Palaeopathology

Congenital

No major congenital abnormalities were detected in the Deal material. However, two skeletons (SK 41, 124) displayed minor variations which are considered to be congenital in origin.

1 Congenital fusion (TV3–4)

In SK 41, an adult female, the third and fourth thoracic vertebrae are solidly fused. The vertebral bodies, articular processes, laminae and spinous processes are all fused, without loss of contour. The pedicles and transverse processes are normal. By visual inspection, the intervertebral disc space is practically nonexistent: the maximum height appears to be 0.5mm and it is only visible on the right superior aspect of the vertebrae. On radiographic examination, the disc space narrowing was confirmed and, in addition, the normal facets (zygapophyseal joints) were absent (pl. XIV).

The fusion of the bodies, without osteophytic outgrowths and absence of any visible disease process, argues in favour of a congenital causation, so-called blocked vertebrae. The radiographic appearance suggests that congenital fusion has occurred due to failure of normal articular joint development. It is possible that the lack of mobility in the upper thoracic spine predisposes this area to fusion. In SK 41 the fifth and sixth thoracic vertebrae display degenerative changes, enlargement and porosity of the articular surfaces. It is highly probable that the degeneration has occurred as a result of the congenital fusion. An identical example, also in the upper thoracic spine, has been identified as congenital in origin (Chandraraj 1987). Similar blocked vertebrae are known in an Iron Age skeleton from the Near East (Kunter 1976).

2 Lumbar Rib

In SK 124, an elderly adult, possibly female, the development of an additional rib could be ascertained. The rib itself was not recovered. However, a smooth costo-vertebral facet on the right side of the first lumbar vertebra confirmed its presence. The left side was damaged post-mortem, consequently it is not possible to decide if the manifestation was bilateral.

In modern clinical practice, cervical ribs are reported much more frequently than lumbar ribs. This is due to the fact that cervical ribs may compromise the brachial plexus, which results in loss of sensation in the lower arms and hands (Todd 1911). Lumbar ribs, however, being asymptomatic, are only recorded as incidental findings (Birmingham 1891; Decker 1915; Launay 1894; Shepherd 1881) and, as such, they are clearly underrepresented. Indeed, it has been suggested that lumbar ribs may be eight times more frequent than cervical (Lanier 1944).

Only by the careful examination of dry bone material will the true frequency of different costal anomalies be established. The fact that additional ribs are known to be familial (Donaldson 1909; Purves and Wedin 1950; Serck-Hanssen 1935) suggests that these, largely neglected, congenital variants may be of value for the assessment of biological groupings.

'Arthritic' Conditions

1 Primary Degenerative Joint Disease (DJD)

Based on the recognised classification (presence of eburnation or both pitting and deformation of the joint contour), there is very little evidence for primary DJD. The site of predilection is the mandible. Temporomandibular joint involvement occurs in an adult female (SK 47), an adult male (SK 44) and an elderly male (SK 108). Based on individual condyles, this represents a prevalence of 10.7% (3/28), or by individuals 17.6%. In the elderly male, the teeth were very heavily worn, with exposure of the pulp canals; the other male had lost thirteen teeth during life. The dentition of the only female involved was not heavily worn. In two cases the degeneration was unilateral, on the left side; and in SK 108 only the left condyle was available for study.

In modern material a prevalence of 8% has been recorded (Toller, 1973) and its occurrence is rare under 40 years of age (Öberg et al. 1971). Very few Iron Age sites have been studied, but analysis of the Maiden Castle material gave a figure of 14.8% (12/81) (Hodges 1991), which is quite similar to our sample. Much higher prevalences have been recorded in Anglo-Saxon and medieval samples (ibid.). It has been suggested that this is related to stringent living conditions (Griffin et al. 1979). In the Deal sample, although attrition is quite severe and a large number of teeth were lost during life (see below Oral Health), the prevalence of TMJ degeneration is not unduly high.

Only two other examples of DJD were noted. In an elderly female (SK 42) the right acromio-clavicular joint is enlarged and displays marked porosity. The left side was unavailable for examination. Based on available acromio-clavicular joints the overall prevalence of DJD of the shoulder is 10%.

The right humerus displays two roughened bone overgrowths. The larger corresponds to the insertion of the pectoralis major: a muscle which is responsible for adduction of the shoulder and is important in climbing (Sinclair 1966, 345–8). The smaller enthesopathy is probably related to the latissimus dorsi, an extensor of the shoulder, which is important in climbing and swimming (ibid.). The left humerus was available but did not display any osseous pathology. In modern-day material the shoulder is not a normal location for DJD, except in the elderly. In SK 42 it is possible that overuse of the upper arm and shoulder muscles (climbing or swimming?) was a contributory factor in the development of the degeneration.

The third example of DJD involved the third right metacarpophalangeal (MCP) joint of an elderly female (SK 24). Both hands are practically complete. However, no other hand joints displayed any evidence of degeneration. The morphology of the affected joint, including the eburnation, is pathognomonic of DJD. However, the MCP site is atypical for primary degeneration. It is not possible to ascertain why the degenerative change is confined to a single atypical articulation.

2 Secondary Degenerative Joint Disease (DJD)

Secondary DJD refers to joint degeneration which occurs as the result of an existing disease or it may be secondary to a developmental defect or else the sequelae of trauma. It is never as frequent as primary DJD and unlike the former it can occur at any age and will display a different pattern of joint involvement.

There are two examples of secondary DJD, both occurring as a result of congenital anomalies. We have already discussed the possibility of the third tarsometatarsal joints suffering degenerative alteration secondary to congenital cubo-navicular bridging (see above SK 31). The second case, involves the spine of SK 41, in which the third and fourth thoracic vertebrae were congenitally fused (see above). In the latter the degeneration is confined to the articular facets of the fourth, fifth and sixth thoracic and the left costo-vertebral facets of the sixth and eighth vertebrae. It is very likely that the reduced mobility of the blocked vertebrae has led to increased stress and movement of thoracic five and six and consequently secondary DJD has developed.

3 Vertebral Degeneration

I. DJD

Exactly half the males (3/6) (SK 15, 31, 44) and just under half (6/14) (SK 24, 41, 42, 110, 124, 125) of the females displayed vertebral DJD. The earliest onset being in the earlier thirties (SK 15). In both sexes the lower cervical spine was spared. In males, the lower thoracic spine (TV6–12) was free from disease. In females, there is a marked predilection for lumbo-sacral DJD and some 27% of the available joints were affected. There are three such cases: two adults (SK 24; 125) and an elderly female (SK 42). In the two former, the lumbo-sacral articulation is markedly deformed, grossly enlarged and extremely porotic.

The overall prevalence of spinal DJD is quite low. Over half the available spines, including most of the elderly, do not display any degenerative changes. In the adults at both Beckford (Roberts unpub.) and the Yorkshire sites (Stead 1991a) spinal DJD was practically universal. At Wetwang Slack the prevalence of spinal DJD is much lower: 37% of adult males; 32% of adult females affected (Dawes unpub.). This is similar to our findings from Deal.

It is noteworthy that the two women with marked deformation of the lumbo-sacral articulations (SK 24, 125) both display large, well-defined squatting facets. This leads one to speculate that the bone alterations may be occupationally linked. Possibly they were engaged in fairly strenuous activities which involved long periods of squatting as well as repeated lower back strain (cleaning skins, grinding corn?).

II. OSTEOPHYTES

Eighteen spines contained vertebral bodies which could be examined for osteophytic outgrowths. 60% of males (SK 15, 31, 44) and 50% of females (SK 24, 30, 41, 42, 43, 110, 124) displayed osteophytic development. It is noticeable that there is a strong correlation between spines with osteophytes and with DJD (see above). In both males (SK 15, 44) and females (SK 41, 42) osteophytic spines also presented with porotic intervertebral surfaces. There was no clear evidence for laterality in our small sample. The earliest onset being in a female in her early twenties (SK 30). In this case, the outgrowths, confined to the fifth lumbar vertebra, had probably developed as a result of spondylolysis (see below). In both sexes the site of predilection was the lumbar spine, with the second, fourth and fifth vertebrae being most frequently involved. Other sites frequently involved included the mid-lower thoracic (TV 6, 7, 9, 11) and lower cervical spine (CV 6).

In our Iron Age material the location of the outgrowths (the lumbar spine, mid-lower thoracic, and lower cervical) correspond to the areas of greatest curvature. This finding, coupled with the evidence of a male bias in our sample, suggests that the pattern of osteophytic outgrowths at Deal equates closely with the normal distribution. In our sample the male lumbar spine is the site of predilection. The marked disc degeneration of the lower spines in males may be partly due to repeated compressional forces, as would occur when carrying heavy loads.

III. SCHMORL'S NODES

Schmorl's nodes were not very frequent: definite nodes were not recorded in any male skeletons and occurred in only two females: a young adult (SK 123) and an adult (SK 41). In the latter the defects were confined to the inferior surfaces of TV 8 and 9. In the former a single node was present on the dorsal aspect of superior TV 12.

It is generally accepted that node formation is directly related to severe strain, especially compressional forces, which cause the intervertebral disc to rupture (Knowles 1983). It is possible that the cavitations will more readily develop during adolescence, while the vertebral bodies are still plastic (ibid.). The infrequency of Schmorl's nodes in the Deal material suggests that the Iron Age community were not subjecting their spines to heavy stress during adolescence. However, the combination of osteophytes and DJD in several (no. 7) adult spines argue that vertebral strain and stress did develop in both sexes during adulthood.

IV. OTHER INTERVERTEBRAL ABNORMALITIES: SCHEUERMANN'S DISEASE

One skeleton (SK 26), a male juvenile, aged 17–19 years deserves special mention. The two lower thoracic vertebrae displayed irregular defects in the middle of the superior surface of the vertebral body. The edges of the lesions are slightly irregular in outline and the defects are clearly larger internally than externally. In addition the height of the ventral aspect of the lower thoracic vertebrae is reduced, leading to kyphotic curvature.

The radiographic appearance of the lower spine reveals vertebral end-plate irregularities; kyphosis and sclerotic-edged cavitations of the superior aspect of the two lower thoracic vertebrae is pathognomonic of Scheuermann's disease (pl. XV). The rare group of genetic diseases, the mucopolysaccharidoses, can lead to vertebral irregularities but these can be excluded since the typical changes to the hands and possible long bone deformities were not present (Ortner & Putschar 1985, 335–6).

Scheuermann's disease has only been rarely reported in the archaeological literature (Kunter 1976; Møller-Christensen 1958, 165; Wells 1961). This is almost certainly due to the lack of radiographic evidence from archaeological specimens. However, in skeletal samples, the majority of cases may not be recognised and the early onset of vertebral DJD and marked osteophytic outgrowths may be the only evidence of the healed disease.

Earlier work suggested that there might be a direct relationship between heavy manual labour and Scheuermann's disease (Wassman 1951). However, more recent work has negated this view (Fisk et al. 1984). One clear finding is that the disease is closely related to the growth spurt. It occurs more in taller males (Fisk et al. 1984) and earlier in girls, related to the fact that the female growth spurt occurs earlier than the male (Alexander 1977). Clinical manifestations are highly variable. In some individuals the disease is totally asymptomatic. In others, symptoms include: kyphotic curvature, fatigue and back pain, which may be made worse during periods of physical exertion (Resnick and Niwayama 1981, 2903).

As such it is not possible to confirm that the Iron Age juvenile was carrying out hard physical tasks. Nor can it be ascertained if he was aware of the disease, which may have been asymptomatic. As far as we are aware, only one other example of Scheuermann's disease has been reported from British archaeological material (Wells 1961). It is possible that other examples do exist but, without radiographic examination, they have not been recognised.

V. SPONDYLOLYSIS (NEURAL ARCH SEPARATION)

Two males (SK 44, 46) and two females (SK 30, 120) displayed neural arch separation, an overall prevalence of 18.2%, which is much higher than the 3–7% found in modern populations (Resnick & Niwayama 1981, 2253). Two cases (SK 30, 44) are particularly interesting in so far as the fifth lumbar vertebra is perfectly normal and the fourth lumbar vertebra presents with a separate neural arch. Occasionally, multiple lumbar vertebrae may be involved, but in these cases the fifth is normally affected (Barkley 1978; Roberts unpub.).

The favoured interpretation of the defect is a stress or fatigue fracture that fails to heal (Resnick and Niwayama 1981, 2253). As such it appears that the prevalence of spondylolysis may give a clue to levels of vertebral stress in earlier populations. However, the possibility that a genetic weakness in the spine may predispose to neural arch separation cannot be ignored (Hensinger 1989).

There is no evidence that the affected bones have been displaced, so-called spondylolisthesis. It is probable that the defects did not cause any pain or discomfort, since in modern practice spondylolysis is often asymptomatic. In our sample there is no clear relationship between vertebral degeneration and spondylolysis. Only one of the four skeletons with separation of a neural arch had distal tibiae sufficiently preserved to record squatting facets. It is interesting that in this one case (SK 30) spondylolysis of the fourth lumbar vertebra was associated with squatting facets. However, it is possible that, in a small Iron Age community, genetic influence and inbreeding are also playing an important part in the development of spondylolysis.

Trauma

Apart from SK 112, only two possible traumatic bone lesions were discovered, both in males, a juvenile (SK 26) and an adult (SK 44). In the former, the fourth metatarsals present with diaphyseal swelling, more advanced on the right side. These isolated swellings probably represent the sequelae of repeated minor trauma.

The second example of trauma was noted in the spine of an adult male (SK 44). The eleventh thoracic vertebra displays marked anterior collapse, evidence of wedge or compression fracture. The other vertebrae displayed DJD and osteophytic outgrowths, but no other evidence of disease was noted. The radiographic appearance did not suggest a metastatic lesion; nor is there any evidence of infection within any of the bones. Overall reduction of bone quantity, osteoporosis, can lead to collapse of the vertebrae. The fact that only a single bone is affected does not support a general loss of bone quantity. Consequently, a traumatic aetiology is the favoured interpretation.

Unlike other Iron Age sites there was no evidence of weapon injury on any of our bones. At Beckford one male skull displayed an unhealed blade injury which had probably caused death (Roberts unpub.). An adult male at

Wetwang Slack had suffered a sword cut to the occipital bone (Dawes unpub.). At Rudston a female skull showed a healed cut on the frontal bone (Stead 1991a).

Infection

The possibility of a spinal infection in SK 112 has already been mentioned (see above). There was only one other possible, but not definite, infective lesion. It occurred in the upper jaw of an adult male (SK 44). A small (8×5mm) oval lesion is sited on the body of the right maxilla directly inferior to the border of the nasal aperture. The inferior aspect of the defect presents with a small raised area of smooth, dense and very finely porotic bone. The major part of the lesion is a more coarsely grained shallow depression. The fine porotic nature of the lesion is rather suggestive of a bone reaction, secondary to localised infection.

Similar to our findings at Deal, in the larger samples from the Yorkshire sites (Stead 1991a) and Wetwang (Dawes unpub.) there were very few examples of bone infection. However, at Beckford there were eight cases of infection (including sinusitis and two pulmonary infections) out of 18 males (Roberts unpub.).

Metabolic (Nutritional)

The only evidence for metabolic bone disease is a single case of cribra orbitalia in an adult female (SK 41); this represents an adult prevalence of 12.5%. The lesion does not appear to be aggressive or active. The indistinct appearance is evidence of remodelling, which suggests that the nutritional deficit occurred many years before death, possibly during childhood. The fact that no sub-adult orbits were preserved in the Deal sample means that the prevalence of childhood iron deficiency cannot be ascertained.

At the Roman site of Poundbury, 24.4% (62/254) of adult males and 27.7% (81/292) of adult females presented with cribra orbitalia (Stuart-Macadam 1989). At Beckford 29.4% of adults displayed cribra orbitalia (Roberts unpub.) and at Danebury just under half, 47.9% of the skeletons were involved (Hooper 1984). In comparison, the single adult example (12.5%) suggests that lack of iron, either due to inadequate diet or parasitic infestation, was not a major problem for the Iron Age population at Deal; which is more than can be said for many modern urban children (Ehrhardt 1986).

Neoplasm

There was no clear evidence of neoplastic growths in the recently excavated Deal material. However, an extant cranial vault from an earlier excavation in the region of the South-West Cemetery (Woodruff 1904) exhibited a vascular disturbance, which may represent a meningioma, a benign brain tumour. The right middle meningeal artery presents as a deep sulcus with clear cystic cavitation (30×10mm) of its terminal branch (pl. XVI).

Meningiomas are variable in presentation. In dry bone material those associated with visible hyperostosis will be readily recognised (Anderson 1991). Clinical evidence, however, suggests that 75–80% of cases do not present with external bone overgrowth (ibid.). Campillo (1991), in a detailed study, has pointed out that minor endocranial lesions may be the only evidence for meningiomatous involvement. These changes include localised bone exostosis, cavitation and increased diameter of the vascular grooves (ibid.).

Our possible example of meningioma is similar to a Neolithic specimen from Spain (Campillo 1991, fig. 2). Both present with cystic cavitation (hypervascularisation) of an enlarged middle meningeal artery, which may equate with a diagnosis of osteolytic meningioma. In modern practice, meningiomas are known to be more frequent in females (Anderson 1992, Table 3) and symptoms are rare before the age of 30 (Helseth et al. 1988). The sex of our skeleton is uncertain; the age 30–40, estimated by sutural closure and dental attrition, would not be incompatible with a diagnosis of meningioma.

It must be stressed that the presented pathology is not diagnostic for meningioma. According to Campillo (1991) exostotic alterations are more frequent than osteolysis; also enlargement of vascular grooves is not specific to meningiomatous causation. However, the available evidence points to the possibility of an Iron Age benign brain tumour.

In large modern day samples, meningiomas account for 18–28% of intra-cranial tumours (Helseth et al. 1988; Preston-Martin 1989). This contrasts strongly with the rarity of meningiomatous alteration in earlier societies. In British material there is a possible case of meningioma from Burton Fleming, Yorkshire (Stead 1991a). It is probable that careful examination of discrete endocranial lesions will lead to a more accurate understanding of the palaeopathology of meningioma.

Miscellaneous

In dry bone material enigmatic lesions, which cannot be definitely diagnosed, are occasionally encountered. One such case occurs in SK 31, an adult male from the Central Cemetery. The lesion presents on the inner surface of the right greater wing of the sphenoid, just superior to a (bipartite) foramen rotundum. The localised defect consists of smooth-edged, cystic cavitation, with exposure of the underlying diploë (pl. XVII).

The smooth-edged nature of the defect rules out both post-mortem defect and malignant neoplasm. Consideration was given to a benign neoplasm, such as meningioma or haemangioma, as a possible causation. The former may present with minor endocranial bone alteration (Campillo 1991). However, the cystic cavitation of SK 31 does not appear typical of meningiomatous involvement. The trabeculae are not thickened and the diagnostic 'spoke-wheel' radiographic appearance of haemangioma (Resnick and Niwayama 1981, 2671) was not visualised in our specimen.

At the time of writing, the aetiology of this smooth-edged, non-aggressive defect is uncertain. A benign neoplasm is a remote possibility but, on the available evidence, the conclusion is one of idiopathic cystic cavitation.

Oral Health

Tooth Loss

In the Deal material four males (40%) and eight females (57%) displayed ante-mortem tooth loss. Based on individual teeth, it was possible to ascertain an overall ante-mortem tooth loss of 12.6%. In agreement with both modern and archaeological samples, female tooth loss was much higher than male (Table 33). The maxilla was slightly more involved than the mandible and this preference was more noticeable in females than in males (Table 33).

Detailed dental studies are infrequent on Iron Age material. However, there is a much lower tooth loss than was found in the Yorkshire series; in the latter the overall tooth loss was just over 2% (Table 34). In Iron Age Denmark the overall percentage of ante-mortem tooth loss was 7.7% (Bennike 1985, Table 35).

Caries

Approximately 70% of males and 64% of females presented with carious cavities. In both sexes the upper jaw was more frequently involved than the lower. There was no marked sexual predilection but males were slightly more involved than females. A total of 65 carious cavities were discovered, two teeth presenting with two cavities (SK 54). When sub-divided by size, the majority (53.8%) were classed as extensive. The most serious case was an adult male (SK 31) in which eight teeth were carious, three presenting with complete destruction of the crown. Occlusal caries was distinctly rare, accounting for 7.7% of all cavities.

Examination of individual teeth revealed an overall prevalence of 12.9%. In comparison to the Yorkshire sites this is a very high figure, in the latter the overall caries frequency was just over 2%, rising to almost 3% in females (Table 34) and at Danebury just over 7% of teeth were carious (Hooper 1984). At Wetwang Slack 44% of males and 51% of females displayed carious cavities (Dawes unpub.), which is much lower than the 75% in our sample. The caries frequency in Scottish Iron Age material is 6.6% and, unlike Deal, no cases of gross destruction were noted (Lunt 1974). In the early Iron Age in Germany caries prevalence varied between 2.2–5.4% (Claassen 1991) and in Iron Age Denmark the overall frequency was 8.6% (Bennike 1985, Table 31). Only at Beckford was a similar prevalence of 11.5% recorded (Roberts unpub.).

Abscesses

In our sample 37.5% of dentitions presented with abscesses, with exactly half the males and 28.6% of females affected. Abscess cavities affected 3.7% of 675 erupted tooth positions. In both sexes abscesses were more frequent in the maxilla and males were more involved than females (Table 33).

The most advanced case was in an adult male (SK 20), in which six sinuses were discovered in the upper jaw. Where teeth are available, 83% of abscesses are associated with carious teeth. The direct relationship is due to infection subsequent to pulp cavity exposure by carious destruction (pl. XVIII). Compared to our findings, a slightly higher prevalence was noted at Beckford, 5.4% (Roberts unpub.). Abscesses were much less frequent in the Yorkshire series, with an overall prevalence of only 1% (Table 34) and at Wetwang Slack only 21% of males and 13% of females displayed abscesses (Dawes unpub.).

Calculus

In our sample only a third of available dentitions displayed calculus deposits. Just under 24% of all teeth were affected, with the highest prevalence being in the female mandibles (Table 33). A total of 170 calculus deposits were recorded. The majority were minimal (77.8%) with only four extensive deposits. The latter were all located in female mandibles (SK 42, 43, 47).

Roberts (unpub.) reports that 64% of teeth from Beckford displayed calculus deposits, with slightly more (72%) on the lower jaw. Similarly, at Wetwang Slack 63% of teeth were affected by calculus, with 16% presenting with extensive deposits (Dawes unpub.). Although only a third of our sample displayed calculus formation, in vivo the incidence would have been much higher. Calculus when dry is very friable and easily lost. Even allowing for the fact that some of the Deal calculus had been lost post-mortem, it appears that calculus was less frequent in our material, than at other Iron Age sites.

The distribution of calculus follows the normal human pattern, with the heaviest deposits being found on the lingual surfaces of the lower anterior teeth, and the buccal surfaces of the upper posterior teeth. This distribution is related to the position of the three pairs of major salivary glands, the parotid, sub-mandibular and sub-lingual (Buckley 1980).

Periodontal Disease

Following the work of Kerr (1989), all the adults displayed some evidence of periodontal disease. Male periodontal disease was slightly more marked (mean figure 3.07) than female (2.93). In both sexes the maxilla showed slightly more evidence of disease than the mandible. Alveolar bone loss has been documented in early hominid material (Hildebolt & Molnar 1991), but in general, little work has been carried out on the occurrence of periodontal disease in archaeological remains.

Hypoplasia

Hypoplastic lines represent defects in the enamel formation during the growth of the tooth. They occur in response to some form of childhood stress (Dobney and Goodman 1991). Once formed they remain visible throughout life.

In the Deal skeletons, when sub-adult material was included, a total of 27 dentitions could be examined for enamel hypoplasia. Only two cases of hypoplasia were recorded, a prevalence of 7.4%. In one case, a young adult female (SK 30), the defects (no. 2) were confined to an upper right central incisor, this may represent localised trauma rather than systemic disease. In the second case, an adult male (SK 46), 25 teeth were available and 14 each displayed a single hypoplastic line. This is highly suggestive of a single episode of childhood illness, possibly, from the position of the defects, occurring between 3-5 years of age.

In a small sample of dentitions from Beckford three cases of hypoplasia were noted, a prevalence of 13.6% (Roberts unpub). From 85 well-preserved dentitions, five presented with hypoplastic defects, a prevalence of 5.9% (Stead 1991a). Recent work suggests a frequency of 14.9% at Dürrnberg during the Hallstatt period (Claassen 1991). The general absence of hypoplastic lines in the Deal population gives an indication that the wide range of diseases (Soames and Southam 1988, 6) associated with these defects were relatively uncommon.

Malocclusion

There was very little evidence for malocclusion in the Deal material. Only one skeleton, an adult female (SK 51), displayed malocclusion: her lower left central incisor had been rotated 80° disto-lingually. The absence of overcrowding in our sample may be attributed to the high level of attrition. This is probably dietary in origin, rather than cultural or occupational. Their flour was almost certainly contaminated by abrasive particles due to the use of the locally produced coarse sandstone querns (Keller 1989). Fragments of these Lower Greensand querns were found during earlier excavations of the St Richard's Road site (Stebbing 1934; Parfitt 1985, 213).

An interesting case is shown in a mature female, SK 124, showing extensive tooth loss (pl. XIX). The area of note is the upper left first molar which is grossly carious with the palatal root having been fractured away from the rest of the tooth. Due to secondary occlusal trauma the remains of the crown have been moved palatally, forcing the disto-buccal root through the alveolar bone and overlaying mucosa. Friction with the cheek has polished the root for its entire length (pl. XIX).

This condition is seldom encountered clinically but is relatively pain free, as the tooth involved must have lost its blood supply which is via the apical foramina. The only discomfort is from a chronic periodontal infection. With this degree of tooth loss, mastication of all but the softest food must have been very laborious and time-consuming. From the degree of alveolar bone loss, however, this situation must have existed for several years.

Abnormalities

There were very few abnormalities in the Deal teeth. An adult female (SK 43) presented with hypoplastic roots. In one case, an elderly female (SK 110), seven teeth were congenitally absent (partial anodontia). Three second premolars were congenitally absent, the right maxillary region was unavailable and it is very likely that the second premolar had also been absent in this quadrant. Both upper lateral incisors were congenitally absent and on the left side the deciduous tooth, worn down to its root, had been retained. Higher than normal frequencies of missing teeth have been reported in small isolated communities (Graber 1978).

In the Deal material congenital absence of the third molars was a frequent finding: 20% of males and nearly 43% of females were involved. In the adult sample, 19% of the scoreable third molars were absent. In males 6.3% of maxillary and 10% of mandibular third molars were congenitally absent. In females third molar absence was much higher: 28.6% in the maxilla and 32% in the mandible. At Danebury only 4.9% of third molars were congenitally absent (Hooper 1984). In the Yorkshire series absence was more frequent in females, with the greatest absence occurring in the lower jaw, 14.1% (Stead 1991a). In the small sample from Beckford an overall absence of 13.6% was recorded (Roberts unpub.).

Based on 2,500 dentitions the frequency of third molar absence in southern England today is 12.7% (Shinn 1976), rather less than our findings from Iron Age Deal (19%). The aetiology of the absence is not fully understood. The fact that third molars may be missing in large dental arches, suggests that reduction in jaw size and inadequate space is not the only factor in the absence (Brothwell et al. 1963, 185). There is some evidence for a familial link in congenital absence (Graber 1978). Since impacted third molars may lead to chronic sepsis, it is possible that absence is a selective advantage (Brothwell et al. 1963, 187).

Conclusion

The Deal material has provided the first opportunity to examine the bones of an Iron Age community from Kent. The absence of weapon injuries suggests that their existence was peaceful. The overall standard of health was quite high, with very little evidence for infection or metabolic bone disease. The high prevalence of squatting facets, especially in females, support the hypothesis of a farming community involved in preparing hides and grinding corn, activities which involve prolonged squatting.

The lack of degeneration, especially in the lower limb, argues that working conditions were not too arduous. Possibly farming was restricted to easily tilled soil, on flat, even ground. The lack of non-metric alteration of the femoral neck supports the view that walking and running over hill sides was infrequent. The lower standard of oral health may be partially related to a coarse diet, including the gnawing of bones. The presence of several congenital anomalies could be evidence of a restricted gene pool.

The presence of these rare anomalies may be of great value for we hope to examine the Deal Anglo-Saxon skeletons to assess how closely related they are to the earlier Iron Age community. Our present examination has shown that much can be learned from even a small fragmentary skeletal sample when it has been carefully excavated. The knowledge we have gained from the Iron Age bones bears out the motto of the Paleopathological Society, *Mortui viventes docent.*

TABLE 11: SKELETAL COMPLETENESS AND BONE CONDITION

CODE	ALL	SW CEMETERY
SKELETAL COMPLETENESS		
1	3	0
2	5	0
3	8	7
4	11	7
5	2	2
6	6	5
7	3	3
0	0	3
TOTAL	38	27
BONE CONDITION		
a	1	0
b	3	0
c	5	1
d	19	14
e	10	9
0	0	3
TOTAL	38	27

CODES	COMPLETENESS %	CONDITION
1	>95	a Excellent, all solid
2	80-95	b V. good, mainly solid
3	60-80	c Good, some fragmented, repairable
4	40-60	d Largely fragmented
5	20-40	e V. badly fragmented
6	5-20	f Powdery stain, some bone
7	< 5	g Stain only
0	0	0 No bone or stain

TABLE 12A: THE DEAL SKELETONS GROUPED BY AGE AND SEX (SW Cemetery)

SK	SEX	AGE	STATURE	PRESERVATION	FINDS	PATHOLOGY
Infans II (1-6 years)						
55	?	1-6?	—	0		
113	?	1-2	—	6d		
116	?	0-4?	—	0		
117	?	2-4	—	7e		
Infans III (6-12 years)						
52	?	6-10	—	7e		
107	?	5-10	—	7e		
118	?	9-11	—	6e		
122	?	6-7	—	6e	*	
128	?	6-12?	—	0		
Juvenile (12-20 years)						
115	F	17-19	—	4d		
48	?	13-15	—	4d		
121	?	18-20	—	4d	*	
126	?	11-13	—	5c		
MALE						
Young Adult						
54	M?	27-32	—	4e		
127	M	22-27	1.727	3d	*	
Adult						
46	M	35-45	—	3e		Spondylolysis
114	M?	35-45	1.720	3d		
Mature						
108	M?	40-50	—	4e	*	DJD: Mandible
FEMALE						
Young Adult						
123	F?	20-25	—	3d	*	Schmorl's Nodes
Adult						
47	F	28-35	1.543	3d	*	DJD: Mandible
50	F?	35-45	—	4d	*	
51	F	30-40	—	5d		
120	F	30-40	—	6d		Spondylolysis
125	F	28-35	1.610	3d		Spinal DJD
Mature						
119	F	45-55	—	4d		
124	F?	40-50	1.500	3d		Lumbar rib
SEX UNKNOWN						
Grown						
49	?	?	—	6e		

TABLE 12B: THE DEAL SKELETONS GROUPED BY AGE AND SEX (excluding SW Cemetery)

SK	SEX	AGE	STATURE	PRESERVATION	FINDS	PATHOLOGY
Juvenile (12-20 years)						
26	M?	17-19	—	2b	*	Scheuermann's disease; trauma
28	F	16-18	—	6a		
MALE						
Young Adult						
3	M	25-30	1.735	2b		
Adult						
15	M	30-35	1.704	1c		Spinal DJD
20	M	30-35	1.636	1c		
31	M	35-45	1.792	1b		Spinal DJD; hand & foot anomalies; 2ndy DJD; ?cyst
44	M	35-45	1.654	2e	*	Spine & mand DJD; infection?; trauma; cong; spondylolyis
112	M	30-35	1.605	4d	*	Spinal DJD; trauma?
FEMALE						
Young Adult						
30	F?	20-25	1.606	3d	*	Spinal osteophytes; spondylolysis
Adult						
24	F?	35-45	1.604	2c		Spinal & hand DJD
41	F	35-40	1.564	2d		Spinal & 2ndy DJD;Schmorl's Nodes; cribra orbitalia; cong
43	F	28-33	1.640	4c		Spinal DJD (osteophytes)
Mature						
42	F	45-55	1.564	4d		Spinal & shoulder DJD
110	F	50-60	—	4d	*	Spinal DJD

TABLE 13: SUB-ADULT MORTALITY IN IRON AGE BRITAIN

SUB-ADULT MORTALITY (%)	SITE	SOURCE
4.5 (11/246)	various Yorks	Stead (1991a)
7.9 (3/38)*	Maiden Castle	Goodman & Morant (1940)
17.6 (12/68)	Maiden Castle	Goodman & Morant (1940)
18.9 (81/429)	Wetwang Slack	Dawes (unpub.)
31.6 (12/38)*+	Deal	present report
43.8 (14/32)	Beckford	Roberts (unpub.)
52.6 (??/??)*	Poundbury	Molleson (1992)

* Late Iron Age
+ Including the child graves without bones (Nos 55; 116; 128) and the previously reported juvenile (SK 5), the sub-adult mortality at Deal is 38.1%.

TABLE 14: ADULT MALE STATURE IN IRON AGE BRITAIN

MEAN STATURE	RANGE	SITE	SOURCE
1.645 (no. 15) 5'5"	1.570-1.750 5'2"-5'9"	Danebury	Hooper (1984)
1.660 (no. ??) 5'5½"	???-1.712 ???-5'7½"	Poundbury	Molleson (1992)
1.678 (no. 122) 5'6¼"	???-???	Wetwang Slack	Dawes (unpub.)
1.686 (no. 26) 5'6½"	1.572-1.812 5'2"-5'11½"	Maiden Castle	Goodman & Morant (1940)
1.700 (no. 8) 5'7"	1.605-1.792 5'3¼"-5'10¾"	Deal	present report
1.707 (no. 73) 5'7½"	1.590-1.799 5'2¾"-5'11"	various Yorks	Stead (1991a)

TABLE 16: DEAL: MALE CRANIOMETRIC MEANS

METRIC	SYMBOL	MEAN	NO.	RANGE
Maximum cranial length	L	188.7	6	181.0–196.0
Maximum cranial breadth	B	139.0	5	119.0–151.0
Minimum frontal breadth	B'	100.7	7	92.2–109.2
Maximum frontal breadth	B"	122.25	4	115.0–123.0
Basion-Bregmatic height	H'	140.5	4	137.0–144.0
Basion-Nasion length	LB	106.4	5	102.0–112.0
Frontal Arc	S_1	130.4	5	115.0–139.0
Frontal Chord	S'_1	110.0	5	102.3–117.3
Parietal Arc	S_2	136.75	4	123.0–147.0
Parietal Chord	S'_2	120.6	4	110.0–128.2
Occipital Arc	S_3	124.8	5	114.0–129.0
Occipital Chord	S'_3	102.3	5	99.1–107.5
Basion-Alveolar length	GL	98.0	2	98.0
Opisthion-Metopion	OM	167.3	3	165.0–169.0
Biasterionic breadth	BiastB	108.0	4	94.0–115.0
Upper facial height	G'H	70.15	2	69.2–71.1
Total facial height	GN	114.2	2	113.6–114.8
Total facial breadth	J	—	—	—
Mid facial breadth	GB	95.85	2	95.0–96.7
Orbital breadth (right)	O_1R	40.95	2	40.6–41.3
Orbital breadth (left)	O_1L	41.0	3	40.6–41.3
Orbital height (right)	O_2R	32.95	2	32.8–33.1
Orbital height (left)	O_2L	32.6	3	32.0–33.1
Nasal breadth	NB	24.9	3	22.0–28.0
Nasal height	NH'	50.4	3	49.0–51.1
External palatal length	G''_1	54.15	2	52.6–55.7
External palatal breadth	G''_2	63.9	2	62.4–65.4
Internal palatal length	G'_1	45.55	2	44.7–46.4
Internal palatal breadth	G'_2	35.3	4	30.9–37.5
Mastoid length (right)	MastLR	26.0	9	19.0–32.0
Mastoid length (left)	MastLL	24.8	6	19.0–32.0
Foramen magnum length	LFM	39.0	5	34.3–43.1
Foramen magnum breadth	WFM	31.2	5	29.8–31.8
MANDIBLE				
Bicondylar breadth	W_1	123.5	3	118.5–129.2
Bigonial length	GoGo	100.4	6	95.2–107.2
Ramus height (right)	CrH	61.8	5	50.3–69.9
Ramus height (left)	CrH	69.5	5	56.3–80.7
Maximum ramus breadth (right)	RB"	46.75	2	44.6–48.9
Maximum ramus breadth (left)	RB"	47.8	3	47.2–48.4
Mimimum ramus breadth (right)	RB'	32.8	7	29.8–36.0
Minimum ramus breadth (left)	RB'	33.6	8	28.2–36.2
Maximum mandibular length	ML	102.7	3	97.0–107.0
Mandibular body height (r)	M_2H	33.0	3	26.7–34.7
Mandibular body height (l)	M_2H	30.1	5	25.7–33.9
Mandibular body breadth (r)	M_2B	16.2	6	15.2–17.3
Mandibular body breadth (l)	M_2B	15.5	7	13.7–17.7
Symphyseal height	H'	33.8	3	32.2–35.0

TABLE 15: ADULT FEMALE STATURE IN IRON AGE BRITAIN

MEAN STATURE	RANGE	SITE	SOURCE
1.562 (no. 168) 5'1¾"	???-???	Wetwang Slack	Dawes (unpub.)
1.564 (no. 7) 5'1¾"	1.504-1.602 4'11¼"-5'3¼"	Danebury	Hooper (1984)
1.567 (no. 16) 5'1¾"	1.450-1.677 4'9"-5'6"	Maiden Castle	Goodman & Morant (1940)
1.580 (no. 8) 5'2¼"	1.500-1.610 4'11¼"-5'3½"	Deal	present report
1.582 (no. 49) 5'2½"	1.499-1.712 4'11¼"-5'7½"	various Yorks	Stead (1991a)
1.623 (no. 6) 5'4"	1.552-1.686 5'1¼"-5'6½"	Poundbury	Molleson (pers. comm.)

TABLE 17: DEAL: FEMALE CRANIOMETRIC MEANS

METRIC	SYMBOL	MEAN	N	RANGE
Maximum cranial length	L	183.4	10	171.0 –192.0
Maximum cranial breadth	B	136.7	7	129.0 –146.0
Minimum frontal breadth	B'	95.6	9	90.1– 98.1
Maximum frontal breadth	B"	118.3	3	114.0–123.0
Basion-Bregmatic height	H'	136.3	3	129.0–143.0
Basion-Nasion length	LB	103.7	3	100.0–109.0
Frontal Arc	S_1	130.4	12	114.0–142.0
Frontal Chord	S'_1	111.1	12	98.0–120.8
Parietal Arc	S_2	131.3	11	120.0–154.0
Parietal Chord	S'_2	115.6	11	104.5–128.0
Occipital Arc	S_3	112.6	7	103.0–120.0
Occipital Chord	S'_3	98.5	7	94.4–104.2
Basion Alveolar length	GL	96.1	1	96.1
Opisthion-Metopion	OM	159.1	7	152.0–165.0
Biasterionic breadth	BiastB	109.9	7	106.0–116.0
Upper facial height	G'H	65.05	2	63.1–67.0
Total facial height	GN	114.85	2	111.2–118.5
Total facial breadth	J	127.2	1	127.2
Mid facial breadth	GB	92.9	1	92.9
Orbital breadth (right)	O_1R	40.0	1	40.0
Orbital breadth (left)	O_1L	39.7	2	39.5–39.9
Orbital height (right)	O_2R	33.1	1	33.1
Orbital height (left)	O_2L	34.5	3	32.3–38.5
Nasal breadth	NB	21.7	1	21.7
Nasal height	NH'	47.0	1	47.0
External palatal length	G''_1	55.6	1	55.6
External palatal breadth	G''_2	55.0	3	54.3–62.4
Internal palatal length	G'_1	38.6	1	38.6
Internal palatal breadth	G'_2	30.9	4	28.2–34.4
Mastoid length (right)	MastLR	22.8	6	17.0–26.0
Mastoid length (left)	MastLL	22.6	8	18.0–27.0
Foramen magnum length	LFM	36.7	3	36.0–37.9
Foramen magnum breadth	WFM	29.2	3	28.1–30.3
MANDIBLE				
Bicondylar breadth	W_1	116.1	1	116.1
Bigonial length	GoGo	95.4	4	89.0–101.2
Ramus height (right)	CrH	54.0	4	50.5–58.7
Ramus height (left)	CrH	52.75	2	51.2–54.3
Maximum ramus breadth (right)	RB"	40.6	4	37.3–43.7
Maximum ramus breadth (left)	RB"	46.9	3	39.6–50.8
Mimimum ramus breadth (right)	RB'	32.05	8	29.6–34.4
Minimum ramus breadth (left)	RB'	31.6	6	29.5–34.8
Maximum mandibular length	ML	99.25	2	96.6–102.0
Mandibular body height (r)	M_2H	28.55	4	25.8–32.9
Mandibular body height (l)	M_2H	29.7	5	25.3–34.8
Mandibular body breadth (r)	M_2B	15.0	10	10.6–17.6
Mandibular body breadth (l)	M_2B	14.6	11	11.6–19.2
Symphyseal height	H'	32.9	5	28.6–39.2

TABLE 18: DEAL: ALL CRANIOMETRIC MEANS

METRIC	SYMBOL	MEAN	NO.	RANGE
Maximum cranial length	L	185.3	16	171.0–196.0
Maximum cranial breadth	B	137.7	12	119.0–151.0
Minimum frontal breadth	B'	97.9	16	90.1–109.2
Maximum frontal breadth	B"	120.6	7	114.0–123.0
Basion-Bregmatic height	H'	138.7	7	129.0–144.0
Basion-Nasion length	LB	105.4	8	100.0–112.0
Frontal Arc	S_1	130.4	17	115.0–139.0
Frontal Chord	S'_1	110.8	17	98.3–120.8
Parietal Arc	S_2	132.9	15	120.0–154.0
Parietal Chord	S'_2	117.1	15	104.5–128.2
Occipital Arc	S_3	117.7	12	103.0–129.0
Occipital Chord	S'_3	100.1	12	94.4–107.5
Basion-Alveolar length	GL	97.3	3	96.1–98.0
Opisthion-Metopion	OM	161.6	10	152.0–169.0
Biasterionic breadth	BiastB	109.2	11	94.0–116.0
Upper facial height	G'H	67.6	4	63.1–71.1
Total facial height	GN	114.5	4	111.2–118.5
Total facial breadth	J	127.2	1	127.2
Mid facial breadth	GB	94.9	3	92.9–96.7
Orbital breadth (right)	O_1R	40.6	3	40.0–41.3
Orbital breadth (left)	O_1L	40.3	5	39.5–41.3
Orbital height (right)	O_2R	33.0	3	32.8–33.1
Orbital height (left)	O_2L	33.6	6	32.0–38.5
Nasal breadth	NB	24.1	4	21.7–28.0
Nasal height	NH'	49.5	4	47.0–51.1
External palatal length	G''_1	54.6	3	52.6–55.7
External palatal breadth	G''_2	60.6	5	54.3–65.4
Internal palatal length	G'_1	43.2	3	38.6–46.4
Internal palatal breadth	G'_2	33.1	8	28.2–37.5
Mastoid length (right)	MastLR	24.7	15	17.0–32.0
Mastoid length (left)	MastLL	23.9	14	18.0–32.0
Foramen magnum length	LFM	38.1	8	34.3–43.1
Foramen magnum breadth	WFM	30.4	8	28.1–31.8
MANDIBLE				
Bicondylar breadth	W_1	121.6	4	116.1–129.2
Bigonial length	GoGo	98.3	10	89.0–107.2
Ramus height (right)	CrH	58.3	9	50.3–69.9
Ramus height (left)	CrH	64.6	7	51.2–80.7
Maximum ramus breadth (right)	RB"	42.7	6	37.3–48.9
Maximum ramus breadtth (left)	RB"	47.3	6	39.6–50.8
Mimimum ramus breadth (right)	RB'	32.4	15	29.6–36.0
Minimum ramus breadth (left)	RB'	32.75	14	28.2–36.2
Maximum mandibular length	ML	101.3	5	96.6–107.0
Mandibular body height (r)	M_2H	30.0	7	25.8–34.7
Mandibular body height (l)	M_2H	30.1	10	25.3–34.8
Mandibular body breadth (r)	M_2B	15.4	16	10.6–17.6
Mandibular body breadth (l)	M_2B	15.0	18	11.6–19.2
Symphyseal height	H'	33.3	8	28.6–39.2

TABLE 19: DEAL: CRANIAL METRICS: THE INDICES

SK NO	CRANIAL INDICES 1	2	3	4	5	6	7R	7L	8	9	10	11	12	13	14
MALE															
Young Adult															
3	65.7	75.7	115.1	77.5	—	—	—	—	—	—	—	89.0	90.4	—	—
Adult															
15	70.9	71.4	100.7	74.0	—	—	79.4	77.5	48.1	117.4	80.8	77.3	89.0	78.8	70.1
20	78.6	75.0	95.4	71.7	—	—	—	—	—	—	—	84.4	89.4	79.7	82.4
31	77.2	76.6	99.3	78.4	—	—	81.5	81.5	44.9	118.6	83.9	85.9	84.6	86.9	76.8
44	—	—	—	—	—	—	—	—	—	—	—	86.0	80.4	—	79.1
112	74.6	—	—	75.8	—	—	—	79.4	54.9	—	—	—	—	84.6	93.9
MALE AVERAGE	73.4	74.7	102.6	75.5	—	—	80.5	79.5	49.3	118.0	82.4	84.5	86.8	81.9	80.5
FEMALE															
Young Adult															
123	78.9	—	—	—	—	—	—	—	—	—	—	86.0	86.1	—	—
Adult															
24	69.6	—	—	71.8	—	—	—	—	—	—	—	86.3	88.2	94.8	—
41	74.0	74.5	100.7	68.9	52.7	93.2	—	82.0	46.2	112.2	—	84.3	90.9	87.6	81.4
43	—	—	—	—	—	—	81.8	—	—	—	—	86.4	—	82.8	—
47	69.1	—	—	71.7	—	—	—	—	—	—	—	84.3	87.4	—	—
50	80.2	—	—	66.4	—	—	—	—	—	—	—	86.4	86.8	—	—
51	72.9	71.4	97.9	—	—	—	—	—	—	—	—	83.8	83.1	86.7	74.1
120	—	—	—	—	—	—	—	—	—	—	—	81.7	90.9	—	—
125	72.9	—	—	75.2	—	—	—	—	—	—	—	86.3	87.2	82.9	—
Mature															
42	—	74.6	—	—	—	—	—	—	—	—	—	87.7	90.2	92.8	83.9
110	—	—	—	—	—	—	—	—	—	—	—	82.2	88.4	—	—
124	—	—	—	—	—	—	—	—	—	—	—	87.1	91.0	86.2	—
FEMALE AVERAGE	73.9	73.5	99.3	70.8	52.7	93.2	81.8	82.0	46.2	112.2	—	85.2	88.2	87.7	79.8
ALL AVERAGE	73.6	74.2	101.5	72.8	52.7	93.2	80.9	80.3	46.4	116.1	82.4	85.0	87.8	85.9	78.3

TABLE 20A: DEAL: THE CRANIAL INDICES: SUB-DIVIDED BY CLASSIFICATION

INDEX	M (%)	NO.	F (%)	NO.	ALL (%)	NO.
1) Cranial Index						
Hyperdolichocranic (v. long)	20.0	1	28.6	2	23.1	3
Dolichocranic	40.0	2	42.8	4	46.1	6
Mesatocranic	40.0	2	14.3	1	23.1	3
Brachycranic	—		14.3	1	7.7	1
Hyperbrachycranic (v. broad)	—		—		—	
2) Height-Length Index						
Chamecranic (low skull)	—		—		—	
Othocranic	25.0	1	100	3	57.1	4
Hypsicranic (high skull)	75.0	3	—		42.9	3
3) Height-Breadth Index						
Tapeinocranic (low skull)	—		—		—	
Metriocranic	—		50.0	1	16.7	1
Acrocranic (high skull)	100	4	50.0	1	83.3	5
4) Frontal Index						
Stenometopic (narrow)	—		—		—	
Metriometopic	—		40.0	2	20.0	2
Eurymetopic (broad)	100	5	60.0	3	80.0	8
5) Upper Facial Index						
Only one index (female) available: Mesenic (medium)						
6) Total Facial Index						
Only one index (female) available: Leptoprosopic (narrow)						
7) Orbital Index						
Five male indices (two right; three left) and two female indices. All mesoconchic (medium orbit)						
8) Nasal Index						
Leptorrhinic (narrow)	33.3	1	100	1	60.0	3
Mesorrhinic	33.3	1	—		20.0	1
Platyrrhinic (broad)	33.3	1	—		20.0	1
9) External Palatal Index						
Dolichuranic (narrow)	—		—		—	
Mesuranic	—		100	1	33.3	1
Brachyuranic (broad)	100	2	—		66.7	2
10) Internal Palatal Index						
Only two indices (male) available: both mesostaphyline (medium palate)						
11- 13) Frontal, Parietal, Occipital Curves: No classification established.						
14) Foramen Magnum Index						
Microsemic (narrow)	60.0	3	66.7	2	62.5	5
Mesosemic	20.0	1	33.3	1	25.0	2
Megasemic (broad)	20.0	1	—		12.5	1

TABLE 20B: MAIDEN CASTLE: THE CRANIAL INDICES: SUB-DIVIDED BY CLASSIFICATION

INDEX	M (%)	NO.	F (%)	NO.	ALL (%)	NO.
1) Cranial Index						
Hyperdolichocranic (v. long)	9.5	2	—		4.6	2
Dolichocranic	38.1	8	50.0	11	44.2	19
Mesatocranic	47.6	10	36.4	8	41.9	18
Brachycranic	4.8	1	9.1	2	7.0	3
Hyperbrachycranic (v. broad)	—		4.5	1	2.3	1
2) Height-Length Index						
Chamecranic (low skull)	5.9	1	13.6	3	10.2	4
Othocranic	70.6	12	63.6	14	66.7	26
Hypsicranic (high skull)	23.5	4	22.7	5	23.1	9
3) Height-Breadth Index						
Tapeinocranic (low skull)	11.8	2	11.8	2	11.8	4
Metriocranic	35.3	6	29.4	5	32.3	11
Acrocranic (high skull)	52.9	9	58.8	10	55.9	19
4) Frontal Index						
Stenometopic (narrow)	20.0	5	10.5	2	15.9	7
Metriometopic	28.0	7	21.1	4	25.0	11
Eurymetopic (broad)	52.0	13	68.4	13	59.1	26
5) Upper Facial Index						
Hypereuryene (v. broad)	—		—		—	
Euryene	12.5	1	12.5	1	12.5	2
Mesene	50.0	4	50.0	4	50.0	8
Leptene	37.5	3	25.0	2	31.25	5
Hyperleptene (v. narrow)	—		12.5	1	6.25	1
6) Total Facial Index						
This index, as defined by Bass (1987, 75), was not taken on the Maiden Castle skeletons. The authors used the mid facial breadth (GB) instead of total facial breadth (J).						
7) Orbital Index						
This is based on the left side.						
Chamaeoconchic (low orbit)	36.4	4	30.8	4	33.3	8
Mesoconchic	54.5	6	69.2	9	62.5	15
Hypsiconchic (high orbit)	9.1	1	—		4.2	1
8) Nasal Index						
Leptorrhine (narrow)	33.3	3	38.5	5	36.4	8
Mesorrhine	44.4	4	38.5	5	40.9	9
Platyrrhine (broad)	22.2	2	23.0	3	22.7	5
9) External Palatal Index						
This index was not used by Goodman & Morant on the Maiden Castle skeletons.						
10) Internal Palatal Index						
Leptostaphyline (narrow)	80.0	8	100	10	90.0	18
Mesostaphyline	10.0	1	-		5.0	1
Brachystaphyline (broad)	10.0	1	-		5.0	1
11- 13) Frontal, Parietal, Occipital Curves: no classification established.						
14) Foramen Magnum Index						
Microsemic (narrow)	41.2	7	61.5	8	50.0	15
Mesosemic	17.6	3	7.7	1	13.3	4
Megasemic (broad)	41.2	7	30.8	4	36.7	11

TABLE 22: MEAN MANDIBULAR MEASUREMENTS: DEAL AND MAIDEN CASTLE

	W_1	NO.	GOGO	NO.	Crh	NO.	rb'	NO.
MALE								
Deal	123.5	(3)	100.4	(6)	65.6	(10)	33.2	(15)
Maiden Castle	121.5	(19)	99.5	(25)	70.6	(28)	33.1	(33)
FEMALE								
Deal	116.1	(1)	95.1	(4)	53.6	(6)	31.9	(14)
Maiden Castle	117.5	(12)	90.8	(18)	60.2	(25)	30.4	(24)

W_1 maximum length
GoGo bigonial breadth
Crh coronoid height
rb' minimum ramus breadth
For the latter two measurements the Deal metrics have been pooled.

TABLE 21: THE MEAN CRANIAL INDICES, DEAL, MAIDEN CASTLE, YORKSHIRE, WETWANG SLACK

	CRANIAL INDICES																													
	1	No.	2	No.	3	No.	4	No.	5	No.	6	No.	7R	No.	7L	No.	8	No.	9	No.	10	No.	11	No.	12	No.	13	No.	14	No.
MALE AVERAGE																														
D	73.4	5	74.7	4	102.6	4	75.5	5	—	0	—	0	80.5	2	79.5	3	49.3	3	118.0	2	82.4	2	84.5	5	86.8	5	81.9	3	80.5	5
MC	74.5	21	73.6	17	97.6	17	69.3	25	53.8	8	—*		—*		77.6	11	48.0	9	—*		75.8	10	87.1	17	89.8	20	82.0	19	83.5	17
Y	72.3	41	74.3	22	100.9	21	—*		—*		—*				85.2*	26*	43.5	19	—*		85.1	27	—*		—*		—*		81.0	27
WS	73.6	101	—*		—*		—		—*		—*		82.6	57	—*		45.4	64	—*		—*		—*		—*		—*		—*	
FEMALE AVERAGE																														
D	73.9	8	73.5	3	99.3	2	70.8	5	52.7	1	93.2	1	81.8	1	82.0	1	46.2	1	112.2	1	—	0	85.2	12	88.2	11	87.7	7	79.8	3
MC	75.8	22	73.6	22	98.2	17	69.5	19	54.8	8	—*		—*		78.2	13	50.1	13	—*		73.8	10	87.0	21	89.3	18	83.4	16	80.9	13
Y	72.2	44	73.7	22	97.1	24	—*		—*		—*				88.7*	25*	49.5	17	—*		86.0	23	—*		—*		—*		84.5	23
WS	73.9	144	—*		—*		—*		—*		—*		82.8	46	—*		47.0	64	—*		—*		—*		—*		—*		—*	
ALL AVERAGE																														
D	73.6	12	74.2	7	101.5	6	72.8	9	52.7	1	93.2	1	80.9	3	80.3	4	48.5	4	116.1	3	82.4	2	85.0	17	87.8	16	85.9	10	78.5	7
MC	75.2	43	73.6	39	97.9	34	69.4	44	54.3	16	—*		—*		77.9	24	49.2	22	—*		74.8	20	87.0	38	89.6	38	82.6	35	82.4	30
Y	72.2	85	74.0	44	98.9	45	—*		—*		—*				86.9*	51*	46.4	36	—*		85.5	50	—*		—*		—*		82.6	50
WS	73.8	245	—*		—*		—*		—*		—*		82.7	103	—*		46.2	128	—*		—*		—*		—*		—*		—*	

D Deal
MC Maiden Castle
WS Wetwang Slack
— no measurements available
—* not calculated at Maiden Castle, Yorkshire Sites (Stead), Wetwang Slack
* Yorkshire: orbital index sides pooled?

TABLE 23: DEAL: MALE POST-CRANIOMETRIC MEANS

METRIC	SYMBOL	MEAN	NO.	RANGE
CLAVICLE				
Maximum length (r)	ClL_1	144.0	2	140.0–148.0
Maximum length (l)	ClL_1	154.0	1	154.0
Mid-shaft circumf. (r)	ClC	40.7	6	35.5–44.5
Mid-shaft circumf. (l)	ClC	39.5	8	35.5–44.5
HUMERUS				
Maximum length (r)	HuL_1	332.3	3	317.0–344.0
Maximum length (l)	HuL_1	310.0	2	295.0–325.0
Vert. diam. of head (r)	$HuHD_1$	48.65	2	47.7–49.6
Vert. diam. of head (l)	$HuHD_1$	45.9	1	45.9
Max mid-shaft diam. (r)	HuD_1	23.45	8	20.9–26.1
Max mid-shaft diam. (l)	HuD_1	23.5	6	23.0–26.7
Min mid-shaft diam. (r)	HuD_2	18.0	7	16.7–20.0
Min mid-shaft diam. (l)	HuD_2	18.3	7	15.9–20.0
Mid-shaft circumf. (r)	HuC	69.9	7	68.0–73.5
Mid-shaft circumf. (l)	HuC	67.9	7	57.0–76.0
Epicondylar width (r)	HuE_1	72.5	1	72.5
Epicondylar width (l)	HuE_1	64.5	3	60.0–71.5
RADIUS				
Maximum length (r)	RaL_1	252.3	3	248.0–256.0
Maximum length (l)	RaL_1	260.0	1	260.0
ULNA				
Maximum length (r)	UlL_1	280.0	3	274.0–281.0
Maximum length (l)	UlL_1	257.5	2	249.0–266.0
FEMUR				
Maximum length (r)	FeL_1	444.5	6	398.0–477.0
Maximum length (l)	FeL_1	447.8	5	403.0–481.0
Oblique length (r)	FeL_2	442.5	6	397.0–475.0
Oblique length (l)	FeL_2	444.6	5	401.0–480.0
Vert. diam. of head (r)	$FeHD_1$	46.8	6	42.3–50.8
Vert. diam. of head (l)	$FeHD_1$	46.6	5	43.0–49.8
Sub-troch. a-p diam. (r)	FeD_1	25.2	11	20.4–28.5
Sub-troch. a-p diam. (l)	FeD_1	26.0	11	20.3–29.9
Sub-troch. transv diam. (r)	FeD_2	34.2	11	30.9–39.4
Sub-troch. transv diam. (l)	FeD_2	35.6	11	32.4–40.6
Mid-shaft a-p diam. (r)	FeD_3	28.85	10	25.0–33.4
Mid-shaft a-p diam. (l)	FeD_3	29.2	10	27.1–33.0
Mid-shaft transv diam. (r)	FeD_4	28.5	10	25.4–32.5
Mid-shaft transv diam. (l)	FeD_4	28.6	10	25.7–33.4
Mid-shaft circumf. (r)	FeC	89.1	10	84.0–103.0
Mid-shaft circumf. (l)	FeC	91.1	10	86.0–103.0
Bicondylar width (r)	FeE_1	80.0	2	76.0–84.0
Bicondylar width (l)	FeE_1	85.75	2	85.5–86.0
TIBIA				
Maximum length (r)	TiL_1	377.0	5	352.0–406.0
Maximum length (l)	TiL_1	376.5	4	345.0–409.0
Prox. bicond. width (r)	TiE_1	73.0	1	73.0
Prox. bicond width (l)	TiE_1	80.0	2	80.0
Nut. for. a-p diam (r)	TiD_1	35.9	9	31.3–42.3
Nut. for. a-p diam (l)	TiD_1	36.0	9	32.8–41.6
Nut. for. transv. diam (r)	TiD_2	24.2	9	21.9–26.9
Nut. for. transv. diam (l)	TiD_2	23.9	9	21.3–26.4
FIBULA				
Maximum length (r)	FiL_1	374.25	4	351.0–408.0
Maximum length (l)	FiL_1	370.0	1	370.0
CALCANEUS				
Maximum length (r)	CaL_1	82.3	5	80.5–83.5
Maximum length (l)	CaL_1	81.25	4	78.5–84.0
TALUS				
Maximum length (r)	TaL_1	53.8	5	53.0–54.0
Maximum length (l)	TaL_1	53.8	6	53.0–54.6

TABLE 24: DEAL: FEMALE POST-CRANIOMETRIC MEANS

METRIC	SYMBOL	MEAN	NO.	RANGE
CLAVICLE				
Maximum length(r)	ClL_1	136.0	1	136.0
Maximum length (l)	ClL_1	139.7	3	132.0–149.0
Mid-shaft circumf. (r)	ClC	35.9	9	32.5–43.0
Mid-shaft circumf. (l)	ClC	35.3	9	32.0–41.0
HUMERUS				
Maximum length (r)	HuL_1	305.8	5	295.0–313.0
Maximum length (l)	HuL_1	296.7	3	292.0–303.0
Vert. diam. of head (r)	$HuHD_1$	41.0	2	40.8–41.2
Vert. diam. of head (l)	$HuHD_1$	40.8	4	39.0–43.6
Max mid-shaft diam. (r)	HuD_1	21.9	11	18.0–25.4
Max mid-shaft diam. (l)	HuD_1	21.2	13	16.8–24.0
Min mid-shaft diam. (r)	HuD_2	16.4	11	15.2–18.5
Min mid-shaft diam. (l)	HuD_2	16.2	13	14.4–18.2
Mid-shaft circumf. (r)	HuC	64.1	11	54.0–71.0
Mid-shaft circumf. (l)	HuC	62.1	13	52.0–70.5
Epicondylar width (r)	HuE_1	58.35	4	57.0–59.8
Epicondylar width (l)	HuE_1	58.2	4	54.6–61.0
RADIUS				
Maximum length (r)	RaL_1	223.75	4	216.0–230.0
Maximum length (l)	RaL_1	220.4	5	213.0–225.0
ULNA				
Maximum length (r)	UlL_1	248.3	3	241.0–255.0
Maximum length (l)	UlL_1	242.7	3	237.0–249.0
FEMUR				
Maximum length (r)	FeL_1	417.3	3	400.0–427.0
Maximum length (l)	FeL_1	412.75	4	388.0–431.0
Oblique length (r)	FeL_2	413.0	2	400.0–426.0
Oblique length (l)	FeL_2	408.0	4	385.0–427.0
Vert. diam. of head (r)	$FeHD_1$	42.3	3	39.9–46.6
Vert. diam. of head (l)	$FeHD_1$	43.3	5	39.3–47.7
Sub-troch. a-p diam. (r)	FeD_1	23.25	10	21.5–26.7
Sub-troch. a-p diam. (l)	FeD_1	23.6	10	21.0–28.4
Sub-troch. transv diam. (r)	FeD_2	32.0	10	29.5–35.6
Sub-troch. transv diam. (l)	FeD_2	32.6	10	30.0–34.3
Mid-shaft a-p diam. (r)	FeD_3	25.6	10	23.8–27.5
Mid-shaft a-p diam. (l)	FeD_3	25.7	9	23.1–28.4
Mid-shaft transv diam. (r)	FeD_4	26.0	10	21.7–28.9
Mid-shaft transv diam. (l)	FeD_4	26.7	9	24.2–29.2
Mid-shaft circumf. (r)	FeC	81.45	10	72.0–84.5
Mid-shaft circumf. (l)	FeC	82.8	9	78.5–87.0
Bicondylar width (r)	FeE_1	–	–	–
Bicondylar width (l)	FeE_1	74.75	2	74.0–75.5
TIBIA				
Maximum length (r)	TiL_1	335.0	3	327.0–343.0
Maximum length (l)	TiL_1	335.0	4	322.0–345.0
Prox. bicond. width (r)	TiE_1	–	–	–
Prox. bicond width (l)	TiE_1	71.25	2	69.0–73.5
Nut. for. a-p diam (r)	TiD_1	32.2	8	30.5–34.4
Nut. for. a-p diam (l)	TiD_1	32.15	8	29.4–35.4
Nut. for. transv. diam (r)	TiD_2	22.0	8	18.4–26.6
Nut. for. transv. diam (l)	TiD_2	22.4	8	18.9–26.7
FIBULA				
Maximum length (r)	FiL_1	–	–	–
Maximum length (l)	FiL_1	–	–	–
CALCANEUS				
Maximum length (r)	CaL_1	75.5	1	75.5
Maximum length (l)	CaL_1	74.5	1	74.5
TALUS				
Maximum length (r)	TaL_1	49.2	4	44.6–54.5
Maximum length (l)	TaL_1	50.0	5	49.0–52.4

TABLE 25: DEAL: ALL POST-CRANIOMETRIC MEANS

METRIC	SYMBOL	MEAN	NO.	RANGE
CLAVICLE				
Maximum length (r)	ClL_1	141.3	3	136.0–148.0
Maximum length (l)	ClL_1	143.25	4	132.0–154.0
Mid-shaft circumf. (r)	ClC	37.8	15	32.5–44.5
Mid-shaft circumf. (l)	ClC	37.3	17	32.0–44.5
HUMERUS				
Maximum length (r)	HuL_1	315.75	8	295.0–344.0
Maximum length (l)	HuL_1	302.0	5	292.0–325.0
Vert. diam. of head (r)	$HuHD_1$	44.8	4	40.8–49.6
Vert. diam. of head (l)	$HuHD_1$	41.8	4	39.0–45.9
Max mid-shaft diam. (r)	HuD_1	22.6	18	18.0–26.1
Max mid-shaft diam. (l)	HuD_1	21.9	20	16.8–26.7
Min mid-shaft diam. (r)	HuD_2	17.1	18	15.2–20.0
Min mid-shaft diam. (l)	HuD_2	16.9	20	14.4–20.0
Mid-shaft circumf. (r)	HuC	66.4	18	54.0–73.5
Mid-shaft circumf. (l)	HuC	64.1	20	52.0–76.0
Epicondylar width (r)	HuE_1	61.2	5	57.0–72.5
Epicondylar width (l)	HuE_1	60.9	7	54.6–71.5
RADIUS				
Maximum length (r)	RaL_1	236.0	7	216.0–256.0
Maximum length (l)	RaL_1	227.0	6	213.0–260.0
ULNA				
Maximum length (r)	UlL_1	264.0	6	241.0–281.0
Maximum length (l)	UlL_1	248.6	5	237.0–266.0
FEMUR				
Maximum length (r)	FeL_1	435.4	9	398.0–477.0
Maximum length (l)	FeL_1	432.2	9	388.0–481.0
Oblique length (r)	FeL_2	435.6	8	397.0–475.0
Oblique length (l)	FeL_2	428.3	9	385.0–480.0
Vert. diam. of head (r)	$FeHD_1$	45.3	9	39.9–50.8
Vert. diam. of head (l)	$FeHD_1$	44.9	10	39.3–49.8
Sub-troch. a-p diam. (r)	FeD_1	24.2	22	20.4–28.5*
Sub-troch. a-p diam. (l)	FeD_1	24.9	21	20.3–29.9
Sub-troch. transv diam. (r)	FeD_2	33.2	22	29.5–39.4*
Sub-troch. transv diam. (l)	FeD_2	34.2	21	30.0–40.6
Mid-shaft a-p diam. (r)	FeD_3	27.3	21	23.8–33.4*
Mid-shaft a-p diam. (l)	FeD_3	27.6	19	23.1–33.0
Mid-shaft transv diam. (r)	FeD_4	27.1	21	21.7–32.5*
Mid-shaft transv diam. (l)	FeD_4	27.7	19	24.2–33.4
Mid-shaft circumf. (r)	FeC	85.6	21	72.0–103.0*
Mid-shaft circumf. (l)	FeC	87.2	19	78.5–103.0
Bicondylar width (r)	FeE_1	80.0	2	76.0–84.0
Bicondylar width (l)	FeE_1	80.25	4	74.0–86.0
TIBIA				
Maximum length (r)	TiL_1	365.0	7	327.0–406.0
Maximum length (l)	TiL_1	355.75	8	322.0–409.0
Prox. bicond. width (r)	TiE_1	73.0	1	73.0
Prox. bicond width (l)	TiE_1	75.6	4	69.0–80.0
Nut. for. a-p diam (r)	TiD_1	34.1	17	30.5–42.3
Nut. for. a-p diam (l)	TiD_1	34.2	17	29.4–41.6
Nut. for. transv. diam (r)	TiD_2	23.2	17	18.4–26.9
Nut. for. transv. diam (l)	TiD_2	23.2	17	18.9–26.4
FIBULA				
Maximum length (r)	FiL_1	374.25	4	351.0–408.0
Maximum length (l)	FiL_1	370.0	1	370.0
CALCANEUS				
Maximum length (r)	CaL_1	81.2	6	75.5–83.5
Maximum length (l)	CaL_1	79.7	5	74.5–84.0
TALUS				
Maximum length (r)	TaL_1	51.8	9	44.6–54.0
Maximum length (l)	TaL_1	52.1	11	49.0–54.6

* Includes measurement from unsexed individual, SK 49.

TABLE 26: DEAL: THE POST-CRANIAL METRICS: THE INDICES

	HUMERUS				FEMUR						TIBIA	
SK	Brachic		Robust		Meric		Pilast		Robust		Cnemic	
NO.	R	L	R	L	R	L	R	L	R	L	R	L
Inf II												
113	—	—	—	—	—	—	115.7	106.7	—	—	—	—
Inf III												
118	80.9	—	—	—	—	—	—	—	—	—	—	—
Juv: sex												
26 M?	86.5	85.1	13.3	13.7	66.5	67.4	93.4	89.3	12.0	12.2	78.5	80.1
115 F	79.2	80.3	—	—	—	—	—	—	—	—	—	—
48 ?	—	—	—		72.8	73.7	89.7	95.1	—	—	67.6	69.3
98 ?	77.2	72.3	—	—	—	74.0	114.3	111.1	—	—	75.3	74.1
121 ?	66.7	77.1	—	—	80.4	82.3	119.6	111.8	—	—	—	74.5
126 ?	69.7	77.1	—	—	—	—	—	—	—	—	—	—
MALE												
Young Adult												
3	71.3	73.6	—	—	67.6	70.3	102.3	104.9	13.1	12.6	76.5	80.5
54	79.9	83.2	—	—	64.7	70.6	82.8	94.4	—	—	—	—
127	—	—	—	—	75.4	75.8	108.0	114.4	—	—	72.2	69.8
Adult												
15	82.3	82.0	12.9	—	75.4	75.3	99.7	97.0	14.1	—	62.9	66.2
20	77.7	—	—	—	88.0	88.3	109.1	104.7	13.3	13.8	75.1	71.3
31	66.7	67.4	13.0	13.8	72.3	73.6	102.8	98.8	13.9	13.8	63.6	61.8
44	79.1	81.5	—	—	83.4	76.9	103.7	98.6	—	—	70.9	73.3
46	78.3	79.6	—	—	71.8	70.8	101.8	100.4	—	—	64.5	58.7
112	—	83.6	—	—	83.1	76.7	108.7	116.0	—	—	63.0	58.7
114	—	—	—	—	71.1	68.2	97.8	97.1	12.0	11.9	60.5	60.3
Mature												
108	—	—	—	—	61.1	58.2	—	—	—	—	—	—
MALE ADULT AVERAGE												
	76.5	78.7	13.0	13.8	74.0	73.2	101.7	102.6	13.3	13.0	66.7	66.7
FEMALE												
Young Adult												
30	72.6	79.3	—	—	63.3	66.1	86.9	81.8	—	12.4	—	—
123	84.4	85.8	—	—	68.7	67.5	109.7	100.8	—	—	73.4	71.1
Adult												
24	61.9	68.3	13.0	13.3	80.9	82.0	105.7	106.0	—	—	—	—
41	77.4	70.9	12.9	12.9	75.1	70.3	103.0	98.2	—	13.7	89.0	90.8
43	75.0	73.8	11.2	—	—	—	—	—	—	—	—	—
47	87.0	85.7	12.2	—	78.0	71.7	97.7	84.6	13.1	—	57.3	62.4
50	85.2	89.4	—	—	73.6	70.0	99.6	101.7	—	—	59.3	62.2
51	63.8	64.9	—	—	—	—	—	—	—	—		71.0
120	78.6	75.4	—	—	—	—	—	—	—	—	—	—
125	74.3	75.2	—	—	85.8	89.9	99.6	104.4	12.4	—	76.6	82.5
Mature												
42	70.7	81.3	12.4	12.5	—	—	—	—	—	—	65.0	—
110	—	79.4	—	—	59.6	70.8	83.7	—	—	—	—	—
119	87.7	86.6	—	—	65.4	67.6	103.0	101.1	—	—	62.5	62.1
124	—	76.5	—	—	80.4	69.0	99.6	92.4	—	—	67.2	59.3
FEMALE ADULT AVERAGE												
	76.5	78.0	12.3	12.9	73.1	72.5	98.8	96.8	12.8	13.1	68.8	70.2
SEX?												
Grown												
49	—	—	—	—	69.0	—	117.2	—	—	—	—	—
ALL ADULT AVERAGE												
	76.5	78.3	12.5	13.1	72.9	72.6	100.6	99.0	13.1	13.0	68.5	69.0

TABLE 27: THE MEAN POST-CRANIAL INDICES, DEAL, YORKSHIRE AND WETWANG SLACK

SK	HUMERUS				FEMUR						TIBIA	
	Brachic		Robusticity		Meric		Pilasteric		Robusticity		Cnemic	
NO	R NO.	L NO.	R NO.	L NO.	R NO.	L NO.	R NO.	L NO.	R NO.	L NO.	R NO.	L NO.
MALE ADULT AVERAGE												
D	76.5 (7)	78.7 (7)	13.0 (2)	13.8 (1)	74.0 (11)	73.2 (11)	101.7 (10)	102.6 (10)	13.3 (5)	13.0 (4)	67.7 (9)	66.7 (9)
Y	84.7 (40)	—	—	—	70.2 (87)	—	—	—	—	—	67.0 (82)	
WS	—	—	—	—	70.1 (121)	73.7 (116)	90.8 (122)	92.0 (121)	—	—	66.2 (114)	66.6 (114)
FEMALE ADULT AVERAGE												
D	76.5 (12)	78.0 (14)	12.3 (5)	12.9 (3)	73.1 (10)	72.5 (10)	98.8 (10)	96.8 (9)	12.8 (2)	13.1 (2)	68.8 (8)	70.2 (8)
Y	83.2 (30)	—	—		72.2 (101)	—	—	—	—	—	69.7 (90)	
WS	—	—	—	—	70.1 (171)	72.2 (176)	95.5 (175)	96.7 (172)	—	—	69.5 (155)	69.7 (159)
ALL AVERAGE												
D	76.5 (19)	78.3 (21)	12.5 (7)	13.1 (4)	73.4 (22)*	72.8 (21)	101.1 (21)*	99.9 (19)	13.1 (7)	13.0 (6)	68.2 (17)	68.4 (17)
Y	84.1 (70)	—	—	—	71.3 (188)	—	—	—	—	—	68.4 (172)	
WS	—	—	—	—	70.1 (292)	72.8 (292)	93.6 (297)	94.8 (293)	—	—	68.1 (269)	68.4 (273)

The raw measurements for these indices were not taken on the Maiden Castle material.
The three indices calculated for the Yorkshire sites were not sub-divided by side.

* includes unsexed individual SK 49.

TABLE 28: THE POST-CRANIAL INDICES SUB-DIVIDED BY CLASSIFICATION

	M(%)	NO.	F(%)	NO.	ALL(%)	NO.
FEMUR						
MERIC INDEX						
Platymeric (broad)	95.2	(20)	90.0	(18)	95.1*	(39)
Eurymeric	4.8	(1)	10.0	(1)	4.9	(2)
Stenomeric (narrow)			—		—	
TIBIA						
CNEMIC INDEX						
Platycnemic (broad)	38.9	(7)	43.75	(7)	41.2	(14)
Mesocnemic	22.2	(4)	12.5	(2)	17.6	(6)
Eurycnemic (narrow)	38.9	(7)	43.75	(7)	41.2	(14)

* Includes unsexed individual, SK 49.
Notes: no classifications have been established for the brachial and pilasteric indices.

TABLE 29: PLATYCNEMIA AND SQUATTING

	CNEMIC INDEX			
	R	NO.	L	NO.
MALE ADULT				
All tibiae	68.3	(8)	67.7	(8)
Tibiae with squatting facets	62.9	(4)	61.7	(4)
FEMALE ADULT				
All tibiae	68.8	(8)	70.2	(8)
Tibiae with squatting facets	68.0	(2)	65.2	(3)
ALL ADULTS				
All tibiae	68.5	(16)	69.0	(16)
Tibiae with squatting facets	64.6	(6)	63.2	(7)

TABLE 30: SELECTED CRANIAL NON-METRICS

TRAIT NO	M		F		ALL	
1	0	(0/10)	21.4	(3/14)	12.5	(3/24)
6	42.9	(6/14)	41.2	(7/17)	41.9	(13/31)
8	0	(0/15)	17.6	(3/17)	9.4	(3/32)
13	33.3	(5/15)	36.0	(9/25)	35.0	14/40)
14	53.3	(8/15)	44.0	(11/25)	47.5	(19/40)
15	0	(0/16)	18.2	(4/22)	10.5	(4/38)
16	58.3	(7/12)	7.7	(1/13)	32.0	(8/25)
17	40.0	(2/5)	66.7	(8/12)	58.8	(10/17)
19	28.6	(4/14)	35.3	(6/17)	32.3	(10/31)
27	20.0	(3/15)	9.1	(1/11)	15.4	(4/26)
28	75.0	(6/8)	57.1	(4/7)	66.7	(10/15)
30	9.1	(1/11)	0	(0/9)	5.0	(1/20)
35	12.5	(2/16)	8.7	(2/23)	10.5	(4/38)
37	0	(0/16)	18.7	(3/16)	9.4	(3/32)

Trait No: (1) Metopism; (6) Lambdoid ossicle; (8) Asterionic ossicle; (13) Supra orbital foramen; (14) Frontal notch present; (15) Parietal foramen present; (16) Mastoid foramen absent; (17) Mastoid foramen exsutural; (19) Zygomatico-facial foramen absent; (27) Hypoglossal canal bipartite; (28) Posterior condylar canal patent; (30) Pre-condylar tubercle; (35) Mandibular tori; (37) Mylohyoid bridge.

TABLE 31: SELECTED POST-CRANIAL NON-METRICS

TRAIT NO	M		F		ALL	
1	15.4	(2/13)	14.3	(2/14)	14.8	(4/27)
2	0	(0/9)	20.0	(2/10)	10.5	(2/19)
8	16.7	(1/6)	0	(0/6)	8.3	(1/12)
10	14.3	(1/7)	20.0	(2/10)	17.6	(3/17)
13	0	(0/3)	16.7	(2/12)	13.3	(2/15)
14	7.7	(1/13)	0	(0/17)	3.3	(1/30)
15	5.3	(1/19)	0	(0/25)	2.2	(1/44)
18	18.2	(2/11)	0	(0/6)	11.8	(2/17)
20	0	(0/18)	7.7	(1/13)	3.2	(1/31)
21	36.4	(8/22)	36.8	(7/19)	37.5	(15/41)
23	7.7	(1/13)	0	(0/10)	4.4	(1/23)
25	62.5	(5/8)	87.5	(7/8)	75.0	(12/16)
26A	58.3	(7/12)	50.0	(6/12)	54.2	(13/24)
26B	33.3	(4/12)	50.0	(6/12)	41.6	(10/24)
26C	8.4	(1/12)	0	(0/12)	4.2	(1/24)

Trait No: (1) Atlas Facet Double; (2) Atlas Posterior Bridge; (8) CV6 BFT; (10) Accessory Sacral Facets; (13) Supra Scapular Foramen; (14) Septal Aperture; (15) Supracondylar Spur; (18) Plaque; (20) Third Trochanter; (21) Hypotrochanteric Fossa; (23) Emarginate Patella; (25) 'Squatting Facets' Lateral; (26) Calcaneal Facet Form.

TABLE 32A: DEAL: ADULT ORAL HEALTH (MAXILLA)

Caries	R															L	
TOOTH	8	7	6	5	4	3	2	1	1	2	3	4	5	6	7	8	TOTAL
MALE																	
n	6	7	6	7	9	9	7	7	7	8	8	11	4	5	7	8	116
carious	2	3	0	1	1	1	0	0	0	0	1	2	1	2	4	4	22
%	33.3	42.9	0	14.3	11.1	11.1	0	0	0	0	12.5	18.2	25.0	40.0	57.1	50.0	19.0
FEMALE																	
n	4	8	7	8	8	9	4	6	6	8	10	8	6	9	9	3	113
carious	2	1	2	0	3	0	1	0	0	0	2	0	0	4	2	0	17
%	50.0	12.5	28.6	0	0	0	25.0	0	0	0	20.0	0	0	44.4	22.2	0	15.0
ALL																	
n	10	15	13	15	17	18	11	13	13	16	18	19	10	14	16	11	229
carious	4	4	2	1	4	1	1	0	0	0	3	2	1	6	6	4	39
%	40.0	26.7	15.4	6.7	23.5	5.6	9.1	0	0	0	16.7	10.5	10.0	42.9	37.5	36.4	17.0

Calculus	R															L	
TOOTH	8	7	6	5	4	3	2	1	1	2	3	4	5	6	7	8	TOTAL
MALE																	
n	6	7	6	7	9	9	7	7	7	8	8	11	4	5	7	8	116
calculus	2	2	0	2	2	3	2	2	2	2	2	2	0	1	0	1	25
%	33.3	28.6	0	28.6	22.2	33.3	28.6	28.6	28.6	25.0	25.0	18.2	0	40.0	0	12.5	21.6
FEMALE																	
n	4	8	7	8	8	9	4	6	6	8	10	8	6	9	9	3	113
calculus	1	4	2	2	1	1	0	1	1	2	3	1	2	1	1	1	24
%	25.0	50.0	28.6	25.0	12.5	11.1	0	16.7	16.7	25.0	30.0	12.5	33.3	11.1	11.1	33.3	21.2
ALL																	
n	10	15	13	15	17	18	11	13	13	16	18	19	10	14	16	11	229
calculus	3	6	2	4	3	4	2	3	3	4	5	3	2	2	1	2	49
%	30.0	40.0	15.4	26.7	17.6	22.2	18.2	23.1	23.1	25.0	27.8	15.8	20.0	14.3	6.2	18.2	21.4

TABLE 32A: DEAL: ADULT ORAL HEALTH (MAXILLA) (continued)

Abscess	R															L	
TOOTH	8	7	6	5	4	3	2	1	1	2	3	4	5	6	7	8	TOTAL
MALE																	
n	7	8	8	9	10	10	9	9	9	10	10	11	9	9	9	9	146
abscess	1	1	0	0	0	0	0	0	0	0	2	1	2	3	1	2	12
%	14.3	12.5	0	0	0	0	0	0	0	0	20.0	9.1	22.2	33.3	11.1	22.2	8.2
FEMALE																	
n	9	9	10	9	10	12	11	11	12	13	13	12	11	11	8	5	162
abscess	0	0	0	0	0	0	1	0	0	1	2	0	0	1	1	0	6
%	0	0	0	0	0	0	9.1	0	0	7.7	15.4	0	0	9.1	12.5	0	3.7
ALL																	
n	16	17	18	18	20	22	20	20	21	23	23	23	20	20	17	14	308
abscess	1	0	0	0	0	0	1	0	0	1	4	1	2	4	2	2	18
%	6.2	0	0	0	0	0	5.0	0	0	4.3	17.4	4.3	10.0	20.0	11.8	14.3	5.8

A-M loss	R															L	
TOOTH	8	7	6	5	4	3	2	1	1	2	3	4	5	6	7	8	TOTAL
MALE																	
n	7	8	8	9	10	10	9	9	9	10	10	11	9	9	9	9	146
a-m loss	0	0	2	2	1	0	1	1	0	0	0	0	0	1	1	1	10
%	0	0	25.0	22.2	10.0	0	11.1	11.1	0	0	0	0	0	11.1	11.1	11.1	6.8
FEMALE																	
n	9	9	10	9	10	12	11	11	12	13	13	12	11	11	8	5	162
a-m loss	2	2	3	1	2	3	2	2	3	3	3	3	4	2	0	0	35
%	22.2	22.2	30.0	11.1	20.0	25.0	18.2	18.2	25.0	23.1	23.1	25.0	36.4	18.2	0	0	21.6
ALL																	
n	16	17	18	18	20	22	20	20	21	23	23	23	20	20	17	14	308
a-m loss	2	2	5	3	3	3	3	3	3	3	3	3	4	3	1	1	45
%	12.5	11.8	27.8	16.7	15.0	13.6	15.0	15.0	14.3	13.0	13.0	13.0	17.4	15.0	5.9	7.1	14.6

TABLE 32B: DEAL: ADULT ORAL HEALTH (MANDIBLE)

Caries	R															L	
TOOTH	8	7	6	5	4	3	2	1	1	2	3	4	5	6	7	8	TOTAL
MALE																	
n	9	9	6	10	11	10	8	7	8	10	11	10	10	8	10	9	146
carious	0	1	2	2	0	0	0	0	0	0	0	0	1	2	4	2	14
%	0	11.1	33.3	20.0	0	0	0	0	0	0	0	0	10.0	25.0	40.0	22.2	9.6
FEMALE																	
n	4	10	8	8	9	11	11	9	7	11	13	11	9	10	10	5	146
carious	0	3	1	0	0	0	0	0	0	1	1	1	1	2	2	0	12
%	0	30.0	12.5	0	0	0	0	0	0	9.1	7.7	9.1	11.1	20.0	20.0	0	8.2
ALL																	
n	13	19	14	18	20	21	19	16	15	21	24	20	19	18	20	14	292
carious	0	4	3	2	0	0	0	0	0	1	1	1	2	4	6	2	26
%	0	22.1	21.4	11.1	0	0	0	0	0	4.8	4.2	5.0	10.5	22.2	30.0	14.3	8.9

Calculus	R															L	
TOOTH	8	7	6	5	4	3	2	1	1	2	3	4	5	6	7	8	TOTAL
MALE																	
n	9	9	6	10	11	10	8	7	8	10	11	10	10	8	10	9	146
calculus	3	3	3	2	1	2	2	2	2	2	2	2	2	1	2	1	32
%	33.3	33.3	50.0	20.0	9.1	20.0	25.0	28.6	25.0	20.0	18.2	20.0	20.0	12.5	20.0	11.1	21.9
FEMALE																	
n	4	10	8	8	9	11	11	9	7	11	13	11	9	10	10	5	146
calculus	3	4	3	2	2	1	1	2	2	4	4	5	3	5	3	2	46
%	75.0	40.0	37.5	25.0	22.2	9.1	9.1	18.2	28.6	36.4	30.8	45.5	33.3	50.0	30.0	40.0	31.5
ALL																	
n	13	19	14	18	20	21	19	16	15	21	24	21	19	18	20	14	292
calculus	6	7	6	4	3	3	3	4	4	6	6	7	5	6	5	3	78
%	46.2	36.8	42.9	22.2	15.0	14.3	15.8	25.0	26.7	28.6	25.0	33.3	26.3	33.3	25.0	21.4	26.7

TABLE 32B: DEAL: ADULT ORAL HEALTH (MANDIBLE) (continued)

Abscess	R															L	
TOOTH	8	7	6	5	4	3	2	1	1	2	3	4	5	6	7	8	TOTAL
MALE																	
n	11	11	11	11	11	11	10	8	9	10	11	11	11	10	11	11	167
abscess	0	0	3	0	0	0	0	0	0	0	0	0	0	1	0	0	4
%	0	0	27.3	0	0	0	0	0	0	0	0	0	0	10.0	0	0	2.4
FEMALE																	
n	12	13	12	12	13	13	11	12	12	13	13	13	13	12	13	13	200
abscess	0	1	0	0	0	0	0	0	0	0	0	0	0	1	1	0	3
%	0	7.7	0	0	0	0	0	0	0	0	0	0	0	8.3	7.7	0	1.5
ALL																	
n	23	24	23	23	24	24	21	20	21	23	24	24	24	22	24	24	367
abscess	0	1	3	0	0	0	0	0	0	0	0	0	0	2	1	0	7
%	0	4.2	13.0	0	0	0	0	0	0	0	0	0	0	9.1	4.2	0	1.9

A-M loss	R															L	
TOOTH	8	7	6	5	4	3	2	1	1	2	3	4	5	6	7	8	TOTAL
MALE																	
n	11	11	11	11	11	11	10	8	9	10	11	11	11	10	11	11	167
a-m loss	0	1	4	1	0	0	1	0	0	0	0	1	1	2	0	0	11
%	0	9.1	36.4	9.1	0	0	10.0	0	0	0	0	9.1	9.1	20.0	0	0	6.6
FEMALE																	
n	12	13	12	12	13	13	11	12	12	13	13	13	13	12	13	13	200
a-m loss	3	3	3	3	2	1	0	1	3	0	0	0	2	2	3	3	29
%	25.0	23.1	25.0	25.0	15.4	7.7	0	8.3	25.0	0	0	0	15.4	16.7	23.1	23.1	14.5
ALL																	
n	23	24	23	23	24	24	21	20	21	23	24	24	24	22	24	24	367
a-m loss	3	4	7	4	2	1	1	1	3	0	0	1	3	4	3	3	40
%	13.0	16.7	30.4	17.4	8.3	4.2	4.8	5.0	14.3	0	0	4.2	12.5	18.2	12.5	12.5	10.9

TABLE 33: DEAL: ADULT ORAL HEALTH

	Deal — % of Teeth with Dental Diseases							
	CARIES		CALCULUS		ABSCESS		A.M.LOSS	
MALE								
Maxilla	19.0	(22/116)	21.6	(25/116)	8.2	(12/146)	6.8	(10/146)
Mandible	9.6	(14/146)	21.9	(32/146)	2.4	(4/167)	6.6	(11/167)
All	13.7	(36/262)	21.8	(57/262)	4.8	(15/313)	6.7	(21/313)
FEMALE								
Maxilla	15.0	(17/113)	21.2	(24/113)	3.7	(6/162)	21.6	(35/162)
Mandible	8.2	(12/146)	31.5	(46/146)	1.5	(3/200)	14.5	(29/200)
All	11.2	(29/259)	27.0	(70/259)	2.5	(9/362)	17.7	(64/362)
MALE & FEMALE								
Maxilla	17.0	(39/229)	21.4	(49/229)	5.8	(18/308)	14.6	(45/308)
Mandible	8.9	(26/292)	26.7	(78/292)	1.9	(7/367)	10.9	(40/367)
All	12.5	(65/521)	24.4	(127/521)	3.7	(25/675)	12.6	(85/675)

TABLE 34: THE YORKSHIRE SITES: ADULT ORAL HEALTH

	Yorkshire Sites — % of Teeth with Dental Diseases				
	CARIES	NO.	ABSCESS	A.M.LOSS	NO.
MALE					
Maxilla	1.5	(1070)	1.4	2.4	(1169)
Mandible	1.3	(2273)	1.2	2.6	(2467)
All	1.3	(3343)	1.3	2.5	(3636)
FEMALE					
Maxilla	3.9	(1007)	0.9	1.3	(1113)
Mandible	2.5	(2359)	0.8	2.0	(2462)
All	2.9	(3366)	0.8	1.8	(3575)
MALE & FEMALE					
Maxilla	2.6	(2399)	1.2	1.9	(2637)
Mandible	1.9	(5212)	1.0	2.3	(5653)
All	2.1	(7611)	1.0	2.2	(8290)

The Cremated Bones

Five cremations were examined, and the results are summarised in Tables 35 and 36; full details are recorded in the archive. All individuals are adult, but the disappointing lack of dental evidence did not permit tighter age definition. Only two teeth fragments survived, both from Cremation 132; Cremation 4 had the only surviving alveolar, which was sizeable but without teeth. None of the cremations had any evidence of pathology.

There is evidence for the burning of the whole body in four burials; Cremation 2 has no feet fragments, but that is not significant because so few of the bones have survived (total weight only 191g). All the cremated bones are well burnt but incompletely calcined. In most, the cortical bone is white and the cancellous bone pale brown. Cremations 2 and 130 are well burnt with some horizontal fissuring of the skull. Cremation 4 is less well burnt – the cortical bone is mostly creamy white, the cancellous bone ginger coloured, some heavy long bone fragments have dark grey interiors, and there are colour variations from pinkish brown to dark grey. The differences in the right and left petrous temporal bones are worth noting. The right is mostly dark grey and larger with sharp contours. The left is smaller though less burnt, brownish and very worn. It is difficult to believe that they come from the same cremation, let alone the same individual. There is no other evidence for another individual.

Graves 2 and 4 were adjacent, and the two cremations are remarkable for their lack of small and tiny fragments. Unlike Graves 130–32 they had not been disturbed in Roman times. An estimated average length of the smaller fragments is 25mm. It should also be noted that the identification of the fragments in the two burials is mutually exclusive although Cremation 2, only a sixth of the weight of Cremation 4, has far less material for comparison. Most of the skull fragments in Cremation 4 are split horizontally and most of those in Cremation 2 are not, but there are some fragments that are similar in appearance. An attempt was made to discover a join between the single femur fragment with a linea aspera in Cremation 2 and four such fragments in Cremation 4, but it proved impossible. It was also found that the thickness of the fragment in Cremation 2 was significantly smaller (2–3mm) than those in Cremation 4.

The excavator suggested that Cremations 130 and 132 might be from the same burial. There is no indisputable evidence, although on balance it seems likely that they were different individuals. Both have the area of frontal bone (skull) with the internal crest, but for 130 it is the anterior end of the crest and for 132 the posterior. The fragments do not join. A small split fragment from Cremation 132 is probably the right supra orbital limit, which certainly exists for 130. A small radius fragment from 132 could be from the left radius, and is much more slender than the definite left radius of Cremation 130. The cranial fragments from 132 are mostly thinner than 130 and have more iron salt staining. It is unlikely that Cremations 130 and 132 represent the same individual.

Several cremated fragments from Cremations 4 (2.5g) and 131 (1g) were considered as possible animal bone and submitted to A. J. Legge, who identified: Cremation 4, rib fragments, possibly animal; Cremation 131, animal, probably not rib fragments. No more positive identification was possible.

TABLE 35: CREMATED BONES: SUMMARY

GRAVE	AGE	SEX	WEIGHT (g)	MAX. SIZE OF FRAGMENTS (MM) SKULL	LONG-BONE
2	Adult	?	191	53 x 34	77
4	Adult <30	?Male	1124	51 x 32	85
130	Adult	Male	321	50 x 48	79
131	Adult	?	265	28 x 24	73
132	Adult	?	271	34 x 20	46

TABLE 36: CREMATED BONES: IDENTIFIABLE BONES

GRAVE		2	4	130	131	132
CRANIUM:	parietal	L	X	X		X
	frontal		R	X		X
	sphenoid		R L	X		
	petrous temporal		R L			R L
	squamous temporal		L			X
	ethmoid		X			
	occipital	X	X	X	X	
	zygomatic arch				L	
	malar		R			
	maxilla		L	R		
	maxilla alveolar		R			
MANDIBLE:	alveolar		X			
	coronoid		R			
	other		L	L		
TEETH:	pre-molar					upper
	molar					lower
UPPER EXTREMITY:	clavicle		X			
	scapula		X			R
	humerus	X	R L		X	X
	radius		R L	L	X	L
	ulna	L	X	L	R	
	carpal		X			X
	metacarpal		X			R
	phalanges	X	X			X
STERNUM						X
RIBS		X	X	X	X	X
VERTEBRAE:	atlas		X			
	axis/dens		X			X
	cervical		X			X
	thoracic		X		X	X
	lumbar		X	X		X
	saccral		X			X
PELVIS			X	L	X	R
LOWER EXTREMITY:	femur	X	R L	R	X	X
	patella					X
	tibia	L	X	X	X	
	fibula				X	
	tarsal		X	R	X	X
	calcaneum		X	X	X	
	metatarsal		R			
	phalanges			X		
ANIMAL BONES			?		X	

X=fragment present; R, right; L, left.

A Horse Burial and Other Grave Offerings

Grave 53 – a horse burial (pl. v; fig. 6)

Grave 53 contained the skeleton of an entire horse, which had been placed in the burial pit on its left side. In order to fit into the rather narrow grave pit the forelegs were tightly flexed at the carpal joint, while the hind legs were extended backwards.

Because of the rather hostile burial environment the bones are very brittle and all have some degree of surface erosion, particularly so at the limb extremities. The cranial bones were also very eroded. Fragmentation had taken place due to the pressure of soil and some further damage to the cranium was sustained during excavation. Some measurements could not therefore be taken with complete accuracy and these are designated as estimated in the list of measurements given below.

Two Iron Age or early Roman horse burials have been described from Yorkshire (Legge 1991), and these are used here as a basis for comparison with the Mill Hill Horse.

The Mill Hill horse

Identification

An examination of the dentition shows that the specimen is a true horse *Equus caballus*. The cheek teeth have the wide lingual folds of enamel and the degree of penetration of the buccal fold which separate the horse from other equid species.

Age of the horse

All of the bones of the appendicular skeleton were fully fused with the exception of the proximal femurs and tibias, where the fusion line was still partially open, but in a very late stage of fusion. Of the axial skeleton, the cervical, thoracic and lumbar vertebrae all have fused proximal articular surfaces, but unfused distal surfaces. The exception is in the last lumbar vertebra which is unfused both proximal and distal. The individual sacral vertebra were also unfused both proximal and distal, though fragmentation of the bones prevents a judgement of the extent of fusion of these vertebrae at their lateral margins. The age for the fusion of these bones is commonly quoted as 3.5 years for the later fusing limb bones and 5 years for the vertebral bodies (Habermehl 1975). This would suggest that the horse was less than five years old at the time of death.

Age may also be estimated from the dentition, both from the wear pattern on the incisors and by height loss due to wear on the permanent cheek teeth. In younger horses age estimation is fairly reliable from the incisors as the cavity at the centre of the tooth (the infundibulum) rapidly changes its form with progressive tooth wear. The Mill Hill horse has the full adult dentition in wear, likely to be attained only after the age of four years (Huidekoper 1891, Habermehl 1974). The roots of the upper and lower dentition are still open with the exception of the left M^1 where the roots are closed.

However, the incisor teeth are of limited help for age estimation of the Mill Hill horse as the infundibulae are imperfectly formed on some incisors, and are represented only by shallow enamel folding on the lingual surface of the tooth. The upper lateral incisors have the infundibulum fully isolated by a surround of dentine with the exception of a small notch on the lingual surface. The remaining four incisors have no infundibulae (right and left I^2) or weakly developed infundibulae (right and left I^1). Of the lower dentition, the lateral incisors again have no infundibulae. The central four incisors are in an early state of wear and the infundibulae are enclosed by dentine. The wear on the incisor teeth can be judged to correspond with the age of six or seven years as illustrated by Huidekoper (1891, figs 88, 91) though, due to the abnormality of the infundibulae in these teeth, this estimate cannot be given a high reliability.

Age is probably best estimated from the crown height of the permanent premolars and molars (Levine 1982, table 1). That study gives the mesio-distal diameters (the L dimension of Von den Driesch 1976, figs 6b, 19b) of a small sample of New Forest pony teeth; the Mill Hill horse teeth are very close in size to these, and can therefore be directly compared. Levine's graphs of crown height loss in relation to age (1982, figs 10–15) allow the following age estimates to be made:

TABLE 37: MILL HILL HORSE: RIGHT MANDIBLE

TOOTH:	P2	P3	P4	M1	M2	M3
crown height:	45.5	70.7	60.8	55.5	67.0	71.5
estimated age:	7	6	7	7	6	6

These methods of age estimate provide a good measure of agreement, and show the horse to be a young adult, of an age of about six or seven years.

Sex of the horse

The pelvis of the Mill Hill horse was fragmented on lifting, but it has been largely reconstructed on the bench. The pelves of male and female horses are illustrated in Sisson and Grossman (1953, fig. 90). There is little doubt that the Mill Hill horse pelvis corresponds well with that of the female. The shafts of the ilium and pubis are slender and the pelvic inlet is large and rounded. The sciatic notch forms a wide, smooth curve.

The male horse almost always has canine teeth ('tushes') in both the upper and lower jaws, while these are small or more commonly absent in the female. Although the cranium of the horse could not be lifted intact, all of the teeth are present, and there are no canine teeth among them. It is concluded that the horse was female.

Stature and bone size of the horse

A comparison is made between the Mill Hill horse and two entire horse skeletons from Yorkshire (full measurements given by Legge 1991), a sample from Danebury (Grant 1984), and the horse bones which survive from the King's Barrow at Arras, Yorkshire (Legge 1984; see below for measurements).

Figs 51–3 show the dimensions of entire specimens of the metacarpal, tibia and radius from these sites,

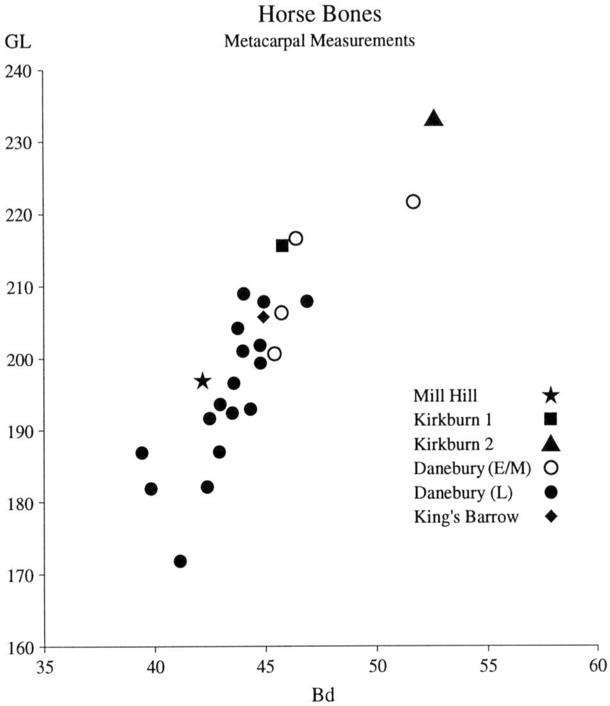

Figure 51. Iron Age horses, metacarpal measurements.

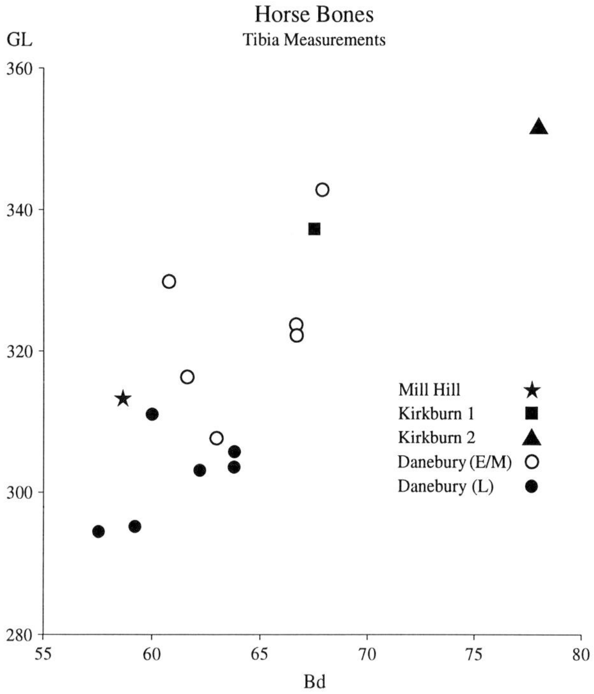

Figure 52. Iron Age horses, tibia measurements.

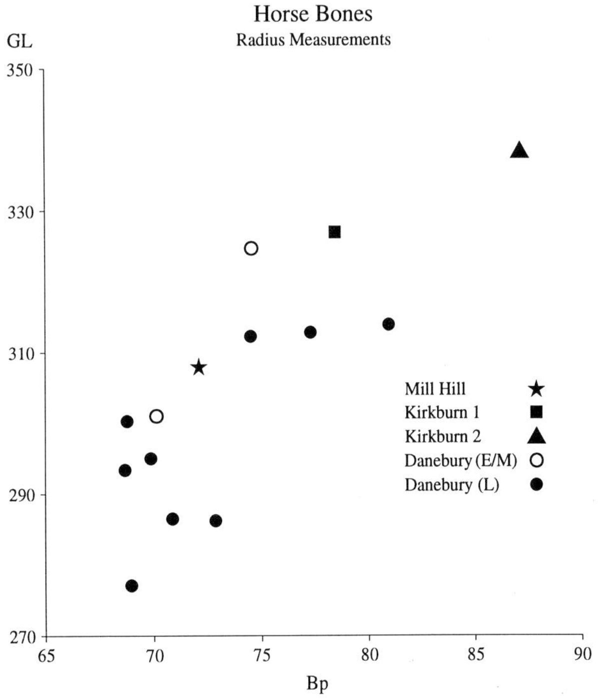

Figure 53. Iron Age horses, radius measurements.

plotting length (GL) against an articular width (Bp or Bd). Grant (1984) has noted the fact that the horses from the earlier phases of the Danebury sequence are larger than those from later phases. This is shown well in fig. 51 (metacarpal) and fig. 52 (tibia). Four specimens have been excluded from the diagram as their measurements appear to be those of metatarsals. The sample of entire radii (fig. 53) from the early period at Danebury is small, though again the Mill Hill specimen falls within the range of the Late Phase specimens.

Length measurements of horse limb bones can be used to estimate withers heights, by means of Kiesewalter's factor (Boessneck 1970). The following withers heights (in cm) have been determined:

TABLE 38: ESTIMATED WITHERS HEIGHTS OF FOUR IRON AGE HORSES

	MILL HILL	KNPY	KRDB	KING'S BARROW
metacarpal	122	144	134	130
metatarsal	125	141	133	133
tibia	128	147	134	—
mean:	125	144	133.6	131.5

In the British horse measurement of the 'hand' (1 hand=10.16 cm), the Mill Hill horse has an average stature of slightly more than 12 hands, while the largest horse in the table above, specimen KNPY, was a little over 14 hands. However, the larger size of the Yorkshire horse may be due to a rather later date than the Mill Hill specimen.

These measurements correspond well with other reports on samples of Iron Age horse bones:

Asheville (Wilson 1978)	120–142 cm
Gussage (Harcourt 1979)	102–145 cm
West Stow (Crabtree 1989)	110–136 cm

The Mill Hill horse is thus typical of the small animals that were used during the Iron Age, only the larger of which attained the size of the modern New Forest pony.

Pathology of the specimen

As would be anticipated in a young adult animal the skeleton shows no signs of joint disease, though inflammatory lesions in the foot bones were found in a horse of seven-nine years of age from Kirkburn in Yorkshire (Legge 1991). The only evidence of disease comes from the right P^2 which has a severe erosion caused by infection around the anterior root, forming a cavity 25×14 mm and which penetrates deeply into the body of the tooth. The margins of the cavity are thickened and rounded suggesting a long-standing infection, likely to have caused considerable pain to the animal. The skull is very fragmented and it was not possible to identify the socket of this tooth, so that the extent to which the bone was affected by the infection could not be determined.

There is no bit wear on either P_2, which was again recognised in one of the two horses from Kirkburn (Legge 1991).

Dog bones in Grave 47

The disarticulated bones of a fully adult but very small dog (*Canis familiaris*) were found with the human skeleton in Grave 47. Those present are listed below. As bones from the skull, vertebrae, ribs and both front and hind limbs were found it is probable that the whole animal was originally buried.

The bones are so small that it was necessary to check carefully that they were not those of a fox (*Vulpes vulpes*) as the bones of a male fox in the writer's collection are of very similar size. However, the putative dog bones show a higher degree of robusticity, especially in the shaft and articular dimensions. The measurements Dp divided by the length measurement GLC gives the following figures:

TABLE 39: COMPARISON OF ROBUSTICITY OF DOG AND FOX BONES

SPECIMEN	GLC/DP
Grave 47	0.27
modern fox 1	0.22
modern fox 2	0.22
modern fox 3	0.22

The mandibles too show different characteristics; the mandibular bone from Grave 47 is significantly more robust than that of the three modern fox specimens. The teeth also show differences, in that the cusps of the M_1 (particularly the paraconid and the metaconid) are more rounded and more robust in the specimen from Grave 47 than in the foxes. The latter also show a strong development of the lingual protocone, which is very weakly developed in the specimen from Grave 47 and in other modern dog specimens when compared with the foxes.

The small size of the dog, bearing in mind its date, is not surprising. Harcourt (1974) reviewed the body size of dogs in British archaeology. The humerus of this specimen, at a little under 120mm in length, would fall at the lower end of size for those identified as Iron Age dogs (Harcourt 1974, fig. 5, table 9). However, in the early Romano-British period, small dogs become common. Limb bone lengths have a suggestion of bimodality (ibid. fig. 8), and are divisible into lap dogs and working dogs. The specimen from Grave 47 falls into the small lap dog size range and was probably a household pet rather than a working dog. The humerus length (119.8mm) suggests a standing height of only 38.5cm in the living dog, using the factor quoted by Harcourt (ibid. 154), who found a range of 30cm to 64cm in 31 dog humeri from this period.

BONES IDENTIFIED FROM THE DOG IN GRAVE 47
left and right mandibles:
left mandible:
1=199.0 2=97.5(E) 8=53.9 10=25.7 11=28.7
left and right humerus:
left humerus:
GLI=119.8 GLC=118.2 Dp=31.6 Bd=22.5 SD=8.4
Other bones (poorly preserved):

cranium:	fragment of left temporal bone
scapula:	left, glenoid only
radius:	right distal articulation
ulna:	right distal
tibia:	right and left shafts
metatarsal:	1 proximal articulation
ribs:	3 right rib articular ends, fused
vertebrae:	2 cervical, fused
	1 thoracic, fused
	1 lumbar, fused
	1 caudal, fused

Other bone finds from the graves

GRAVE 2

Pig (Sus scrofa)
Probably the entire vertebral column, from atlas to sacrum, had been deposited. The bones are eroded and fragmentary, though it is evident that most were unfused. The following bones can be identified with some certainty: at least four cervical vertebrae, nine or ten thoracic vertebrae, five lumbar vertebrae, all with unfused proximal and distal articular surfaces. Axis vertebra with unfused posterior articulation and sacrum with fusing proximal articulation.

TABLE 40: IDENTIFICATION OF FOWL BONES FROM GRAVE 2

	right side	left side
Limb bones:		
coracoid		whole
scapula	proximal	
humerus	proximal	
tibiotarsus	distal	distal missing
femur	proximal	
carpometacarpus	fragment	whole
tarsometatarsus	proximal	whole
furcula		proximal
Vertebrae:		
thoracosynsacralis		
1 cervical		

Fowl (Gallus gallus)
In the lists, the designation 'whole' implies that most of the bone is present; erosion or other damage has, in most cases, prevented measurement; those which were possible are listed in the appendix of measurements (Table 40).

Mole (Talpa europaea)
pelvis (appears recent)

GRAVE 4

Pig
Probably a complete vertebral column of pig was deposited, but it is now very fragmentary and poorly preserved. All fragments of vertebral bodies are unfused: four or five lumbar vertebrae, one caudal vertebra, and 13 other vertebral fragments were identified, all very eroded.

Fowl

TABLE 41: IDENTIFICATION OF FOWL BONES FROM GRAVE 4

	right side	left side
Limb bones:		
coracoid		whole
scapula	whole	whole
humerus	distal missing	whole
radius		whole
carpometacarpus	distal	whole
femur	distal	whole
tibiotarsus		whole
ulna	proximal	whole
furcula fragment		
Vertebrae:		
thoracosynsacralis		
1 cervical		

Discussion of the grave offerings

Graves 2 and 4 contained articulated animal bones which appear to represent very modest offerings. In some Yorkshire Iron Age graves (Legge 1991) it appeared that substantial joints of pig meat had been deposited, though most graves had part of a pig skull or even single sheep bones. However, even where larger joints were deposited, there was some evidence that the meat had been removed before burial of the bones. The Mill Hill examples appear to follow this pattern, in that the offering was of limited value, with the deposition of the vertebral column rather than head or leg bones. Unfortunately the poor condition of the bones precluded the examination of the vertebrae for possible filleting cuts.

The presence of vertebrae only is very unlikely to be the product of differential preservation. In most species, the vertebrae are of low density and survive poorly in most archaeological assemblages, so that it is improbable that vertebrae would survive in conditions where limb bones did not.

Although the pig bones represent a modest grave offering, the burial of a young horse in Grave 53 is more substantial, as with the Kirkburn horse burials. The evidence of a rather long standing tooth infection might be taken to imply that a horse in less than full health had been chosen. It was noted that one specimen at Kirkburn had a foot ailment, and that at least one horse from the King's Barrow (Legge 1984) was of extreme age. It seems likely that, at least in some instances, less than perfect specimens had been placed in graves; this, of course, assumes that killing was deliberate in these circumstances.

The fowls appear to have been fully adult, with at least the body entire. Though the bones are rather poorly preserved, it is evident that most parts of the body were present. The absence of foot bones, except for the tarsometatarsi from grave 2, and any but the last neck vertebra, suggests that these had been placed in a prepared, possibly even cooked, condition. The fowls were very small; the few bone measurements that were possible (see below) are very close to those from the bones of a bantam hen in the writer's collection, which had an entire live weight of 420g.

The tarsometatarsi from Grave 2 lack spurs and no unfused spurs were found among the bone fragments, nor did the tarsometatarsus show any evidence of spur development. Bearing in mind the caution of Sadler (1991) on spur development in the fowl, it is probable that the specimen is a hen. That from Grave 4 lacks the tarsometatarsi, but its small size suggests that it too was female.

The archaeological evidence is that the fowl was introduced into Britain only in the later Iron Age; Coy (1974) reports only seven fowl bones from Danebury. Of these, six come from the Late (b) Phase, and only one, possibly intrusive, was found in the earlier Late (a) Phase. This distribution is confirmed by further work on the Danebury bird bones, where Sergeantson (1991) has reported a further five fowl bones, again all from the late period. The occurrence of fowls in graves of the first century AD at Mill Hill thus accords with this evidence.

The rarity of fowl bones from that period need not be taken to suggest that the species was particularly rare as Walters (1984) reported that only a single fowl bone survived of 180 discarded at a recent camp site due to the activities of scavenging dogs.

Acknowledgement
I am grateful to Christine Whatrup for her assistance in the benchwork on the bones.

Mill Hill, Deal; measurements of animal bones from graves 2, 4 and 53

All limb bone measurements correspond to those illustrated for equid bones by Von den Dreisch 1976, with exceptions for the distal humerus, where two extra measurements are taken on the distal articulation. The measurement HT represents the maximum dimension of the articulation at its medial margin in the line of the long axis of the bones (Legge 1981, fig. 53B; given there as measurement T). HTC is the dimension of the constricted central part of the articulation, measured again parallel to the long axis of the bone.

The tooth measurements are those illustrated by Levine 1982, fig. 2, 228. Certain bones of the horse skeleton are badly eroded by adverse burial conditions. The bone measurements taken are those not markedly affected by postmortem erosion or damage, though all of the bone surfaces are eroded to some degree. While this effect is not significant for bone length measurements in most cases, width measurements are more obviously affected. Those with obvious surface erosion or other slight damage are designated (E) at the end of the measurement to indicate that it is *estimated.* Where bones are too damaged for a particular measurement to be taken this is indicated by NP=measurement *Not Possible* (Tables 42, 43, pp. 151–2).

Fowl bone measurements
Some of the bones are quite heavily eroded. Those measured are the better preserved. While the length measurements will be relatively little affected, articular width measurements should be used with caution. The figures given in italics are the measurements of a modern bantam hen of deadweight 750 g.

TABLE 44: FOWL BONE MEASUREMENTS

GRAVE 2				
tarsometatarsus	(left)	GL=64.8	Bp=10.8	
modern		*GL=63.4*	*Bp=11.9*	
GRAVE 4				
humerus	(left)	GL=66.6	Bp=17.9	
modern		*GL=60.6*	*Bp=16.3*	
carpometacarpus	(left)	GL=34.7		
modern		*GL=32.1*		
femur	(left)	GL=72.3	Lm=68.5	Bd=13.4
modern		*GL=66.8*	*Lm=62.3*	*Bd=13.2*
ulna	(left)	GL=66.2		
modern		*GL=58.6*		

Some further measurements of Iron Age horse bones
The measurements in Table 45 were taken from horse bones surviving from the 1816 excavation of the King's

TABLE 42: HORSE BURIAL; GRAVE 53. BONE MEASUREMENTS.

Scapula (R)						
SLC=50.0	GLP=78.4	LG=50.0	BG=42.0			
Scapula (L)						
SLC=50.5	GLP=78.5	LG=50.0	BG=42.0			
Humerus (R)						
GL=253.0	GLl=252.4	GLC=243.4	Bp=NP	SD=26.4	Bd=69.0	
Bt=63.8	HT=39.8	HTC=30.6				
Humerus (L)						
GL=255.0	GLl=249.2	GLC=244.2	Bp=75.2	SD=26.8	Bd=70.0	
Bt=65.0	HT=39.5	HTC=31.7				
Radius/ulna (R)						
GL=374.0	GLl=NP					
Radius/ulna (L)						
GL=373.0	GLl=370.0					
Radius (R)						
GL=308.0	GLl=300.9(E)	Ll=249.2(E)	SD=NP	Bp=72.0		
BFp=66.3(E)	Bd=NP	BFd=NP				
Radius (L)						
GL=306.5	GLl=300.1	Ll=294.0	SD=29.1	Bp=72.0		
Bfp=65.9	Bd=62.0	Bfd=53.6				
Ulna (R)						
SDO=41.0	DPA=51.4	LO=69.0				
Ulna (L)						
SDO=40.3	DPA=51.5	LO=67.7				
Metacarpal (R)						
GL=198.0	GLl=NP	Ll=NP	Bp=NP	Dp=NP	SD=NP	Bd=NP
Metacarpal (L)						
GL=197.0	GLl=195.0	Ll=190.0	Bp=43.7	Dp=29.2	SD=NP	Bd=41.3(E)
Phalanges heavily eroded: not measurable						
Femur (R)						
GL=349.0	GLC=326.0	Bp=NP	SD=30.3(E)	Bd=NP		
Femur (L)						
GL=352.0	GLC=324.0	Bp=93.0	SD=32.5(E)	Bd=NP		
Tibia (R)						
GL=313.0	Ll=297.0	Bp=NP	SD=29.6(E)	Bd=NP	DD=NP	
Tibia (L)						
GL=316.0	Ll=300.0	Bp=74.0	SD=29.7(E)	Bd=58.0	DD=35.7(E)	
Metatarsal (R)						
GL=241.0	GLl=238.0	Bp=42.3	Bd=NP	SD=24.2(E)		
Metatarsal (L)						
GL=239.5	GLl=234.5	Bp=41.9	Bd=41.5(E)	SD=23.8(E)		
Astragalus (R)						
GH=48.1	Bfd=43.3					
Astragalus (L)						
GH=47.5	Bfd=43.6					
Calcaneum (R)						
GL=NP						
Calcaneum (L)						
GL=95.7						

Phalanges very eroded: not measurable.
Cranium very fragmented: no measurements possible.

Barrow, Arras, Yorkshire, now held in the Yorkshire Museum. These consist of a left metacarpal and metatarsal, five left maxillary teeth (apparently from a single tooth row) and part of a left mandible. The mandible is from a very old horse, worn to the extent that the enamel folds are eliminated from the occlusal surface. It is evident that the maxillary and mandibular dentition do not come from the same animal. The maxillary teeth come from a horse that was nine–ten years old at death, while the mandible comes from a very old horse of 25 or more years at death. A brief note on these horse bones was published by Legge (1984), but without the bone measurements which are given in Table 45.

TABLE 45: HORSE BONES, KING'S BARROW, ARRAS

Metacarpal (L)					
GL=205.6		LI=203.2	Bp=45.5	SD=29.8	Bd=45.0
Metatarsal (L)					
GL=253.0		LI=250.0	Bp=46.0	SD=27.4	Bd=45.0
Tooth crown measurements					
Maxilla					
RIGHT	P3	P4	M1	M2	M3
height	44.5	49.3	45.5	48.2	38.8
mesiodistal	28.0	26.5	24.0	24.5	28.0
Mandible					
RIGHT	P3	P4	M1	M2	M3
height	NP	NP	NP	12.5	—
mesiodistal	24.9	24.5	21.9	24.0	—

TABLE 43: HORSE BURIAL, GRAVE 53. MANDIBULAR AND TOOTH CROWN MEASUREMENTS

Right mandible fragmented						
Left mandible						
6a=163.0	7=78.5	7a=77.0	8=89.8	8a=87.2	15=NP	
19=170.0	20=169.5	21=NP	22a=86.3	22b=69.0	22c=43.8	
Tooth crown measurements:						
Maxilla						
RIGHT	P2	P3	P4	M1	M2	M3
height	*	60.0	64.6	57.6	63.0	62.5
mesiodistal	35.4	27.8	27.6	23.9	24.2	23.8
LEFT	P2	P3	P4	M1	M2	M3
height	50.5	64.2	67.6	61.6	67.0	NP
mesiodistal	36.2	27.6	27.6	24.3	23.8	NP#
Mandible						
RIGHT	P2	P3	P4	M1	M2	M3
height	45.5	60.8	70.7	55.5	67.0	71.5
mesiodistal	31.6	27.0	27.3	24.2	24.5	29.0
LEFT	P2	P3	P4	M1	M2	M3
height	NP	63.3	NP	NP	NP	NP
mesiodistal	32.2	27.6	27.2	24.5	25.0	29.2

* = tooth missing
NP = tooth tightly rooted in socket; height measurement not possible.
# = diseased tooth roots

4

RADIOCARBON RESULTS

Radiocarbon determinations have been made on material from the Mill Hill cemetery in three separate laboratories. An initial single measurement was produced in 1988 at Harwell (HAR–8444) and has since been supplemented by a further six determinations carried out in 1992 and 1993 at the British Museum (BM–2840, –2867 and –2868) and at Oxford (OxA–2966 to –2968). Both British Museum and Harwell laboratories used conventional liquid scintillation counting methods while the Oxford Laboratory employs accelerator mass spectrometry, thus requiring much smaller sample sizes.

Technical details for the Harwell measurement are given in Walker et al. 1990, for the British Museum in Ambers et al. 1991, and for Oxford in Hedges et al. 1989. Both BM and OxA results were produced after the quality control recommendations made in *Radiocarbon*, 32(3), 1990 and both laboratories maintain concordant quality assurance procedures. The results of the recent IAEA organised interlaboratory comparison (Rozanski 1992) indicate no interlaboratory offsets between the two.

All the samples were of bone, and only well-preserved protein extracts (produced as described in the references quoted above) were used for dating. The results are given below in Table 46, quoted in the form recommended by Stuiver and Polach 1977, in uncalibrated years BP (before 1950), and corrected for isotopic variation (measured or estimated as shown in the table). Calibrations listed were generated from the curve of Stuiver and Pearson 1986, as calculated using revision 2.0 of the University of Washington Quaternary Laboratory Radiocarbon Calibration Program (CALIB, published in Stuiver and Reimer 1987) and the probabilistic method of calibration. Calibrated date ranges are quoted in the form recommended by Mook 1986, with the end points rounded outwards to five years. An effect of this is slightly to overestimate the date range for a given confidence interval. Calibrated ranges for the results are also shown diagrammaticality in figs 54 and 55. Fig. 54 shows the one and two sigma age ranges as lines, while fig. 55 shows the full probability distribution.

TABLE 46: RADIOCARBON DETERMINATIONS ON HUMAN BONE FROM GRAVES IN THE MILL HILL CEMETERY

LAB REF	GRAVE	RADIOCARBON RESULT (BP)	$\delta^{13}C$ (‰)	CALIBRATED AGE RANGE (CALENDAR YEARS) 1σ (68% PROBABILITY)	2σ (95% PROBABILITY)
BM-2867	29	1630±35	−18.6	345 to 450 AD	335 to 535 AD
BM-2840	110	1860±35	−20.1	90 to 95 AD or 110 to 215 AD	75 to 230 AD
OxA-2966	15	1975±70	−22.4	80 BC to 85 AD	170 BC to 145 AD or 165 to 195 AD
OxA-2968	44	1950±70	−18.7	40 BC to 125 AD	115 BC to 225 AD
OxA-2967	20	2030±65	−20.9	155 to 145 BC or 120 BC to 55 AD	200 BC to 115 AD
BM-2868	31	2130±50	−21.0 estimated	355 to 310 BC or 210 to 95 BC	356to 275 BC or 265 TO 45 BC
HAR-8444	5	2390±60	−21.4	755 to 705 BC or 535 to 395 BC	765 to 385 BC

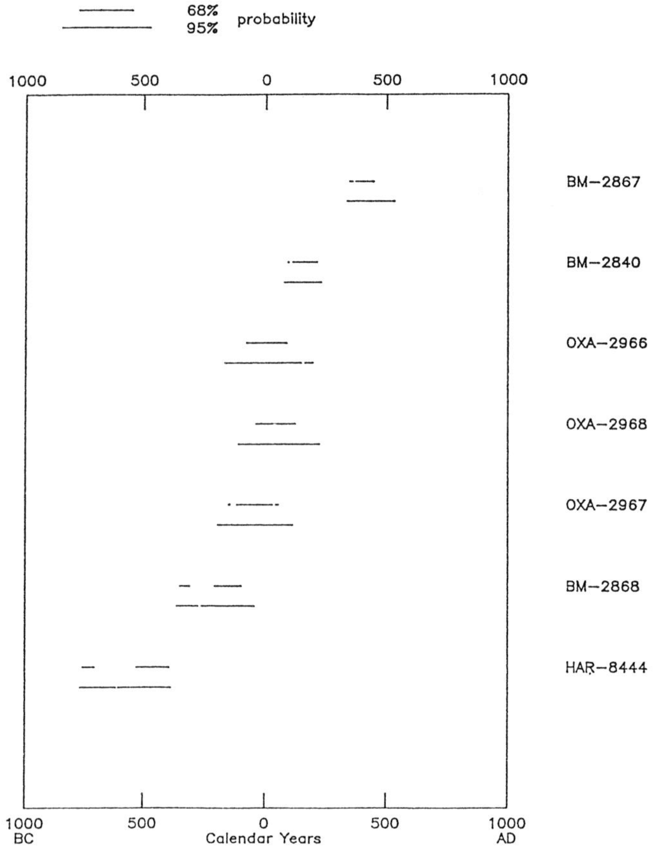

Figure 54. Calibrated age ranges for the radiocarbon results shown as simple lines for summed 68% and 95% confidence limits.

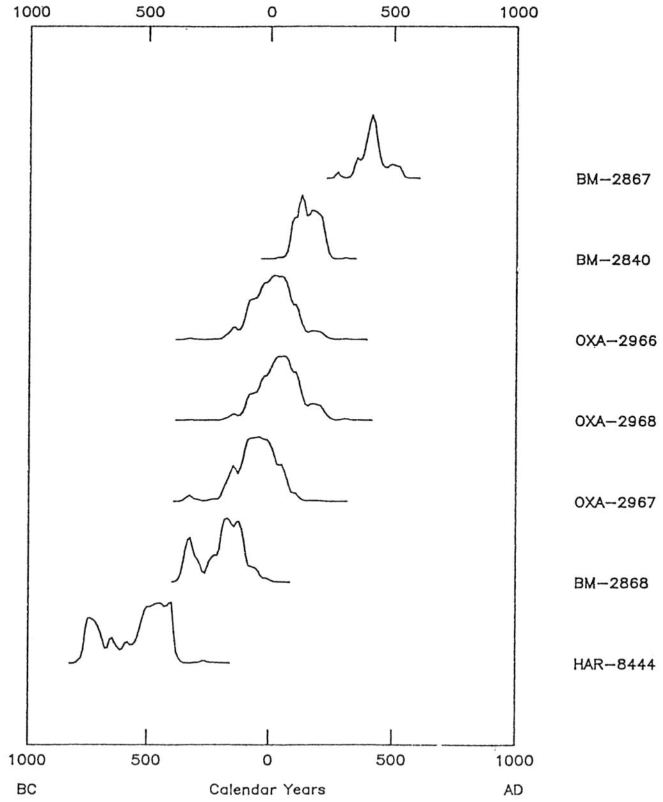

Figure 55. Calibrated age ranges for the radiocarbon results given as probability distributions of possible calendar age.

5

DISCUSSION

Some 45 Iron Age burials were excavated at Mill Hill between 1984 and 1989, but many more were disturbed by nineteenth-century chalk quarrying. The cremations alone rate this site among the most significant British Iron Age cemeteries, whilst the number of inhumations is unparalleled in southeastern England.

The predominant burial rite at Mill Hill in the Iron Age was inhumation and the graves covered a considerable time span, starting with an isolated and tightly crouched inhumation (Grave 5) dated by carbon-14 between the eighth and fourth centuries BC. The large Bronze Age round barrow at the centre of the site had no surviving burial to provide a local context for the origins of the inhumation rite, but elsewhere in East Kent both cremations and inhumations are known from the Bronze Age, although too few have been examined to indicate which was the more common rite. Cremations were found in four urns under an Early Bronze Age round barrow on Free Down at Ringwould (Woodruff 1874, 22), and in Middle Bronze Age bucket urns at Kingsdown and Great Mongeham (Champion 1982, 34–5). Inhumation is represented by a crouched burial under a small barrow above Otty Bottom, Kingsdown, to the southeast of the Ringwould mound (Woodruff 1874, 26) whilst on Mill Hill itself salvage work at the northwest end of the ridge in 1977 revealed a ring-ditch enclosing two graves provisionally dated to the Bronze Age (Philp 1978). On the present site, however, there seems to have been a significant break in the burial sequence between the construction of the Bronze Age barrow and the establishment of the Iron Age cemeteries.

At least two centuries after Grave 5, probably early in the second century BC, another isolated burial (Grave 112) was interred some 50m northwest of the centre of the Bronze Age barrow. Its proximity to this once prominent monument was probably intentional and it may be significant that the main axis of the grave is aligned on the centre of the area enclosed by the ring-ditch. It is the earliest extended inhumation at Mill Hill, introducing a rite that remained the norm for inhumations here for the rest of the Iron Age and into the Roman period. Grave 112 contained the skeleton of a rather short young man of slightly feminine build wearing a fine bronze crown and buried with an impressive range of metalwork including a sword and shield. This exceptional grave-group, one of the finest from Iron Age Britain, is unsurpassed in terms of its artwork, for no other British Iron Age burial has included so many decorated items. In an earlier age such a rich asssemblage buried almost within sight of the continent, would have been casually accepted as the equipment of an immigrant. But all the artefacts are distinctively British. Its parallels may lie with other isolated warrior burials in Britain, such as those from Shouldham, Norfolk (Clarke and Hawkes 1955), St Lawrence, Isle of Wight (Jones and Stead 1969) and Great Brackstead, Essex (unpub.). Perhaps the most relevant comparison is with the burial from Newnham Croft, Cambridgeshire (Fox 1923, 81) whose grave-group included a couple of fine decorated artefacts as well as, it now seems likely, the remains of a crown. Less well recorded burials at Leckhampton, Ogmore Down and Cerrig-y-Druidion can be added to the list of Iron Age notables buried with headdresses.

The interment of the high status individual in Grave 112 marks the start of a long, probably continuous burial sequence on the site in two separate inhumation cemeteries. The 28 graves excavated in the South-West Cemetery belonged to a larger cemetery partially destroyed by the nineteenth-century chalk quarry. Grave-goods were rare, but those that can be dated show that the cemetery was used during the second and first centuries BC. The second-century involuted brooch from Grave 127 is the earliest artefact from the cemetery, and all three La Tène III brooches might well be pre-Caesarian. As with Grave 112, the grave-goods in the South-West Cemetery are British and there is no reason to suggest an immigrant population (though the joiner's dogs in Grave 123 can be better matched in continental rather than British burials).

Some Iron Age inhumations had been disturbed by the chalk quarry, including one (Grave X2, with two spoons) that was plotted on a sketch plan. But most of the destroyed graves seem to have been cremations of the first century BC and later. Southeast of the quarry Aylesford Culture and Roman cremations (including Graves 2, 4, 6 and 7 in the South-East Cemetery) may effectively belong to the same burial-ground. It could have started in the second century BC with inhumations mainly at the west end, and over the next three centuries gradually progressed to the Roman cremations at the east end.

The Central Cemetery is represented by a quite separate group of inhumations whose full extent was contained within the excavated area. But the precise number of Iron Age graves is unknown because many have no grave-goods and some were certainly Roman. In the field 13 graves were classified as Iron Age, but radio-carbon dates have shown that one (Grave 29) is probably Saxon and another (Grave 110) is Roman. Six inhumations (Graves 15, 20, 26, 30, 31 and 44) are likely to date between the third century BC and first century AD, and five others (Graves 24, 28, 41, 42 and 43) could be Iron Age or Roman. The few Iron Age grave-goods were strikingly different from the finds in the South-West Cemetery (no one type occurred in both, Table 47); in particular, the absence of brooches in the Central Cemetery is curious because it seems to have been used at a time when brooches were common.

The slight remains of a ring-ditch round Grave 123 probably shows that it had been covered by a small mound, and judging from the grave spacings and interrelationships, Graves 46, 114 and 127 also in the South-West Cemetery could have been covered by barrows too. Grave 5, the early crouched burial with later burials grouped around it, and Grave 112, the warrior that starts the extended inhumation tradition, may also have been marked in some way. Other possible funerary monuments may perhaps be represented by the six- and four-post features near Grave 5. Such arrangements of post holes are common in Iron Age contexts, and possible explanations have included platforms for exposing the dead (Ellison and Drewett 1971, 190–92); but they are usually features on settlements and could have served a domestic function here because there are traces of Iron Age settlement at Mill Hill. Perhaps more relevant to the funerary rituals is the unusual shaft (Feature 58, see fig. 2), 2.5m deep that gave access to a small underground chamber located roughly mid-way between the Central and South-East Cemeteries. It has been suggested that this structure was a subterranean shrine, filled in during the second century AD (Parfitt 1986; Parfitt and Halliwell 1986). Amongst the finds was a small carved chalk figurine that might well have once occupied a niche in the wall of the chamber (Parfitt and Green 1987). The shaft must have been contemporary with at least some of the burials described here and it emphasises the religious significance of this hill-top to ancient man.

TABLE 47: GRAVE-GOODS WITH INHUMATIONS

	SOUTH-WEST CEMETERY	CENTRAL CEMETERY
Brooches	6	—
Bracelet	1	—
Pin	1	—
Joiner's dogs	5	—
Handle	—	1
Pot	—	1
Coin	—	1
Finger-ring	—	1
Knife	—	1
TOTAL NUMBER OF GRAVES	28	12

A curious feature of the South-West Cemetery was the burial of a horse in a grave aligned with, and presumably contemporary with, those for humans. Horse skeletons have been discovered on Iron Age settlements (Tollard Royal, P. F. Bird, in Wainwright 1968, 146; Blewburton Hill, Berks – though also at the edge of an Anglo Saxon cemetery, Harding 1976, 143 and fig. 5; Danebury, Hants, Grant 1984, 533–43) but they are rare in cemeteries. In the King's Barrow at Arras two horses had been buried in the same grave as a man and the remains of a two-wheeled vehicle (Stead 1984, 38, with A. J. Legge's comments p. 41), and the cranium of a horse was found with one of the King Harry Lane inhumations (Burial 194, Stead and Rigby 1989, 322). The skeleton of a horse found in 1840 in a cemetery outside the walls of the Roman town at Dorchester, Dorset, had an Iron Age bridle-bit in its mouth (RCHM 1970, 574; Palk 1984, 41–2, no. SJ4, fig. C27). One of a pair of horses formally buried at Kirkburn, East Yorkshire, each under a small round barrow, was dated by carbon-14 to the first century AD, or early in the second century AD (Stead 1991a, 27, and A. J. Legge's report, pp. 144–7). But in none of these was the animal's skeleton in a separate grave alongside a human burial. From that point of view there are perhaps better analogies with other animals in French Iron Age cemeteries. At Châlons-sur-Marne a boar had been buried in a separate grave alongside a cart-burial (Lemoine 1905, 105–6; the plan is most accessible in Piggott 1983, fig. 123), and in the cemetery at Villeneuve-Renneville, Marne, a grave aligned with the others contained the skeleton of a deer wearing a bridle-bit (Bretz-Mahler and Brisson 1958, 289–98).

In the past, ill-equipped graves such as those found on Mill Hill would have attracted little attention. In Kent, unaccompanied extended inhumations have invariably been assigned to the Anglo-Saxon period, for the county is rich in such burials, but it is now clear that they occurred in late Iron Age and Roman times as well. Even the occasional ring-ditch, another feature of excavated Anglo-Saxon cemeteries in Kent, now also can be assigned to the late Iron Age.

The only close local comparison for the late Iron Age cemeteries at Deal seems to be the poorly recorded site at Highsted, Sittingbourne, 49km to the west. Apparently 20 inhumations and six cremations were found 'with Belgic pottery and a La Tène (presumably III) brooch' (Kelly 1978, 267; Thompson 1982, 820–21). A few isolated Iron Age inhumations have also been discovered in the South-East: there are brief references to an Iron Age inhumation with a simple iron brooch found in 1960 at Dumpton Gap, Broadstairs, Kent (*Arch. Cant.* 76, 1961, lvi; Birchall 1965, 256, 257); an isolated inhumation in a purpose-cut grave at Slonk Hill, Shoreham, West Sussex, was accompanied by an involuted brooch and a shale bracelet (Hartridge 1978, 80, Grave 2; a second Iron Age inhumation, Grave 1, was in a domestic pit); and an inhumation with a Barrel Beaker was found at Willingdon near Eastbourne, East Sussex (Bugden 1931). Although never as common as cremation, the tradition of burial by inhumation does seem to have continued into the early Roman period. At Julliberries's Grave Neolithic long-barrow, near Canterbury, two late first-century AD inhumations were found cut into the upper ditch filling (Jessup 1937), whilst on Mill Hill itself, Grave 110 must be post-Conquest. Further afield, too, inhumation is occasionally found as a minority rite in cremation cemeteries (e.g. King Harry Lane, St Albans, Stead and Rigby 1989, 81).

The Iron Age inhumation cemeteries at Mill Hill, virtually without parallel in southeast England, are not closely matched elsewhere in Britain. In Yorkshire the Arras Culture graves were generally covered by a barrow (Stead 1979, 1991a), whereas most of the Deal graves were flat; the Yorkshire barrows were square in plan, unlike the surviving traces of the Deal barrow which was round; and the predominant rite was crouched or contracted inhumation, in contrast to the typical extended skeletons at Deal. Outside Yorkshire there are Iron Age inhumation cemeteries in southwest England where crouched inhumation in flat graves was the normal rite (e.g. Whimster 1977; 1981, 60–74; Aitken and Aitken 1990; Nowakowski 1991). The Deal rite may have been inspired by the continent, where Iron Age cemeteries of extended inhumations in flat graves are common, but the Mill Hill grave-goods do not reflect close continental links.

At some time in the second half of the first century BC cremation was introduced to Deal as elsewhere in south-east England. In comparison with the Iron Age inhumations, relatively few cremations have been recovered from Mill Hill but it is still one of the more important Aylesford Culture cemeteries. If the main criterion for defining size is the number of recorded burials, then Swarling (19 burials) is the largest late Iron Age cremation cemetery in the South-East; however, Aylesford, with eight recorded burials but 49 pots was almost certainly larger. Mill Hill compares well with both, containing more recorded burials than Aylesford and at least as many surviving vessels as Swarling. It also includes the inhumation burials, many predating the cremation rite, which Aylesford and Swarling appear to lack.

Surviving finds from about 20 cremations indicate that Mill Hill continued to be used as a cemetery until the late second century AD. Samian replaced Gallo-Belgic wares as the popular imported fine table ware in the mid-first century AD, while wheel-thrown, sand-tempered, kiln-fired Roman coarse wares were substituted for grog-tempered vessels. Continuity from the late Iron Age into the Roman period may have been quite usual, for most sites listed in the Gazetteer (pp. 179–93) include Roman cremations spanning the period from the later first to the end of the second century AD. But neither Aylesford nor Swarling has any definitely post-Conquest cremation, so Mill Hill survived later as well as being established earlier.

With the odd exception (e.g. Grave 1, fourth century AD, and perhaps Grave 29) Mill Hill was not used for burial in the later Roman period, and for a while it seems to have been occupied by shallow chalk quarries. Then, in the sixth century AD, the funerary tradition was revived by the Anglo Saxons: their 70 or so graves, once again focused on the Bronze Age barrow, will be the subject of another report.

TABLE 48: GRAVES AND GRAVE-GOODS: SUMMARY

GRAVE	CREM	LOCATION:				ARTEFACT	C14	NOTES
		SE	CEN.	SW	ISOL.			
2	X	X				X		
3		X						
4	X	X				X		
5		X					X	Early Iron Age
15			X			X	X	
20			X				X	? R–B
24			X					
26			X			X		
28			X					
30			X			X		
31			X				X	
41			X					
42			X					
43			X					
44			X			X	X	
46				X				
47				X		X		Includes dog
48				X				
49				X				
50				X		X		
51				X				
52				X				
53				X				Horse burial
54				X				
55				X				
107				X				
108				X		X		
110			X			X	X	R–B
112					X	X		
113				X				
114				X				
115				X				
116				X				
117				X				
118				X				
119				X				
120				X				
121				X		X		
122				X		X		
123				X		X		
124				X				
125				X				
126				X				
127				X		X		
128				X				
130	X				X			
131	X				X	X		
132	X				X	X		

6

INVENTORY OF GRAVES AND GRAVE-GOODS

From 1984–89 excavations

The original grave numbers allocated on site have been retained; thus, missing numbers within the sequence relate to other burials, mostly Saxon, not reported here. The grave number is followed by reference to the illustration of the grave-plan, the sex, age and condition of the skeleton (for condition codes see p. 125), the radiocarbon date (see p. 153) and grave-goods with references to illustrations. Grave axes given are foot to head alignments, calculated in degrees from true north. Depth measurements are for the distance into the natural chalk, rather than from ground level, since the cuts could not be traced through the topsoil overlying the chalk.

The Central Cemetery (fig. 4)

(NB: The relationship of the individual graves of the Central Cemetery to a series of probably Roman quarry pits occupying the same area remains uncertain; see p. 21).

Grave 15: (fig. 56); M, 30–35, condition 1c; radiocarbon date.
Grave-goods: Bowl (fig. 58, G15).
Axis 236°. Ovoid, 2.02m×0.59m and 0.92m deep. Pick marks on all sides. Very steep sides and a slightly rounded base. Filled with a grey-brown loam with chalk lumps and grits which contained some 60 joining sherds, forming more than half of a necked and cordoned bowl of grog-tempered ware, together with one small flint-tempered sherd. Well-preserved skeleton, supine, legs straight; right arm slightly bent across pelvis, left arm straight. Head facing left. Possibly cut by Saxon Grave 16.

Grave 20: (fig. 56); M, 30–35, condition 1c; radiocarbon date; no grave-goods.
Axis 239°. Rectangular with rounded corners, 1.97m×0.57m and 0.52m deep. Three adze marks on northeast end. Sloping sides and a flat base. Filled with a cream-brown clay loam with large chalk lumps and chalk grits containing two flint-tempered potsherds. Well preserved skeleton, supine, right leg bent to left, left leg straight. Right arm bent across pelvis, left arm straight. Head facing half left. Cuts pit (F. 223); apparently cut by Saxon Grave 23.

Grave 24: (fig. 56); F?, 35–45, condition 2c; no grave-goods.
Axis 223°. Oval, 1.63m×0.78m and 0.49m deep. Steep sides and a flat base. Filled with a brown clay loam with small chalk lumps containing five flint-tempered potsherds and three grog-tempered sherds, struck flints and a few fragments of animal bone. Well-preserved skeleton on right side, right leg bent to right, left leg straight; arms bent double. Head facing right. Apparently cut by (double) Saxon Grave 25.

Grave 26: (fig. 56); M?, 17–19, condition 2b.
Grave-goods: Bronze handle (fig. 48, no. 4) over lower backbone.

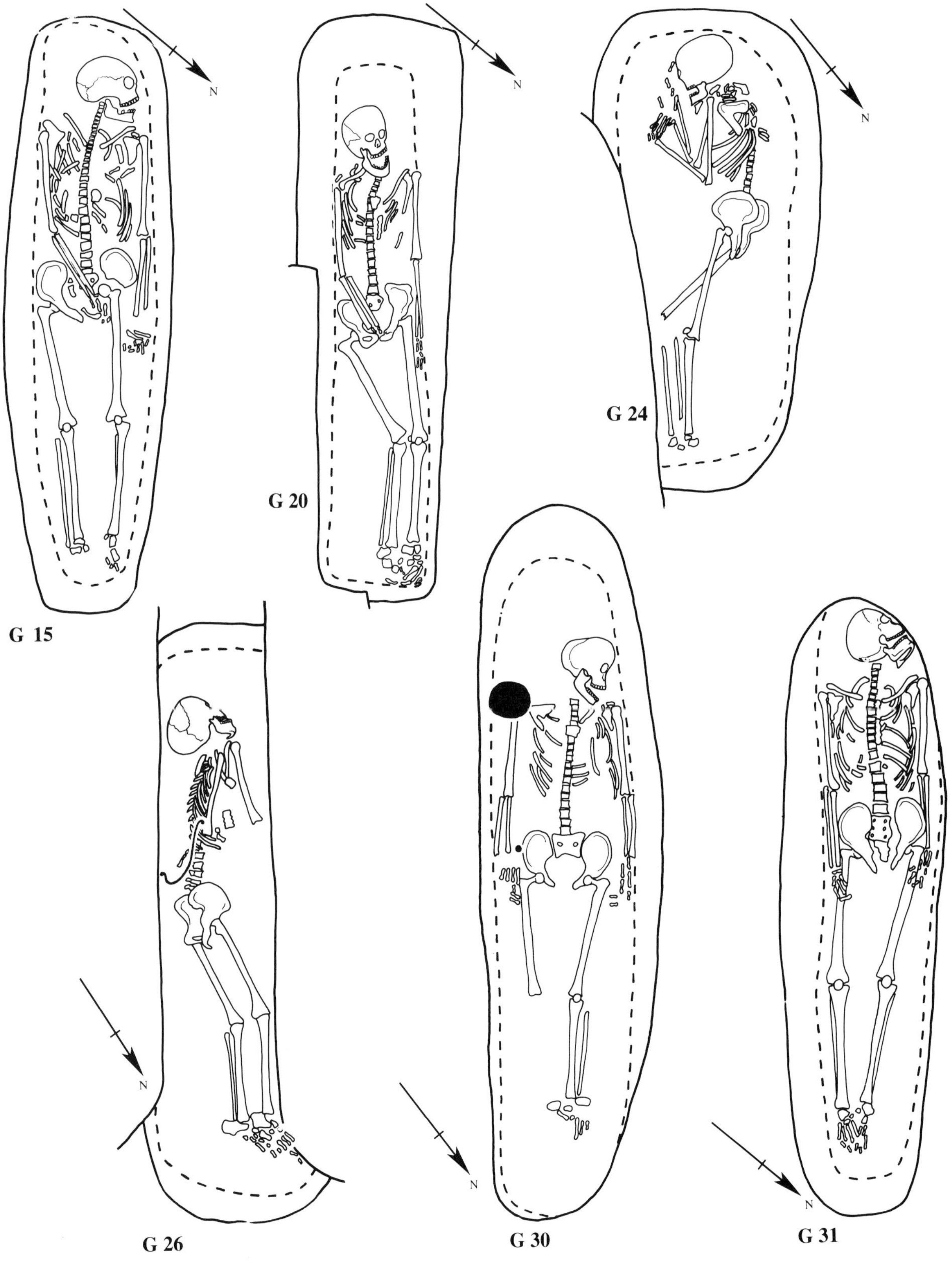

Figure 56. Central Cemetery, grave plans. (Scale 1/20)

Axis 216°. Sub-rectangular with rounded corners, 2.03m×0.66m and 0.61m deep. Four pick marks on northeast end. Steep sides and a slightly rounded base. Filled with a dark grey clay loam with occasional large chalk lumps and chalk grits containing eight sherds of flint-tempered ware and three grog-tempered sherds, together with a single probably intrusive rim of Roman sandy ware, several struck flints and a few fragments of animal bone. Well-preserved skeleton on left side, legs bent to left; arms bent double. Head facing left and rolled backwards. Apparently cut by Saxon Graves 25 and 27.

Grave 28: (not illustrated); F, 16–18, condition 6a, no grave-goods.
Axis 020°. Largely destroyed by Saxon Grave 25, rounded southern end of grave only remained, 0.80m (min.)×0.59m and 0.60m deep. Steep sides and a flat base. Filled with a dark grey clay loam with some large chalk lumps and chalk grits containing no finds. Well-preserved lower leg and foot bones only.

Grave 30: (fig. 56); F?, 20–25, condition 3d.
Grave-goods: Jar (fig. 58, G30) over right shoulder; coin (p. 112) on base of grave by right pelvis.
Axis 224°. Ovoid, 2.41m×0.64m and 0.82m deep. Two pick marks on the northwest side and northeast end. Steep vertical sides and a slightly rounded base. Filled with a light grey loam with much small chalk. Moderately well-preserved skeleton, supine, legs straight, lower right cut away by Grave 29; arms straight. Head facing left. Cut by Saxon Grave 29.

Grave 31: (fig. 56); M, 35–45, condition 1b; radiocarbon date; no grave-goods.
Axis 235°. Ovoid, 2.08m×0.57m and 0.81m deep. Adze marks on northeast end. Steep vertical sides and a flat base. Filled with a brown loam with large chalk lumps containing no finds. Well-preserved skeleton, supine, legs and arms straight. Head facing left, pushed hard against the grave side.

Grave 41: (fig. 57); F, 35–40, condition 2d; no grave-goods.
Axis 140°. Sub-rectangular with rounded ends, 2.07m×0.58m–0.75m and 0.70m deep. Pick marks on the northwest and southeast ends. Steep sloping sides and a

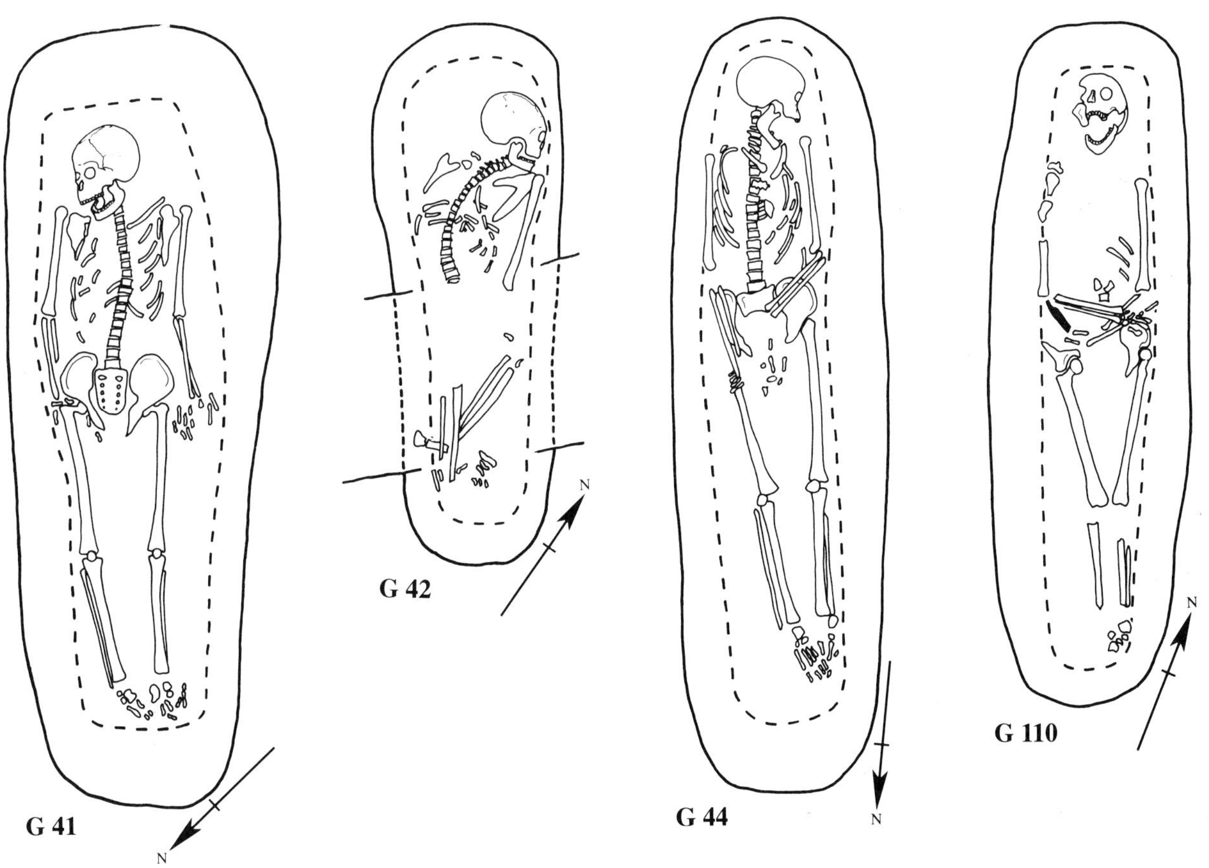

Figure 57. Central Cemetery, grave plans. (Scale 1/20)

sloping base. Filled with a light grey loam with small chalk rubble containing no finds. Well-preserved skeleton, supine, legs and arms straight. Head facing right.

Grave 42: (fig. 57); F?, 45–55, condition 4d; no grave-goods.
Axis 328°. Sub-rectangular/oval, 1.43m×0.39m–0.51m and 0.38m deep. Steep sides and a flat base. Filled with a brown clay loam with occasional small chalk lumps containing no finds. Partially disturbed skeleton, crouched, on left side. Legs and arms apparently bent. Femurs and pelvis destroyed. Head facing left. Touches end of Grave 44. Apparently cut by Roman field boundary ditch (Feature 211).

Grave 43: (not illustrated); F, 28–33, condition 4c; no grave-goods.
Axis 139°. Sub-rectangular with rounded corners, 1.97m (min.)×0.78m and 0.93m deep. Steep sloping sides and a flat base. Filled with a grey-brown clay loam with much small chalk containing no finds. Fairly well-preserved skeleton partially cut away by later graves. Supine, legs largely destroyed but probably straight; right arm straight, left arm bent across right pelvis. Head facing right. Cut by Saxon Graves 33, 39 and 45.

Grave 44: (fig. 57); M, 35–45, condition 2e; radiocarbon date.
Grave-goods: Finger-ring (fig. 48, no. 3) below pelvis among finger bones.
Axis 180°. Sub-rectangular with rounded ends, 2.06m× 0.49m and 0.79m deep. Steep sloping sides and a slightly undulating base. Filled with a cream-brown clay loam with much small chalk containing no finds. Well preserved skeleton, supine, legs straight; right arm straight over right pelvis, left arm bent over left pelvis. Head facing left. Touches end of Grave 42.

Grave 110: (fig. 57); F, 50–60, condition 4d; radiocarbon date.
Grave-goods: Knife (fig. 49, no. 1) above right pelvis (tang upwards).
Axis 347°. Sub-rectangular with rounded ends, 1.80m× 0.56m and 0.81m deep. Pick marks on base and two sides. Steep sides and a flat base. Filled with a cream loam with much chalk rubble containing no finds. Moderately well-preserved skeleton – principally the skull, pelvis and long bones. Supine, legs straight, arms bent across pelvis (right over left).

Grave 130: (not illustrated); M, adult.
Redeposited cremation in a circular pit 0.63m in diameter and 0.21m deep, cut into the partially filled Roman quarry pit complex. Steep sides and a slightly rounded base. Filled by a dark grey loam with small chalk lumps; scattered throughout the filling were fragments of cremated bone but no pottery.

Grave 131: (fig. 58); sex ?, adult.
Grave-goods: Jar (fig. 58, G131a); Pedestal Jar (fig. 58, G131b) containing the cremation.
Cremation of an adult contained within a circular pit at least 0.42m in diameter and 0.19m deep. Steep sides and a flat base. Filled by a dark brown loam with occasional small chalk lumps. Cut by Roman quarry pit complex.

Grave 132: (not illustrated); sex?, adult.
Grave-goods: Throughout the filling were fragments from at least three pots (fig. 58, G132a–c).
Redeposited cremation scattered in an oval pit measuring 0.63m (N–S)×1.10m (E–W) and 0.21m deep, cut into the partially filled Roman quarry pit complex. Steep sides and a slightly rounded base. Filled by a dark grey loam with small chalk lumps.

The South-West Cemetery (fig. 5)

Grave 46: (fig. 59); M, 35–45, condition 3e; no grave-goods.
Axis 184°. Sub-rectangular with rounded corners, 1.76m× 0.59m and 0.30m deep. Steep sides and a flat base. Filled with a brown clay loam with much small chalk containing no finds. Fairly well-preserved skeleton, supine, legs bent to left; right arm bent across body, left arm bent double. Head facing half left.

Grave 47: (fig. 59); F, 28–35, condition 3d.
Grave-goods: Brooch (fig. 40, no. 4 on the chest); disarticulated bones of a lap-dog (p. 148).
Axis 197°. Ovoid, 1.95m×0.61m and 0.80m deep. Steep sides and a flat base. Two pick marks were noted on the east wall of the grave and three on the south (end) wall. Filled with a cream-brown clay loam with much small chalk containing two sherds of flint-tempered pottery. Fairly well-preserved skeleton extended, supine; legs straight, arms bent across right pelvis. Head pushed forward, facing half left.

Grave 48: (not illustrated); sex?, 13–15, condition 4d; no grave-goods.
Axis 026°. Rectangular with rounded corners; northern end cut by a modern post hole; 1.67m×0.64m and 0.43m deep. Steep sides and a flat base. Filled with a cream-brown clay loam with much small chalk containing no finds. Poor to moderately well-preserved skeleton – principally the long bones and pelvis – prone, legs bent back at knees, arms straight by sides (right hand under pelvis). Skull missing.

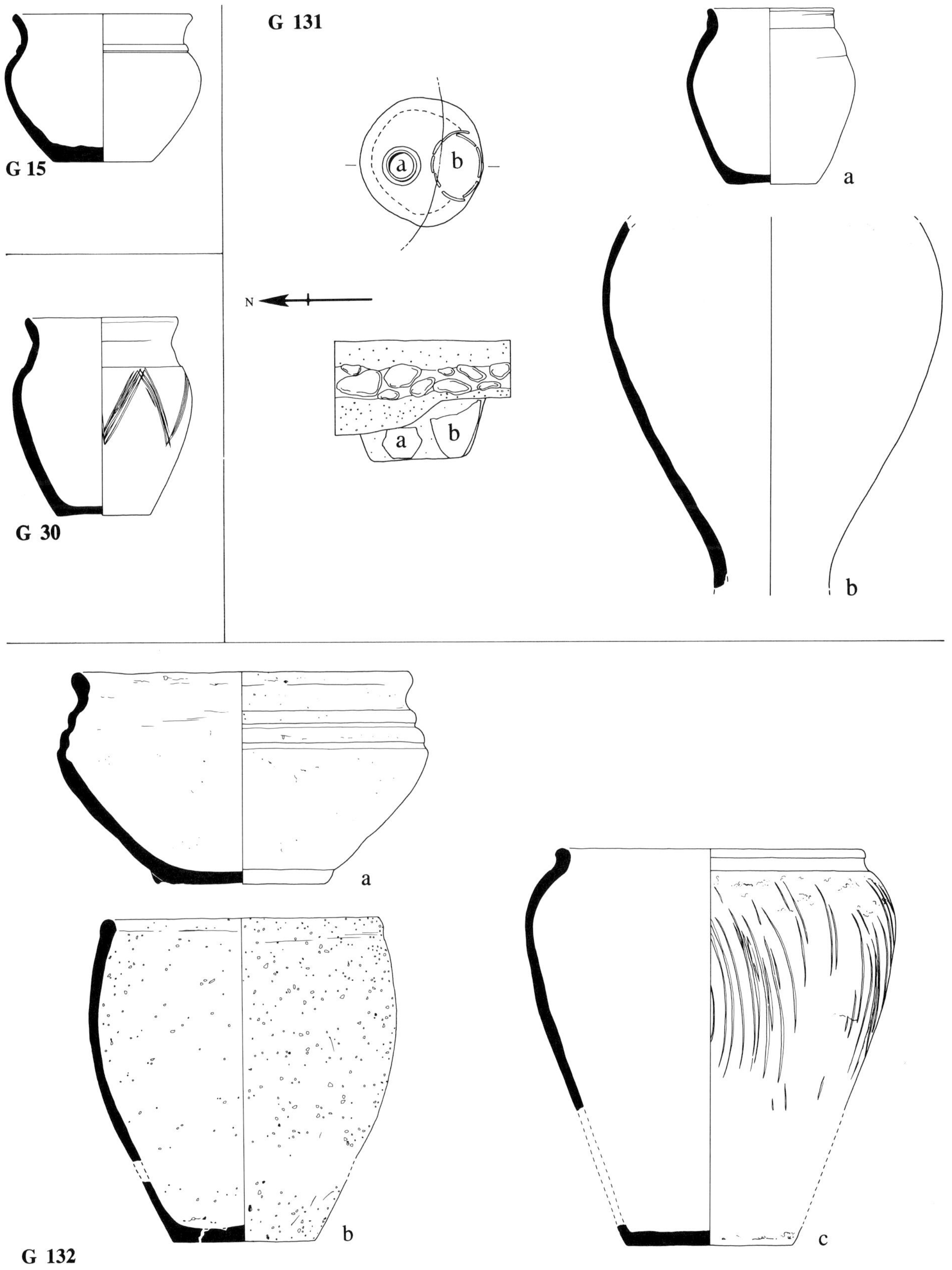

Figure 58. Grave 131, plan and section, and pottery from Graves 15, 30, 131 and 132. (Scales, pottery 1/4; plan and section of Grave 131, 1/20)

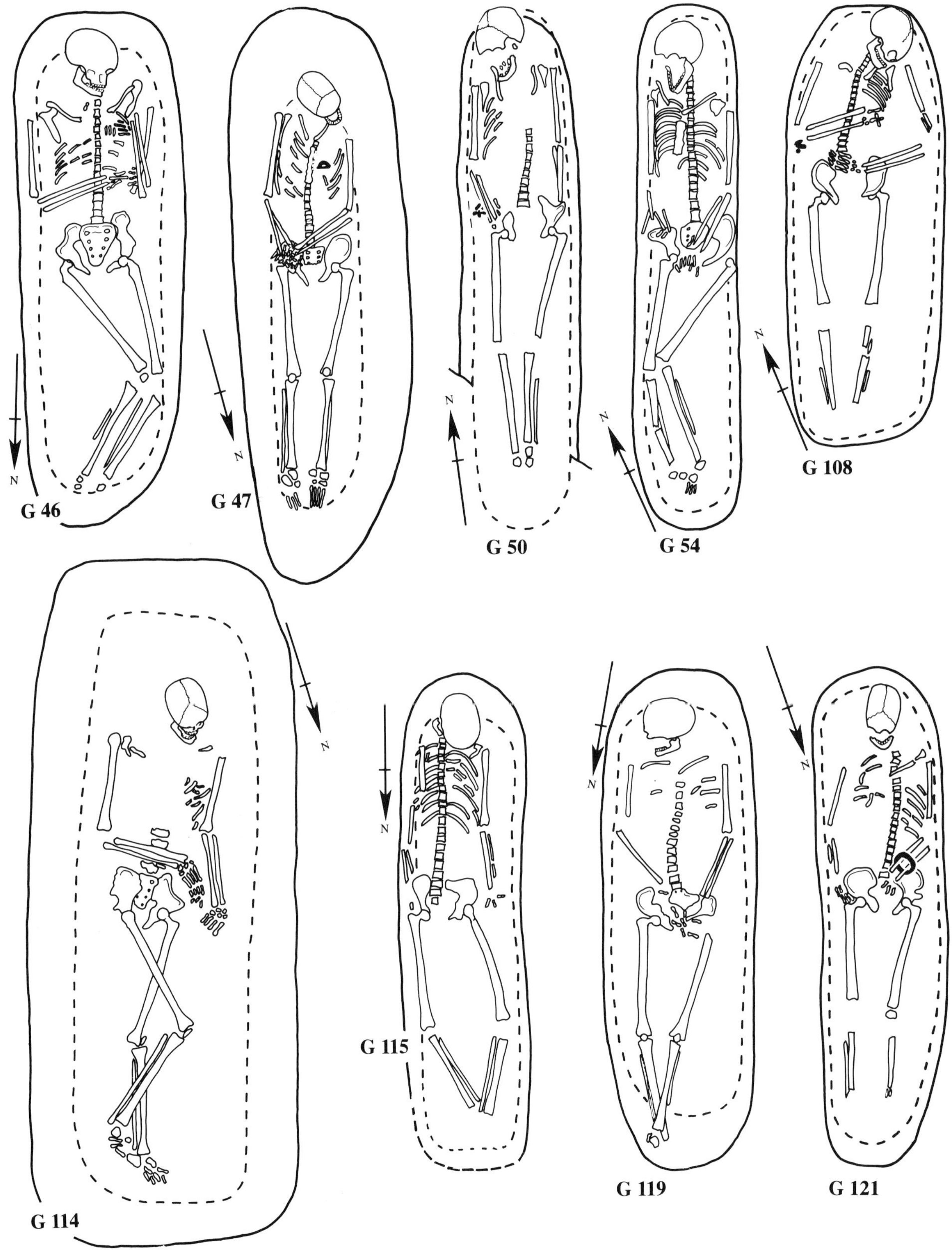

Figure 59. South-West Cemetery, grave plans. (Scale 1/20)

Grave 49: (not illustrated); sex?, adult, condition 6e; no grave-goods.
Axis 205°. Rectangular with rounded north end. South end cut away by modern wall foundation. Minimum of 1.30m×0.61m and 0.10m deep. Steep sides and a flat base. Filled with a brown clay loam with much small chalk containing no finds. Only the lower part of the skeleton, extended, supine; legs straight, upper part of body disturbed.

Grave 50: (fig. 59); F?, 35-45, condition 4d.
Grave-goods: Brooch (fig. 40, no. 6) in fragments beside and under the right forearm.
Axis 013°. Rectangular with rounded ends; south end partially cut away by modern wall foundation; 1.76m×0.43m and 0.30m deep. Generally steep sides with undercut north end; flat base. Filled with a cream-brown clay loam with some small chalk containing a few struck flints. Poor to moderately well-preserved skeleton, extended, supine; legs straight, arms straight by sides. Head facing half right.

Grave 51: (not illustrated); F, 30–40, condition 5d; no grave-goods.
Axis 013°. Sub-rectangular with rounded corners; western side partially destroyed by modern foundation trench; 1.67m×0.44m and 0.30m deep. Steep vertical sides and a flat base. Filled with a cream-brown clay loam with much small chalk containing no finds. Poorly- to moderately well-preserved skeleton but femurs robbed, supine, bent at waist to fit in grave; legs crossed at ankle (right over left), arms by sides. Head facing left.

Grave 52: (not illustrated); sex?, 6–10, condition 7e; no grave-goods.
Axis 231°. Rectangular with rounded ends, 1.46m×0.45m and 0.16m deep. Steep sides and a flat base. Filled with a brown clay loam with small chalk lumps containing no finds. Very poorly-preserved skeleton – the fragmentary skull and long bones only, extended, supine; legs straight; right arm straight, left arm decayed. Body laid down right side of grave.

Grave 53: (Horse Burial, fig. 6, p. 146); no grave-goods.
Axis 037°. Sub-rectangular with rounded corners, 2.44m × 0.94m and 0.60m deep. Steep vertical sides and a flat base. Filled with a cream-brown clay loam, containing two sherds of flint-tempered pottery and a few prehistoric struck flints, over loose small chalk rubble. Well-preserved skeleton of a young horse on its left side, back legs straight, front legs bent to fit grave.

Grave 54: (fig. 59); M?, 27–32, condition 4e; no grave-goods.
Axis 031°. Rectangular with rounded ends, 1.79m×0.38m and 0.27m deep. Adjacent to horse burial (Grave 53). Steep sides and a slightly rounded base. Filled with a cream-brown clay loam with small chalk lumps containing no finds. Moderately well-preserved skeleton, supine, legs bent to right, arms bent across pelvis. Head facing half right. Grave far too small for body.

Grave 55: (not illustrated); sex?, 1–6 (judging from size of grave), no bones survived; no grave-goods.
Axis uncertain, 019–199°. Sub-rectangular with rounded corners, 1.06m×0.40m and 0.17m deep. Steep sides and a flat base. Filled with a cream-brown clay loam with much small chalk containing no finds.

Grave 107: (not illustrated); sex?, 5–10, condition 7e; no grave-goods.
Axis 004°. Rectangular with rounded corners, 1.18m×0.43m and 0.10m deep. Steep sides and a flat base. Filled with a brown loam with chalk lumps containing a single sherd of flint-tempered pottery and a few prehistoric struck flints. Very poorly-preserved skeleton – fragmentary leg bones only – probably extended, supine; legs straight.

Grave 108: (fig. 59); M?, 40–50, code 4e.
Grave-goods: Brooch (fig. 40, no. 5), three fragments, infilling at a depth of 0.15m, over right elbow.
Axis 029°. Sub-rectangular with rounded corners, 1.50m×0.55m and 0.19m deep. Steep sides and a flat base. Filled with a brown loam with chalk lumps containing no finds. Fairly well-preserved skeleton (4e) of a probable male aged 40 to 50. Extended, supine; legs straight; right arm bent across chest, left arm bent across pelvis. Head pushed forward, facing half left.

Grave 113: (not illustrated); sex?, 1–2, condition 6d; no grave-goods.
Axis 014°. Rectangular with rounded corners, 1.02m×0.36m and 0.35m deep. Steep vertical sides and a flat base. Filled with a cream-brown clay loam with chalk lumps containing no finds. Very poorly-preserved skeleton – only the crushed skull and fragmentary leg bones, probably supine; legs bent to right, arms decayed.

Grave 114: (fig. 59); M?, 35–45, condition 3d; no grave-goods.
Axis 202°. Rectangular with rounded corners, 2.34m×0.96m and 0.50m deep. Sloping sides and a flat base. Filled with a brown clay loam with chalk lumps containing three sherds of flint-tempered pottery, together with three sherds of Neolithic Grooved Ware, three small fragments of animal bone and a few prehistoric struck

flints. Fairly well-preserved skeleton, extended, supine; left leg straight with right leg over, bent at knee; right arm bent across body, left arm straight. Head facing half left.

Grave 115: (fig. 59); F, 17–19, condition 4d; no grave-goods.
Axis 185°. Sub-rectangular with rounded south end; northern end destroyed by modern post hole; minimum of 1.65m×0.45m and 0.26m deep. Steep sides and a flat base. Filled with a cream-brown clay loam with chalk lumps containing no finds. Moderately well preserved skeleton, extended, supine; legs bowed outward, touching at ankle; arms straight by sides. Head pushed forward.

Grave 116: (not illustrated); sex?, 0–4 (judging from the size of the grave), no bones survived; no grave-goods.
Axis unknown, 016–196°. Sub-rectangular with rounded corners; east side cut by modern post hole; 0.94m×0.37m and 0.16m deep. Steep sides and a flat base. Filled with a brown clay loam with much small chalk containing no finds.

Grave 117: (not illustrated); sex ?, 2–4, condition 7e; no grave-goods.
Axis 187°. Sub-rectangular with rounded corners 1.04m× 0.49m and 0.42m deep. Steep sides and a flat base. Filled with a cream-brown clay loam with chalk lumps containing no finds. Only small skull fragments and two loose teeth.

Grave 118: (not illustrated); sex ?, 9–11, condition 6e; no grave-goods.
Axis 234°. Rectangular with rounded corners, 1.45m× 0.45m and 0.32m deep. Steep sides and a flat base. Filled with a cream-brown clay loam with chalk lumps containing a single sherd of Neolithic Grooved Ware. Poorly-preserved skeleton – only skull, vertebral column and fragmentary long bones, extended, supine; legs straight, fragmentary right arm only.

Grave 119: (fig. 59); F, 45–55, condition 4d; no grave-goods.
Axis 175°. Rectangular with rounded ends, 1.70m× 0.55m and 0.39m deep. Steep vertical sides and a slightly rounded base. Filled with a brown clay loam with many chalk lumps containing no finds. Moderately well-preserved skeleton, extended, supine; legs crossed at ankle (left over right), arms bent across pelvis. Head facing right.

Grave 120: (not illustrated); F, 30–40, condition 6d; no grave-goods.
Axis 360°. Rectangular with rounded north end; south end destroyed by modern chalk quarry; minimum of 1.60m×0.46m and 0.29m deep. Steep sides and a flat base. Filled with a brown clay loam with many chalk lumps containing no finds. Largely robbed skeleton, probably extended, supine; legs destroyed, lower arms destroyed. Head facing left.

Grave 121: (fig. 59); sex ?, 18–20, condition 4d.
Grave-goods: Bracelet (fig. 48, no. 2) around left forearm.
Axis 202°. Sub-rectangular with rounded ends, 1.70m× 0.45m and 0.36m deep. Steep sides and a flat base. Filled with a brown clay loam with many chalk lumps containing no finds. Fairly well-preserved skeleton, extended, supine, legs straight, arms bent across pelvis. Head pushed forward.

Grave 122: (fig. 61); sex ?, 6–7, condition 6e.
Grave-goods: Brooch (fig. 40, no. 7) on right side of skeleton.
Axis 319°. Rectangular with rounded ends, 1.09m×0.38m and 0.38m deep. Steep sides and a flat base. Filled with a brown clay loam with many chalk lumps containing no finds. Poorly-preserved skeleton – crushed skull and long bones only – supine, legs bent to right, arms partially decayed.

Grave 123: (fig. 60); F?, 20–25, condition 3d.
Grave-goods: (fig. 60) Five joiner's dogs, 1, 2 and 4, amongst foot bones, 3, to right of feet, 5, in two parts above and to left of skull; 6, Brooch on right ribs; 7, Pin on vertebrae.
Axis 041°. Grave partially enclosed by ring gully, 4.50m in diameter, suggesting the former existence of a small covering mound or barrow. Grave rectangular with rounded corners, 1.58m×0.73m and 0.58m deep. Steeply sloping sides and a flat base. Filled with a brown clay loam with many chalk lumps containing three sherds of flint-tempered pottery, together with three sherds of Neolithic ?Grooved Ware and three small fragments of animal bone. Fairly well-preserved skeleton, extended, supine; legs crossed at knee (left over right); right arm straight by side, left arm across pelvis. Head pushed forward. Grave too short for body; feet on wall.

Grave 124: (fig. 61); F?, 40–50, condition 3d; no grave-goods.
Axis 036°. Rectangular with rounded ends, 1.78m× 0.53m and 0.34m deep. Steep sides and a flat base. Filled with a cream clay loam with much small chalk containing no finds. Fairly well-preserved skeleton, extended, supine, legs crossed at ankle (left over right), arms straight by sides. Head pushed forward, facing half left. Right side of body rests on side of grave.

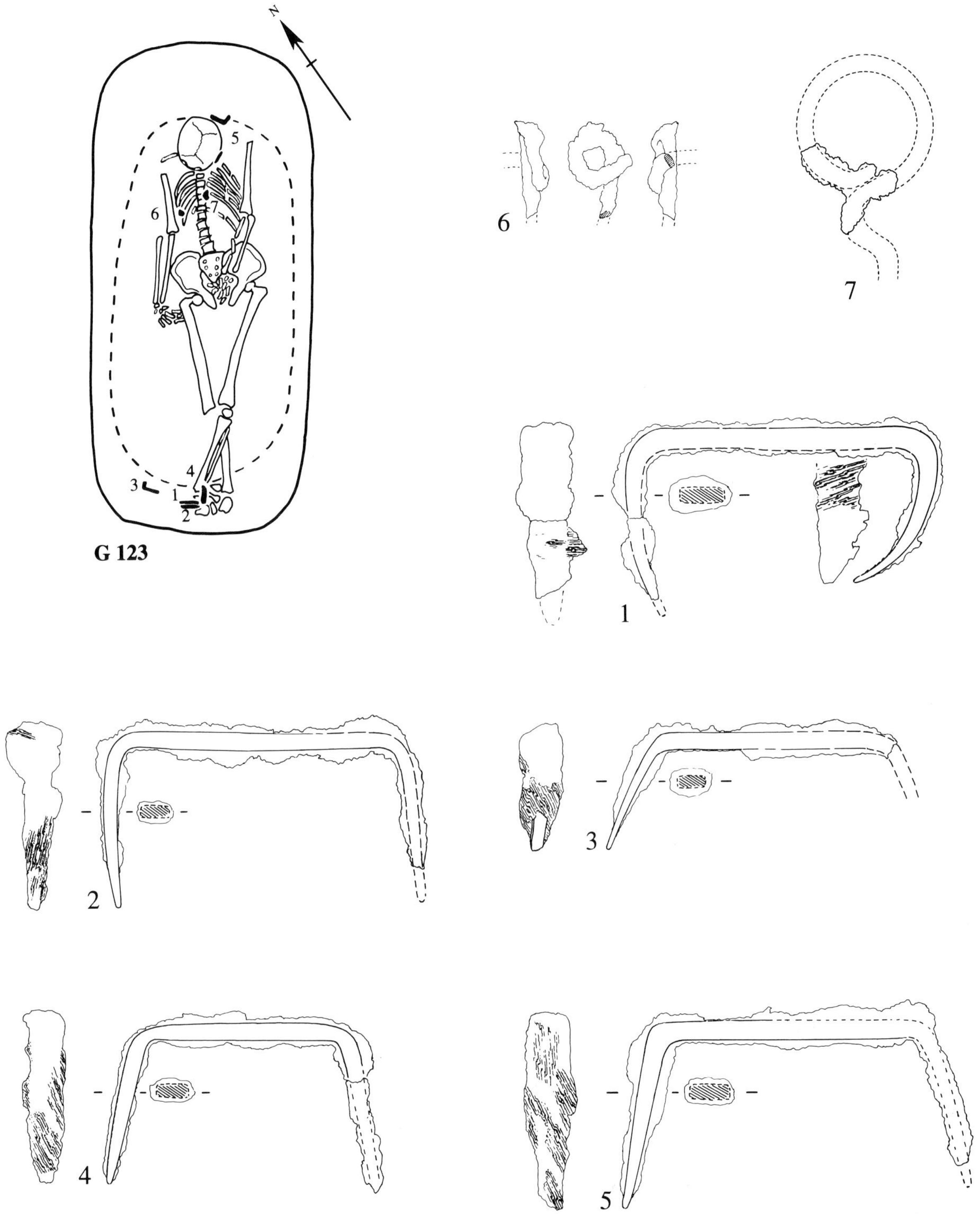

Figure 60. South-West Cemetery, Grave 123 and iron grave-goods. (Scales, plan 1/20; iron artefacts 2/3)

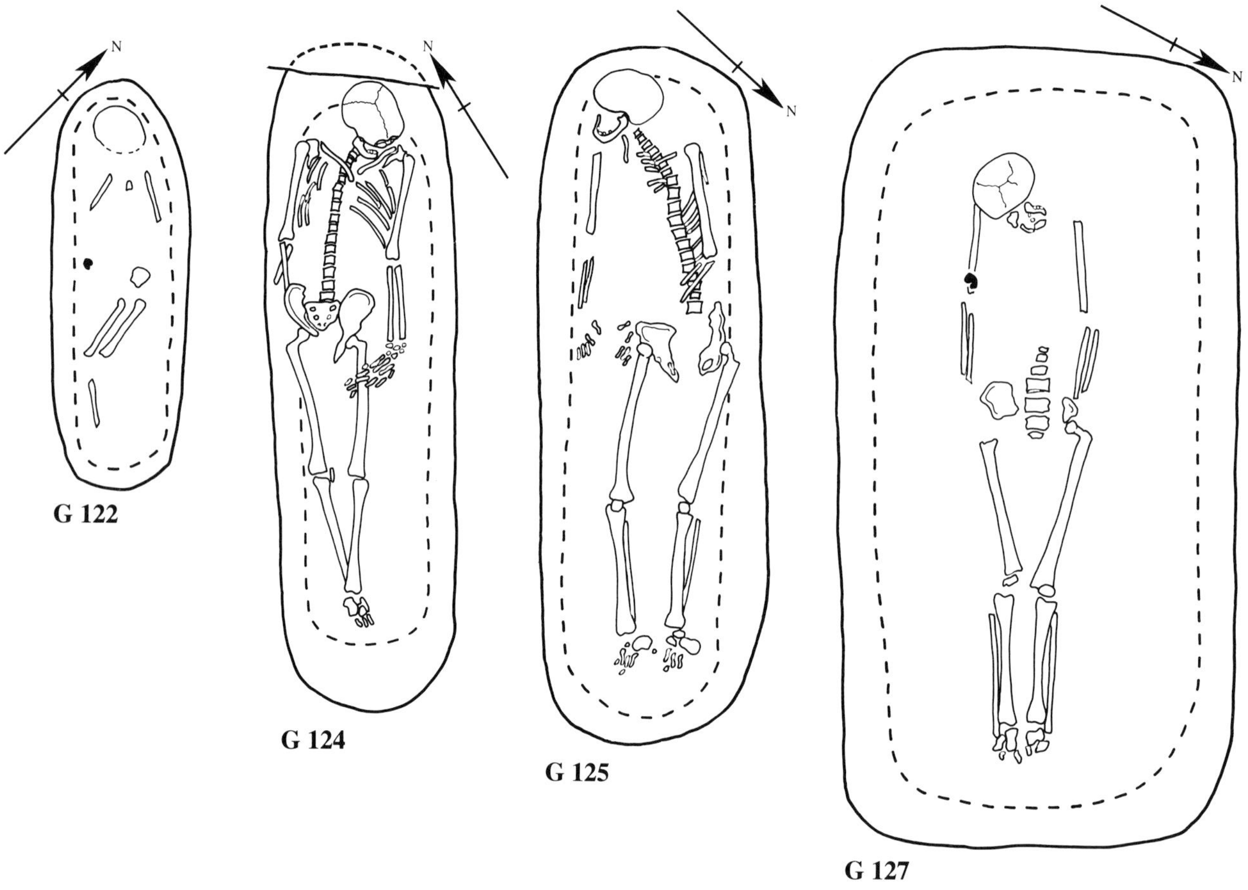

Figure 61. South-West Cemetery, grave plans. (Scale 1/20)

Grave 125: (fig. 61); F, 28–35, condition 3d; no grave-goods.
Axis 231°. Rectangular with rounded ends, 1.85m× 0.62m and 0.41m deep. Steep sides and a flat base. Filled with a cream clay loam with much small chalk containing no finds. Fairly well-preserved skeleton, extended, supine; legs straight; right arm straight by side, left arm bent across right pelvis. Head facing right.

Grave 126: (not illustrated); sex?, 11–13, condition 5c; no grave-goods.
Axis 016°. Rectangular with rounded ends, 1.39m× 0.39m and 0.22m deep. Steep sides and a flat base. Filled with a brown clay loam with very occasional chalk grits containing no finds. Poorly-preserved skeleton – principally the skull and long bones – supine; legs bent to right, arms mostly decayed.

Grave 127: (fig. 61); M, 22–27, condition 3d.
Grave-goods: Brooch (fig. 40, no. 3) on lower end of right humerus.
Axis 250°. Rectangular with rounded corners, 2.13m× 1.10m and 0.47m deep. Steep sloping sides and a slightly rounded base. Filled with a cream clay loam with much small chalk containing no finds. Moderately well-preserved skeleton, extended, supine, legs straight, arms straight by sides.

Grave 128: (not illustrated); sex?, 6–12 (judging from the size of the grave), no bones survived; no grave-goods.
Axis uncertain, 36°–216°. Sub-rectangular with rounded ends, 1.27m×0.30m and 0.07m deep. Steep sides and a flat base. Filled with a brown clay loam with chalk grit containing no finds.

The South-East Cemetery (fig. 7)

Grave 2: (fig. 62); sex?, adult.
Grave-goods: (fig. 62) a, cup inverted in west corner; b, platter broken, base in west corner and rim – b(i) – to the southeast of it; c, bowl, in sherds, between b and b(i);

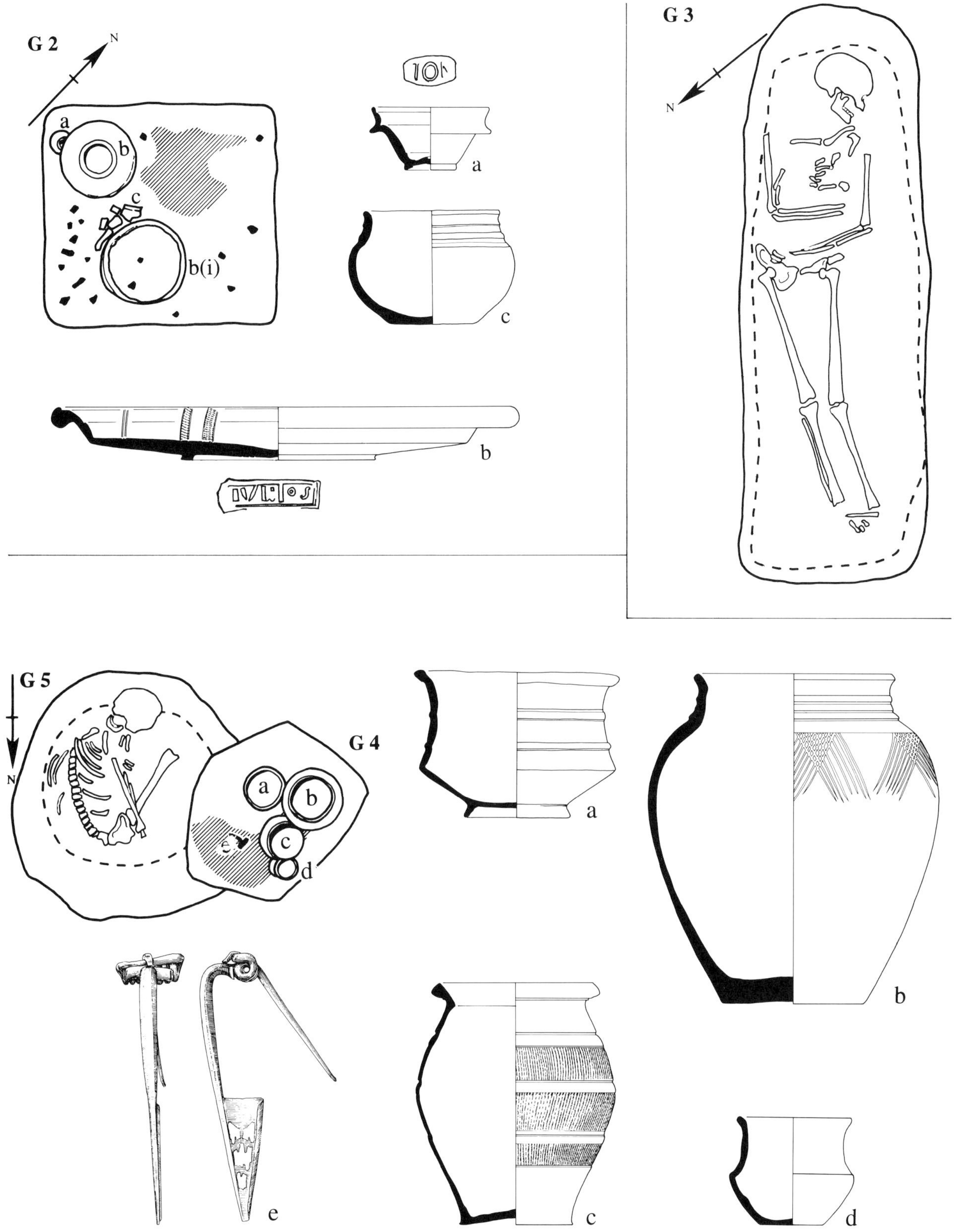

Figure 62. South-East Cemetery, grave plans and grave-goods; in the plans of Graves 2 and 4 the distribution of cremated bones is shaded. (Scales, plans 1/20; pottery 1/4; bronze brooch 1/2)

unburnt pig and fowl bones (p. 149) at southwest side.
Cremation on the floor of a rectangular pit measuring 0.80m (NE–SW) by 0.75m (NW–SE) and 0.56m deep. Vertical sides and a sloping base. Filled with a brown clay loam with small chalk lumps. Disturbed in antiquity.

Grave 3: (fig. 62); M, 25–30, condition 2b; no grave-goods.
Axis 125°. Sub-rectangular, 1.95m×0.55m–0.65m and 0.43m deep. Steep vertical sides and a flat base. Filled by a light grey-brown loam with many small chalk lumps devoid of finds. Well-preserved skeleton, extended, supine but bent slightly to the right at the waist; legs straight, arms bent at right angles across body. Head facing left. Cut by Roman gully, Feature 76.

Grave 4: (fig. 62); M?, <30.
Grave-goods: (fig. 62) a, tazza; b, jar; c, beaker; d, bowl; e, brooch (fig. 43, no. 19); unburnt pig and fowl bones (p. 149) among the cremated human bones.
Cremation on the floor of a five-sided pit measuring 0.63m (NE–SW) by 0.52m (NW–SE) and 0.48m deep. Steep vertical sides and a flat base. Filled with a grey-brown loam with many small chalk lumps. Cuts Grave 5.

Grave 5: (fig. 62); F?, 10–15; radiocarbon date; no grave-goods.
Roughly circular, 0.85m in diameter and 0.37m deep. Sloping sides and a slightly rounded base. Filled by a brown clay loam with many small chalk lumps devoid of finds. Moderately well-preserved skeleton, tightly crouched, on left side with head at south end. Cut by late Iron Age cremation, Grave 4.

From earlier excavations

Summary of the archive sources

BM Archive – correspondence, with photographs, 1905–09 between Stephen Manser and R. A. Smith, Assistant Keeper, Department of British and Medieval Antiquities.
Letters:

1. to S.M., missing

(R.A.S. visited Mill Hill chalkpit with S.M. before Letter 2).

2. 22/1/03 to R.A.S., with Photos A–E
3. 24/8/05 to S.M.
4. 7/9/05 to R.A.S., with Photos F and G
5. 7/11/05 to R.A.S., with Photos H-M
6. 18/11/05 to S.M.
7. 16/3/07 to R.A.S., with Photo Q
8. 4/7/08 to R.A.S., with Photos R and S

(R.A.S. visited Deal Town Hall 3/2/09)

9. 18/6/09 to R.A.S., with Photos T and U
10. 23/6/09 to S.M.
11. 23/9/09 to R.A.S., with Photos V–Y
12. 24/9/09 to S.M.
13. 3/10/13 to R.A.S. (does not refer to Mill Hill site)

Photographs

A. Grave X2, skull and spoons
B. Context X3, Roman finds (published by Woodruff 1904, pl. iv)
C. Context X3, selection of five artefacts shown in Photo B
D. [not located]
E. Two pots and glass vessel from Lower Walmer (cf. Woodruff 1902, pl. i – a larger collection including these three vessels, and pl. ii – the glass vessel alone)
F. Context X4, three pots (pl. XX)
G. Samian sherds from North Deal
H. Context X4, five La Tène III brooches and a pin; a different photograph of these brooches was published by Bushe-Fox 1925, pl. xv, 16
I. Artefact X6, La Tène I brooch
J. Showcase in the Town Hall at Deal (pl. VII)
K.–P. [not located]
Q. Context X7. Two photographs, showing different views of the two brooches (pl. XXI)
R. Grave X8, grave-group (pl. XXII)
S. Spearhead, not from Mill Hill
T. and U. Artefact X10, two views of ring-headed pin
V. Grave X11, pottery in grave-group (published by Bushe-Fox 1925, pl. iv, fig. 2)
W. Grave X11, two brooches
X. Grave X11, toilet set (published by Bushe-Fox 1925, pl. iv, fig. 3)
Y. Chalkpit section in 1909, showing Graves X11 and X12 (pl. VI)

KMSI = Kent Museum Service Inventory taken in 1978 when the artefacts were still displayed in Deal Castle. They were numbered D1 to D123, but include material from sites other than Mill Hill, Deal; a further batch of old acquisitions, D125–35 was added in 1985. The Inventory correlates published sources, original Manser labels and other manuscripts which cannot be traced, but it contains errors, some of which may be explained by loose labels.

Label = Original labels in Manser's hand giving details of provenance and used for the display in Deal Town Hall. Serial numbers in the top left corner presumably refer to Manser's manuscript catalogue of the collection, and some were included in the KMSI. Because they could be placed inside pots, more pot labels survive than for other artefacts; they therefore provide more information (not necessarily correct, however) about provenance.

(i) kept in pots displayed in Deal Library until October 1992
(ii) with pots in boxes stored in Dover Castle in July 1992

Newington NB = Diary of acquisitions and notes on local finds kept by Captain Charles Newington 1907–15, entitled 'Record of old things found by me or bought in Deal & district etc'.

Burials and finds recovered before the excavations of 1984–89 and listed below have been given the prefix X:

Grave X = Burial recorded in the archive
Context X = Objects from burials, but the association cannot be traced in the archive
Artefact X = Objects with recorded, or deduced provenance at Mill Hill, but no other details can be traced in the archive.

Inventory

Artefact X1, 1900 (or earlier)
La Tène III brooch (fig. 42, no. 9) published by Woodruff (1904, 12–13, pl. iv, no. 2) who records that it was found

in the same vicinity as the other Mill Hill finds, 'but whether in connection with sepulchral remains I have not been able to ascertain, for it had been thrown out with the chalk and removed to some distance'.

BM Register 1900 7–25 1 – i.e. registered in 1900; presented by W. R. Cave, of Deal.

Grave X2, ?1902 (no later than January 1903); see also Artefact X15.
Two bronze spoons (figs. 46 and 47) in a grave, published by Woodruff (1904, 11–12, pl. iv, no. 1): 'A skeleton was found lying at full length about north-east and south-west, and on each side of the skull the curious spoon-shaped objects ... had been placed'. The cranial vault survives, see p. 122.
BM Archive – Letter 2, 22/1/03 with Photograph A. Letter 4, 7/9/05, gives a sketch of the location of the grave (cf. figs 8 and 9).
KMSI–D57

Context X3, ?1902 (no later than January 1903)
Roman pottery and other finds.
BM Archive – Letter 2, 22/1/03, with Photographs B and C. Letter 4, 7/9/05, also refers to Roman pottery found about the same time as Grave X2 but at the opposite side of the chalkpit (sketch included, cf. figs 8 and 9).
1 Iron triangular knife (fig. 49, no. 2)
KMSI–D129
2 Bronze brooch (Colchester-derivative) (fig. 44, no. 24)
BM Archive – Photograph B (cf. Woodruff 1904, pl. iv) back row, centre; Photograph C, centre.
KMSI–D48
The pottery is Roman, so is not included in the present report; the brooch (D48) is also Roman, so perhaps the triangular knife is Roman also.

Context X4, (?1904)
BM Archive – Letter 4, 7/9/05: 'Romano British urns near ... (Context X3) ... and two or three small fibula of the same type as that given to the Museum by Mr Cave of Deal' 'One of the fibula was in the shortest urn' (i.e. in no. 3, below); Photograph F (pl. XX), (sent 7/9/05) shows three vessels annotated 'Romano-British found in chalkpit at Upper Deal, with fibulas, they contained burnt human bones'; the three pots in Photograph F are all on the top shelf in Photograph J (pl. VII) see below; Letter 5, 17/11/05: 'you will see the urns that were found with brooches in the top left hand corner', referring to Photograph J and the brooches in Photograph H – i.e. the pots from Context X4, no. 2 and Context X5, no. 1 (and perhaps no. 2) were found with the brooches from Context X4, nos. 4–8. Smith annotated a copy of Photograph J accordingly, but a copy of Photograph H he annotated 'Deal (not with Pottery)'.

1. Conical Jar (fig. 63)
   BM Archive – Photograph F (pl. XX), left; Photograph J (pl. VII), shelf 1, 5th from left.
   Label (i)–'Found in chalkpit Waterworks Road in 1909'.
   KMSI–D2, repeats information of label, which must have been replaced in the wrong pot because the vessel had been found by 1905.
2. Pedestal Jar (fig. 63)
   BM Archive – Photograph F (pl. XX), centre; Photograph J (pl. VII), shelf 1, first left.
   Label (ii)–'Romano British Upper Deal Feb. 1904 GHD'
   KMSI–not recorded.
3. Ripple-necked Jar (fig. 63; Thompson B2–4)
   BM Archive – Letter 4, 7/9/05: this must be the 'shortest urn' that contained one of the brooches (see no. 8, below)
   Photograph F (pl. XX), right; Photograph J (pl. VII), shelf 1, fourth from left.
   Label (i) – 'Found in G.H. Denne's Chalk-pit, Upper Deal'
   KMSI–D26

4–5. Two La Tène III brooches (fig. 42, nos 10 and 11), possibly worn as a pair.
   BM Archive – Photograph H
   KMSI–D56

6–7. Two La Tène III brooches (fig. 42, nos 13 and 14), possibly worn as a pair.
   BM Archive – Photograph H
   KMSI–D56

8. La Tène III brooch (fig. 42, no. 12), the only odd one in the group so it may have been the one in pot no. 3.
   BM Archive – Photograph H
   KMSI–D56
9. Pin [not located, ?Roman or Saxon].
   BM Archive – Photograph H

Context X5, 1905
BM Archive – Letter 4, 7/9/05: 'One or two urns of the same kind (as Context X4) found since'

1. Pedestal Jar (fig. 63)
   BM Archive – Photograph J (pl. VII) sent 17/11/05, shelf 1, second from left.
   Label – none; found July 1992 in Stebbing Collection boxes in the Dover Castle store of English Heritage, classed as part of Deal Town Hall Collection.
   KMSI–not recorded.
2. Pedestal Tazza (fig. 63; Thompson F3–4)
   BM Archive – Photograph J (pl. VII), shelf 1, third from left.
   Label – none

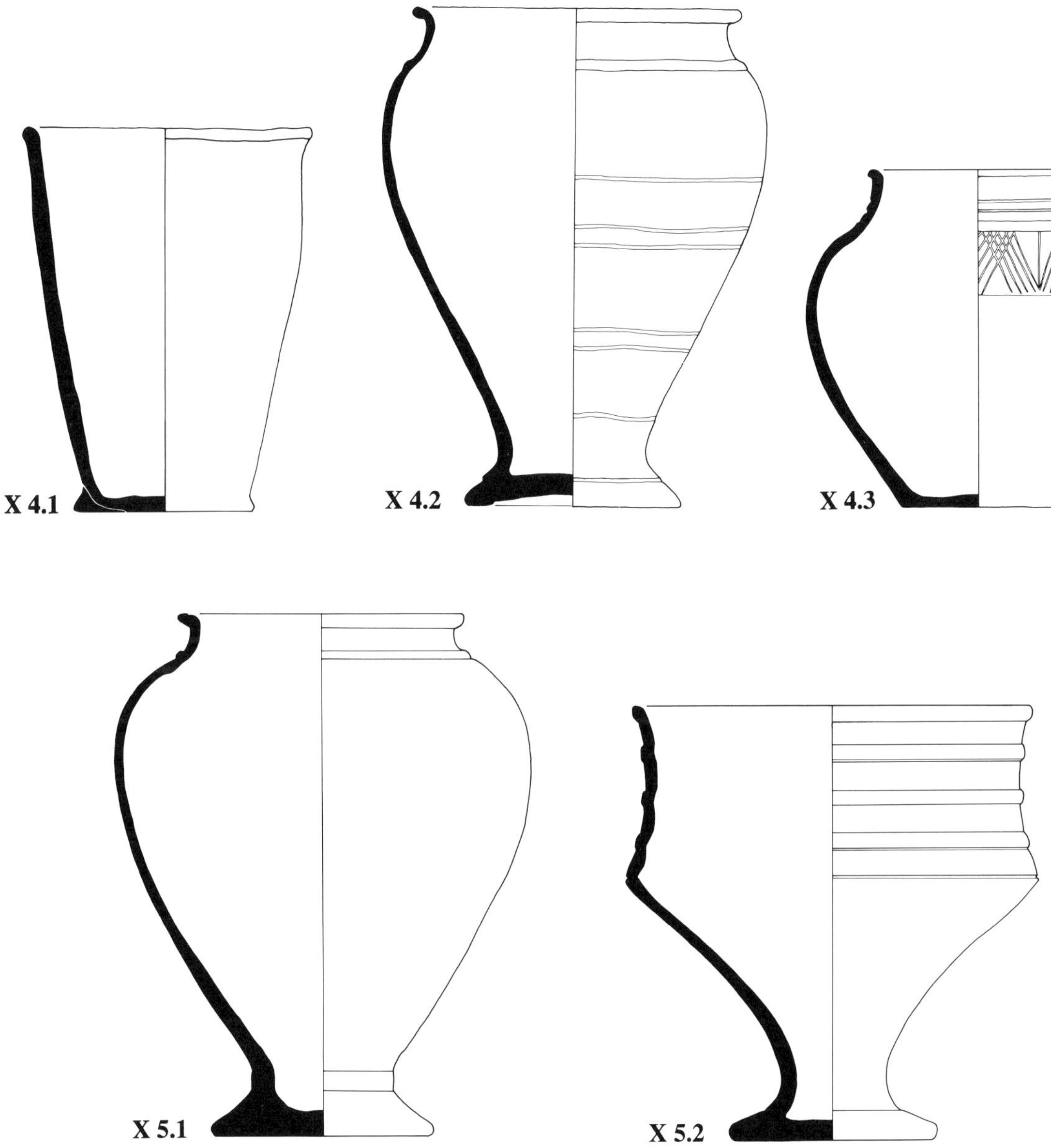

Figure 63. Pottery from Contexts X4 and X5. (Scale 1/4)

KMSI–D21, provenance recorded as Upper Deal, Deal Kent, grave-group 1 1904. Deal Town Hall Collection. Ogilvie and Dunning 1967, 224, note 13 'The pot is marked '3' and formerly belonged to the collection of the late Captain C.F. Newington. No details of its finding are known, beyond that it was found at Mill Hill between 1907 and 1915'. But it must have been found by 1905 (Photograph J), before Newington started collecting, and it is not no. 3 in his notebook. Perhaps the 1904 date given in KMSI is correct, but KMSI records most of the artefacts from Grave X8 (1908) as 'grave group I 1904'.

Artefact X6, 1905 or earlier
La Tène I brooch (fig. 40, no. 1) published by Hawkes 1940.
BM Archive – Letter 5, 17/11/05: 'found in the neighbourhood but I could not find out the exact place'.
KMSI–D58

Context X7, 1907 or earlier
Two bronze brooches (fig. 43, no. 16 and fig. 44, no. 22). [not located]
BM Archive – Letter 7, 16/3/07: 'found near Deal but I do not know the exact spot. The man who found them said it was in the marshes but there is chalk in the springs and catch so I think they may have come from some of the chalk pit'; Photograph Q (pl. XXI).
KMSI–not recorded.

Grave X8 1908
(fig. 64; pl. XXII); grave-group published by Bushe-Fox 1925, 18–19, pl. iv, fig. 1; 43, pl. xiii, nos. 7 and 8; Birchall 1965, 249, grave-group I.
BM Archive – Letter 8, 4/7/08, includes a sketch to give dimensions, because the photograph has no scale; Photograph R (pl. XXII) shows three brooches and seven pots, but all published versions of the group have two brooches (omitting no. 10, below) and only six pots. Bushe-Fox 1925, pl. iv, fig. 1, omits a pedestal jar (no. 6, below); Birchall 1965, fig. 11, and Thompson 1982, 691, include that pedestal jar but omit another (i.e. they include no. 6 but omit no. 7 which was published by Bushe-Fox).
Label – 'Presented by G.H. Denne Esq. 1908'
KMSI–Most of the entries record this wrongly as 'grave group I 1904', and D21 is included (see above, Context X5, no. 2).

1. Ribbed Open Bowl (Thompson L5)
   KMSI–D8
2. Shapeless Bowl with omphalos base (Thompson E2–4)
   KMSI–D6
3. Cordoned Bowl (Thompson E2–3)
   KMSI–D4
4. Ripple-shouldered Bowl (Thompson E2–3)
   KMSI–D5
5. Narrow-necked Jar (Thompson B3–8)
   KMSI–D7
6. Pedestal Jar (Thompson A1)
   KMSI–D27
7. Pedestal Jar [not located]
   BM Archive – Photograph R (pl. XXII; Bushe-Fox 1925, pl. iv, fig. 1)
   KMSI–not recorded
8. and 9. Bronze brooches (fig. 43, no. 20 and fig. 44, no. 21)
   KMSI–D53
10. Spring and pin of a bronze brooch (not illustrated, p. 99, no. 15)
   BM Archive – Photograph R (pl. XXII), front
   KMSI–D134

Context X9, 1909
BM Archive – Letter 9, 18/6/09: 'I have just received some more Keltic urns from Mr G H Denne's chalk pit. They were found near the same spot as the others. I was told that they also found a grave with a skeleton but nothing with it'. There is a sketch of two pots and a reference to a third having been kept by Denne, but none has been certainly identified.

1. Ripple-necked or ripple-shouldered Bowl [probably Artefact X18]
2. Ripple-necked Jar [probably Artefact X19]
3. Another pot, no information [possibly Artefact X20]

Artefact X10, 1909 or earlier
Ring-head pin (fig. 45) published by Dunning 1966b, 15, pl. v, 5.
BM Archive – Letter 9, 18/6/09: 'Mr Denne has a small object of bronze found in the top earth near the same place'; Photographs T and U; submitted to Smith (delivered by and returned to a Mr Adkins). Identification in Letter 10, 23/6/09.
KMSI–D59

Grave X11, 1909
(fig. 65); grave-group first published by Bushe-Fox 1925, 19, pl. iv, figs. 2 and 3; 43, pl. xiii, no. 9; Birchall 1965, 249, grave-group II.
BM Archive – Letter 11, 23/9/09: 'They [the grave-goods] were found in a square hole about 2ft deep you will see the end of hole (sic) in the small photo of chalk pit. The man who found them told me there were burnt bones over and round the urns and the brooches &c were beside the urns. They were brought to me with their contents but when I cleaned them out there did not seem any bones in them only fine chalk'; four pots described and dimensions given. Photograph V shows pots, W and X show other finds; photograph Y (pl. VI) is of the chalkpit showing Graves X11 and X12 in section. A Saxon grave that produced knives, spearhead and shield found 'some years ago' just in front of Grave X11 may well have been one of those shown in fig. 9.
Label (i) – G.H. D(enne) autumn 1909 2 black and one light brown urns and large red bottle in pieces, 2 brooches, toilet set from square hole in chalkpit.

1. Barrel Beaker, KHL Type 1A1
   KMSI–D9
2. Flagon or Lagena Copy, with 3-ribbed handle (Thompson G6)
   KMSI–D12
3. Waisted Carinated Bowl (Thompson E1–4)
   KMSI–D11
4. Cordoned Necked Bowl (Thompson E3–2)
   KMSI–D10
5. Bronze brooch (fig. 43, no. 17)
   KMSI–D54
6. Bronze brooch (not illustrated; p. 103, no. 18)
   BM Archive – Photograph W
   KMSI–D133
7. Bronze toilet set (fig. 48, no. 1)
   KMSI–D55

Grave X12, 1909
BM Archive – Letter 11, 23/9/09: 'in the round hole in right corner of pit they had just found two black urns with burnt bones in them. I hope to photograph them soon' but no photograph seems to have been sent. The

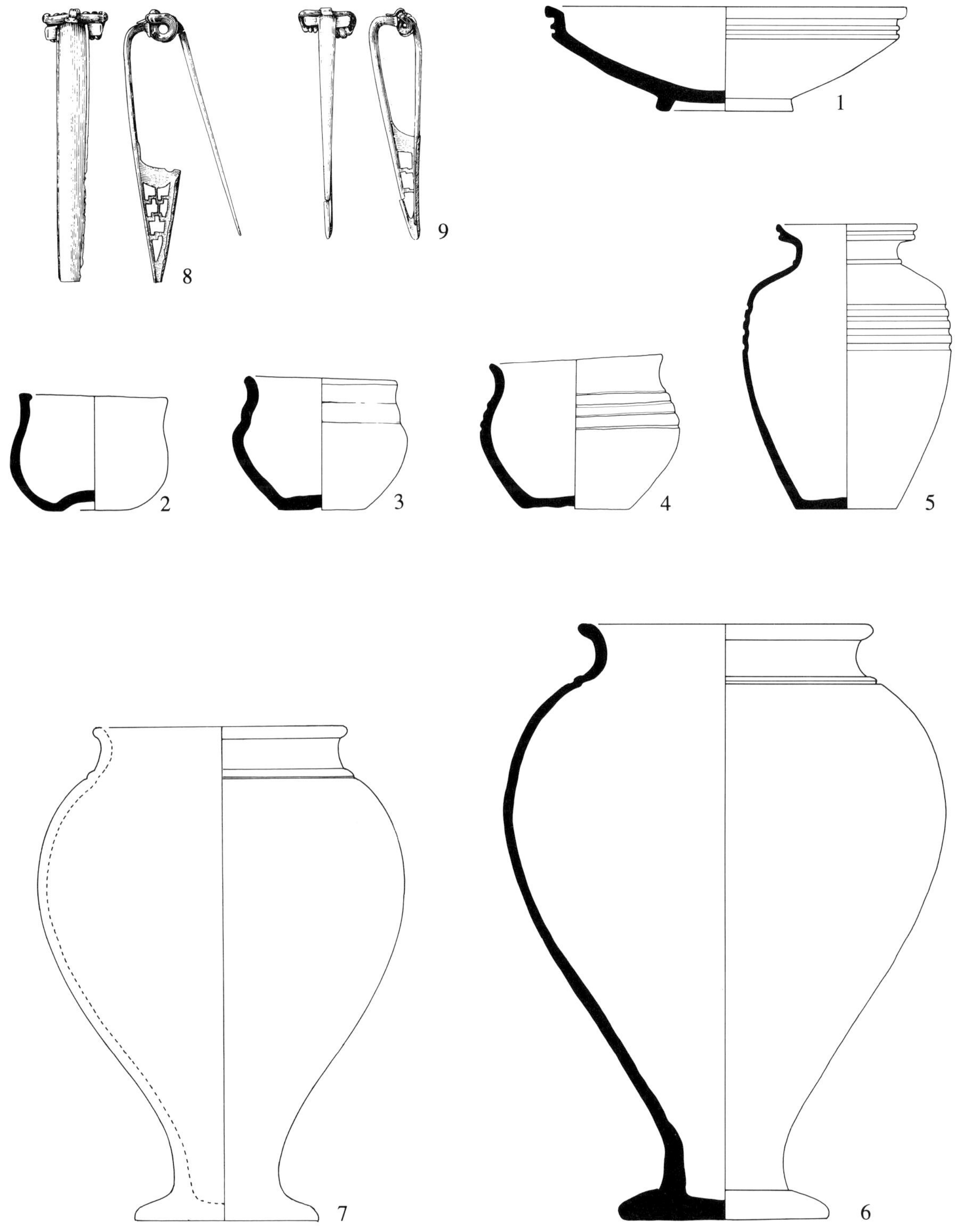

X 8

Figure 64. Grave X8, grave-group. (Scales, pottery 1/4; bronze brooches 1/2)

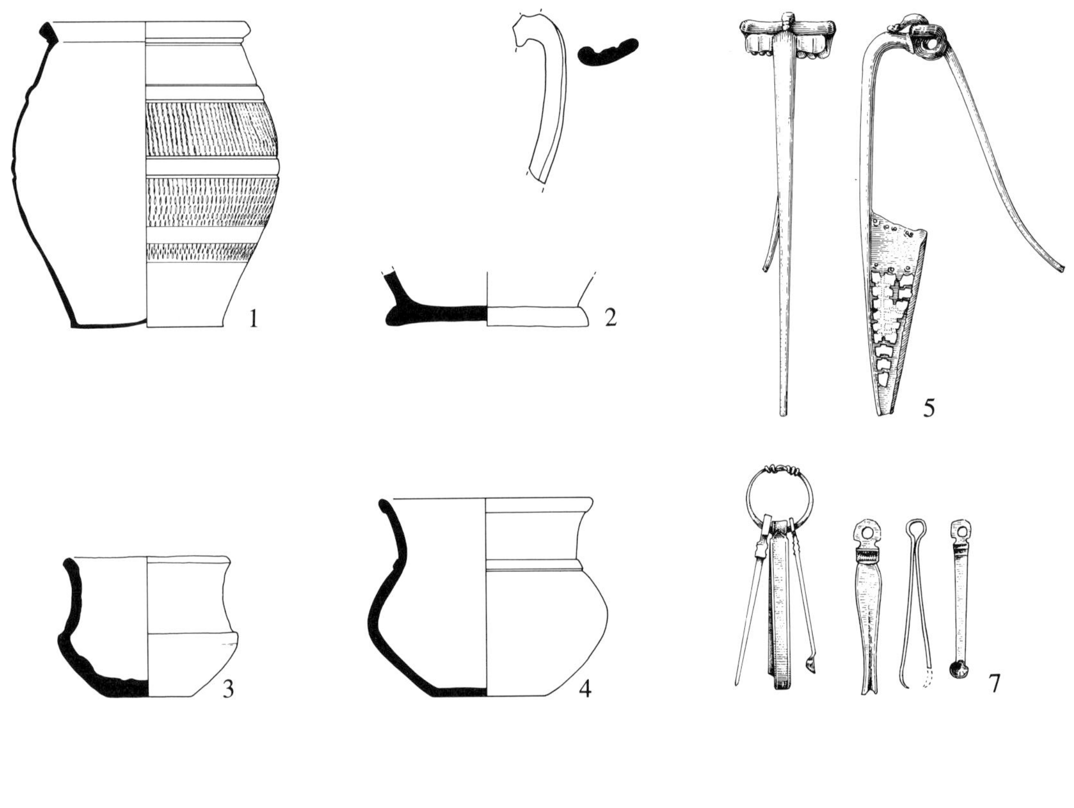

Figure 65. Grave X11, grave-group. (Scales, pottery 1/4; bronze objects 1/2)

pots not identified, but there are two vessels with matching labels for 1909 which appear to fit the record.

1. Ripple-necked Bowl (fig. 66; Thompson E2–3)
   Label (i) – one of two late Celtic urns from Upper Deal–G.H.D.
   KMSI–D14, 29 (29 is the Manser catalogue number)
2. Ripple-necked Jar (fig. 66; Thompson B2–3)
   Label (i) – one of two black urns found in a hole at Mr G.H. Denne's chalkpit near Upper Deal 1909
   KMSI–D33

Grave X13, 1910

Newington NB – 1910 (no. 31), 'Celtic Bronze bracelet found with skeleton in the smaller chalk pit near the Waterworks, Walmer it was on the arm bone ... purchased'.

The accompanying sketch is useless for identification purposes and the bracelet cannot now be found.

Grave X14, October 1913

Newington NB – 1 October 1913 (nos 97–100) 'Grave in Roman cemetery Upper Walmer G Denne's chalk pit B.L.W.'
KMSI–not recorded

1. platter, Drag 18 Samian (fig. 66)
   Newington NB 100
2. Cup, Drag 27 Samian [not located]
   Newington NB 99 – 'Samian bowl potters name – VADI $1^{1}/_{2}$" by $3^{1}/_{5}$". broken but put together except small piece, same pattern as 65, only smaller'
3. Butt Beaker Copy (fig. 66)
   Newington NB 97
4. Butt Beaker Copy (fig. 66)
   Newington NB 98

Artefact X15

Newington NB – 18 November 1913 (no. 108) 'bronze ring Keltic most likely from the grave where the two [spoons? or spears?] that are in Deal Museum for it was found in the dirt just under the grave in the pit, G. Dennes chalk pit Upper Walmer across $1^{7}/_{20}$"'. The artefact has not been located but Newington provides a sketch which enables it to be identified as a penannular brooch (fig. 44, no. 25).

Artefact X16

Barrel Beaker Copy (fig. 66; Thompson G5–1)

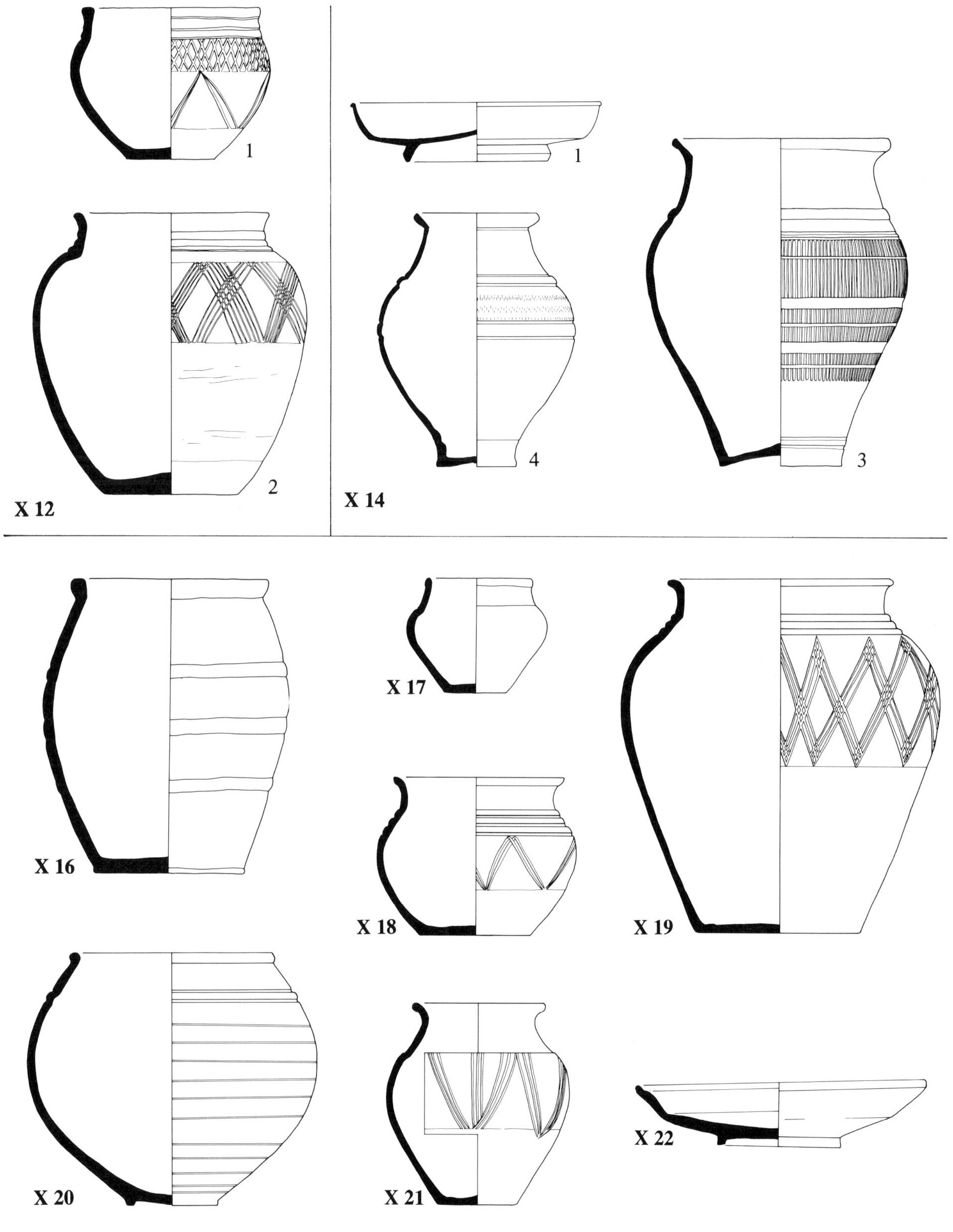

Figure 66. Pottery from Graves X12 and X14, and single pots from the Mill Hill Cemetery. (Scale 1/4)

Newington NB – 20 December 1913 (no. 109) 'From Mr Dunn who found it about 20 years ago near the chalk pit of G.Denne Upper Deal near the windmill.'
Label (i) – 10/9/1915 bought from Mr Dunn(?) who dug it up. From Roman cemetery Upper Walmer Waterworks Road [and a completely illegible final line]
KMSI–D3 where find dated *c*.1885. Purchased 1912 from Mr Brown (?misreading of the name on the label)

Artefact X17
Necked Bowl (fig. 66; Thompson E3–1)
BM Archive – Photograph J (pl. VII) sent 17/11/05, shelf 3, centre.
Label (i) – Small urn found in trench Waterworks Road when laying water main 190[?].
KMSI–D15

Artefact X18
Ripple-shouldered Bowl (fig. 66; Thompson E3–1)
Label (i) – Cremation urn . . .Upper Deal
This could be one of the missing pots noted in Letter 9 (see Context X9, 1)
KMSI–D13. 30 (30 is the Manser catalogue number)

Artefact X19
Ripple-necked Jar (fig. 66)
Label (ii) – From Upper Deal GHD, (20) changed to (23) – these are Manser catalogue numbers.
This is probably one of the additional pots found in 1909 (see Context X9, 2)
KMSI–not recorded

Artefact X20
Bead-rimmed Bowl (fig. 66)
Label – no original label, but old envelope addressed to S. Manser Esq. bears the scribbled note 'all on this shelf Manser'.

Exhibited at some time and accompanied by a typed display label reading: 'Globular Bowl of bright red ware with bead rim and cordon on the upper part of the body and foot-ring. Found in G.H. Denne's chalkpit Upper Deal. Deal Town Hall Collection.'
KMSI–not recorded
This may be the third vessel retained by Mr Denne in 1909 (see Context X9, 3).

Artefact X21
Long-necked Jar (fig. 66; Thompson E3–1)
Label – illegible
KMSI–D51

Artefact X22
Foot-ring Platter (fig. 66; Thompson G1–1 or G1–4)
Label – none, no information about its provenance but always displayed with the Mill Hill finds.
KMSI–D1

Artefact X23
Colchester brooch (fig. 66, no. 23)
KMSI–D52, recorded merely as Upper Deal.

7

GAZETTEER OF GAULISH IMPORTS IN BURIALS AND CEMETERIES

A gazetteer of Gaulish imported fine wares found in burials and cemeteries has been compiled from published sources and museum collections. Thirty imports and three other pots from 17 sites are catalogued below.

The range of imports comprises 'Arretine Ware' from Italy and Gaul, Gallo-Belgic Wares – Terra Rubra and Terra Nigra, Fine Parchment and White Pipeclay Wares – and Lead-glazed Wares presumed to originate in Central Gaul. The functional range includes cups, platters, beakers, flagons and lagenae and unguent flasks: the typology is summarised in fig. 11.

Sites have been grouped by county, then arranged in alphabetical order of parish and usual site name. Imports are illustrated in Gazetteer order, and those found in recorded burials are accompanied by their associated vessels (figs. 67–70), while the most complete examples form the typological sequence (fig. 11).

The small number of finds and their manner of discovery and recovery renders the current distribution pattern of limited value (figs 71, 72). Most burials were found in the nineteenth century as the result of railway construction and associated quarrying. Some finds have been lost or dispersed and surviving records lack detail; however, in this the South-East is no different to the rest of Britain. Numerous undiscovered cemeteries must remain in the region.

Kent

1. AYLESFORD

Between 1880 and 1887 a cremation cemetery was disturbed by gravel extraction at a pit lying about 180m northwest of Aylesford church and then owned by Silas Wagon. News of the finds spread to antiquarian circles, and according to his correspondence, even George Payne tried to find the site although he failed. Some finds, including the fittings from a tankard and sherds from accessory pots, were dispersed before A. J. Evans visited the site in 1886 and managed to retrieve what proved to be the richest burial group which had just been uncovered; it included the Aylesford Bucket (the so-called bronze situla, a wooden bucket with three feet, covered with decorated sheet bronze). Six more graves were excavated and recorded by Evans, being termed 'the Family Circle' because they were arranged more or less in a circle; the pots from these graves went to the Ashmolean Museum. Finds from the three richest graves, including the Aylesford Bucket, the bronze-banded tankard and an iron-banded bucket, were separately acquired by the British Museum from Silas Wagon, the owner of the gravel pit, John Hales of Ightham, and Henry Lewis of Camberwell, respectively. In all, 24 pots were acquired from the latter. Because of their accidental recovery and dispersal to collectors, there are no reliable, contemporary records, and what survives is contradictory. Registration took place between 1886 and 1888.

Correspondence in the British Museum archives is limited and not particularly informative. There is a letter from Silas Wagon, Junior, dated 16 November 1886, concerning the discovery of the Aylesford Bucket Grave but no reply, and four from Henry Lewis, negotiating a price for his collection of pots, with one reply.

In his letter, Wagon describes the stratigraphy of the Aylesford Bucket Grave, but with no useful detail. He claims never to have heard of John Hales, the vendor of the Tankard Burial, and says that anything Hales acquired was from workmen at the pit, a practice opposed by his father. The activities of Arthur and John Evans are not mentioned. Wagon is sure that only Henry Lewis received objects from the Aylesford pit, and they were confined to pots similar to others already at the British Museum; perhaps he was disregarding, or was ignorant of the iron fittings from a bucket. In his letter of November 1887, even Henry Lewis only mentions 24 vases and parts of 50 others as being on offer to the British Museum; the iron objects warrant no mention.

There are problems with the attribution of pots to the three main burials. Brooches found with the cremation in the Aylesford Bucket belong to the mid-first century BC and provide valuable dating evidence for the associated pots (Stead 1976). Evans published a reconstruction drawing of the burial but only one of the pots illustrated there can be equated with those ascribed to the Bucket Burial in the British Museum Register, and the text of the publication is no help (Evans 1890, fig. 1). The most notable absentees are two Pedestal Jars, shown with unusually narrow necks and decorated with cordons. Thompson (1983, 598) argues persuasively that a mix-up could have occurred, since artefacts from both the Bucket and Tankard Graves were in the British Museum at the same time, and were actually registered in reverse order of the date of discovery. Unfortunately such an explanation does not establish whether the error is in the illustration or in the registration lists.

An original label, existing at the time of acquisition, ties the iron-banded bucket firmly into the Lewis collection. It is inscribed 'British Cemetry [sic] Relics consisting of two rings and band of a wooden receptacle [sic] containing urns no. 8, 9, 10 and 11 with the calcined bones of the dead'. The statement that four pots were contained in the bucket was dismissed by the British Museum registrar as an error of syntax, judging by the comment he wrote on the back. There is more confusion here, for although pots with the correct Lewis collection numbers, 8–12 inclusive, can be identified in the publication and the British Museum Register, there is an additional illustrated vessel with the caption 'in iron-banded bucket' which has no Lewis collection number (Evans 1890, pl.ix, fig. 5, list no. 24, Lewis coll. 8; pl.viii, fig. 2, list no. 33, Lewis coll. 9; not illustrated, list no. 20, Lewis coll. 10; pl.viii, fig. 7, list no. 32, Lewis coll. 11. pl.ix, fig. 7, list no. 16, Lewis coll. no. number). Judging from the size of the bucket and the pots, it would have been a very tight fit for the designated four, not to mention the fifth.

In the same letter, there is also a note of the recent discovery (Autumn 1887) of a complete pot, in another part of the cemetery. Lewis includes a relatively accurate sketch of the rather shapeless oddity, difficult to reconcile with the rest of the Aylesford pots, which was appended to the 1888 registration sequence (Birchall 1965, fig. 11, 85; Thompson 1983, 1391). It may have had no connection with the late Iron Age cemetery.

From existing records there are ten burial groups but only those from the 'Family Circle' can be reconstructed with certainty (Evans 1890). There are 20 ungrouped vessels for which no associations were recorded, and amongst these is an imported Butt Beaker Cam. 113 (Evans 1890, pl. ix, 9 – but list no. 12, not 13).

The Butt Beaker Cam. 113 cannot have been manufactured before AD20, therefore the cemetery continued in use at least until that date. The grave-goods include locally made copies of functionally specific imports, a platter and a butt beaker in Graves B and C of the Family Circle, whilst the ungrouped vessels include a copy of a barrel beaker. The earliest date by which the prototypes could have arrived in southern Britain is also AD20; moreover, typological study gives a date of manufacture in the Claudio-Neronian period, so that the copies could be post-Conquest. The Aylesford Cemetery was in use for approximately a century, the brooches found in the Aylesford Bucket provide a date in the mid-first century BC for its start, and the pottery suggests a terminal date as late as AD40–50.

Fig. 67, 1 (Ashmolean Museum 1891.607)

Butt Beaker Cam.113/KHL variant 6D2. Typical Fine Parchment Ware, with occasional red grog inclusions; the upper and lower zones were rouletted separately, the lower zone was then further sub-divided by adding a groove. Condition: complete.

It is an unusual small variant with a wide shoulder and hence a curvaceous shape characteristic of Tiberio-Claudian imports. However, the deep, fully developed rim has both an external cordon and internal cornice so that the vessel could have been imported in the pre-Conquest period, sometime after AD20.

2a. Elms Vale, Maxton, DOVER

In the nineteenth century, at least two imported vessels were found in the Maxton area of Dover. The first, a Barrel Beaker Cam.113, survives, and is said to have been found 'one mile from Dover Market Square, near Maxton'; it was also described and illustrated by Payne (1889, 202–4, photo opp. p. 204, pot C, back row, extreme right) who wrongly attributed it to the Buckland Cemetery. The second survives only in two published descriptions and the same Payne photograph, but it can be identified as an Ovoid Beaker Cam.112 in TR3 (Astley 1867, 279; Payne 1889, 202–4, photo opp. p. 204, pot A,

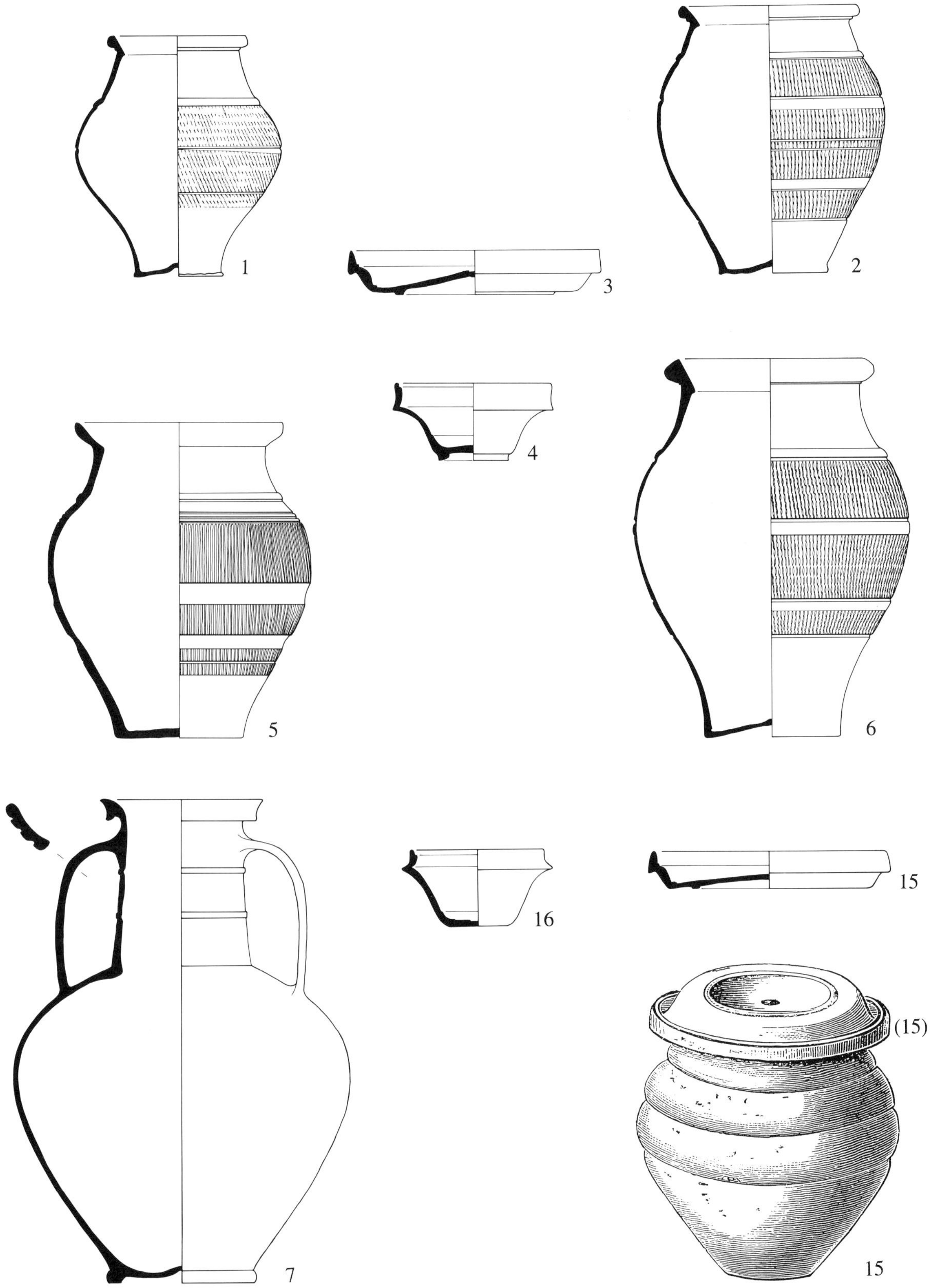

Figure 67. Gaulish imports and associated local products in cremation burials in Kent: 1. Aylesford; 2. Elms Vale, Maxton, Dover; 3. King's Field, Faversham; 4. Oare, Faversham; 5 and 6. Radnor Park, Folkestone; 7. Tassell's Quarry, Allington, Maidstone; 15. Rainham Creek, Rainham; 16. Shorne. (Scale 1/4)

back row, extreme left). The published descriptions leave no doubt that both authors were referring to the same red urn which they say had been broken and repaired with many rivets in antiquity, and contained cremated bone and a fibula.

According to the records in Dover Museum, Payne's published attribution (1889) of all the vessels in his photograph to a cemetery in the Buckland area of Dover is incorrect. Astley (1867) locates the site of the cemetery he was describing 'in a valley a short distance from the high road that leads from Dover to Folkestone' and the area has been identified as Elms Vale by a recent researcher (Philp 1981, B5). Both imports could be from the same cemetery.

The photograph includes at least six other vessels from late Iron Age or early Roman burials; one (B) is also from Elms Vale, and is recorded as containing burnt bones (Astley 1867; Payne 1889, 204–5, nos B, H, M–O). The types include a Embossed Barrel Beaker Copy similar to one found in Burial vii at Cheriton, Kent (Tester and Bing 1949, fig. 2, 19). There are also two Tazza-bowls each with a single cordon at the waist (M and N), and two Necked Bowls (H and O). Thirteen other pots are Roman, mainly late third or fourth century in date (ibid. E, G, I–L, P–T). The finds and original photographs went to Dover Museum, but some are now lost probably as a result of war damage.

Burial A
Urn containing bones and a fibula (Dover Museum Collection, not located).

Ovoid Beaker Cam. 112. Red ware ?TR3. Decoration: combed stripes. Broken in antiquity and repaired with bronze rivet-plates. Condition: broken and repaired in antiquity; fragmented after excavation, but restored to complete for the photograph.

Urn C
No mention of a cremation, therefore possibly an accessory vessel.

Fig. 67, 2 (Dover Museum O.1346)

Barrel Beaker Cam.113/KHL variant 1C2. Typical Fine Parchment Ware, pinky-buff matrix and surfaces. Decoration: three zones of rouletting, the middle zone further divided with a pair of burnished lines. Condition: restored to almost complete.

2b. Priory Hill, DOVER

Twenty-one vessels from a field behind Dover College, on Priory Hill were recorded and photographed, but not all survive (Payne 1889, 202–4; Philp 1981, fig. 2, B2). Amongst the missing vessels is at least one import, a TN platter Cam. 8, with a central stamp (ibid. photo opp. p. 203, pot 17 – 'patera, black, stamped IVINOF'). The remaining vessels include a Butt Beaker Copy with raised cordons, similar to the example found in the Sholden burial, and a Tazza-bowl with a broad cordon on the waist (Ogilvie and Dunning 1967). No typological detail can be distinguished on either a squat Necked Jar or a Necked Bowl, and they could be Roman (ibid. 15, 8 and 14). No cremated bone is recorded, which may indicate that it was separate in the grave and not inurned. The remaining vessels are from a Roman burials of the mid- to late second century AD; four are recorded as containing cremations.

Small moulded platter, probably Cam.8/KHL 13. Probably TN.

IVINOF. Central stamp. (Dover Museum collection, not located).

The potter cannot be identified with certainty from the record, but Jul(l)ios is a strong possibility. The die on the TN platter found in MHC Grave 2 reading IVLI:OS could have been misread (fig. 62b, p. 41). Imported *c.*AD25–65.

3. King's Field, FAVERSHAM

Extensive Roman and Anglo-Saxon cemeteries were disturbed during the construction of the London, Chatham and Dover railway, and subsequent brickearth digging between 1846 and 1869. William Gibbs acquired a large collection of antiquities which he bequeathed to the Victoria and Albert Museum in 1870, and which was catalogued by C. Roach Smith in 1871: in 1875, the collection was transferred to the BM. Smith included one TN platter (1353.70), but no details survive about its context; however, since it is substantially complete it may be presumed to have been part of a grave-group.

Sixteen late Iron Age and Roman brooches survive. Three are considered to belong to the earliest phase of the Aylesford-Swarling culture so that the cemetery was established by the first century BC (Stead 1976). Ten are types represented in the KHL Cemetery; they span the first half of the first century AD and match the date range of the TN platter. The remainder belong to the later first or second centuries AD.

Fig. 67, 3 (BM 1353.70)

Small platter Cam.8/KHL 13. TN – pale blue-grey, fine-grained matrix; blue-black surfaces; badly flaked and laminated, no finish survives; typical fabric quality for Ben(t)ios.

[BEИ]TO bordered. Central stamp.

Ben(t)ios die 2A3. Stamps from this die, all on small TN platters, five the same Cam.8: Camulodunum and

Sheepen (6), London and Cemetery S, Nijmegen. The London example was found in a Neronian context (information provided by the Museum of London). Stamps from related dies have been found in a number of burials and probable burials, all are on small platters in TN and where classifiable Cam. 8: Rainham Creek, Grave 1 (see below no. 8), KHL Cemetery, Grave 6, Ardleigh, Noyelles-Godault, Grave 23, Cemeteries O, E and S, Nijmegen (16), Trier. Also at Bagendon, Camulodunum and Sheepen (3), Canterbury, Silchester, Paris. Ben(t)ios was clearly an important supplier of TN to the Lower Rhineland and Britain.

The KHL example was found in one of the late areas of the cemetery in a grave which postdates AD50. Generally, the dates for Ben(t)ios are AD25–60.

Source: probably the Marne-Vesle potteries; the name is recorded at Sept-Saulx, but the die-style is unrelated.

4. Church Field, Oare, FAVERSHAM

In 1838, while digging gravel in Church Field, 20m from the road to the ferry for the Isle of Sheppey, an extensive Roman cemetery was disturbed, many pots were lost, enough 'to have filled a cart', before the tenant, Mr Amos, ordered that they should be preserved (Smith 1842, 221). The finds were deposited at Canterbury Museum, and include an imported cup presumably belonging to the earliest phase of use, and South Gaulish samian dating to the second half of the first century AD.

Fig. 67, 4 (R.M.Canterbury 980)

Small cup Cam.56(A)/KHL 17. TN – brown fine-grained matrix; blue-grey surfaces; abraded, no finish survives. Condition: complete.

Central Mark – dotted St Andrew's cross.

Stamps from the same die, all on TN cups:- Sheepen (2). Stamps from related dies, all on TN cups:- Camulodunum (4), Stansted Airport Cemetery (three identical TN cups) Cemeteries E and OH, Nijmegen (2), Speyer, Bavay and Kiln 3, Courmelois (2 examples).

Source: likely to be Courmelois in the Marne-Vesle potteries, although Bavay remains a possibility since TN production is also claimed there. *c.*AD 40–65.

5. Radnor Park, FOLKESTONE

Three cremations were found on allotments at the junction of Julian and Wilton Road, in Radnor Park, Burials 1 and 2 in close proximity in February 1918, and Burial 3 about 90m distant in December of the same year. The associations were recorded but there is no additional information (Winbolt 1925; Bushe-Fox 1925, 20–1)

Burial 1

Fig. 67, 5 (Folkestone Museum 1918.231.458)

URN

Butt Beaker Copy. Same fabric and decorative combed finish as MHC Grave X14, 3 (Bushe-Fox 1925, pl. v, fig. 3 and pl. ix, 4). Technically this vessel dates to the period between AD50 and 75.

Burial 2 (not illustrated)

Found near Burial 1, comprises three pots and dates to the Neronian-early Flavian period (ibid. pl. v, fig. 1 and pl. xiv, 11–12). The cremation urn also contained a Hod Hill and a Colchester brooch.

URN

a. Pedestal Jar Copy. Wheel-thrown. Fine sand-tempered ware; blue-grey burnished slip on the exterior. Kiln-fired. Late first or second century.

ACCESSORY VESSELS

b. Cup Drag. 27g. Stamp illegible. South Gaulish. Pre-Flavian

c. Cup-mouthed Flagon. Wheel-thrown. Buff coarse sand-tempered ware. Kiln-fired. Late first or second century.

Burial 3

The final burial was found over one hundred yards away from the previous discoveries and comprises a single urn containing cremated bone and a Colchester brooch (ibid. pl. v, fig. 2 and pl. xi, 5). It is the earliest of the three and the only one which could be pre-Conquest in date.

URN

Fig. 67, 6 (Folkestone Museum 1920.2A.F455)

Butt Beaker Cam.113/KHL variant 2C2. Typical Fine parchment ware, with occasional red grog inclusions. Condition: restored to complete.

Evidence from the KHL cemetery suggests a date of manufacture between AD25 and 50 (Stead and Rigby 1989, 137–141).

6. Tassel's Quarry, Allington, MAIDSTONE

In about 1860, a cremation cemetery was disturbed by quarrying and the finds deposited in Maidstone Museum. Nineteen late Iron Age and four Romano-British pots, one iron and two copper alloy brooches survive, but no associations were recorded, and only one vessel contains cremated bone (Thompson 1978).

The brooch-types can be paralleled in the KHL cemetery indicating a date in the first half of the first century AD. The single imported vessel, a Lagena Cam. 161, is evidence that the cemetery continued in use until

AD15 when the type was first imported, and possibly even after the Roman invasion since the overall date range for the type is AD15–50.

Fig. 67, 7 (Maidstone Museum 4ALB)

Collared Lagena Cam.161/KHL GL6. Typical White Pipeclay Ware, with few impurities. Condition: complete.

7. East Hall, MURSTON

Between 1870 and 1878 more than 20 cremation burials were discovered during the digging of brickearth. Workmen used to inform George Payne when they were to move to another area so that he could visit the site and rescue finds, and thus he amassed a collection of 70 pots, two glass vessels, five brooches and two glass beads from the site for his museum. The pots are included in the *Catalogue of my Museum of Local Antiquities* (Payne 1882, 95–159). He also published an account of the discovery of the actual grave-groups in his major work on Kentish archaeology *Collectiana Cantiana* (Payne 1893). Most of the finds, but not all, were ultimately sold to the BM. (Payne 1893, 33–42. BM 1883, 12–13, 228–289 and 539–551).

Using his personal copy of the *Catalogue* held at Rochester Museum, which includes two original water-colour sketch plans of the finds of 1872, with the account and pot drawings in the *Collectiana Cantiana* and the entry in the BM Register, reconstruction of the grave groups can begin, but the present documentation is inadequate to complete them. One grave-group appears secure and complete, the pedestal jar with the imported lagena (Payne 1893, 35, lower, 9–10). A second containing an early Gaulish import can be recognised from the illustration on page 35, but only one pot, a butt beaker, can be identified (Payne 1893).

Six imported vessels survive, two TR platters, a TN cup, a butt beaker, a lagena and an Arretine cup and they comprise the largest and most varied group of early imports found in a cremation cemetery in the region. The date range is between *c.*AD1 and 60, only the Arretine cup could be late Augustan, but the Gaulish products could be pre-Conquest imports. Seven brooches also have the East Hall provenance, and all are types represented in the KHL Cemetery – four Colchesters, a Thistle and a Nertomaros variant – and they have a similar date range to the imported pottery (Stead and Rigby 1989, figs 48–9, types C, F and J).

The cemetery served a relatively rich community in the early Roman period since the collection also includes 17 samian vessels, mainly dishes and cups Dragendorff forms 18 and 27, but also the plain forms 15/17, 18/31, 31 and 33, and decorated bowls 29 and 30, with an overall date range of over a century from the Neronian to the Antonine period. There is also one roughcast colour-coated beaker which dates to the mid-second century AD. The East Hall Cemetery, or cemeteries, therefore could have been established in the early decades of the first century AD and continued in use until the second half of the second century AD.

i. Fig. 68, 8 (1883, 12–13, 254)

Small Cup Loeschcke form 8. Arretine Ware.

Illegible stamp, probably *in planta pedis*. From Italy or Central Gaul. Late Augusto-Tiberian.

ii. Fig. 68, 9 (1883,12–13, 282)

Small Platter Cam.8/KHL GB 13. TR 1(C) – orange fine-grained matrix; darker slip; badly abraded surfaces, no finish survives. Condition: complete.

ASSINNO bordered. Central stamp.

Assin(n)o die ?3C1?, stamp too abraded for certain identification. Stamps from this die, on TN platters: Camulodunum and Trier (2). The Trier examples are from a local source, the fabrics being noticeably distinct from the typical range of export quality TN. Stamps from other dies: Andernach, Arlon and Cologne, no further information.

Source: at least some vessels stamped with die 3C were made at Trier, but this is perhaps an unlikely source for the remainder. *c.*AD25–60.

iii. Fig. 68, 10 (1883, 12–13, 283)

Small Platter Cam.8/KHL GB13. TR 1(C) – fabric and condition as above.

Illegible central stamp. The die-face, form and fabric are sufficiently similar to suggest that it is from the same source as no. 11 above.

iv. Fig. 68, 11 (1883, 12–13, 253)

Small Cup Cam.56B/KHL 17. TN – light blue-grey matrix; very abraded dark blue-grey surfaces, no finish survives. Condition: about half survives.

Stamp missing, covered by restoration. Probably from the Marne-Vesle potteries. Tiberio-Claudian.

v. Fig. 68, 12 (1883, 12–13, 231)

Butt Beaker Cam.113/KHL 2E2. Typical Fine Parchment Ware. Condition: complete.

The variant with a simple offset at the neck base and the decorative zone divided by grooves is comparatively rare

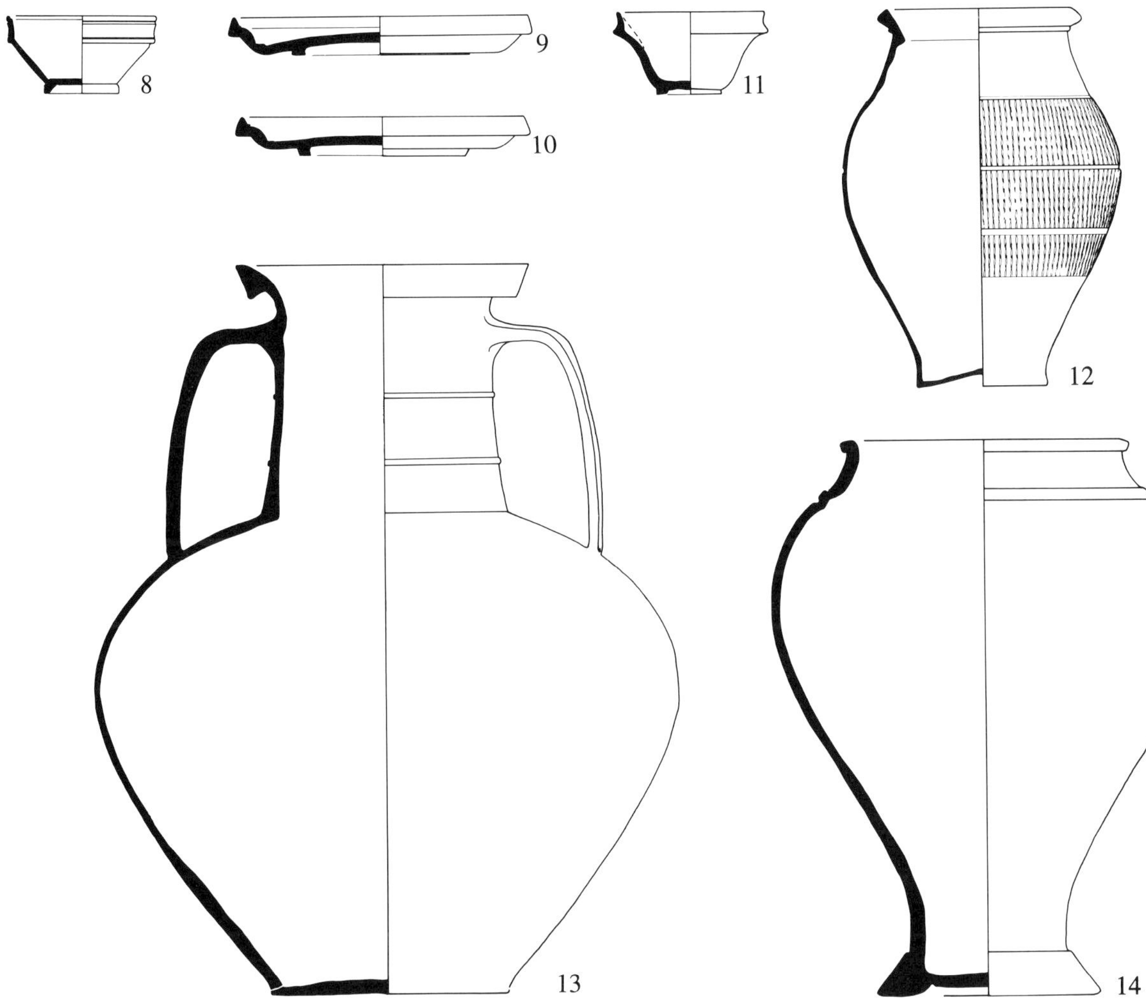

Figure 68. Imported fine wares in cremation burials at East Hall, Murston, Kent. (Scale 1/4)

and only three examples were found in the KHL Cemetery. None occurred in an early, pre-Conquest group nor in early areas of the cemetery so that a post-Conquest date is likely for its manufacture (Stead and Rigby 1989, 137–141, fig. 166, Burial 373).

The vessel is illustrated by Payne and is part of the first burial group which he describes (Payne 1893, p. 35 upper group, no. 1). The grave contained a separate cremation as well as two bronze brooches and two other pots which cannot be identified (ibid. nos. 2–3).

vi. Fig. 68, 13 (1883, 12–13, 228)

Collared Lagena Cam.161/KHL GL6. Typical White Pipeclay Ware. Condition: complete but for base.

The lagena is the only import in the cemetery with a recorded association, and since it was found with a large pedestal jar, it may well be the earliest grave (Payne 1893, p. 35 lower, nos. 10 and 11).

vii. Fig. 68, 14 (1883, 12–13, 240)

Pedestal Jar. Grog-tempered Ware; variegated brown surfaces; burnished finish. Associated with vi.

8. Rainham Creek, RAINHAM

In January 1881, a group of seven vessels, three with lids, were found while digging for clay between Barlett Ness and Nor Marsh (Wood 1883, 108–10). They were standing in a circle about 1m in diameter, 6m from the water's edge and 3–4m below the surface. The three jars with covers contained cremated bone, the remaining four did not and were presumably accessory vessels, but no associations were recorded. The pots were acquired by Humphrey Wood, and then wholly, or in part, passed on to S. Evans, a collector living in Somerset, whose collection was purchased by Folkestone Museum in 1921. By then the platter had lost its cremation urn and provenance; however, reidentification has been possible from the published illustration carefully executed by Sara Bowles. The platter had been used as a cover for one of the urns and even the reverse impression of the stamp on the underside is shown.

The Humphrey Wood collection was sold at Sotheby's late in 1902. Unfortunately, none of the lots has a Rainham provenance, nor can any of the pots be identified from the catalogue entries. Three pots with a possible Rochester provenance, acquired by the British Museum from the same sale, bear the inscription '1860 Ray' in red on the underside, as well as labels giving their saleroom catalogue number. None resembles the pots in the Bowles illustration, while the find dates do not match; it seems improbable therefore that 'Ray' was an abbreviation for Rainham, and that they were part of the Rainham Marshes find.

Fig. 67, 15 (Folkestone Museum 174)

Small Platter Cam.8/KHL 13. TN – brown fine-grained matrix; very abraded dark grey surfaces, no finish survives. Condition: complete.

BENTO bordered. Central stamp.

Ben(t)ios die 1A2. Stamps from this die:- Grave 6, KHL Cemetery, assigned to the post-Conquest period (Stead and Rigby 1989, 274), Chichester and Cemetery S, Nijmegen (6).

Source: likely to be the Marne-Vesle potteries. *c.*AD25–60. (For further discussion see above p. 182).

9. SHORNE

In 1848, Mr Crafter noted the discovery of a large number of Roman vases, fibulae and large iron nails during gravel-digging; he was able to save about 50 vessels. The find was reported to the British Archaeological Association and published along with illustrations of some of the finds including what is surely an imported Ovoid Beaker in TR3 (Crafter 1849, 406, pot second from left). There is a TR cup at Maidstone Museum which may be part of the group, but is not recognisable in the figure. In his records, Payne has several more manuscript sketches of pots found at Shorne than were published. One is of interest here, a Necked Bowl, with two raised cordons on the neck, which should be of late Iron Age rather than Roman date (Payne's manuscript journal vol. ii).

A Colchester brooch said to be from a Roman burial place near Shorne, Kent was also published (Crafter 1849, 406; Smith 1850, 80–81). Payne's manuscript record of the find notes that two brooches were found (Payne's manuscript journal vol.ii).

i. Fig. 67, 16 (Maidstone Museum)

Small cup Cam. form 56A, clumsy version. TN – grey matrix; grey-black surfaces, badly flaked and laminated, no finish survives. Condition: complete but for the footring which could have been left in the ground.

ΛSSI[IN(N)O] Central stamp.

Assi die 1B1, possibly an abbreviation of Assin(n)os (see above p. 184). Stamps from related dies, all on TN four Cam.56 cups and one Cam.5 platter:- Camulodunum (3), Trier and Cobern. It is likely that this die was mainly intended for use on cups, where space is restricted.

Source: probably the Marne-Vesle potteries. *c.*AD20–60.

ii. Crafter 1849

Ovoid Beaker Cam.112. TR3. Decoration: upper zone, combed lattice; middle zone, rouletting; lower zone, incised chequerboard.

The identification is from the published sketch and could be wrong. It may be a cornice-rimmed beaker in colour-coated ware with barbotine lattice on the upper zone and two varieties of rouletting on the middle and lower.

10. TONG

In May 1924, while clay digging, seven early Roman vessels were found about 230m west of Tong vicarage and 320m south of the old road from Rochester to Canterbury (Whiting 1926). The find comprised three lagenae in white pipeclay, each said to contain cremated bones.

A South Gaulish Crater Drag.11, only the second to be recorded in a cremation burial in Britain, two samian dishes and a cup, forms 18 and 10 respectively, were found at the same time but no associations were recorded. The account records that similar finds already made nearby, had been dispersed.

The vessels which were displayed in the Maison Dieu, Ospringe, are in the English Heritage store at Dover Castle (July 1992).

i. Fig. 69, 17 (686)

Collared Lagena Cam.161/KHL GL 6. Typical white pipeclay. Condition: restored to complete.

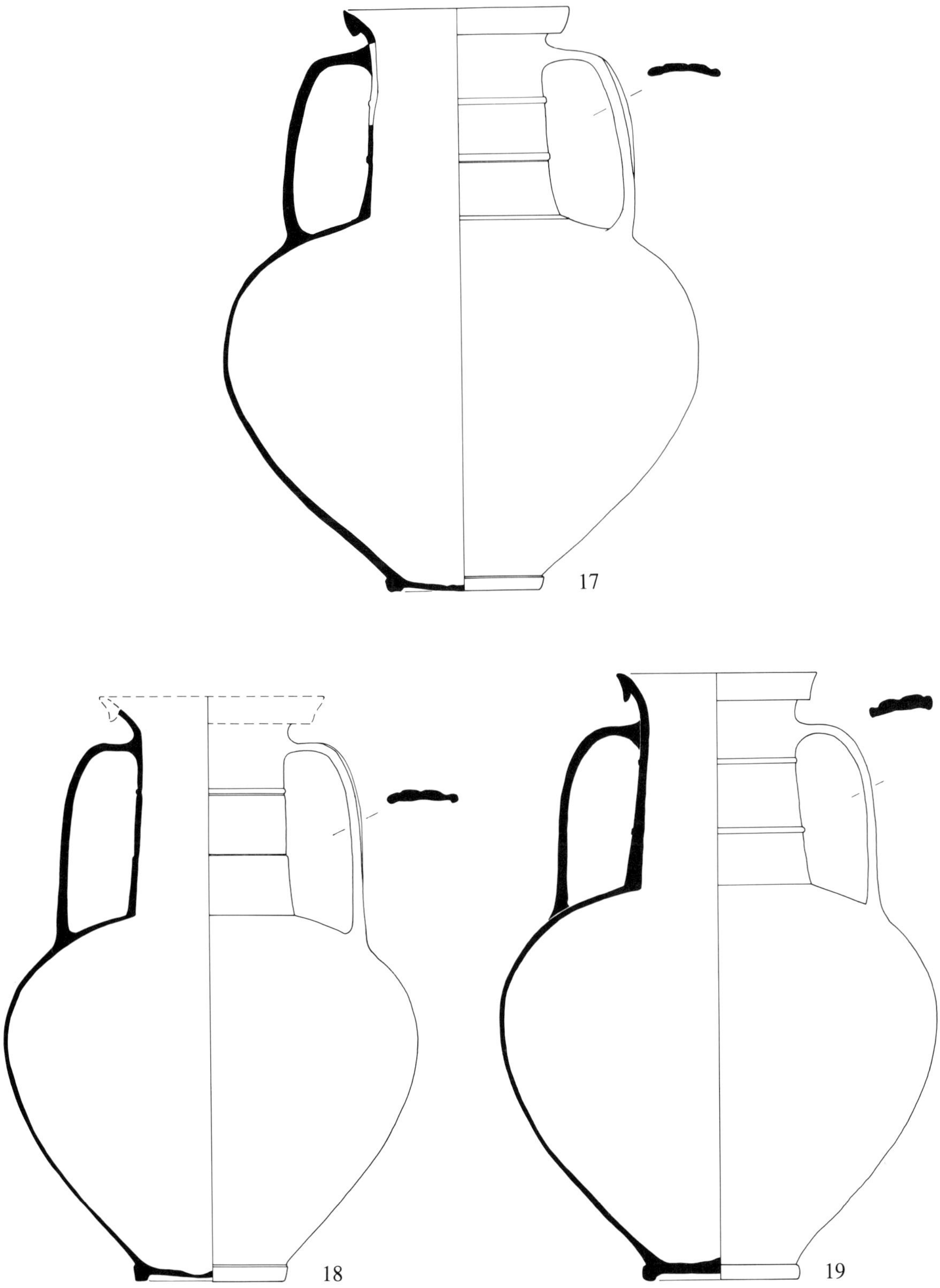

Figure 69. Gaulish imports in cremation burials at Tong, Kent. (Scale 1/4)

ii–iii. Fig. 69, 18–19 (688–689)

Collared Lagenae Cam.161/KHL GL 6. Typical White Pipeclay Ware. Condition: both complete when deposited in the grave, possibly some plough damage, which most probably occurred at the time of discovery.

11. Bolderwood Way, WEST WICKHAM

In 1932, five cremation burials which may have been previously disturbed by ploughing, were found by the owner of a newly built house when digging the garden (Cook and McCarthy 1933). Group E comprises a small flask with moulded decoration and a locally-made copy of a butt beaker.

Burial Group E

i. Fig. 70, 20 (Maidstone Museum)

Lid-seated Flask with pedestal foot, similar to Greene form 2. ?Lead-glazed Ware – off-white fine-grained, micaceous fabric; highly abraded surfaces, no trace of an original lead glaze survives, however given the form and decoration it is likely that the vessel was originally glazed. Decoration: one zone on the shoulder of scallops (Greene 2.25) with ivy-leaf terminals (cf. Greene C20). Condition: complete.

The flask-form is paralleled by an identical example found in a grave at Sanderstead, although different motifs were used for the moulded decoration (fig. 70, 22). It is a hithertoo unidentified type, previous finds were flagons, with narrow strap handles.

ii. Fig. 70, 21 (Maidstone Museum)

Butt Beaker Copy. Fine sand-tempered red ware; abraded surfaces. Decoration: two zones of rouletting.

The vessel was made locally in the Nero-Flavian period. It is similar to the example in MHC Grave X14, which is in a fine-grained reduced fabric which probably qualifies as 'Upchurch Ware'. Another oxidised version in Maidstone Museum with a Canterbury provenance is complete; it is considered to be from a burial and is contemporary.

SURREY

12. Kings Wood, SANDERSTEAD

During an excavation in 1959, a small Roman cremation cemetery was discovered attached to a rural settlement (Little 1961). Unusually, the interments were all of young children. Four of the five burials were accompanied by pottery dating to the later first and early second centuries AD, while one comprised just a heap of cremated bones. In Burial 5, the accessory vessel was a small flask imported from Central Gaul.

Burial 5

i. Fig. 70, 22 (Guildford Museum AS241)

Flask with lid-seated rim and a pedestal foot similar to Greene form 2 (1978, figs 3.2–3.3). ?Lead-glazed Ware – off-white fine-grained fabric, with sparse fine mica and occasional red argillaceous pellets; highly abraded surfaces, no trace of an original lead glaze survives; however, given the form and decoration it is likely that the vessel was originally glazed. Decoration: two zones on the shoulder: the upper is a running scroll of daisies (Greene H6): the lower zone is a bordered wreath of upright leaves (cf. Greene C22). Condition: sherds can be restored to a complete profile.

An import from Central Gaul. The form is identical to the example found at West Wickham although the decoration is different (fig. 70, 20).

ii. fig. 70, 23 (Guildford Museum AS13735)

Large Necked Jar, no evidence of precise variant survives. Glauconitic Clay or Grog-tempered Ware – grey matrix with dense stipple of black argillaceous inclusions, either glauconite or grog, coarse sandy texture; dark grey-black abraded surfaces, no finish survives.

EAST SUSSEX

13. Herstmonceux Castle, HERSTMONCEUX

In October 1953, during building work for the Royal Observatory, five cremation urns and an accessory vessel were disturbed (Norris 1956,4–5). The finds were rescued and deposited at Lewes Museum. There is a sketch plan and a brief note recording the find in the archives of the Sussex Archaeological Society at Lewes Museum, but the numbering does not appear to tally with the publication (information kindly provided by Fiona Marsden, Curator).

Burials 1 and 2 each comprised a cordoned jar with a cover, handmade and in typical local grog-tempered fabrics (Green 1980, fig. 27, 6–7). Amongst the cremated bone of Burial 2 were the fragmentary remains of a small Colchester brooch, badly affected by the heat, but apparently a late variant with a cast loop (Hawkes and Hull 1947, type IIIB). The urns of Burials 3 and 4 were also local cordoned jars, but in Burial 5 the urn was an imported Butt Beaker. The account is not entirely clear, but cremated bone was not found in the second import, a Lagena Cam.161.

Both imports could be pre-Conquest, with similar date ranges *c.*AD20–60.

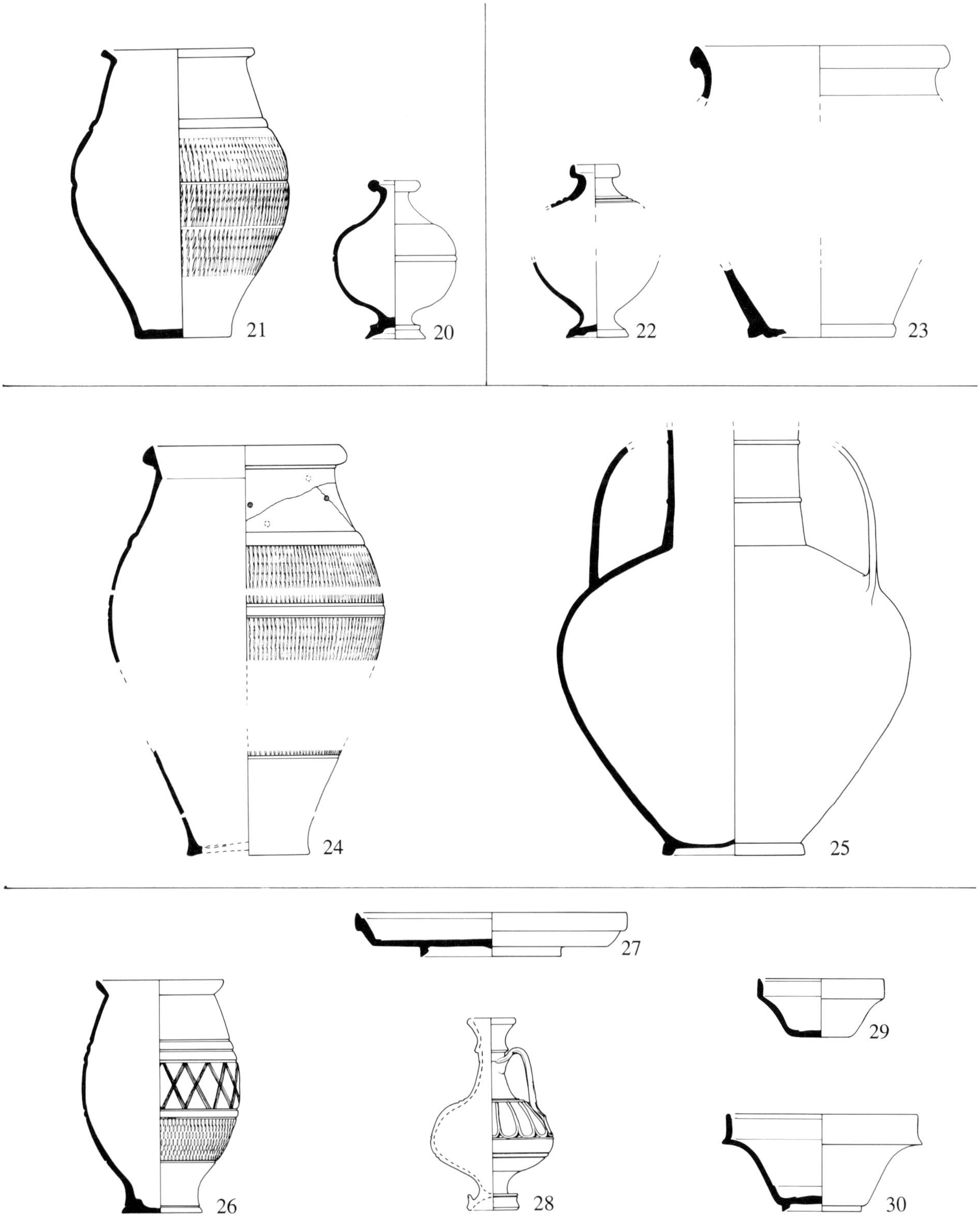

Figure 70. Gaulish imports and associated local products in cremation burials: 20–21, Bolderwood Road, West Wickham, Kent; 22 and 23. Kings Wood, Sanderstead, Surrey; 24–25. Herstmonceux, Sussex; and from possible burials in Kent – 26. Canterbury; 27. Cherry Orchard Way, Maidstone; 28. Bapchild, Sittingbourne; 29 and 30, Canterbury? (Scale 1/4)

Burial 5

i. Fig. 70, 24 (Lewes Museum 1953.61.6)
Butt Beaker Cam.113/KHL 2C2. Typical Fine Parchment Ware, with pinkish buff surfaces streaked by occasional red grog inclusions. Condition: incomplete circuit and profile, but probably complete and standing when buried. Broken in antiquity and repaired with at least four pairs of rivets; white metal corrosion around the holes suggests that lead rivets were used (Stead and Rigby 1989, 203–4).

Context 6

ii. Fig. 70, 25 (Lewes Museum 1953.61.5)
Lagena Cam. 161 variant GL 6, with two cordons on the neck and four-ribbed handles. Typical White Pipeclay Ware. Condition: rim and top of handles missing, possibly lost through plough damage; remainder restored to complete and standing, so presumably complete when buried.

Possible Burials

KENT

14. [CANTERBURY]

There is no information about the circumstances of the find but since the vessel is complete and standing it could well be from a burial (see below no. 17).

Fig. 70, 26 (Canterbury Museum RM1077)

Ovoid Beaker Cam.112Cb/KHL GB25. TR3 – orange-red fine-grained matrix; abraded surfaces; smoky firing line on the inside of rim and the bottom edge of the rouletted zone. Decoration: upper zone: combed crosses made with three-pronged comb; lower zone: rouletted.

Probably imported from the Marne–Vesle potteries. Claudio–Neronian.

15. [Cherry Orchard Way, MAIDSTONE]

Three complete vessels were found in 1920 when a new road was made adjoining the Council School in Tonbridge Road. No cremation was found, and the three vessels form an unlikely association, but they could represent the remnants of a cemetery (Thompson 1982, 778). The platter is one of the earliest G–B imports found in the South-East outside Canterbury.

Fig. 70, 27 (Maidstone Museum)

Small Platter Cam.7/KHL GB11, with a single offset groove below the lip; one bordered rouletted wreath. TN – pale blue-grey, sandy textured matrix; patchy dark blue-grey very abraded surfaces, no finish survives. Condition: complete.

IIOCICI Central stamp; reading uncertain and potter not identified. Stamps from the same die:- a fragment on a TN cup at Camulodunum.

Source: the potter probably worked in the Marne–Vesle potteries sometime in the period 15BC to AD20.

16. [Heywood's gravel pit, Bapchild, SITTINGBOURNE]

In 1929 Roman pottery was rescued which was considered to be from a grave-group because cremation burials had been made previously on the site. There is no further information (Hawkes 1929, pl. xvi, 161–2). The finds which included a small, lead-glazed flagon were deposited in Rochester Museum, from where the flagon was unfortunately stolen.

Fig. 70, 28 (after Hawkes 1929)

Small Flagon Greene type 2, with moulded decoration on the shoulder in the form of simple gadroons. Lead-glazed ware. Condition: complete. Probably pre- or early Flavian. Typical product of the Central Gaulish factories.

17. Probably Kent, possibly Canterbury

No information recorded, the vessels are sufficiently complete to be from burials.

i. Fig. 70, 29 (Canterbury Museum RM1230)

Small cup Cam.56A. TR1(C) – orange fine-grained matrix; darker slip; badly flaked and laminated, no finish survives. Condition: complete but for foot-ring which may have been lost in antiquity, or may not have been recovered.

EB or ER – an abbreviation. Central stamp. The stamp is unique and the abbreviation has not been identified. Probably from the Marne–Vesle potteries. Pre-Claudian.

It is unfortunate that the provenance is unknown since this could be the earliest Terra Rubra vessel yet found in a burial in the region.

ii. Fig. 70, 30 (Canterbury Museum RM1074)

Large Cup Cam.56C. TN – brown fine-grained matrix; very abraded black surfaces, no finish survives. Condition: about two-thirds of the circuit.

IVLLIOS Central Stamp.

Jul(l)ios Die 4G7. Stamps from the same die, on TN:- Duston cemetery, Northants and Camulodunum. Stamps from related dies, all on TN cups Cam.56: Camulodunum (4), the *colonia* at Camulodunum (1), the 'Rich Burial' at Snailwell, Cambs.

Source: probably the Marne–Vesle potteries; an unrelated die of Jul(l)ios occurred at the Louvercy potteries *c.*AD25–60 (For more details see above p. 41, and for discussion of the problems of Jul(l)ios stamps see Rigby 1981).

EAST SUSSEX

18. Motcombe Lane, EASTBOURNE

In 1913, during the construction of a new road, four cremation urns, an accessory vessel and a bronze thistle brooch were disturbed; there is no record of which urn the accessory and brooch accompanied (Ray and Budgen

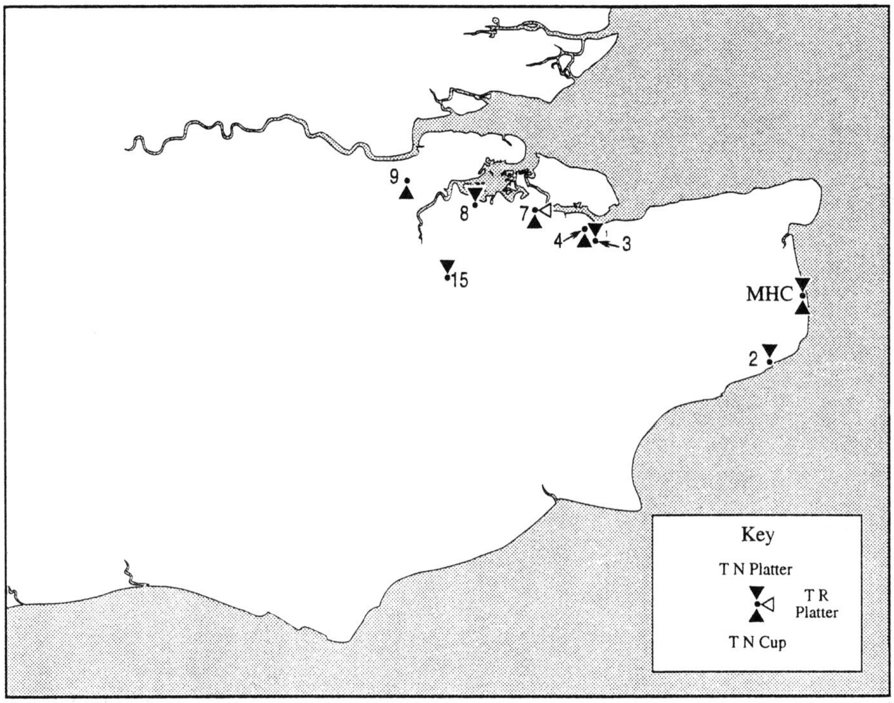

Figure 71. Gallo-Belgic imports from burials in the South-East – cups and platters in TN and TR. Key to figs. 71 and 72: MHC = Mill Hill Cemetery, Deal. Other burials in Kent: 1. Aylesford; 2. Dover; 3. Faversham (King's Field); 4. Faversham (Oare); 5. Folkestone; 6. Maidstone; 7. Murston; 8. Rainham; 9. Shorne; 10. Tong; 11. West Wickham; Surrey: 12. Sanderstead; Sussex: 13. Herstmonceux. Possible burials in Kent: 14. Canterbury; 15. Maidstone; 16. Sittingbourne. For full details see the Gazetteer.

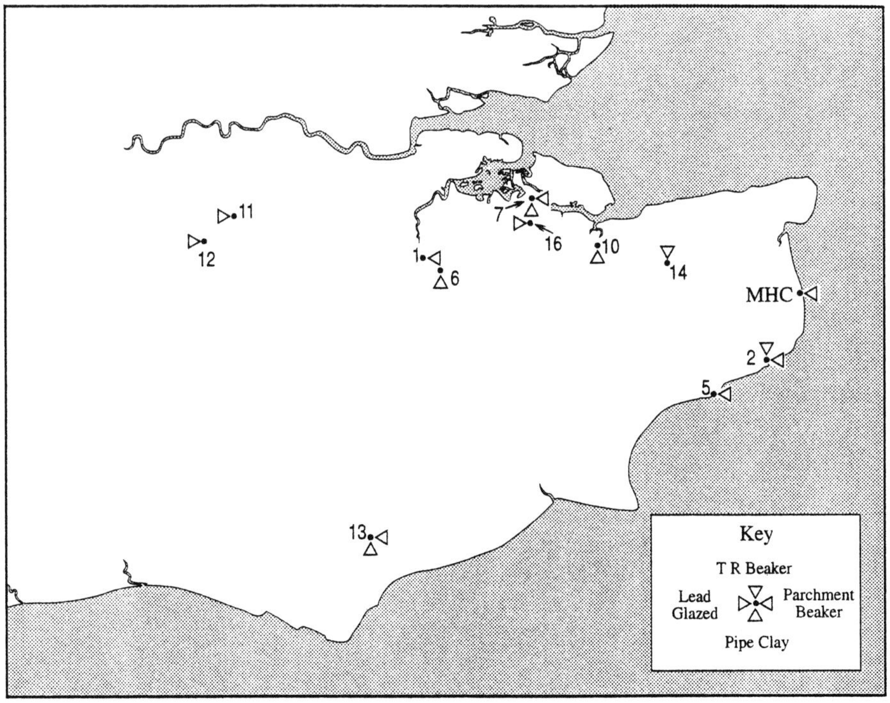

Figure 72. Gallo-Belgic imports from burials in the South-East – beakers, lagenae, flasks and flagons. See caption to fig. 71 for list of sites.

1916, 188-193). Fortunately the group was published with photographs and detailed descriptions, because the finds were destroyed during the war (information kindly provided by Mr and Mrs J. L. Stevens).

The accessory vessel (ibid, fig. 5) is either an imported Butt Beaker, a late variant, or a close copy of the early Roman period, with typical rouletting. The fabric is described as 'hard light grey ware, with a reddish straw-coloured surface and having externally some glaze'. Such a description could fall within the range of imports, however, the pot was examined by Thomas May who compared it with the import from the Aylesford Cemetery (fig. 67, 1), and commented that that was 'the prototype of no. 5, of late Celtic origin. The later examples of the Roman period down to the end of the first century differ in having no cordon or projecting band on the body, and in being of harder, cleaner and better baked clay'. He was probably correct in his assessment, as he so often was.

Plate I. The Bronze Age ring-ditch (F 200) in course of excavation.

Plate II. Grave 112 as excavated, looking southeast.

Plate III. Grave 112, detail showing the crown in situ.

Plate IV. The Central Cemetery in course of excavation, looking southeast.

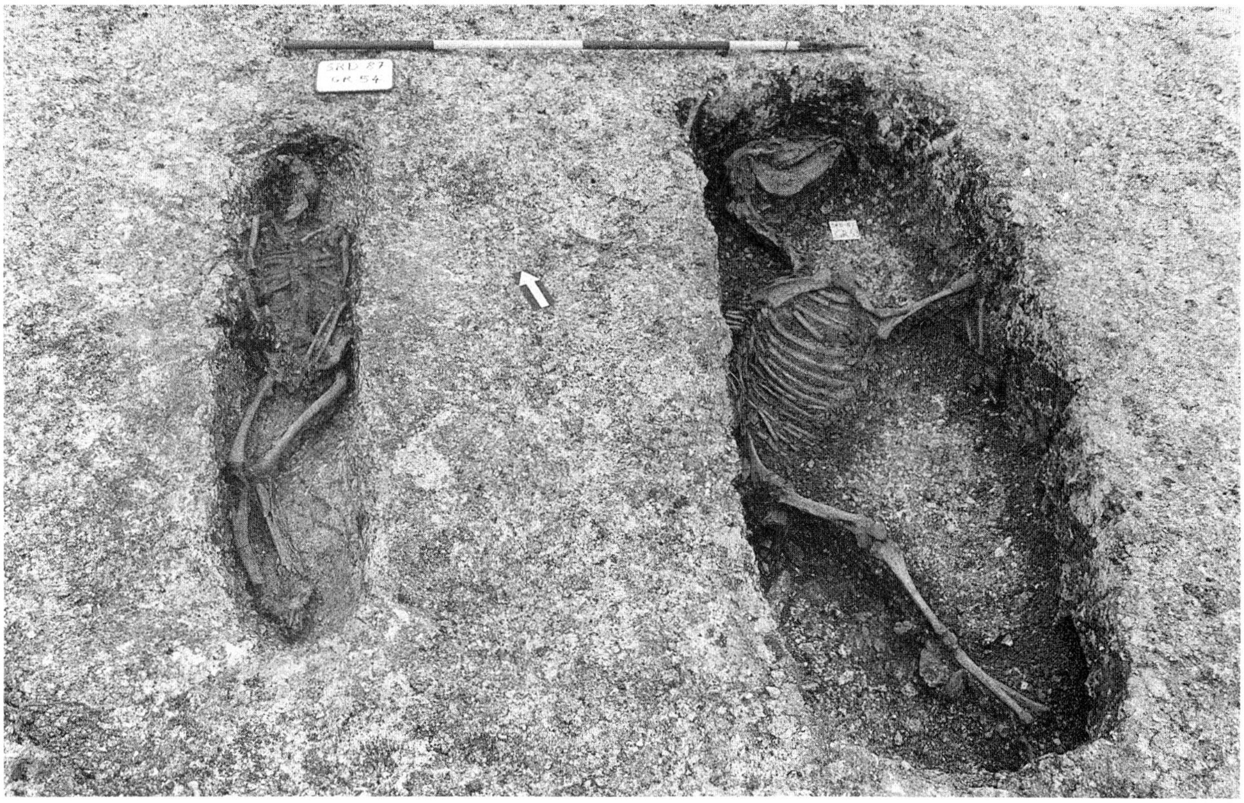

Plate V. Graves 54 and 53 (the Horse burial) in course of excavation.

Plate VI. The face of the quarry in 1909, showing Grave X11 in section in the centre and Grave X12 to the right. Note the pick and shovel, bottom right. (Photo Y, see p. 171).

Plate VII. Showcase at the Town Hall, Deal, in 1905. (Photo J, see p. 171).

Plate VIII. Decorated bronze panel from the top of the scabbard. Scale 2/1

Plate IX. A replica of the crown, as worn.

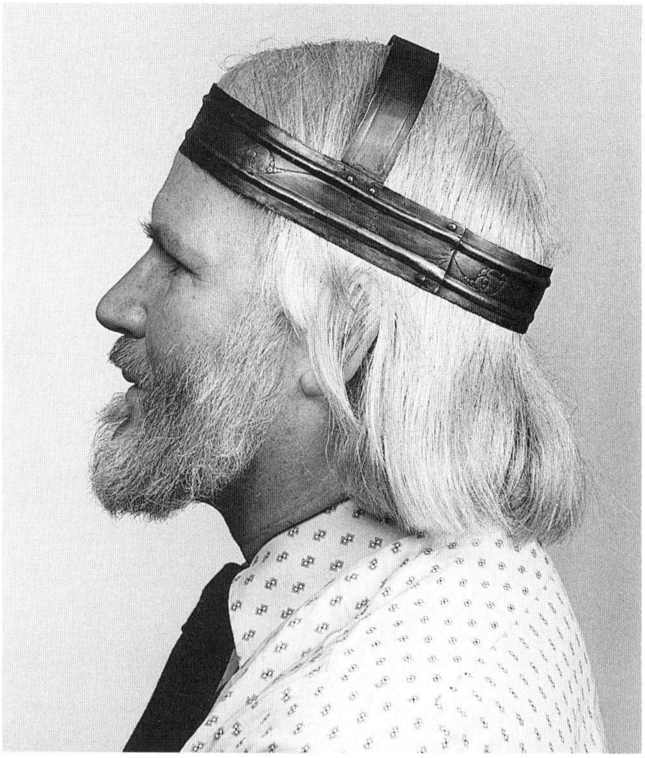

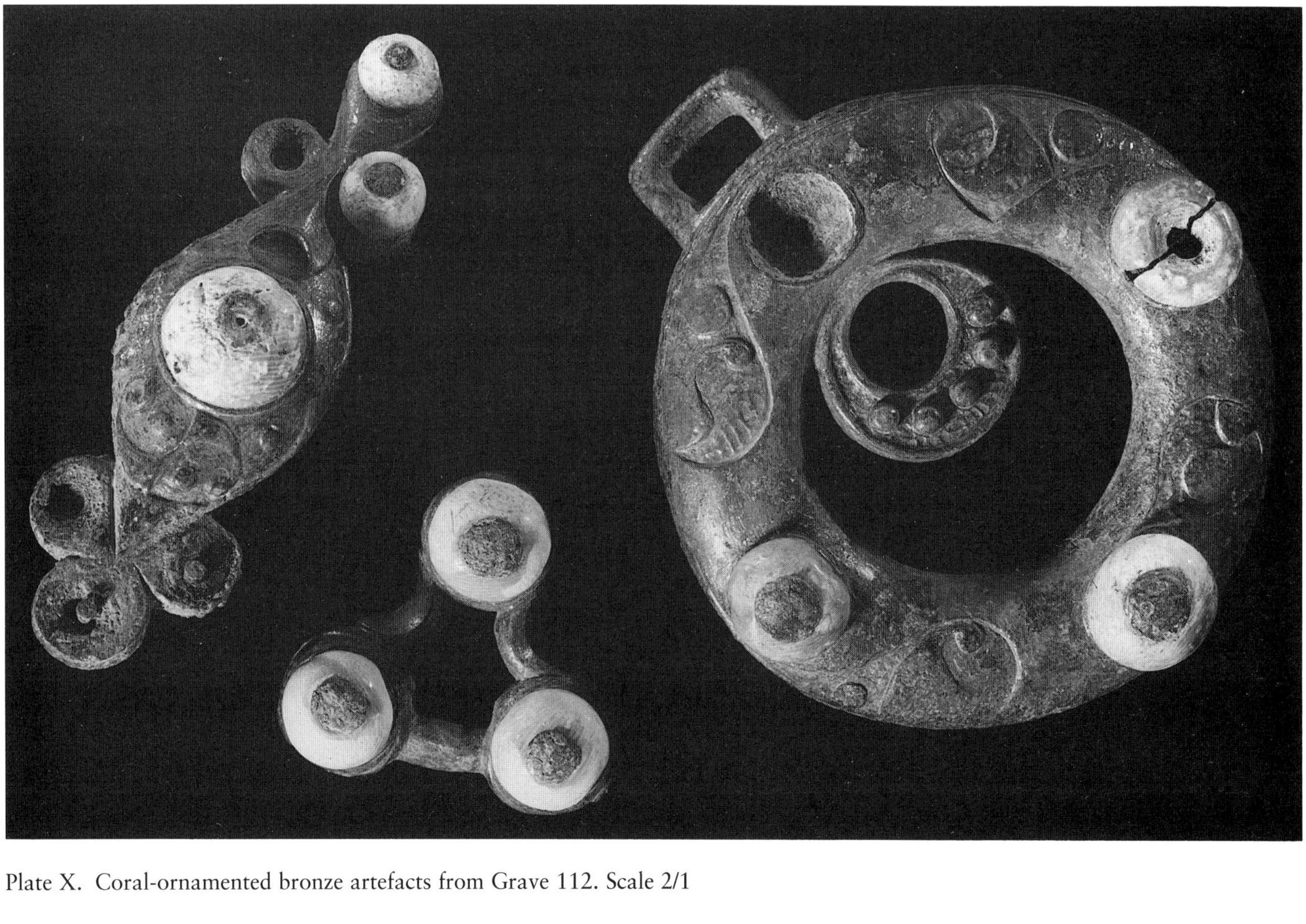

Plate X. Coral-ornamented bronze artefacts from Grave 112. Scale 2/1

XIa

XIb

Plate XI. Coin of Eppillus from Grave 30.

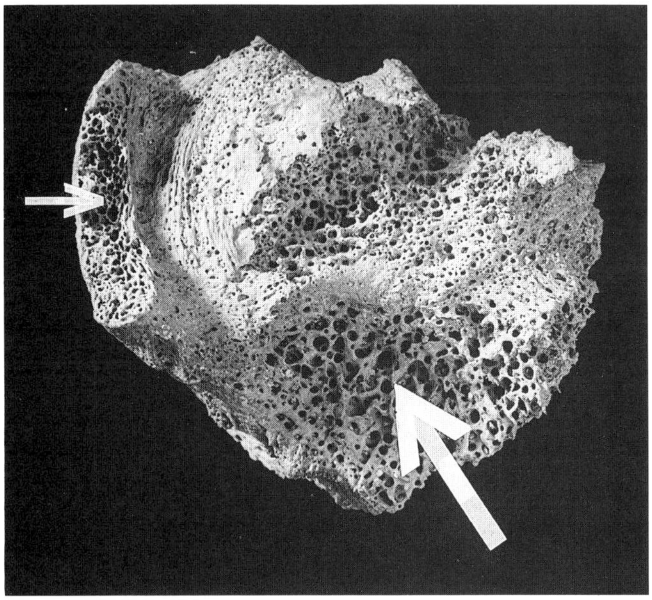

Plate XII. SK 112: Second lumbar vertebra (cranial aspect). The bone is eroded post-mortem but the central area displays an irregular, linear, roughened defect; a roughened porous cavitation is present on the ventral aspect (larger arrow). The broken osteophyte is also visible on the right side (smaller arrow).

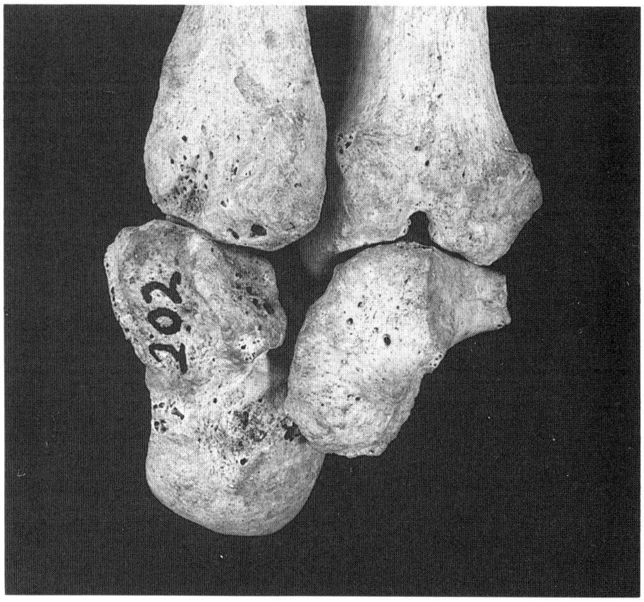

Plate XIII. SK 31: Left hand. Detail of metacarpal III region, showing absence of styloid process. The process originally presented, between metacarpal III and capitate, as a loose ossicle (os metastyloideum).

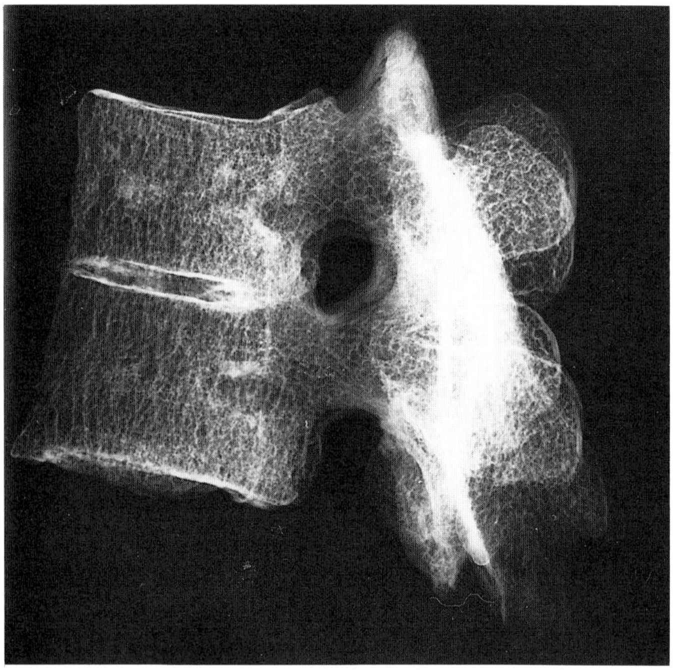

Plate XIV. SK 41: Radiograph of thoracic vertebrae 3 and 4. Note: narrowing of disc space and absence of articular joint facets. These findings, in conjunction with fused laminae and spinous processes, suggest congenital causation, a so-called block vertebra.

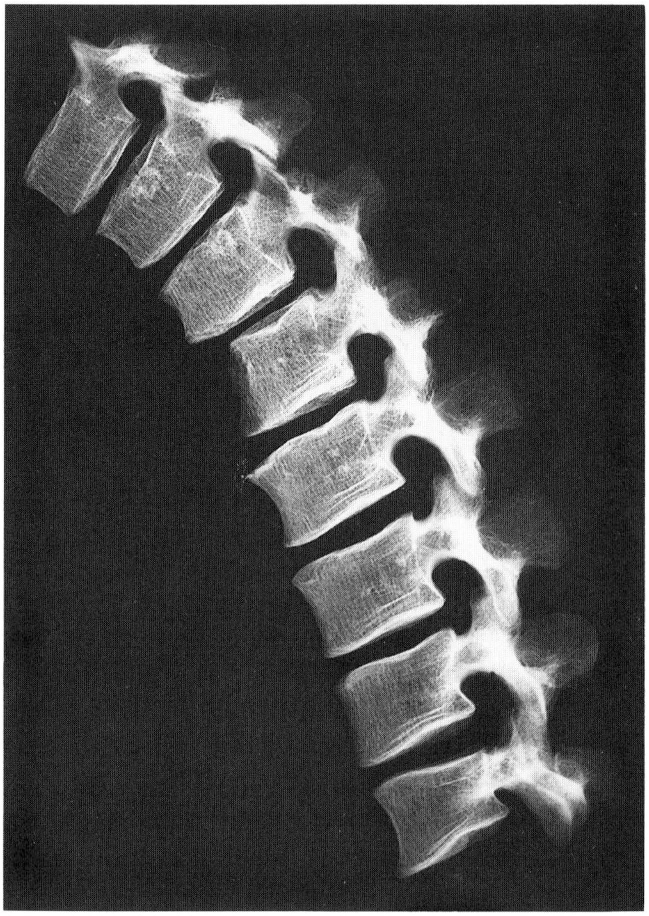

Plate XV. SK 26: Radiograph (lateral projection) of thoracic vertebra 10 – lumbar vertebra 5. The vertebral end plate irregularities and kyphosis support a diagnosis of Scheuermann's disease.

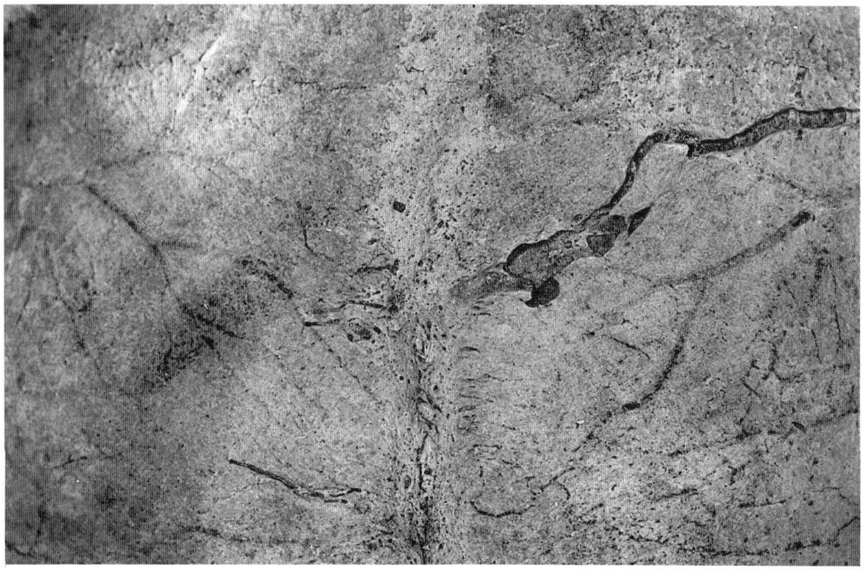

Plate XVI. SK X2: Inner surface of the cranial vault, exhibiting cystic cavitation (hypervascularisation) of a deepened right middle meningeal artery. Possible evidence of a meningioma.

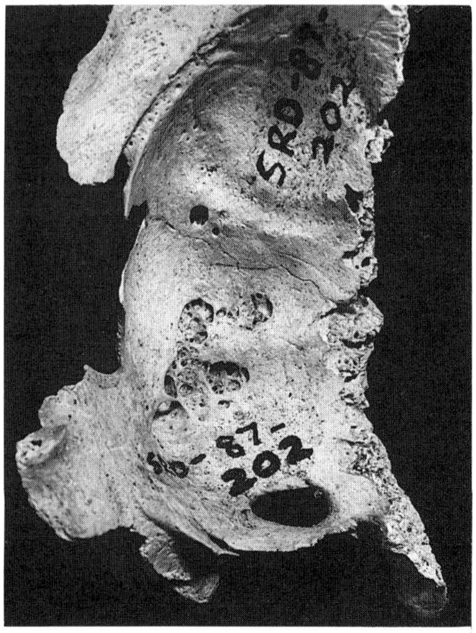

Plate XVII. SK 31: Detail of the inner surface of the right greater wing of the sphenoid, showing localised cystic cavitation.

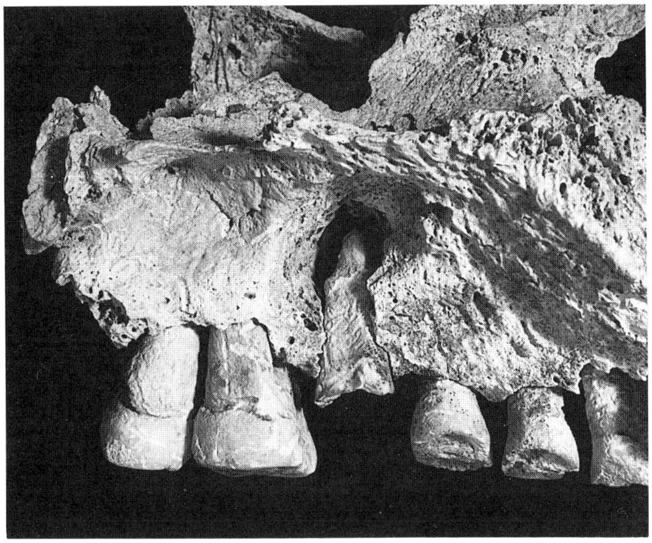

Plate XVIII. SK 51: Left maxilla displaying large penetrating sinus, which has developed secondary to carious destruction of the first molar.

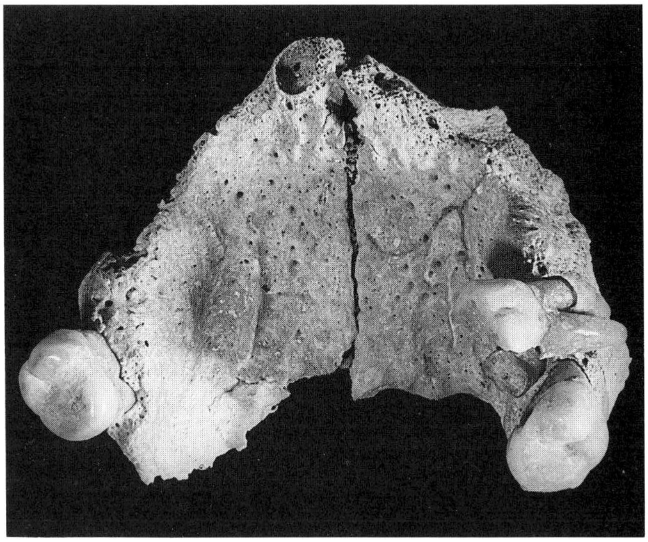

Plate XIX. SK 124: Maxilla showing ante-mortem tooth loss, gross caries and occlusal trauma of the left first molar.

Plate XX. Three pots from Context X4 (Manser's Photo F).

Plate XXI. Two brooches from Context X7 (Manser's Photo Q).

Plate XXII. Grave X8, grave-group (Manser's Photo R).

BIBLIOGRAPHY

Aitken, G. M. and G. N., 1990 'Excavations at Whitcombe, 1965–1967' *Proc. Dorset Nat. Hist. and Archaeol. Soc.* (112) 57–94

Alexander, C. J., 1977 'Scheuermann's disease. A traumatic spondylodystrophy?' *Skeletal Radiology* (1) 209–21

Allen, D. F., 1972 'The fibula of Criciru' *Germania* (50) 122–32

Ambers, J., Mathews, K. and Bowman, S., 1991 'British Museum natural radiocarbon measurements XXII' *Radiocarbon* (33,1) 51–68

Anderson, T., 1987 *Post-cranial non-metric variation: the examination of a neglected subject* (MA thesis, Sheffield University) Sheffield. Appendix Q.

Anderson, T., 1991 'A medieval example of meningiomatous hyperostosis' *Brit. J. Neurosurgery* (5) 499–504

Anderson, T., 1992 'A medieval example of meningiomatous hyperostosis' *J. Paleopathology* (4) 141–54.

Anon, 1846 'Archaeological Intelligence' *Archaeol. J.* (3) 348–61

Anthony, I. E., 1968 'Excavations in Verulam Hills Field, St Albans 1963-4' *Hertfordshire Archaeol.* (1) 9–50

Ashbee, P., 1960 *The Bronze Age round barrow in Britain* London

Astley, E. F., 1867 'Recent discovery of Roman remains, with urns and other relics near Dover' *Archaeol. J.* (24) 279–80

Atkinson, R. J. C., and Piggott, S., 1955 'The Torrs Chamfrein' *Archaeologia* (96) 197–235

Baffet, E., 1911 'A propos de quelques sépultures gauloises' *Mém. Soc. Agriculture Commerce Sciences Arts Marne* (56, 1911–12) 179–86

Barkley, M. S., 1978 'Vertebral arch defects in ancient Egyptian populations' *J. Human Evolution* (7) 553–7

Barnwell, E. L., 1892 'Bronze articles supposed to be spoons' *Archaeol. Cambrensis* (ser. 3, 8) 208–19

Basu, S. S., 1963 'Naviculo-cuneo-metatarso-phalangeal synostosis' *Indian J. Surgery* (25) 750–1

Bennike, P., 1985 *Palaeopathology of Danish skeletons* (Akademisk Forlag) Copenhagen. Tables 31, 35

Birchall, A., 1965 'The Aylesford-Swarling Culture: The Problem of the Belgae reconsidered' *Proc. Prehist. Soc.* (31) 241–367

Bird, D. G., 1987 'The Romano-British period in Surrey' in J. and D. G. Bird (eds), *The Archaeology of Surrey to 1540* Guildford 165–96

Bird, J., 1989 'Romano-British priestly regalia from Wanborough, Surrey' *Antiq. J.* (69) 316–18

Birmingham, A., 1891 'Variability in the level of attachment of the lower limb in vertebral axis in man' *J. Anatomy* (25) 526–34

Bontillot, J., Mordant, C. and D., 1975 'La nécropole des Gobillons à Châtenay-sur-Seine (Seine-et-Marne)' *Bull. Soc. Préhist. Fr.* (72) 416–48

Boon G. C., 1982 'A coin with the head of Cernunnos' *Seaby Coin and Medal Bulletin* (1982) 276–82

Boon, G. C., 1991 '*Tonsor Humanus*: razor and toilet-knife in Antiquity' *Britannia* (22) 21–32

Boon, G. C., and Wymer, J., 1958 'A Belgic cremation burial from Burghfield (Cunning Man Site)' *Berkshire Archaeol. Soc. J.* (56) 46–53

Brailsford, J. W., 1953 *Later Prehistoric Antiquities of the British Isles* London

Brailsford, J. W., 1975 *Early Celtic masterpieces from Britain in the British Museum* London

Brent, J., 1894 'Account of the society's researches in the Anglo-Saxon cemetery at Sarr' *Archaeol. Cantiana* (6, 1864–5) 157–85

Bretz-Mahler, D., and Brisson, A., 1956 'Le cimetière gaulois du Mont Gravet à Villeneuve-Renneville (Marne)' *Rev. Archéol. Est Centre-Est* (9) 193–223 and 289–302

Brothwell, D. R., Carbonell, V. M., Goose, D H., 1963 'Congenital absence of teeth in human populations' in D. R. Brothwell (ed.), *Dental Anthropology* Oxford, 179–90

Bruce-Mitford, R. L. S., and Luscombe, M. R., 1974 'The Benty Grange helmet' and other "helmets" found in Britain' in R. L. S. Bruce-Mitford, *Aspects of Anglo-Saxon Archaeology* (London) 223–52

Buckley, C. A., 1980 'The relationship between congenital teeth, plaque, calculus and gingival disease' *Brit. Dental J.* (149) 67–9

Bugden, W., 1931 'A La Tène III inhumation' *Antiq. J.* (11) 71–3

Bulleid, A., and Gray, H. St G., 1911 *The Glastonbury Lake Village* (1) Taunton

Bullen, R. A., 1912 *Harlyn Bay and the discovery of its prehistoric remains* 3rd edition, Harlyn Bay, Padstow

Burleigh, G.R., 1993 'Some aspects of burial types in the cemeteries of the Romano-British settlement at Baldock, Herts', *Römerzeitliche Gräber als Quellen zu Religion, Bevölkerungs-strukter und Sozialgeschichte*, Mainz

Bushe-Fox, J. P., 1925 *Excavation at the Late-Celtic Urn-field at Swarling, Kent* (Soc. Antiq. London Res. Rep., 5) London

Calder, J., and Calder, A., 1977 'Talo-calcaneal bridging in an Anglo-Saxon' *Medical History* (21) 316–9

Campillo, D., 1991 'The possibility of diagnosing meningiomas in palaeopathology' *International J. Osteoarchaeology* (1) 225–30

Case, H. J., 1949 'The Standlake Iron Age sword' *Oxfordshire Archaeol. Soc. Rep.* (87) 7–8

Cavallaro, D. C., Hadden, R., Ross, H., 1978 'An unusual case of tarsal coalition: a cuboid navicular synostosis' *J. American Podiatric Association* (68) 71–5

Champion, T. C., 1982 'The Bronze Age in Kent' in P. E. Leach (ed.) *Archaeology in Kent to AD1500* (CBA Res. Rep., 48) London, 31–9

Chandraraj, S., 1987 'Failure of articular process (zygapophyseal) joint development as a cause of vertebral fusion (blocked vertebrae)' *J. Anatomy* (153) 55–62

Chapman, H. S., 1921 *The Story of Dola* London

Claassen, H., 1991 'Paläopathologische Befunde am hallstattzeitlichen Menschen der Oberpfalz. Rückschlüsse auf seine Umwelt' *Anthropologische Anzeiger* (49) 217–29

Clark, J. G. D., 1938 'Early Man' in L. F. Salzman (ed.), Victoria County History, *Cambridgeshire and The Isle of Ely* (1) London, 247–303

Clarke, L. C. G., 1926 'Prehistoric and Romano-British objects from England in the University Museum of Archaeology and of Ethnology, Cambridge' *Antiq. J.* (6) 175–80

Clarke, R. R., and Hawkes, C. F. C., 1955 'An iron anthropoid sword from Shouldham, Norfolk, with related continental and British weapons' *Proc. Prehist. Soc.* (21) 198–227

Coles, J. M., 1987 *Meare Village East* (Somerset Levels Papers, 13)

Collis, J. R., 1973 'Burials with weapons in Iron Age Britain' *Germania* (51) 121–33

Collis, J. R., 1977 'Owslebury, Hants, and the problem of burials in rural settlements' in R. Reece (ed.) *Burial in the Roman world* (CBA Res. Rep., 22) London 26–34

Cook, N. and MacCarthy, M. J., 1933 'A Roman cemetery at West Wickham, Kent' *Archaeol. Cantiana* (45) 188–92

Cotton, M. A., and Richardson, K. M., 1941 'A Belgic Cremation site at Stone, Kent' *Proc. Prehis. Soc.* (7) 134–41

Crabtree, P. J., 1989 *West Stow, Suffolk; Early Saxon Animal Husbandry* (East Anglian Archaeol., 47) Suffolk County Planning Department

Crafter, W., 1849 (untitled note) *Brit. Archaeol. Ass. J.* (4) 406

Cra'ster, M. D., 1973 'Iron Age grave group from Newnham Croft, Cambridge' *Proc. Cambridge Antiq. Soc.* (64) 25

Craw, J. H., 1924 'On two bronze spoons from an Early Iron Age grave near Burnmouth, Berwickshire' *Proc. Soc. Antiq. Scotland* (58, 1923–4) 143–60

Crummy, P., 1992 'Royal Graves' *Colchester Archaeol.* (5, 1991–2) 1–5

Cunliffe B. W., 1984 *Danebury: an Iron Age hillfort in Hampshire* (CBA Res. Rep., 52) London

Cunliffe, B. W., 1991 *Iron Age communities in Britain* 3rd edition, London

Cunliffe, B. W., and Poole, C., 1991 *Danebury 5* (CBA Res. Rep., 73) London

Dawes, J. (unpub.) *Wetwang Slack human bone report* (unpub. MS)

Déchelette, J., 1914 *Manuel d'Archéologie* 2, 3, *Second âge du fer ou époque de La Tène* Paris

Decker, H. R., 1915 'Report of the anomalies in a subject with a supernumerary lumbar vertebra' *Anatomical Record* (9) 181–9

de Freitas, V., Madeira, M. C., Toledo, J. L., Chagas, C. F., 1979 'Absence of the mental foramen in dry human mandibles' *Acta Anatomica* (104) 353–5

Del Sel, J. M., and Grand, N. E., 1959 'Cubo-navicular synostosis. A rare tarsal anomaly' *J. Bone and Joint Surgery* (41B) 149

Demmin, A., 1870 (trans. C. C. Black) *Weapons of War* London

de Navarro J. M., 1952 'The Celts in Britain and their Art' in M. P. Charlesworth (ed.) *The Heritage of Early Britain* London

de Navarro, J. M., 1972 *The finds from the site of La Tène, 1, scabbards and the swords found in them* London

Dent, J. S., 1982 'Cemeteries and settlement patterns of the Iron Age on the Yorkshire Wolds' *Proc. Prehist. Soc.* (48) 437–57

Dent, J. S., 1983 'A summary of the excavations carried out in Garton Slack and Wetwang Slack 1964–1980' *East Riding Archaeol.* (7) 1–14

Dent, J. S., 1985 'Three cart burials from Wetwang, Yorkshire' *Antiquity* (59) 85–92

Dent, J. S., 1990 'Changes in the later Iron Age of East Yorkshire' in A. Duval, J. P. Le Bihan and Y. Menez, *Les Gaulois d'Armorique* (Rev. archéol. de l'ouest, supplément 3) Rennes, 223–31

Dilly, G., 1978 'Céramique de tradition de "La Tène" à Frencq (Pas de Calais)' *Cahiers Archéol. Picardie* (5) 127–34

Dobney, K., and Goodman, A. H., 1991 'Epidemiological studies of dental enamel hypoplasias in Mexico and Bradford: their relevance to archaeological skeletal studies' in H. Bush and M. Zvelebil (eds) *Health in past societies. Biocultural interpretations of human skeletal remains in archaeological contexts* (Brit. Archaeol. Rep., Supplementary Ser, 567) Oxford, 81–100

Donaldson, R., 1909 'Notes on double cervical rib, with an illustrative case' *Brit. Medical J.* (2) 931–2

Dowker, G., 1900 'Deal and its environs' *Archaeol. Cantiana* (24) 108–21

Drury, P. J., 1978 *Excavations at Little Waltham 1970–71* (CBA Res. Rep., 26) London

Dunning, G. C., 1934 'The swans-neck and ring-headed pins of the Early Iron Age in Britain' *Archaeol. J.* (91) 269–95

Dunning, G. C., 1966a 'Neolithic occupation sites in East Kent' *Antiq. J.* (46) 1–25

Dunning, G. C., 1966b 'The Museum' in B. H. St J. O'Neil, *Deal Castle, Kent*, London, 14–21

Duval, P.-M., 1977 *Les Celtes* Paris

Duval, P.-M., and Kruta, V., 1982 *L'Art Celtique de la période d'expansion, IVe et IIIe siècles avant notre ère* (Ecole pratique des Hautes Etudes, IVe section, III, 13) Geneva/Paris

Ehrhardt, P., 1986 'Iron deficiency in young Bradford children from ethnic groups' *Brit. Medical J.* (292) 90–3

Ellison, A. and Drewett, P., 1971 'Pits and post-holes in the British Early Iron Age: some alternative explanations' *Proc. Prehist. Soc.* (37) 183–94

Ettlinger, E., 1973 *Die römischen Fibeln in der Schweiz* Bern

Ettlinger, E., 1990 *Conspectus formarum. Terrae sigillatae Italico modo confectae* (Materialien zur römisch-germanischen Keramik, 10) Bonn

Evans, A. J., 1890 'On a Late-Celtic Urn-Field at Aylesford, Kent, and on the Gaulish, Illyro-Italic, and Classical Connexions of the Forms of Pottery and Bronze-work there discovered' *Archaeologia* (52) 315–88

Evison, V. I., 1987 *Dover: Buckland Anglo-Saxon cemetery* (English Heritage, Archaeol. Rep., 3) London

Fell, C. I., 1936 'The Hunsbury hill-fort, Northants: a new survey of the material' *Archaeol. J.* (93) 57–100

Feugère, M., 1985 *Les fibules en Gaule Méridionale de la conquête à la fin du Ve siècle après J.-C.* (Rev. Archéol. Narbonnaise, Supplément 12)

Fingerlin, G., 1971 'Dangstetten, ein augusteisches Legionslager am Hochrhein' *Ber. R. G. K.* (51–2, 1970–71) 197–232

Fisk, J. W., Baigent, M. L., and Hill, P. D., 1984 'Scheuermann's disease. Clinical and radiological survey of 17 and 18 year olds' *American J. Physical Medicine* (63) 18–30

Fitzpatrick, A., and Megaw, J. V. S., 1987 'Further finds from the Le Câtillon hoard' *Proc. Prehist. Soc.* (53) 433–44

Fox, C., 1923 *The Archaeology of the Cambridge Region* Cambridge

Fox, Sir Cyril, 1946 *A find of the Early Iron Age from Llyn Cerrig Bach, Anglesey* Cardiff

Fox, Sir Cyril, 1958 *Pattern and Purpose* Cardiff

Francis, G. G., 1871 'On ancient bronze helmets found in 1818 at Ogmore Down, Glamorganshire' *Archaeologia* (43) 553–6

Franks, A. W., 1865 'Additions made to the collections of British antiquities at the British Museum during the year 1864' *Proc. Soc. Antiq. London* (2nd ser., 3, 1864–7) 83–94

Franks, A. W., 1866 (untitled exhibit note, the Thames helmet) *Proc. Soc. Antiq. London* (2nd ser., 3, 1864–7) 342–4

Frere, S. S., 1954 'Canterbury excavations, summer, 1946: the Rose Lane sites' *Archaeol. Cantiana* (68) 101–143

Frey, O.-H., 1974 'Akanthusornamentik in der keltischen Kunst' *Hamburger Beitr. Archäol.* (4) 141–57

Furger-Gunti, A., 1979 *Die Ausgrabungen im Basler Münster* I (Basler Beiträge zur Ur- und Frühgeschichte, 6) Derendingen–Solothurn

Furger-Gunti, A., and Berger, L., 1980 *Katalog und Tafeln der Funde aus der spätkeltischen Siedlung Basel-Gasfabrik* (Basler Beiträge zur Ur- und Frühgeschichte, 7) Derendingen-Solothurn

Gebhard, R., 1991 *Die Fibeln aus dem oppidum von Manching* (Die Ausgrabungen in Manching, 14) Stuttgart

Gerlach, G., 1976 *Das Gräberfeld "Die Motte" bei Lebach* (Saarbrücker Beiträge zur Altertumskunde, 16) Bonn

Gilbert, H. M., 1978 'The Felmingham Hall hoard, Norfolk' *Bull. Board Celtic Stud.* (28, part 1) 159–87

Goodman C. N., and Morant, G. M., 1940 'The human remains of the Iron Age and other periods from Maiden Castle, Dorset' *Biometrika* (31) 295–312

Graber, L. W., 1978 'Congenital absence of teeth: a review with emphasis on inheritance patterns' *J. American Dental Association* (96) 266–75

Grant, A., 1984 'Animal husbandry', in B. W. Cunliffe 1984, 496–548 and microfiche 16–17

Gray, H. St G., and Bulleid, A., 1953 *The Meare Lake Village* (2) Taunton

Green, C., 1949 'The Birdlip Early Iron Age burials: a review' *Proc. Prehist. Soc.* (15) 188–90

Green, C., 1980 'Handmade pottery and society in late Iron Age and Roman East Sussex' *Sussex Archaeol. Coll.* (118) 59–86

Greene, K., 1978 'Mould-decorated Central Gaulish glazed ware' in P. Arthur and G. B. Marsh (eds) *Early Fine Wares in Roman Britain* (Brit. Archaeol. Rep., British Ser., 57), Oxford, 31–60

Greenwell, W., 1906 'Early Iron Age Burials in Yorkshire' *Archaeologia* (60) 251–324

Gregory, T., 1991 *Excavations in Thetford 1980-1982, Fison Way* (East Anglian Archaeol., 53)

Griffin, C. J., Powers, R., and Kruszynski, R., 1979 'The incidence of osteoarthritis of the temporomandibular joint in various cultures' *Australian Dental J.* (24) 94–106

Grinsell, L. V., 1992 'The Bronze Age Round Barrows of Kent', *Proc. Prehist. Soc.*, (58) 355–84

Habermehl, K.-H., 1975 *Die Altersbestimmung bei Haus- und Labortieren* Berlin

Haffner, A., 1974 'Zum Ende der Latènezeit im Mittelrheingebiet unter besonderer Berücksichtigung des Trierer Landes' *Archäol. Korrbl.* (4) 59–72

Haldane, J. W., 1975 'The excavations at Stokeleigh Camp, Avon' *Proc. Univ. Bristol Spelaeol. Soc.* (14, 1) 29–63

Harcourt, R. A., 1974 'The dog in prehistoric and early historic Britain' *J. Archaeol. Science* (1) 151–75

Harcourt, R. A., 1979 'The animal bones' in G. J. Wainwright, *Gussage All Saints; an Iron Age Settlement in Dorset* (DOE Res. Rep., 10) London

Harding, D. W., 1972 *The Iron Age in the Upper Thames Basin* Oxford

Harding, D. W., 1976 'Blewburton Hill, Berkshire: Re-excavation and Reappraisal' in D. W. Harding (ed.) *Hillforts* 1976, London/New York/San Francisco, 133–46

Hartridge, R., 1978 'Excavations at the Prehistoric and Romano-British site on Slonk Hill, Shoreham, Sussex' *Sussex Archaeol. Coll.* (116) 69–142

Haselgrove, C., 1987 *Iron Age coinage in South-east England: the archaeological context* (Brit. Archaeol. Rep., British Ser., 174) Oxford

Hattatt, R., 1989 *Ancient brooches and other artefacts* Oxford

Hauser, G., and de Stefano, G. F., 1989 *Epigenetic variants of the human skull* Stuttgart, pp. 102 and 230

Hawkes, C. F. C., 1929 'Jug of St Rémy ware found in Kent' *Antiq. J.* (10) 161–2

Hawkes, C. F. C., 1940 'La Tène I brooches from Deal, Preston Candover, and East Dean' *Antiq. J.* (20) 276–9

Hawkes, C. F. C., and Hull, M. R., 1947 *Camulodunum* (Soc. Antiq. London Res. Rep., 14) London

Hedges, R. E. M., Law, I. A., Bronk, C. R., and Housley, R. A., 1989 'The Oxford accelerator mass spectrometry facility: technical developments in routine dating' *Archaeometry* (31, 2) 99–114

Helseth, R. A., Langmark, F., and Mørk, S. J., 1988 'Neoplasms of the central nervous system in Norway. II. Descriptive epidemiology of intracranial neoplasms 1955–84' *APMIS* (96) 1066–74

Hencken, T. C., 1938 'The excavation of the Iron Age Camp on Bredon Hill, Gloucestershire, 1935–1937' *Archaeol. J.* (95) 1–111

Hensinger, R. N., 1989 'Spondylolysis and spondylolisthesis in children and adolescents' *J. Bone and Joint Surgery* (71A) 1098–1107

Hildebolt, C. F., and Molnar, S., 1991 'Measurement and description of periodontal disease in anthropological studies' in M. A. Kelley and C. S. Larsen (eds) *Advances in Dental Anthropology* New York, 225–40

Hodges, D. C., 1991 'Temporo mandibular joint osteoarthritis in a British skeletal population' *American J. Physical Anthropology* (85) 367–77

Hodson, F. R., 1968 *The La Tène cemetery at Münsingen-Rain* (Acta Bernensia, 5) Bern

Hodson, F. R., 1971 'Three Iron Age brooches from Hammersmith' in G. de G. Sieveking (ed.) *Prehistoric and Roman Studies* (*Brit. Mus. Quarterly*, 35), 50–57

Hogg, A. H. A., 1965 'Early Iron Age Wales' in I. Ll. Foster and G. E. Daniel (eds) *Prehistoric and Early Wales*, London, 109–150

Holman, D., Forthcoming 'Iron Age coins from Worth and Archer's Low Farm, Sandwich'

Holmes, J., 1952-4 'Romano-Belgic Burials' *East Herts. Archaeol. Soc. Trans.* (13, 2) 209–11

Hooper, B., 1984 'Anatomical considerations' in B. W. Cunliffe 1984, 463–74

Huidekoper, R. S., 1891 *Age of the Domestic Animals* Philadelphia

Hull, M. R., 1942 'An Early Claudian Burial found at Colchester' *Antiq. J.* (22) 59–65

Hull, M. R., and Hawkes, C. F. C., 1987 *Corpus of Ancient Brooches in Britain: Pre-Roman Bow Brooches* (Brit. Archaeol. Rep., British Ser., 168) Oxford

Jacobi, G., 1974 *Werkzeug und Gerät aus dem Oppidum von Manching* (Die Ausgrabungen in Manching, 5) Wiesbaden

Jacobsthal, P., 1944 *Early Celtic Art* Oxford

Jones, J. D., and Stead, I. M., 1969 'An Early Iron Age warrior-burial found at St Lawrence, Isle of Wight' *Proc. Prehist. Soc.* (35) 351–4

Jope, E. M., 1960 'The beginnings of La Tène ornamental style in the British Isles' in S. S. Frere (ed.) *Problems of the Iron Age in Southern Britain* 69–83

Keller, P. T., 1989 'Quern production at Folkestone, south-east Kent: an interim note' *Britannia* (20) 193–200

Kelly, D. B., 1963 'Maidstone' (in Researches and Discoveries in Kent) *Archaeol. Cantiana* (78) 194–5

Kelly, D. B., 1978 'Archaeological notes from Maidstone Museum' *Archaeol. Cantiana* (94) 264–8

Kelly, D. B., 1988 'Archaeological notes from Maidstone Museum' *Archaeol. Cantiana* (105) 297–320

Kelly, D. B., 1990 'Archaeological notes from Maidstone Museum' *Archaeol. Cantiana* (108) 281–94

Kemble, J. M., 1863 *Horae Ferales* London

Kendrick, T. D., 1939 'Celtic sword from the River Witham' *Antiq. J.* (19) 194–5

Kerr, N. W., 1989 'A method of assessing periodontal status in archaeologically derived skeletal material' *J. Paleopathology* (2) 67–78

Knowles, A. K., 1983 'Acute traumatic lesions' in G. D. Hart (ed.) *Disease in Ancient Man* Toronto, 61-83

Krämer, W., 1971 'Silberne Fibelpaare aus dem letzten vorchristlichen Jahrhundert' *Germania* (49) 111–32

Kruta, V., 1974 'Remarques sur l'apparition du rinceau dans l'art celtique' *Etudes Celtiques* (14) 21–30

Kruta, V., 1985 'Le port d'anneaux de cheville en Champagne et le problème d'une immigration danubienne au IIIe siècle avant J.-C.' *Etudes Celtiques* (22) 27–51

Kruta, V., and Roualet, P., 1982 'Une série de torques marniens à décor de style végétal continu' in P.-M. Duval and V. Kruta (eds), *Les mouvements celtiques du Ve au Ier siècle avant notre ère* (Paris) 115–35

Kunitz, S., 1987 'Making a long story short: a note on men's height and mortality in England from the first through the nineteenth centuries' *Medical History* (31) 269–80

Kunter, M., 1976 'Wirbelsäulenbefunde bei einer vorderasiatischen skelettpopulation aus dem 5 Jh. v. Chr.' *Homo* (27) 118–27

La Baume, P., 1962/3 'Ein Töpferofen tiberischer Zeit "an der Rechtschule" in Köln' *Kölner Jahrbuch für Vor- und Frühgeschichte* (6, 1962–3) 12–22

Lanier, R. R., 1944 'Length of first, twelfth and accessory ribs in American whites and negroes; their relationship to certain vertebral variations' *American J. Physical Anthropology* (2) 137–46

Larking, L. B., 1845 (untitled communication to the central committee of the British Archaeological Association, read 9 Oct. 1844) *Archaeol. J.* (1) 386–7

Launay, P., 1894 'On lumbar ribs and six pieces of sacrum in same subject' *J. Anatomy* (28) 375

Laver, P. G., 1927 'The excavation of a tumulus at Lexden, Colchester' *Archaeologia* (76, 1926–7) 241–54

Layard, N. F., 1925 'Bronze crowns and a bronze head-dress, from a Roman site at Cavenham Heath, Suffolk' *Antiq. J.* (5) 258–65

Legge, A. J., 1981 'The agricultural economy' in R. J. Mercer, *Grimes Graves, Norfolk; Excavations 1971–72, vol. 1* (DOE, Arch. Rep. 11) London, 79–103.

Legge, A. J., 1984 'The horses from the chariot burials at Arras, Yorkshire' in I. M. Stead 1984c, 41.

Legge, A. J., 1991 'The Animal Bones' in I. M. Stead 1991a, 140–47.

Lemoine, R., 1905 'Epoque marnienne. Sépulture à char découverte du 10 mars 1904, à Châlons-sur-Marne' *Bull. Soc. Préhist. Fr.* (2) 100–116

Lethbridge, T. C., 1953 'Burial of an Iron Age warrior at Snailwell' *Proc. Cambridge. Antiq. Soc.* (47) 25–37

Levine, M., 1982 'The use of crown height measurements and eruption-wear sequences to age horse teeth' in B. Wilson, C. Grigson and S. Payne, eds, *Ageing and Sexing Animal Bones from Archaeological Sites* (Brit. Archaeol. Rep., British Ser., 109), Oxford, 223–251.

Little, R. I., 1961 'The Excavation of a Romano-British settlement at Sanderstead' *Surrey Archaeol. Coll.* (58) 35–46

Logeart, G., 1931 'Coup d'oeil rétrospectif sur les cimetières d'Aussonce' *Bull. Soc. Archéol. Champenoise* (1931) 27–34

Lunt, D. A., 1974 'The prevalence of dental caries in the permanent dentition of scottish prehistoric and medieval populations' *Archives of Oral Biology* (19) 431–7

MacGregor, M., 1976 *Early Celtic Art in North Britain* Leicester

Mack, R. P., 1975 *The coinage of Ancient Britain* 3rd edition, London

Manning, W. H., 1985 *Catalogue of the Romano-British iron tools, fittings and weapons in the British Museum* London

Mariette, H., 1966 'Le site gaulois de la Motte du Vent' *Celticum XV*, suppl. to OGAM, tradition celtique (106) 53–94

Marzke, M. W. and Marzke, R. F., 1987 'The third metacarpal styloid process – human origin and function' *American J. Physical Anthropology* (73) 415–32

May, J., 1991 'Tony Gregory: reflections on a life' *Current Archaeol.* (126) 263–7

May, T., 1930 *Catalogue of Roman Pottery in the Colchester and Essex Museum* Cambridge

Megaw, J. V. S., 1970 *Art of the European Iron Age* Bath

Megaw, J. V. S., and Megaw, M. R., 1989 *Celtic Art* London

Menez, Y., 1985 *Les céramiques fumigées de l'ouest de la Gaule* (Cahiers de Quimper Antique, 2)

Molleson, T., 1992 'The anthropoplogical evidence for change through Romanisation of the Poundbury population' *Anthropologische Anzeiger* (50) 179–89

Møller-Christensen, V., 1958 *Bogen om Æbelholt kloster* København, p. 165

Mook, W. G., 1986 'Business meeting: Recommendations/ Resolutions adopted by the Twelfth International Radiocarbon Conference' *Radiocarbon* (28) 799

Morel, J. P., 1965 *La céramique à vernis noir au forum romain et au palatin* (Ecole française de Rome) 3rd suppl. Paris

Morel, L., 1898 *La Champagne souterraine* Reims

Musson, C. R., 1991 *The Breidden hillfort* (CBA Res. Rep., 76) London

Needham, S. P., 1983 *The Early Bronze Age axeheads of Central and Southern England* (unpub. PhD thesis, University College, Cardiff)

Niblett, R. 1985 *Sheepen: an early Roman industrial site at Camulodunum* (CBA Res. Rep., 57) London

Niblett, R., 1992 'A Catuvellaunian chieftain's burial' *Antiquity* (66) 917–29

Norris, N. E. S., 1956 'Miscellaneous Researches, 1949-56, 3, Romano-British cremations at Herstmonceux' *Sussex Archaeol. Coll.* (94) 4–5

Nowakowski, J. A., 1991 'Trethellan Farm, Newquay: the excavation of a lowland Bronze Age settlement and Iron Age cemetery' *Cornish Archaeol.* (30) 5–242

Öberg, T., Carlsson, G. E., Fajers, C. M., 1971 'The temporo mandibular joint. A morphologic study on human autopsy material' *Acta Odontologica Scandinavica* (29) 349–84

Ogilvie, J. D., and Dunning, G. C., 1967 'A Belgic burial-group at Sholden, near Deal; and a Belgic tazza from Mill Hill, Upper Deal' *Archaeol. Cantiana* (82) 221–6

O'Kelly, M. J., 1961 'The Cork Horns, the Petrie Crown and the Bann Disc: the technique of their ornamentation' *J. Cork Hist. Archaeol. Soc.* (66) 1–12.

O'Neil, H., and Grinsell, L. V., 1960 'Gloucestershire barrows' *Trans. Bristol Gloucestershire Archaeol. Soc.* (79) 1–148

Ortner, D. J., and Putschar, W. G. J., 1985 *Identification of pathological conditions in human skeletal remains* (Smithsonian Institution Press, Contributions to Anthropology, 28) Washington, pp. 116 and 335-6

Painter, K. S., 1971 'Roman bronze crowns from Deeping St James, Lincolnshire' *Antiq. J.* (51) 319–21

Palk, N. A., 1984 *Iron Age bridle-bits from Britain* (University of Edinburgh Department of Archaeology, Occasional Paper, 10)

Parfitt, K., 1985 'Some Iron Age sites in the Deal area' *Kent Archaeol. Rev.* (79) 206–19

Parfitt, K., 1986 'The Deal Man' *Current Archaeol.* (101) 166–8

Parfitt, K., 1989 'A Roman cremation and other finds from Deal' *Kent Archaeol. Rev.* (96) 123–8

Parfitt, K., 1990 'Excavations at Mill Hill, Deal, 1982–1989, an interim report' *Kent Archaeol. Rev.* (101) 9–18

Parfitt, K., 1991 'Deal' *Current Archaeol.* (125) 215–20

Parfitt, K., and Green, M., 1987 'A chalk figurine from Upper Deal, Kent' *Britannia* (18) 295–8

Parfitt, K., and Halliwell, G., 1986 'The Deal Man and a possible underground Roman shrine' *Kent Archaeol. Rev.* (83) 59–62

Partridge, C., 1979 'Excavations at Puckeridge and Braughing 1975-79' *Hertfordshire Archaeol.* (7) 28–132

Payne, G., 1882 *Catalogue of my Museum of Local Antiquities* Sittingbourne

Payne, G., 1883 'On a Roman cemetery discovered at Westbere, near Canterbury' *Archaeol. Cantiana* (15) 318–20

Payne, G., 1889 'On a Roman statue and other remains in the Dover Museum' *Archaeol. Cantiana* (18) 202–5

Payne, G., 1893 *Collectanea Cantiana: or archaeological researches in the neighbourhood of Sittingbourne, and other parts of Kent* London

Payne, G., 1911 'Researches and discoveries in Kent, 1908-1910' *Archaeol. Cantiana* (29) lxxxvi–lxxxv

Peake, H., 1930 'Some unsolved problems in the Newbury district' *Trans. Newbury District Field Club* (5) 17–30

Penninger, E., 1972 *Der Dürrnberg bei Hallein* (1) (Münchner Beiträge zur Vor- und Frühgeschichte, 16) Munich

Petch, D. F., 1957 'Archaeological Notes for 1956' *Lincolnshire Archit. Archaeol. Soc. Rep. Pap.* (7) 1–26

Philp, B. J., 1978 'Ring ditch (Deal, Kent)' *Proc. Prehist. Soc.* (44) 448

Philp, B. J., 1981 *The excavation of the Roman forts of the Classis Britannica at Dover 1970–1977* (Kent Archaeol. Rescue Unit Monograph Ser., 3) Dover

Philp, B. J., 1984 *Excavations in the Darent Valley, Kent* (Kent Archaeol. Rescue Unit Monograph Ser., 4) Dover

Piggott, S., 1950 'Swords and scabbards of the British Early Iron Age' *Proc. Prehist. Soc.* (16) 1–28

Piggott, S., 1983 *The earliest wheeled transport* London

Prescher, A., 1988 'Über Ossa metastyloidea, parastyloidea und pisiformia secundaria' *Gegenbaurs Morphologische Jahrb.* (134) 397–406

Preston-Martin, S., 1989 'Descriptive epidemiology of primary tumours of the brain, cranial nerves and cranial meninges in Los Angeles County' *Neuroepidemiology* (8) 283–95

Probert, L. A., 1976 'Twyn-y-Gaer hill-fort, Gwent: an interim assessment' in G. C. Boon and J. M. Lewis (eds) *Welsh Antiquity* Cardiff 105–19

Purves, R. K. and Wedin, P. H., 1950 'Familial incidence of cervical ribs' *J. Thoracic Surgery* (19) 952–6

RCAHMW 1976 Royal Commission on Ancient and Historical Monuments in Wales, *Glamorgan* (I, part 2) Cardiff

RCHM 1970 Royal Commission on Historical Monuments (England), *County of Dorset* (2) *South-East* London

Raftery, B., 1981 'Iron Age burials in Ireland' in D. O. Corráin (ed.) *Irish Antiquity* (essays and studies presented to Professor M. J. O'Kelly) Cork 173–204

Raftery, B., 1983 *A catalogue of Irish Iron Age antiquities* (Veröffentlichung des vorgeschichtlichen Seminars Marburg, Sonderband 1)

Raftery, B., 1984 *La Tène in Ireland: Problems of Origin and Chronology* (Veröffentlichung des vorgeschichtlichen Seminars Marburg, Sonderband 2)

Raftery, J., 1951 *Prehistoric Ireland* London

Ray, J. E. and Budgen, W., 1916 'Recent finds at Eastbourne (i) Romano-British cinerary urns' *Sussex Archaeol. Coll.* (58) 188–93

Resnick, D., and Niwayama, Gen., 1981 *Diagnosis of bone and joint disorders* Philadelphia, pp. 2253, 2671 and 2903

Richmond, Sir Ian, 1968 *Hod Hill* (2) London

Rigby, V., 1981 'The Gallo-Belgic wares' in C. Partridge, *Skeleton Green: a late Iron Age and Romano-British site* (Britannia Monographs, 2) London, 159–95

Rigby, V., 1981 'The potter Julios – a suitable case for study?' in A. C. and A. S. Anderson (eds) *Roman Pottery Research in Britain and North-West Europe* (Brit. Archaeol. Rep., International Ser., 123) Oxford, 39–50

Rigby, V., 1985 ' The Gallo-Belgic wares' in R. Niblett, 1985, 74–82

Rigby, V., 1986 'Gaulish Fine-Ware Imports' in I. M. Stead and V. Rigby 1986, 223–34

Riha, E., 1979 *Die römischen Fibeln aus Augst und Kaiseraugst* (Forschungen in Augst, 3)

Ritchie, J. N. G., 1968 *Celtic defensive weaponry in Britain and its continental background* (unpub. PhD thesis, Edinburgh University)

Roberts, C., (unpub.) *Beckford, human skeletal report* (University of Bradford) Bradford

Robinson, H. Russell, 1975 *The Armour of Imperial Rome* London

Rozanski, K., Stichler, W., Gonfiantini, R., Scott, E. M., Beukens, R. P., Kromer, B. and van der Plicht, J., 1992 'The IAEA 14C Intercomparison Exercise 1990' *Radiocarbon* (34,3) 506–19

Rozoy, J.-G., 1987 *Les celtes en Champagne* (Mém. Soc. Archéol. Champenoise, 4) 1, étude (2, description = 1986) Charleville-Mézières

Rutland, R. A., 1972 'An Iron Age sword and scabbard from the Thames at Henley, Oxon' *Antiq. J.* (52) 345–6

Sadler, P., 1991 'The use of tarsometatarsi in sexing and ageing domestic fowl (*Gallus gallus* L.), and recognising five toed breed in archaeological material' *Circaea* (8, 1) 41–9.

Savory, H. N., 1984 'Early Iron Age Glamorgan' in H. N. Savory (ed.) *Glamorgan County History* (2) *Early Glamorgan* Cardiff 237–75

Schaaf, U., 1973 'Frühlatènezeitliche Grabfunde mit Helmen vom Typ Berru' *Jahrb. RGZM* (20) 81–106

Schaaf, U., 1974 'Keltische Eisenhelme aus vorrömischer Zeit' *Jahrb. RGZM* (21) 149–204

Scheers, S., 1983 *La Gaule Belgique: Traité de Numismatique Celtique* (Louvain Peeters).

Schmit, E., 1928 'Répertoire abrégé de l'archéologie du Département de la Marne des temps préhistoriques à l'an mille' *Mém. Soc. Agriculture Commerce Sciences Arts Marne* (63, 1926–28), 99–301

Schmorl, G., and Junghanns, H., 1971 *The human spine in health and disease* New York, p. 389

Serck-Hanssen, T., 1935 'Cervical ribs combined with other anomalies of vertebral column as family condition' *Acta Chirurgia Scandinavica* (76) 551–60

Sergeantson, D., 1991 'The bird bones' in B. W. Cunliffe and C. Poole 1991, 479–481.

Shepherd, F. J., 1881 'On some anatomical variations' *J. Anatomy* (15) 292–6

Sherratt, A., 1983 'A newly discovered La Tène sword and scabbard' *Oxford J. Archaeol.* (2) 115–18

Shinn, D. L., 1976 'Congenitally missing third molars in a British population' *J. Dental Research* (4) 42–4

Sinclair, D., 1966 *An introduction to functional anatomy* (3rd ed.) Oxford, 345–8

Sisson, S., and Grossman, J. D., 1955 *Anatomy of the Domestic Mammals* (4th ed.) Philadelphia

Smith, C. R., 1842 'Notices of recent discoveries of Roman antiquities at Strood, Bapchild, Oare and Upchurch, in Kent, with remarks on the site of the Durolevum of Antoninus' *Archaeologia* (29) 217–26

Smith, C. R., 1850 *The Antiquities of Richborough, Reculver and Lymne* London

Smith, C. R., 1852 *Collectanea Antiqua* (2) London

Smith, C. R., 1854 *Collectanea Antiqua* (3) London

Smith, R. A., 1905 *A Guide to the antiquities of the Early Iron Age* London

Smith, R. A., 1908 'Anglo-Saxon remains' in W. Page (ed.) Victoria County History, *Kent* (1) London, 339–87

Smith, R. A., 1925 *A Guide to the antiquities of the Early Iron Age* 2nd ed., London

Smith, R. A., 1926 'Two early British bronze bowls' *Antiq. J.* (6) 276–83

Soames, J. V. and Southam, J. C., 1988 *Oral pathology* (Oxford Medical Publications) Oxford, p. 6

Spratling, M. G., 1970 'The late pre-Roman Iron Age bronze mirror from Old Warden' *Bedfordshire Archaeol. J.* (5) 9–16

Spratling, M. G., 1972 *Southern British decorated bronzes of the Late Pre-Roman Iron Age* (unpub. PhD. thesis, London University)

Stanford, S. C., 1974 *Croft Ambrey* Hereford

Stead, I. M., 1961 'A distinctive form of La Tène barrow in Eastern Yorkshire and on the continent' *Antiq. J.* (41) 44–62

Stead, I. M., 1965 *The La Tène Cultures of Eastern Yorkshire* York

Stead, I. M., 1967 'A La Tène III burial at Welwyn Garden City' *Archaeologia* (101) 1–62

Stead, I. M., 1976 'The earliest burials of the Aylesford Culture' in G. de G. Sieveking et al. (eds), *Problems in Economic and Social Archaeology* 401–16

Stead, I. M., 1979 *The Arras Culture* York

Stead, I. M., 1982 'The Cerrig-y-Drudion "hanging bowl"' *Antiq. J.* (62) 221–34

Stead, I. M., 1983 'La Tène swords and scabbards in Champagne' *Germania* (61) 487–510

Stead, I. M., 1984a 'Some notes on imported metalwork in Iron Age Britain' in S. Macready and F. H. Thompson (eds), *Cross-Channel trade between Gaul and Britain in the Pre-Roman Iron Age* (Soc. Antiq. London Occ. Pap., new ser., 4) 43–66

Stead, I. M., 1984b 'Celtic dragons from the River Thames' *Antiq. J.* (64) 269–79

Stead, I. M., 1984c 'Cart burials in Britain' in M. Guštin and L. Pauli, *Keltski Voz* (Posavski muzej Brežice, 6) 31–41

Stead, I. M., 1985a *Celtic Art in Britain before the Roman Conquest* London

Stead, I. M., 1985b *The Battersea Shield* London

Stead, I. M., 1991a *Iron Age Cemeteries in East Yorkshire* (English Heritage, Archaeol. Rep. 22) London

Stead, I. M., 1991b 'Many more Iron Age shields from Britain' *Antiq. J.* (71) 1–35

Stead, I. M., Hartwell, A. P., Lang, J. R. S., La Niece, S. C. and Meeks, N. D., 1981 'An Iron Age sword and scabbard from Isleham' *Proc. Cambridge Antiq. Soc.* (71) 61–74

Stead, I. M. and Rigby, V., 1986 *Baldock: the excavation of a Roman and pre-Roman settlement 1967–72* (Britannia Monograph, 7) London

Stead, I. M., and Rigby, V., 1989 *Verulamium, the King Harry Lane site* (English Heritage, Archaeol. Rep., 12) London

Stebbing, W. P. D., 1934 'An early Iron Age site at Deal' *Archaeol. Cantiana* (46) 207–9

Stebbing, W. P. D., 1937 *The invader's shore* Deal

Stuart-Macadam, P., 1989 'Porotic hyperostosis: relationship between orbital and vault lesions' *American J. Physical Anthropology* (80) 187–93

Stuiver, M. and Pearson, G. W., 1986 'High-precision calibration of the radiocarbon time scale, AD1950–500BC' in Stuiver, M. and Kra, R. S., (eds), 'Proceedings of 12th Internatl ^{14}C conference' *Radiocarbon* (28, 2B) 839–62

Stuiver, M. and Polach, H. J., 1977 'Discussion: Reporting of ^{14}C data' *Radiocarbon* (19, 3) 355–63

Stuiver, M. and Reimer, P. J., 1987 *Users guide to the programs CALIB and DISPLAY* Rev. 2.1 (Quaternary Isotope Laboratory, University of Washington)

Taylor, A., 1993 'A Roman lead coffin with pipeclay figurines from Arrington, Cambridgeshire' *Britannia* (24) 191–225

Tenney, J. M., 1991 'Comparison of third metatarsal and third cuneiform defects among various populations' *International J. Osteoarchaeology* (1) 169–72

Tester, P. J., and Bing, H. F., 1949 'A first-century urn-field at Chenton, near Folkstone' *Archaeol. Cantiana* (62) 21–36

Thompson, I., 1978 'The Belgic cemetery at Allington' *Archaeol. Cantiana* (94) 127–38

Thompson, I., 1982 *Grog-tempered 'Belgic' Pottery of South-eastern England* (Brit. Archaeol. Rep., British Ser., 108) Oxford

Thomson, A., 1893 'Fourth annual report on the committee of collective investigation of the anatomical society of Great Britain and Ireland for the year 1892–93 Question I' *J. Anatomy* (28) 64–6

Thomson, A., and Buxton, L. H. D., 1923 'Man's nasal index in relation to certain climatic conditions' *J. Royal Anthropol. Inst.* (53) 92–122

Todd, T. W., 1911 'The relation of the thoracic operculum considered in reference to the anatomy of cervical ribs of surgical importance' *J. Anatomy* (45) 293–304

Toller, P. A., 1973 'Osteoarthrosis of the mandibular condyle' *Brit. Dental J.* (134) 223–31

Toynbee, J. M. C., 1962 *Art in Roman Britain* London

Trotter, M., and Gleser, G. C., 1958 'A re-evaluation of estimation of stature based on measurements of stature taken during life and long bones after death' *American J. Physical Anthropol.* (16) 79–123

Van Arsdell, R. D., 1989 *Celtic coinage of Britain* London

Van Endert, D., 1991 *Die Bronzefunde aus dem Oppidum von Manching* (Die Ausgrabungen in Manching, 13) Stuttgart

Van Es, W. A., and Wynia, S. L., 1979 'Quelques observations archéologiques dans la sablière "Les Ursulines", commune de Marck (Pas-de-Calais)' *Rev. Nord* (61, no. 243) 765–82

Verger, S., 1987 'La genèse celtique des rinceaux à triscèles' *Jahrb. RGZM* (34) 287–339

Vermeulen, W. G. J. R., 1932 *Een Romeinsch Grafveld op den Hunnerberg te Nijmegen* Amsterdam

Von Den Dreisch, A., 1976 *A Guide to the Measurement of Animal Bones From Archaeological Sites* (Peabody Mus. of Archaeol. and Ethnol., Bull. 1) Harvard

Wainwright, G. J., 1968 'The excavation of a Durotrigian farmstead near Tollard Royal in Cranbourne Chase, Southern England' *Proc. Prehist. Soc.* (34) 102–47

Walker, A. J., Williams, N., Otlet, R. L., 1990 'Harwell Radiocarbon Measurements VIII' *Radiocarbon* (32) 165–86

Walters, I., 1984 'Gone to the dogs: a study of bone attrition at a central Australian Campsite' *Mankind* (14, 5) 389–400

Warhurst, A., 1953 'A Belgic burial from Borough Green' *Archaeol. Cantiana* (66) 157–60

Wassman, K., 1951 'Kyphosis juvenalis Scheuermann – an occupational disorder' *Acta Orthopedica Scandinavica* (21) 65–74

Waugh, W., 1957 'Partial cubo-navicular coalition as a cause of peroneal spastic flat foot' *J. Bone and Joint Surgery* (39B) 520–3

Way, A., 1855 'Notice of a bronze relique, assigned to the later Roman or the Saxon Age, discovered at Leckhampton, Gloucestershire' *Archaeol. J.* (12) 9–21

Way, A., 1869 'Notices of certain bronze relics, of a peculiar type, assigned to the Late Celtic period' *Archaeol. J.* (26) 52–83

Wells, C., 1961 'A case of lumbar osteochondritis dissecans from the Bronze Age' *J. Bone and Joint Surgery* (43B) 575.

Werner, J., 1955 'Die Nauheimer Fibel' *Jahrb. RGZM* (2) 170–95

Wheeler, R. E. M., 1925 *Prehistoric and Roman Wales* Oxford

Wheeler, R. E. M., 1943 *Maiden Castle, Dorset* (Soc. Antiq. London Res. Rep., 12) Oxford

Wheeler, R. E. M., and T. V., 1932 *Report on the Excavation of the Prehistoric, Roman, and Post-Roman site in Lydney Park, Gloucestershire* (Soc. Antiq. London Res. Rep., 9) Oxford

Whimster, R., 1977 'Harlyn Bay reconsidered: the excavations of 1900–1905 in the light of recent work' *Cornish Archaeol.* (16) 60–88

Whimster, R., 1981 *Burial Practices in Iron Age Britain* (Brit. Archaeol Rep., British Ser., 90) Oxford

White, R. H., 1988 *Roman and Celtic objects from Anglo-Saxon Graves* (Brit. Archaeol Rep., British Ser., 191) Oxford

Whiting, W., 1926 'Further finds from Kent' *Antiq. J.* (6) 309–12

Wild, J. P., 1970 'Button-and-loop fasteners in the Roman provinces' *Britannia* (1) 137–55

Williams, P. L. and Warwick, R., (eds.) 1980 *Gray's anatomy* (36th ed.) Edinburgh, pp. 413 and 1067

Willson, E. J., 1852 (untitled exhibit note) *Proc. Soc. Antiq. London* (2, 1849–53) 199

Winbolt, S. E., 1925 'Pre-Roman finds at Folkestone' *Antiq. J.* (5) 63–7

Wood, H., 1883 'Roman urns found near Rainham Creek, on the Medway' *Archaeol. Cantiana* (15) 108–110

Woodruff, C. H., 1874 'On Celtic tumuli in East Kent' *Archaeol. Cantiana* (9) 16–30

Woodruff, C. H., 1902 'Romano-British interments at Lower Walmer' *Archaeol. Cantiana* (25) 1–10

Woodruff, C. H., 1904 'Further discoveries of Late Celtic and Romano-British interments at Walmer' *Archaeol. Cantiana* (26) 9–16